ECONOMIC CHANGE
AND EMPLOYMENT
POLICY

WARWICK STUDIES IN THE ECONOMICS OF EMPLOYMENT

General Editor:
Robert M. Lindley,
Director, Manpower Research Group, University of Warwick

The Manpower Research Group was established at the University of Warwick in 1975 with a major programme grant from the Manpower Services Commission, following previous research in the general field of labour economics and employment forecasting. The Group has three objectives of which the first is to maintain a regular assessment of Britain's economic prospects over the medium term dealing with output and employment at a highly disaggregated level. The second objective is to conduct special studies of particular segments of the labour market and the third is to develop models of certain general processes which affect the operation of the labour market and its relationship with the rest of the economy.

The Group's first full-scale assessment, *Britain's Medium-Term Employment Prospects,* was published in 1978. Three special studies currently in progress concern the labour markets for engineering craftsmen, skilled construction workers and highly qualified technical manpower. Two others focus on the employment of women and young people. The general modelling work has covered labour supply and demographic accounting, the determinants of labour demand, and the occupational and regional aspects of employment growth in the UK economy.

Warwick Studies in the Economics of Employment will present the results of this research conducted by staff of the Group, sometimes in collaboration with colleagues at other institutions.

ECONOMIC CHANGE AND EMPLOYMENT POLICY

Edited by

Robert M. Lindley

First published 1980 *by*
THE MACMILLAN PRESS LTD
Companies and representatives
throughout the world

Typeset and printed in Great Britain by
Warwick Printing Co. Ltd., Warwick

British Library Cataloguing in Publication Data

Lindley, R M
Economic change and employment policy
1. Manpower policy – Great Britain
2. Great Britain – Economic policy – 1945–
I. Title
331.1'0941   HD5765.A6

ISBN 0-333-28749-5
ISBN 0-333-28750-9 Pbk

Contents

List of Figures

List of Tables

Preface

This book is the first in a series of *Warwick Studies in the Economics of Employment*. It is based upon simulations of economic change in the British economy over the medium term and draws upon various aspects of the work of the Manpower Research Group. This sets it apart somewhat from other studies to be published in the series: these will follow more closely the style of the research monograph.

During the book's preparation a change of government took place which ushered in a new approach to economic management, the spirit of which we wished to capture in the course of our analysis. As a result, the main simulations were completed in September 1979 but, with considerable help from our publishers, it has been possible to arrange publication much more rapidly than would normally be the case.

The outcome is a study of economic growth and its implications for the structure of employment which reflects, rather than evaluates, changes in policy which at the time of writing are only just beginning to emerge. Our concern is with the significance of these and alternative shifts of policy for the underlying employment situation over the medium term. Not only does this put the effects of different measures into better perspective but it also draws attention towards the intermediate problems of adjustment which are so important but frequently ignored in debating economic aspirations and policy.

The present volume not only pursues the analysis of factors underlying industrial, occupational and regional developments in the past and future but also presents some of the results of our more detailed studies concerned with employment prospects for women, the employment of skilled labour in engineering and construction and the labour market for highly qualified technical manpower. All the research findings discussed represent work in progress included at this stage to highlight aspects of the employment situation which deserve particular attention.

Although the production of this assessment has been a team effort, the different chapters are attributed to their main authors. We should like to thank Rosemary Ellis, Pam O'Brien and Anstice Neville for assisting with the editorial work, Carol Davies for her computer programming and several members of the clerical and secretarial staff, notably, Anne Allison, Meena Devlukia, Moira Fair, Maureen Garcia, Valerie Jephcott and Chris Winnett.

We are particularly indebted to staff of the Cambridge Growth Project, especially Terence Barker and William Peterson, for their advice whilst we were setting up the macroeconomic model at Warwick. We have, however, changed the model in significant respects and the MRG is entirely responsible for the results presented in the following chapters. Several government departments and the Manpower Services Commission have provided us with unpublished information for which we are grateful.

Finally, we wish to thank the Manpower Services Commission and the Engineering Industry Training Board for financial support of our research programme but stress that neither is responsible for any of the judgements or opinions expressed in this study. These should be attributed only to the Manpower Research Group.

Robert M. Lindley

List of Contributors

The following research staff and associate fellows contributed to the preparation of this study.

P.A. Dutton	Research Fellow, Manpower Research Group
D.P.B. Elias	Senior Research Fellow, Manpower Research Group
G.T. Keogh	Research Associate, Centre for Industrial Economic and Business Research, University of Warwick
R.M. Lindley	Director, Manpower Research Group
H.C. Murton	Research Associate, Manpower Research Group
D.J.E. Smith	Research Associate, Manpower Research Group
J.D. Whitley	Senior Research Fellow, Manpower Research Group
R.A. Wilson	Senior Research Fellow, Manpower Research Group
D.L. Bosworth	Senior Lecturer, University of Loughborough
G. Briscoe	Senior Lecturer, Lanchester Polytechnic

1 Introduction

British society will need to accommodate a higher level of unemployment well into the 1980s. Forecasters now differ only by degrees of pessimism in their general pronouncements on the economy and employment in the medium term. Whilst there is much less agreement about prospects for the 1990s, the employment situation is likely to continue to deteriorate without significant changes in policy and in attitudes. The seeds of a strategy for coping with such changes must be sown in the next few years. During that period, however, the development of the economy could create an extremely hostile environment for the kind of social and economic experimentation which is now called for. Therefore it is all the more important to establish the likely pattern of economic change over the next five years or so, to discuss those policies required for the long-term benefit of the economy and to consider problems of implementation which are likely to arise on a shorter time-scale. The conflicts which exist between pursuing long-term objectives and the reality of the economic situation in the short term will always be with us. Medium-term policy should provide a means of controlled compromise between the two, through which the rhetoric associated with the former is confronted with the expediency engendered by the latter. In order to do this, however, the policy must be explicit.

As will emerge from the chapters to follow we believe that both the last Labour government and the present Conservative government have failed to enunciate coherent approaches to the medium term. Too much was expected from Labour's industrial strategy and too much is expected from the evolving Conservative policy, particularly in promoting incentives and entrepreneurship. Whilst the fiscal and monetary restraint instituted by the new Government differs in degree and rationale from that practised by Labour, it is nevertheless intended once again to be an accompaniment to more fundamental change being sought by ministers. This involves a shift in economic structure, a regeneration, a reversal of past trends. What seems to be missing from Conservative pronouncements on the economy so far is a sense of how big a job is being assigned to the policy of stimulating better working practices and entrepreneurial activity and how quick must be the response to it. Clearing the way by seeking to cut planned growth in public expenditure and restrict the rate of increase of the money supply would *seem* to be appropriate in the light of the Government's general philosophy but there is a danger that the short-run effects of these measures might lead to an economic environment which would be inimical to the main policy they are intended to facilitate. In our previous study (Lindley, 1978) we argued that the Labour government and the National Economic Development Council were similarly lacking a medium-term perspective on the industrial strategy.

Thus our first objective is to assess the medium-term economic outlook, given an interpretation of present policy, and to evaluate the effects of alternative policies. A discussion of the issues at stake when conducting this sort of analysis is given in Chapter 2. There is sometimes confusion about the nature of such an exercise and our general approach is explained and discussed in the light of recent criticisms of certain British studies of prospects for employment and unemployment.

Chapters 3 to 5 then cover the main elements of the analysis of economic change up to 1985 with particular reference to the structure of employment. Chapter 3 first provides an assessment of economic prospects prior to the introduction of the Conservative government's Budget of June 1979. The chapter then goes on to analyse the implications of the new economic strategy, as represented not only by the specific measures proposed in the Budget but also by more general statements about the style of economic management to be pursued over the longer term. With unemployment rising substantially in both the pre-Budget and post-Budget scenarios, the possibilities for reflation by stimulating further increases in personal rather than public expenditure are examined. The difficulties inherent in this approach lead to a consideration of those mechanisms of structural change which must be made to work in order to extract the British economy from its very weak trade position. Such a solution is highly speculative and clearly eluded the Labour government, despite its explicit commitment to an industrial strategy. Nevertheless it provides a further standpoint from which to view the policy dilemma facing the Conservative government as it seeks to inject a new dynamic into the economy.

The extent of our decline as a trading nation over the last two decades is discussed in some detail in Chapter 4, focussing on its effect upon the structure of industrial employment. The role of productivity growth and exchange rate movements in determining Britain's competitive position is examined for different industries. A more detailed analysis of the post-Budget view and structural change simulation supplements the treatment of these results given in Chapter 3. This includes a rough assessment of the occupational effects of industrial change in the past and over the projection period. Chapter 4 concludes by pinpointing the great difficulty involved for major industries in the economy in starting and maintaining the virtuous circle linking higher productivity to better trade performance to higher output and investment, leading to even higher productivity. This chapter is a particularly long one: it contains a number of large tables and other material which we have chosen to keep within the body of the chapter rather than consign to an appendix. Those wishing to go direct to the occupational projections after reading Chapter 3 can do so, however, by reading section 4.4.

Chapter 5 turns to the geographical distribution of employment. A review of regional developments over the last decade or so is followed by a regional disaggregation of the industrial labour demand projections. Obviously this obscures spatial characteristics which arise *within* regions but should provide a benchmark for more detailed analysis by sub-regional planning authorities etc., incorporating additional information and judgement specific to those areas. The same applies to the regional analysis of labour supply which is also presented in this chapter. The large disparities in regional unemployment rates implied by a simple confrontation of labour demand and supply suggest that adjustments through changing migration patterns and reductions in the rates of growth of certain regional activity rates might significantly reduce the projected regional differences in unemployment. This possibility is investigated and some reference is made to the problems of endogenising regional labour supply.

In Chapters 6 to 8 we move away from dealing with the economy at large in order to investigate the situation in three key areas of the labour market. Each of these chapters uses to some extent the simulation results described in Chapters 3 and 4 but has a more general purpose. None provides a comprehensive treatment of the labour market mechanisms involved, largely because the lack of data precludes the construction of complete empirical models which explain the determination of both wages and employment. On the other hand, these chapters indicate the lines of approach being taken and point to the main problems of analysis which arise.

Chapter 6 investigates the supply of labour and employment opportunities for women. It is well known that increases in activity
rates for married women have provided the major stimulus to the
expansion of the labour force since the 1960s. Whilst this will continue, its relative importance is waning and Chapter 6 discusses the
determinants of past changes in female labour supply and their implications for future patterns of labour force participation. This is
followed by the estimation of employment opportunities for women
based on a model which relates female employment to the growth of
non-manual work and part-time work. Taken at face value the results suggest that not only will female labour supply rise faster than
that of males but so will the availability of job opportunities. The relative worsening of the situation for males in a period of high unemployment is likely to affect their traditional pattern of occupational
and industrial mobility. In these circumstances there may also be
pressures for tempering progress towards supporting the position of
women in the labour market and this is also discussed.

The phenomenon of skill shortages accompanied by high levels of
unemployment amongst skilled manual workers has puzzled many
commentators and has lead to some confusion in the debate about
policy on industrial training. Chapter 7 attempts to clarify the main
issues, particularly as they affect the engineering and construction
industries over the last decade and in the medium term. The
chapter also raises important aspects of labour market policy which
have tended to be ignored when dealing with these groups.

The question of skill shortages also arises in connection with
highly qualified technical manpower. Chapter 8 investigates the determinants of the supply of qualified scientists and technologists and
the demand for their services in different industries and types of
activity.

Finally, Chapter 9 examines the difficulties facing the United
Kingdom in its struggle for growth and higher employment in the
light of the findings of earlier chapters. As industrial countries
approach the 1980s with little prospect for dramatic reductions in
unemployment over the medium term, governments are ex-
perimenting with increasingly differentiated instruments of policy
affecting the labour market. The economic rationale for these
policies has been far from clear, however, and the shifting context in
which they have been implemented has complicated the analysis of
their impact upon the economy and labour market. A review of the
general state of employment policy refers both to changes in the

intellectual climate governing discussion of it and to the evidence available on the effects of various schemes introduced over the last five years or so. The chapter concludes by suggesting that employment policy is in the middle of an uneasy transition and that new areas of economic and social behaviour are now falling within its scope.

Reference

Lindley, R.M. (1978) (ed.) *Britain's Medium-Term Employment Prospects.* Coventry : Manpower Research Group, University of Warwick.

2 Approaches to Assessing Employment Prospects

R.M. LINDLEY

Since all governments intervene in the economy to some extent, they require models which will enable them to assess the consequences of proposed action, suggest alternative possibilities and provide a basis for evaluating the options which emerge as worthy of serious consideration. The difficulties of constructing such models are well-recognised by those involved and a model used for forecasting is subject to a continuous process of development.

Research strategies governing this process will depend upon basic objectives and the resources available.[1] Some economists, particularly those of a monetarist persuasion, have argued that it is inappropriate to seek to model an economy on the scale and with the methodology adopted by the major forecasting groups, strongly influenced by post-Keynesian orthodoxy. This reflects not only a view of the feasibility of building models which are sufficiently reliable representations of an economy to be of use in policy formulation, but also an assessment of how strong are the equilibrating forces within the main developed economies. The latter leads to presuppositions about the scope for effective policy intervention in the first place and the former rules out on practical grounds any residual aspirations we might have for going beyond this. At the centre of the debate are technical issues concerning the econometric estimation of structural parameters, particularly the imposition of *a priori* restrictions which beg crucial questions about the behaviour of the economy.

On the other hand one explanation for the fact that the new equilibrium models (especially those developed by monetarists) are inclined to be 'small but beautiful' is their relatively early stage of development.[2] The predilection for smallness may then be seen as making a virtue of necessity. Moreover, the assumption of a highly competitive market system operating under rational expectations would seem to be more a *belief* than a hypothesis about economic behaviour which is open to testing by reference to the evidence. As a result it is not at all clear under what conditions Lucas and Sargent (1978), for example, would give up the market clearing assumption and pursue a research strategy placing greater stress upon the problems of modelling disequilibrium situations or at least *quantity-constrained* equilibria. Lurking within their paper is a caricature, namely, the macroeconomic model-builder who has no concern for the implications of policy endogeneity, expectations and the econometric techniques used in estimating his model. Furthermore, little attention is given to the trade-off between following the path proposed by these and other authors and attempting to disaggregate.

The pressures for disaggregation are, of course, very strong. This is because the implementation of policies intended to impinge on the disposition of real resources in a very direct way (for example, investment grants, employment sudsidies and job creation schemes) involves intervening at the micro-level such as the firm, the local government district or local labour market. Even a substantial increase in the detail provided by most of the British medium-term models would still fall short of the specific requirements of those administering policies. One option would be to reduce the government's intervention in the labour market in keeping with our ability to assess its impact rather than to hang on until our modelling capability improves. However, subsequent chapters will show that structural aspects of economic change point towards the need for carefully chosen policies acting at the microeconomic level. The approach to disaggregation taken by the Manpower Research Group has been explained elsewhere.[3] It is recognised that the availability of more reliable and detailed data by no means guarantees the success of research work, testing alternative models to explain the behaviour of disaggregate components. This can often be rewarded by sharply diminishing returns. Thus we have no illusions about the accuracy achievable in simulating the effects of alternative policies. This is not just a question of lacking sufficient data. There are clear technical limitations to our ability to model the economy and this applies particularly to the labour market. However, it should nonetheless be possible through combining simulation results and judgement to provide a set of 'points of reference' for policy-makers, indicating the sort of environment which they are likely to face, highlighting the main problem areas, giving some quantitative guide to the scale and dimensions of these problems and attempting some estimates of the impact which different proposals would have upon them. Much research, though, remains to be done before the outcome is a satisfactory basis for policy formulation. The present book is a further step taken by the Manpower Research Group in this direction.

The above process is a world away from the kind of activity portrayed by monetarist critics: the mechanical cranking of large-scale Keynesian models in which the price of disaggregation into different industries etc. is the exogenous treatment of important aggregate variables, such as the rate of wage inflation and the exchange rate. It is precisely the insight obtained by taking the cover off the economy which undermines our faith in the more aggregate models, particularly for medium-term forecasting. Stressing the need for endogenising these variables has become a cliché, like arguing for better dynamic specifications. As usual it is much easier to support the purist line theoretically than to deliver the goods empirically. And because it is so *desirable,* some aggregate model-builders have succumbed to maintaining the semblance of endogeneity by having a set of relevant equations to hand but, in the course of forecasting, over-rule one or more of these equations in the very circumstances where endogeneity has its more crucial policy implications.[4]

It is one thing to claim that wages are responsive to the state of excess demand (among other things) but quite another to assert that the wage system performs its allocative functions reasonably well. The latter automatically denies the economic significance of present high levels of unemployment. Some analysts have gone to extraordinary lengths to attribute a large part of the rise in unemployment during the 1970s to changes in the economy leading to higher *voluntary* unemployment, and failing that there are a number of studies which attempt to manipulate the statistics on unemployment in search of lower estimates of those 'really' unemployed.[5] More sober research (Nickell, 1979) does give support for a modest effect of this kind and it is undoubtedly true that the social welfare implications of the same levels of unemployment differ between the post-war and inter-war periods. But in order to argue that the neoclassical model fits observed behaviour in the British labour market it is necessary to do more than pass over the awkward fact of high levels of unemployment. Some positive evidence of responsive market operation is called for at both the aggregate and disaggregate levels. Despite problems over the Phillips curve and its derivatives, perhaps we could hope for such evidence at the level of different industries, occupations and regions. Most of the detailed studies fail to determine any significant effects of labour market tightness upon wage differentials (see Chapter 7 for the case of engineering). Inevitably there are many qualifications to be attached to usually very simple tests of neoclassical market adjustment, as Fisher (1971) would be quick to point out. But there is something lacking when a theory's main defence seems to be an attack upon the validity of tests which purport to refute it rather than the presentation of results which lend it unequivocal support.

The issues raised above are well illustrated in a recent paper by Beenstock (1979) of the London Business School's Centre for Economic Forecasting. He reviews several studies which, among other things, reach conclusions about prospects for employment in the U.K. Beenstock's mixture of rhetoric and analysis is not unusual for monetarists commenting on the labour market but obscures some striking contradictions related particularly to the British scene. It is therefore worth dealing with the implications of his criticisms, in the light of the comments made earlier. It is argued that Beenstock is carried away by his support of the neoclassical paradigm. His statements about the methods and findings of Leicester (1977), Cripps *et al.* (1978), Barker *et al.* (1979) and Lindley (1978) betray misunderstandings of the models being used and a tendency to extrapolate the findings of these authors in ways calculated to discredit their arguments but not in keeping with their own interpretation and use of the results. Moreover these studies are very different and Beenstock groups them together quite indiscriminately, drawing parallels between them that do not always apply. Of course, having assembled a larger target he is bound to hit parts of it, however erratic his aim. In addition, since Leicester's illustrative projections do suffer from al-.most all of the methodological problems mentioned by Beenstock, there is a strong element of 'guilt by association' transferred to the other studies.[6] The LBS forecasts for 1978–82, contained in *Economic Outlook* (June/July 1979), are not included in Beenstock's review. This conveniently absolves him of the responsibility for criticising the work of his colleagues on the very grounds which he cites when dealing with other forecasts.

Undoubtedly all this is part of a wish to sharpen his own criticism to make way for the contribution of a model which 'goes beyond the traditional trade-off between wages and employment (e.g. the "Phillips curve" effect) to identify a multi-dimensioned set of labour-market responses to changed conditions of demand and

supply.' But one would be more impressed if he had enough faith in
the model to dispense with the parade of straw men against which he
contrives to display it.

Beenstock begins by forcing the four studies into a common
mould in which the projection of GDP is said to be exogenous and
leads to a projection of employment by 'two key steps'.

> 'First there is an assumption about the growth of productivity
> – the more rapid the growth of productivity, the slower the
> growth of employment *for a given growth of output.* Second
> there is an assumption about the relationship between changes
> in output and changes in employment (for a given state of
> technology): the "output elasticity of demand" for labour.'

In fact the first of these is merely a tautology and the second is inconsistent with the first unless the output elasticity is constant
and unity, otherwise the growth of average productivity would
be a function of the growth in output and hence not an independent exogenous assumption. The author *may* have been
trying to distinguish between the long-run and short-run determinants of changes in productivity but that is not clear from
what is actually said. The confusing full quotation may be replaced simply by the initial statement that there is an assumption about the relationship between output and employment.

'Once these technical assumptions have been made, the
forecast of employment follows as a matter of arithmetic' but
as Beenstock asserts at the beginning of his paper 'a sensible
view of the future requires economics as well as arithmetic.'
This jibe loses much of its relevance when we discover that
output is exogenous with respect to productivity only in
Leicester's study and that the employment-output relationships used in all four allow productivity to vary in some way
with output hence actual productivity growth is not itself exogenous.[7] So GDP and output per man are *endogenous* in Cripps,
Barker and Lindley (being partly determined by wage levels).
Beenstock's first technical point is therefore incorrect. His al-
lusion to the lack of 'economics' in fact reflects his insistence
not only that price effects in the determination of output and
factor inputs must be found but that they must take the form of
significant wage effects in the output-employment relationship. The empirical evidence for the UK at the aggregate and
industrial levels does not support this position and whether we
like it or not the short-term employment function of one kind

or another has had the forecasting field to itself for this reason. Thus for the labour demand functions *per se,* market responses are not being suppressed through a perverse refusal to acknowledge readily available econometric evidence.

Beenstock's second main point is that real wages are not allowed to respond to the state of demand. This revelation, although correct, hardly does justice to the degree of discussion on this point contained in Lindley (and previous publications of the two Cambridge groups), in which a case is argued under certain circumstances for holding wages at levels established exogenously, nor to the number of conflicting research studies on wage determination.

The third point is that the working population is treated exogenously in all four studies. Strictly speaking this is not true: the working population as defined in national statistics excludes the unregistered unemployed and is endogenous in Barker, Cripps and Lindley, being dependent upon the propensity to register as unemployed which is a function of the state of demand. However, some measure of *labour supply* is indeed projected as an exogenous variable in the studies reviewed.

As for the LBS model, we find that the labour demand function does contain, in addition to terms in GDP and a time trend, a variable representing the cost of labour relative to output. Unemployment estimates are derived from employment projections via what amounts to a simple registration equation in which only the change in employment influences the change in unemployment. Since unemployment plays no part in the determination of money wages this means that the market clearing device advocated by Beenstock is not featured in the LBS model and labour supply is implicitly exogenous although not in fact identified directly.[8]

It seems reasonable, therefore, to counter the above criticisms of the three main studies cited on the grounds that Beenstock has misrepresented important features of the models concerned. Where there is a clear difference in approach he not only fails to acknowledge that much of the existing evidence on labour demand is contradictory but also that even when significant wage effects in employment functions are identified they tend to be small.[9] This situation is hardly likely to be remedied by the presentation of further results without reference at all to the work of other authors – a methodological deficiency emphasised by Davidson *et al.* (1978) whose econometric approach Beenstock and Warburton (1979) claim to follow.

In the case of labour supply Beenstock completely ignores the measurement problems which dog British empirical work. This partly reflects his assumptions about the efficiency of the labour market mechanism (see below) which lead him to by-pass evidence on unemployment and vacancies and deal purely with the observations of price and quantity exchanged.[10] The difficulties of interpreting the estimates of labour supply parameters in the light of other studies are brushed aside.

This is not the place to discuss in detail the model described by Beenstock and Warburton (1979) whose results Beenstock uses in his attempt to demonstrate that the labour market functions 'adequately enough'. Certain general points should be noted though.

(i) The model incorporates variables which would normally be regarded as endogenous and hence the question of simultaneous equation bias arises, especially given the high level of aggregation adopted.

(ii) The model *assumes* that the labour market tends towards neoclassical equilibrium. We are apparently expected to accept not only that the labour demand and labour supply functions estimated are satisfactory but that this is adequate corroboration for the market clearing condition from which (among other asumptions) they are derived.

(iii) Just in case we have qualms about this much debated methodological position, historical data are presented indicating that the population of working age (15–64 years old) is highly correlated with employment. This is supposed to show that fluctuations in *labour supply* are closely related to fluctuations in employment and that *the absolute difference between labour supply and employment has remained small* throughout the last century. In fact it shows nothing of the sort. The absolute difference (i.e. unemployment) could have been large throughout the period even had the correlation between labour supply and employment been perfect. Furthermore the relation between the population of working age and labour supply is not a sufficiently direct one for the high correlation between employment and the former in the past to apply also to the latter over the medium term.

(iv) Beenstock rather glosses over the fact that his correlation does not in any case prevent the unemployment rate from rising above 10 per cent for two decades during the inter-war period. His reading of the evidence on the impact of the introduction of the Earnings Related Supplement alone allows him to cite an estimate of a 30 per cent increase in unemployment attributable to this measure. *Were we to follow this style of analysis* and allow for the effects of the Welfare State established since the Second World War it is difficult not to conclude that the average unemployment rate of 14 per cent experienced during the period 1921-39 would be equivalent perhaps to 20 per cent and probably more.[11] That would seem on the face of it to provide enough of an historical precedent for unemployment rates of say 15 per cent under present institutional conditions even without the 'cataclysmic' events Beenstock holds responsible for the pre-war debacle. On the other hand, it is certainly the case that an exceptional combination of unfavourable conditions would be required. It is however a reasonable empirical question as to whether such high levels could be generated by sharply introduced monetarist measures against a background of rising potential labour supply, worsening British trade performance and the aftermath of a major world recession from which the developed economies are recovering painfully slowly.

(v) The female labour force participation rate is actually treated as *exogenous* despite the fact that its increase accounts for the major part of the rise in labour supply over the period under study (1948–77). Since the population of working age is also exogenous this amounts to assuming that female labour supply measured as numbers of people is exogenous and that all the supply response operates through female hours of work and male participation and hours of work.

Thus having posed the question 'Do UK labour markets work?' Beenstock answers in the affirmative simply on the basis of his own results using the most aggregate of models possible. His willingness to conclude so much from so little seems to accord such econometric analysis a primacy which in practice it does not deserve. We need to consider the findings of various types of research, including the results of other social scientists, some of whom have studied socio-economic processes at the 'micro' level with very different theoretical perspectives from those commonly found among economists. Industrial relations specialists and industrial sociologists as well as labour economists who have studied decision-making in plants and local labour markets are thus regarded as allies whose research will help us to improve the behavioural content of our theories. And it is quite clear that crucial labour markets do not operate in the neoclassical fashion proposed by Beenstock even though aspects of their behaviour are certainly amenable to quantitative analysis in which price variables have a significant explanatory role to play.[12]

Finally, we return to three issues which affect the interpretation of results derived from models which do not possess the properties of wage endogeneity and responsive supply and demand. The first relates to the fact that a model in which money wages and labour supply are treated exogenously is not necessarily going to lead to incorrect estimates of unemployment even if the market mechanism does operate. This depends upon the values chosen for the exogenous variables. Unless the market mechanism works rapidly, different employment and unemployment forecasts might be due more to different specifications of trade functions than to the treatment of the labour market in a full macroeconomic model. The second issue bears upon the way in which the results are discussed and presented in subsequent chapters. This is the importance attributed to the endogeneity of *policy*. As an expositional device in Lindley (1978) and in the current book a standard view of the economy under present policies can be used to illuminate the underlying position of the economy in the medium term. Alternative policy simulations can then be discussed relative to the standard view together with simulations in which alternative values of the exogenous variables are adopted in the light of the conflicting theories about their determinants.[13] In the case of the labour market, there are some grounds for expecting that policy will react to high levels of unemployment before wages and this approach enables the analysis of the two to be conducted separately.

The third issue is quite simply that the sort of criticisms discussed above, particularly those of the MRG's results, are entirely 'model-bound'. They take no account of the way in which the results are used in reaching *broad* conclusions about prospects for employment and related policy questions.[14] Assumptions about exogenous variables are made in the light of the economic situation being projected; they are not established *a priori* and then fixed throughout the sequence of simulations without reference to the outcome for output, inflation and employment. Such 'informal endogeneity' may offend those who believe they have the complete model but it would seem to be more in keeping with the uncertainties about the evidence and the fact that, in the course of simulating the economy, various adjustments are made to relationships in the model itself which appear for one reason or another to be tracking unsatisfactorily.[15]

It must be said that the desire for identifying market influences and incorporating them into a model of the economy and the labour market is very strong indeed. But this needs to be done at both macroeconomic and microeconomic levels. Our 'special studies' in progress deal with particular labour markets where the significance for policy and aggregate modelling warrants more detailed analysis and where the availability of data makes this possible. Only by synthesising findings at both levels are we likely to improve our understanding of the way in which the labour market works. Otherwise the alacrity with which many economists naturally seize upon aggregate results which apparently fit some version of price theory is liable to blind us to the reality of labour market operation at the disaggregate level, where evidence of market failure or very slow operation of the market mechanism is commonplace. Very few economic policies, whether stressing the use of fiscal or monetary instruments, industrial strategies or the encouragement of incentives, can afford to ignore these problems of structure in the labour market.

Notes

1 For a statement of the research strategy of the Manpower Research Group and a general description of the procedures followed in the course of conducting a medium-term assessment, see Lindley (1976) and (1979a), respectively. Appendix A of the present book summarises the main features of the multisectoral model being used.

2 See Laidler (1978), pp. 35–7.

3 See Lindley (1978), pp. 3–5.

4 For example, Williamson (1978), p.200, notes that the expectations-augmented Phillips curve then used by the National Institute implied a natural rate of unemployment of 11 per cent, well above the level embodied in the policy objectives supported by them.

   'The explanation of this paradox is that whenever expectations get uncomfortably augmented the equation is shut off by introduction of an incomes policy. The conjunction of easy expenditure switching with an absence of any effective demand pressures on the wage-price level leaves me at a loss to understand why the authors are apparently content with unemployment as high as 1.8 per cent'.

5 See, for example, the econometric analysis of Maki and Spindler (1975) and the paring down of the unemployment statistics conducted by Wood (1972).

6 Even so, Beenstock is somewhat ungenerous to Leicester, given the caveats expressed by the latter about his forecasts and the questions for debate he poses at the end of the paper (see pp. 16 and 20), prepared as it was in the form of a simple background paper for a BBC television programme.

7 The medium-term growth in productivity is affected by investment behaviour in the model developed by Barker *et al.* (1979). The model of labour demand used in Lindley (1978) treats *optimal* productivity as exogenous but actual productivity approaches the optimal to a degree depending on the rate of growth of output.

8 The description of the model is that given in Economic Forecasting Unit (1979).

9 Hazledine (1979) provides a recent review of the problems associated with this area of the literature.

10 This cuts him off from the mainstream of American and British research on labour supply in which some significance is attached to measures of the 'labour force' and attempts are made to estimate supply functions from which 'actual' observations may be compared with estimated values. See Greenhalgh and Mayhew (1979) for a review of this research in the British context.

11 The average figure is taken from *British Labour Statistics Historical Abstract 1886–1968,* Table 160, and relates only to the insured labour force.

12 See MacKay *et al.* (1971) for the most extensive of British local labour market studies and Lindley (1979) for a review of the evidence on manpower decision-making with particular reference to the engineering sector. The analysis by Thomas and Deaton (1977) of shortages in certain occupational labour markets is also relevant here.

13 Beenstock takes the standard view registered unemployment projection of 2.3 million for 1982 from Lindley (1978) and claims that the MRG advocates import controls. In fact much of the discussion leads to the conclusion that it might be possible for government to keep unemployment below that level without import controls or an aggressive devaluation, providing the industrial strategy did not produce a major increase in the rate of growth of productivity relative to that in the standard view. Note that the LBS forecasts contained in *Economic Outlook.* June/July 1979, allow registered unemployment to rise to 1.9 million presumably because of the absence of the equilibrating mechanisms proposed by Beenstock. Neither LBS nor the National Institute provides any sensitivity analysis alongside their main forecasts.

14 The policy implications of Beenstock's analysis are discussed in Chapter 9.

15 This practice of making residual adjustments is common to all forecasting groups.

References

Barker, Terry, William Peterson and Alan Winters (1979). 'The Cambridge Multisectoral Dynamic Model: Description and Analysis'. Paper presented to the Seventh International Conference on Input-Output Techniques, Innsbruck.

Beenstock, Michael (1979). 'Do UK Labour Markets Work?'. *Economic Outlook,* June/July, 21–31.

Beenstock, M. and P.W. Warburton (1979). 'A Neoclassical Analysis of Employment and Wage Rates in the UK'. London: London Business School. (mimeographed)

Cripps, F., M. Featherston and T. Ward (1978). 'The Effects of Different Strategies for the UK Economy'. *Economic Policy Review,* 4 (March), 5–21.

Davidson, J.E.H., D.F. Hendry, F. Srba and S. Yeo (1978). 'Econometric Modelling of the Aggregate Time-Series Relationship Between Consumers' Expenditure and Income in the United Kingdom'. *Economic Journal,* 88 (December), 661–92.

Economic Forecasting Unit (1979). 'London Business School Quarterly Econometric Model of the United Kingdom Economy: Relationships in the Basic Model'. London: London Business School.

Fisher, M.R. (1971). *Economic Analysis of Labour.* London: Weidenfeld and Nicholson.

Greenhalgh, Christine and Ken Mayhew (1979). 'Labour Supply in Great Britain: Theory and Evidence'. Treasury/DE/MSC Conference on the Labour Market, Oxford.

Hazledine, Tim (1979). 'Employment Functions and the Demand for Labour in the Short-run'. Paper presented to the Treasury/DE/MSC Conference on the Labour Market, Oxford.

Laidler, David (1978). 'A Monetarist Viewpoint' in Posner, 35–65.

Leicester, Colin (1977). 'Unemployment 2001 A.D.'. Brighton: Institute of Manpower Studies. (mimeographed)

Lindley, R.M. (1976). 'The Research Strategy of the MRG'. Coventry: Manpower Research Group, University of Warwick. (mimeographed)

——(1978) (ed.). *Britain's Medium-Term Employment Prospects.* Coventry: Manpower Research Group, University of Warwick.

—— (1979). 'Economic Decision-Making and Active Manpower Policies'. Paper presented to European Consortium for Political Research, Free University of Brussels, April.

——(1979a) 'Employment Forecasting'. Paper presented to the SSRC Workshop on Employment and Unemployment, London, June.

Lucas, R.E. and T.J. Sargent (1978). 'After Keynesian Macroeconomics'. *After the Phillips Curve: Persistence of High Inflation and High Unemployment.* Proceedings of a conference held at Edgartown, Mass., sponsored by the Federal Reserve Bank of Boston.

MacKay, D.I. *et al.* (1971). *Labour Markets Under Different Employment Conditions.* London: George Allen and Unwin.

Maki, D. and Z.A, Spindler (1975). 'The Effect of Unemployment Compensation on the Rate of Unemployment in Great Britain'. *Oxford Economic Papers,* 27, 3, 440–54.

Nickell, S.J. (1979). 'The Effect of Unemployment and Related Benefits On the Duration of Unemployment'. *Economic Journal,* 89 (March), 34–49.

Posner, Michael (1978) (ed). *Demand Management.* London: Heineman.

Thomas, Barry and David Deaton (1977). *Labour Shortages and Economic Analysis.* Oxford: Basil Blackwell.

Williamson, John (1978). 'The Balance of Payments' in Posner, 200–8.

Wood, J.B. (1972). *How Much Unemployment?* London: The Institute of Economic Affairs.

3 Economic Growth and Employment

R.M. LINDLEY AND J.D. WHITLEY

The United Kingdom could easily squander the benefits of North Sea oil and gas production. The opportunities provided by the discovery and exploitation of this resource will be wasted on temporary increases in private and government consumption if the pattern of economic change over the next five years or so continues to be dictated by short-term considerations, and if governments fail to appreciate that manipulating the conventional fiscal and monetary instruments of policy has not and will not reverse the long-term deterioration in Britain's relative industrial performance.

This chapter explains why we have reached the above conclusion and why the gap between devising short-run measures and stating long-run aspirations must be bridged by some realistic thinking about the medium term. To some extent we have allowed the chronology of recent political developments to dictate the order of presentation of our analysis. This starts with an assessment of the medium-term outlook for the economy and employment prior to the introduction of the June 1979 Budget by the Conservative government and moves on to explore the probable implications of the changes in policy announced or under serious consideration by the Government.

The chapter is in five main sections. The first briefly describes the pre-Budget scenario together with the main assumptions which underlie that projection. This provides a convenient perspective from which to discuss the policies of the present government as indicated in the Budget strategy and related statements about policy over the medium term. Section 3.2 deals with these points of interpretation and analysis of what appears to be a very significant shift in approach to managing or not managing the economy. Section 3.3 then describes our standard view of the implications of current policy for the period up to 1985. The macroeconomic environment is discussed together with the outlook for major industrial groups. The high levels of unemployment being projected suggest that there

may be some equilibrating forces in the economy which are not represented in the model but which might operate to modify this outcome. Our treatment of wages and the exchange rate as exogenous
variables is examined from this point of view. Although we conclude, as already indicated in Chapter 2, that the approach taken
does not obscure some achievable labour market 'equilibrium' at
much lower levels of unemployment, there is a strong likelihood
that policy itself would change in response to the worsening employment situation. In the light of these results, section 3.4 investigates two alternative policy scenarios. In the first, a package of reflationary measures is introduced with the objective of increasing personal income and expenditure rather than government spending.
The second explores a mechanism by which structural change in the
economy might be induced with a view to achieving a substantial
improvement in export performance. Finally, section 3.5
presents our general assessment of the policy dilemma facing the
government.

It is important to emphasise that *none of the projections is a forecast of how the economic situation will actually develop over the next
five years or so.* Obviously our choice of simulations through which
to examine the problem of stimulating higher employment implies a
view of the *potential* scale of the unemployment problem but we
would expect policy to change so as to ameliorate the situation to
some extent. On the other hand, it is shown that there is rather limited scope for stimulating the growth of output *as well as* employment whilst at the same time holding to certain styles of economic
management. Our purpose is to explore the tensions between short-
run and long-run objectives by concentrating on the medium-run
transitional problems which are likely to arise, especially those
which affect the labour market and the social and economic aspirations of the population at work.

3.1 The Pre-Budget Scenario

The simulation results described in this section focus on the underlying economic situation faced by the Conservative government
before introducing their first Budget. Despite the satisfaction of the
previous administration with certain economic indicators, notably
the slight fall in unemployment, some apprehension about the outlook for inflation was clearly warranted not least in connection with
forthcoming public sector wage settlements and rising oil prices. At

an international level the prospects for achieving modest but sustained growth were becoming bleaker.

From the point of view of employment policy, the circumstances of 1975–79 have perhaps tended to foster the illusion that however slow the growth of output, employment would not fall to the extent that past trends in productivity growth might imply. In each of the two decades up to 1974, gross industrial output per man had risen by slightly more than $2^{1}/_{2}$ per cent per annum. Output growth, however, dropped from 3 to 2 per cent per annum between these two periods and employment accordingly fell in the second decade by as much as it had risen in the first, i.e. about $^{1}/_{2}$ per cent per annum. From 1974 to 1978 productivity growth slumped to barely 1 per cent per annum, on the face of it a rather fortuitous response when output was rising on average by less than $^{1}/_{4}$ per cent per annum. Thus the first part of the decade following the oil crisis produced a rather similar rate of decline of employment to that experienced during the decade preceding it but from a combination of quite different records of growth in output and productivity.

This leads us to ask whether or not the rest of the period to 1984/85 will continue this contrast in economic performance. If it is inconceivable that industrial output should not increase more quickly, surely the same would apply to productivity. Since the change in employment is determined by the difference between these two growth rates, clearly the crucial issue in establishing the medium-term outlook concerns the relative speed with which output and productivity recover. Real incomes on the other hand, are determined particularly by the level of productivity achieved. In fact the falling employment projected in the pre-Budget simulation reflects the impact of slow output growth rather than rapid productivity growth. The rest of this section deals with the exogenous assumptions from which this result is derived and summarises the macroeconomic outcome associated with it.

3.1.1 Main exogenous assumptions

World production and prices

For the period 1978–85 world industrial production is expected to grow at about 4 per cent per annum, somewhat below the trend rate for the previous decade and well below the trend of almost 6 per cent per annum established in the twenty years up to the oil crisis of

1973. Our projection anticipates a slow down in 1978–80 followed by an upturn particularly towards the end of the forecast period. The profile of change is perhaps less marked by recession and recovery than that expected by other forecasters. This is largely because we have not assumed that the recent oil price increase will bring about the same degree of synchronised response as was experienced previously. We do not expect the United States to be drawn into line with other developed countries to the same extent as it was in 1974.

Overall, however, the projection reflects our feeling that the impact of the recent increase in oil prices will be to strengthen fears of the inflationary consequences of economic recovery and this will further limit the degree of fiscal and monetary stimulus over the next few years. Problems of world excess capacity in certain industries, notably shipbuilding and metal manufacturing, will probably be exacerbated. The climate of opinion in the major economies is still extremely risk-averse on the subject of resurrecting employment objectives and the latest action of the OPEC producers has provided governments with the chance to bring home once again the need for financial prudence. Indeed, the alacrity with which some have taken this opportunity suggests that an element of Pavlovian response is developing in official and financial circles when addressing the public at large. In addition to the direct impact upon inflation, great stress is placed upon the distributional effects of an oil price increase by which purchasing power is transferred to countries whose capacity for absorbing more imports is very limited, and the further strain it will place upon the international economic system. Much less attention is paid to the fall in the real price of oil since 1974 which has given rise to periodic pressures within OPEC for action to boost the real value of oil revenues. Between 1977 and 1978 OPEC exports fell by 15 per cent and the current account surplus was halved when both are revalued in terms of the world export price of manufactures. The main problems are the uncertainty surrounding OPEC deliberations and the sharp changes in price which result: both have a destabilising effect upon the world economy which exacerbates the deflationary impact of the price increases *per se.*

At present, the real price of oil is about 25 per cent below its 1974 level and the average price of other commodities has only recently regained its 1974 level when expressed in terms of SDRs. Although the underlying market position for oil is not now particularly favourable to producers, a fact which was concealed temporarily by the cut in Iranian supply, the prospects for the next eighteen months are for a considerable rise in the real price of oil, following which we have allowed for a further small gain to 1985. The growth rate for the period as a whole is 10 per cent per annum, about 3 per cent above that assumed for manufactures. Among other commodities, the situation for food products is expected to worsen on average by almost as much as that for oil is expected to improve. Non-food agricultural products, on the other hand, are assumed to hold their own against manufactures, whereas basic materials will experience some loss and minerals and metals some gain. The prices of manufactures are projected to rise at about 7 per cent per annum on average which is also the projected rate of growth of world inflation.

The profile of price changes assumed for 1978–85 is characterised by a general slowing down of all growth rates towards the end of the period but incorporates several significant changes in relative prices during 1978–80, some of which are already foreshadowed by the published statistics for 1978 and the first half of 1979. By 1985, both the world prices of UK imports and competitors' export prices are rising at 6 per cent per annum when weighted by the appropriate trade shares. Allowing for the effects of the domestic economy[1] upon the determination of realised UK import and export prices, the growth rates for 1978–85 are 9 and 11 per cent per annum respectively in the pre-Budget view: by 1985 these rates of change have dropped to 6 and 7 per cent per annum respectively.

Exchange rate and interest rate

In the pre-Budget view, the dollar *exchange rate* is assumed to fall by 10 per cent between 1978 and 1985. This has been set exogenously in the light of various factors, namely, the projections of world prices, domestic wage inflation (see below), the impact of North Sea oil on the balance of payments account and the worsening non-oil trade performance of the UK. The present level of the exchange rate is inconsistent with theories which either see it as being determined principally by competitiveness or attribute the main influence to relative monetary growth. Clearly, at the moment, the beneficial effects of North Sea oil on the current balance of payments and on capital movements (reflecting optimistic expectations about the future state of the current balance) are overriding relationships which would otherwise operate in less exceptional circumstances. The important issue is to what extent will these relationships reassert themselves within the medium term. In particular, how quickly will the present buoyancy of sterling give way to the decline dictated by the underlying weakness of the non-oil economy? Certainly, as we enter the period of peak oil production, attention will gradually begin to shift from the dynamic impetus provided by *rising* contributions to the balance of payments and government income to the uncertainties attached to the period of gradual reduction in oil output. Such a shift will, however, take some time and, as we shall see in the pre-Budget simulation, in the interim a substantial trade surplus could accumulate not only because of the net trade gain from oil but also because import growth generally will be held down by the slow growth of the economy. This will tend to keep the exchange rate considerably higher than we would expect on the basis of maintaining constant competitiveness. Further discussion of the behaviour of the exchange rate over the medium-term is postponed until section 3.3 where the effects of alternative assumptions for both the exchange rate and domestic wage inflation are examined.

Our pre-Budget assumption is that on unchanged policies the dollar rate would fall to 5 per cent below the 1978 average level ($1.92) by 1981. This implies a reduction of 12 per cent from the April 1979 level, i.e. prior to the General Election. A further more modest reduction is allowed for between 1981 and 1985 by which time the exchange rate reaches $1.73. For the period 1978–85 the exchange rate then falls by 1.4 per cent per annum, whereas to maintain constant competitiveness of manufactures it would be necessary to fall by almost 3 per cent per annum.

The *interest rate* used in the model is the consol rate. In our pre-Budget view we have assumed a level of 12 per cent for 1979 (which was about the average rate before the Budget) falling to 8 per cent for 1983–85.

Domestic wage inflation

The average wage in the economy is imposed exogenously. Money wage increases are held at 15 per cent per annum or so for 1978–81 as the effects of past incomes policies upon real wages and relativities begin to unwind. They are then brought down to about 8 per cent per annum by 1985 which, together with an average rate of growth of output per man of roughly 2 per cent per annum, implies that UK manufacturing costs expressed in dollars are growing at about the same rate as UK competitors' export prices.

Optimal productivity and hours

Optimal productivity and hours are those levels of output per man-hour and average hours worked per week to which actual productivity and hours will tend to converge eventually under steady rates of industrial output growth. They are 'optimal' in the sense that hourly labour costs will be at their minimum and capital equipment will be working at peak efficiency (see Appendix B). Since many industries begin the period at well below capacity and output changes are not evenly distributed from year to year, the actual values reached in 1985 are significantly below the optimal values.

The industrial variation in rates of growth of optimal productivity is considerable whether measured as output per man or man-hour (Table 3.1). In aggregate, optimal output per man increases at 1.8 per cent per annum, with manufacturing and services rising at 2.7 and 1.0 per cent per annum respectively. Growth rates within manufacturing are above 3 per cent per annum for chemicals and textiles and below 2 per cent per annum for metals. Optimal output per man in construction (which has a very weak impact upon employment in the labour demand equation) grows more slowly than is the case for services but within the latter, transport and communication has a rate of increase close to that of the manufacturing average, whereas miscellaneous services shows almost no change in productivity at all up to 1985. Much less variation is apparent in the projected changes in optimal hours of work. On average these are reduced by 6 per cent over the period in services and by 4 per cent in manufacturing. Further discussion of these estimates of the underlying trends in optimal productivity will be left until the post-Budget outcome is presented in section 3.3

Labour force

In the previous chapter we mentioned the inherent difficulties that exist with the concept of labour supply. Following the general approach adopted in Lindley (1978) our basis for the analysis of the unemployment implications of medium-term economic growth is a set of population accounts which are projected into the future. The lack of data on flows between the labour force and the rest of the population means that the resulting projections are derived from extremely crude procedures. The *aggregate* labour force figures for males, married females and non-married females are effectively obtained from official projections of the age structure of the population and MRG projections of age-specific economic activity rates.

Table 3.1 Optimal Output per Man and Hours Worked

Index numbers 1978 = 100 or % per annum

SAM groups	Optimal output per man		Optimal weekly hours		Actual output per man as % below optimal in 1978
	1985	1978–85	1985	1978–85	
Agriculture	127	3.5	93	−1.1	21
Mining(1)	119	2.6	94	−0.8	16
Food, drink & tobacco	120	2.6	95	−0.8	2
Chemicals etc.	129	3.7	95	−0.7	14
Metals	109	1.3	97	−0.4	16
Engineering	118	2.3	95	−0.7	8
Textiles & clothing	126	3.4	97	−0.4	9
Manufacturing n.e.s.	117	2.2	97	−0.4	10
Construction	104	0.6	97	−0.4	22
Public utilities	155	6.5	95	−0.7	20
Transport & communication	122	2.9	96	−0.5	2
Distribution	109	1.2	93	−1.0	5
Professional services	108	1.1	93	−1.1	1
Miscellaneous services	101	0.1	94	−0.9	15
Manufacturing	121	2.7	96	−0.6	9
Services	108	1.0	93	−1.0	6
All industries (1)	112	1.6	94	−0.8	10
All industries	115	1.8	94	−0.8	10

Note: (1) Excludes oil and natural gas production.

Table 3.2   UK Labour Force Projections 1978–85

| | Males | | Females | | *Thousands* |
	Level	Change on previous year	Level	Change on previous year	Total
1978	16,283	..	10,454	..	26,737
1979	16,316	33	10,549	95	26,865
1980	16,368	52	10,629	80	26,997
1981	16,430	62	10,791	162	27,221
1982	16,524	94	10,846	55	27,370
1983	16,637	113	10,963	117	27,600
1984	16,746	109	11,074	111	27,820
1985	16,788	42	11,151	77	27,939
1978–85 % change	3.1		6.7		4.5

Sources: Unpublished 1977-based total population projection by GAD; DE *Gazette* (June 1977); MRG estimates (see text).

The margins of error involved in the former are likely to be much less than those affecting the latter. This is because (i) death rates are relatively stable, (ii) young people reaching school-leaving age during 1978–85 have already been born and therefore the relevant cohort sizes are not subject to uncertainties about birth rates, and (iii) migration patterns are not likely to be disturbed sufficiently, either autonomously or through policy changes, to make a significant impact upon the population of working age in the medium term.

MRG activity rate projections are derived from those prepared by the Department of Employment (DE), modified for a slightly different view taken of the labour force participation of married women aged 35–54 and all women aged 60–64. In total, the labour force is reduced by almost 200 thousand because of the lower activity rates adopted for these groups. Between 1978 and 1985 the labour force is then projected to grow by 1.2 million (500 thousand males and 700 thousand females) or 4.5 per cent, as shown in Table 3.2. Female labour force growth is more than twice that for males but when married females are distinguished from non-married females it can be seen that the labour force growth of the latter is in turn more than twice that of the former. Further details of the structure of labour force changes are given in Table 3.3 where the population and activ-

Table 3.3 Changes in the Age Structure of the Labour Force 1978–85

Thousands : Great Britain only

	Labour force		Change 1978–85		Popu-lation effect	Activity effect
	1978	1985	(% of 1978)	(thou-sands)		
Males						
16–19	1,093	1,081	−1.1	−12	36	−48
20–24	1,752	2,049	17.0	297	289	8
25–34	3,790	3,798	0.2	8	12	−4
35–44	3,099	3,543	14.3	444	451	−7
45–54	3,051	2,934	−3.8	−117	−114	−3
55–59	1,520	1,370	−9.9	−150	−149	−1
60–64	1,115	1,215	9.0	100	118	−17
65–69	310	232	−25.2	−78	−35	−43
70 +	143	132	−7.7	−11	16	−27
Total	15,873	16,354	3.0	481	624	−142
Married females						
16–19	70	76	8.6	6	5	−
20–24	546	605	10.8	59	53	7
25–34	1,564	1,493	−4.5	−71	−123	53
35–44	1,836	2,171	18.2	335	247	88
45–54	1,814	1,788	−1.4	−26	−97	71
55–59	675	668	−1.0	−7	−77	70
60–64	263	275	4.6	12	29	−17
65+	100	112	12.0	12	−2	14
Total	6,868	7,188	4.7	320	35	286
Non-married females						
16–19	854	831	−2.7	−23	24	−47
20–24	680	866	27.4	186	177	9
25–34	502	624	24.3	122	137	−15
35–44	308	428	39.0	120	123	−3
45–54	413	413	−	−	1	−1
55–59	278	242	−12.9	−36	−32	−3
60–64	157	131	−16.6	−26	6	−32
65+	141	143	1.4	2	6	−3
Total	3,333	3,678	10.4	345	442	−95
Total	26,074	27,220	4.4	1,146	1,101	49

Source: See Table 3.2.

Note : The population effect is defined as the change in the population between 1978 and 1985, multiplied by the activity rate prevailing in 1978. The activity rate effect is defined as the change in activity rate between 1978 and 1985, multiplied by the population in 1985. The two effects sum to the net change in the labour force during the period.

ity effects are also defined. The significance of the former for males and non-married females was noted in our previous study. The decline in relative importance of the activity effect for married females as a determinant of labour force growth has been a major feature since the middle 1970s. This is due mainly to changes in the age structure of the population towards younger groups and to the postponement of the age of first marriage (and higher divorce rates). The first of these generates large population effects whereas for 1970–76 these were quite small and *negative,* and the second concentrates the female population effect amongst non-married women whose activity rates tend to be higher than those for married women. In addition whilst the aggregate activity effect for males continues to be negative, the likelihood of further reductions in the labour force participation of men aged 65 and above is now less than was the case at the beginning of the decade, unless a policy of earlier retirement is vigorously pursued by the government. However, recent evidence suggests that activity rates for males aged 60–64 have fallen due to an unexpected increase in earlier retirement (a small part of which could be attributed to the Job Release Scheme). If this trend were to continue to 1985 the basic labour force estimate might be reduced by as much as 210 thousand.

Thus the population effects of high birth rates during the late 1950s and early 1960s and low birth rates during the First World War and in the 1920s, combined with the expected larger proportion of non-married women, leads to large net flows into the labour force from males and non-married females during 1978–85 in contrast to the net outflows experienced in the previous decade or so. On the other hand, the tempering of progress towards higher activity rates among married women is more than enough to offset the small increase in the population effect expected up to 1985 and this leads to a marked slowdown in the rate of growth of the married female labour force. Between 1970 and 1978 it rose by 1 million compared with a projection of less than a third of that for 1978–85. A longer discussion of the factors affecting the female labour supply is given in Chapter 6.

Public expenditure and taxation

Table 3.4 gives our pre-Budget projections of general government final consumption and social capital formation respectively. These reflect our reading of the 1979 White Paper on public expenditure (Cmnd 7439).

Table 3.4   Public Expenditure : 1979 White Paper

(a) General government final consumption

			% per annum
	1978–82	1982–85	1978–85
Military defence	1.4	0.4	0.8
National Health Service	2.6	3.6	3.0
Other central government	2.4	3.5	2.9
Education	1.2	2.7	1.8
Other local government	1.9	2.4	2.1
Total	1.9	2.5	2.1

(b) Social capital formation

	% per annum
	1978–85
Dwellings	0.4
Education	−2.2
Health	0.3
Roads	1.9
Other	0.9
Total	0.5

(c) Nationalised industries' investment

	% per annum
	1978–85
Coal mining	2.0
Iron & steel	−1.8
Gas	5.1
Electricity	2.6
Water	0.5
Communications	1.5
Total	1.7

Sources: Cmnd 7439 and MRG estimates for 1983–85.

We estimate that there has been an element of shortfall on current expenditure on goods and services of nearly £100m (1970 prices) in 1978. Some of this may be attributed to cash limits and in section 3.2 we shall discuss how cash limits may influence spending in 1979–81. For the present we have assumed that the contingency reserve remains unspent and that the extent of the shortfall in 1978 persists in future years.

The White Paper only provides projections to financial year 1982–83. Between 1978 and 1982 expenditure on health and 'other central government' rises faster than average. Subsequently we assume that they maintain their momentum relative to expenditure growth in education and 'other local government' but these four categories together expand by 1 per cent per annum faster than is the case during 1978–82. Military defence, in contrast, experiences a reduced rate of growth in the second half of the period. Overall, government consumption increases by 2 per cent per annum with health and 'other central government' growing most quickly at 3 per cent per annum.

Social capital formation also shows a shortfall in 1978 relative to planned expenditure, particularly in housing, and this is assumed to continue. The slow growth anticipated for 1978–85 incorporates a period of recovery to 1980 from which little further increase is envisaged. Capital formation for education suffers most of all, declining at 2 per cent per annum whereas the road programme *increases* expenditure at about that rate. In total, social investment progresses very slowly at 0.5 per cent per annum; expenditure on dwelling reflects the average growth.

Nationalised industry investment for 1978–82 is also derived from the White Paper. For 1983–85 we have assumed little change in the level of investment in most of the nationalised industries, with the exception of electricity where some tailing-off in expenditure is assumed after the rapid rise expected in 1982–83. In total, investment by nationalised industries grows by 1.7 per cent per annum over the period, much faster than the outcome for investment by private industry which is almost unchanged between 1978 and 1985. In the pre-Budget view, gross fixed capital formation for the economy as a whole grows by $1\frac{1}{2}$ per cent per annum, a large part of which is due to investment in private dwellings which increases by over $4\frac{1}{2}$ per cent per annum as against barely $\frac{1}{2}$ per cent per annum in the public sector.

Current and capital transfers together with net lending are projected from Cmnd 7439 for 1978 to 1982 and then extrapolated to 1985 in the light of the policy of the Labour government. This incorporates growth in real terms for current grants to persons from public authorities.

Direct tax rates on personal and corporate income and tax allowances are set at the pre-1979 Budget levels. Allowances and tax bands are then indexed for inflation from 1978.

3.1.2 Pre-Budget prospects for 1978–85

In our pre-Budget scenario, GDP grows at only 1.3 per cent per annum to 1985, sustained particularly by private consumption

Table 3.5   Macroeconomic Summary of Pre-Budget Scenario

	1978–85 % p.a.	
GDP and its components	1970 prices	1975 prices
GDP at market prices	1.3	1.3
Consumers' expenditure	1.8	1.8
General government final consumption	1.6	1.8
Gross fixed capital formation	1.5	0.5
Exports of goods and services	4.1	4.4
Imports of goods and services	5.3	5.0
Labour market, prices and incomes		
Employment	−0.3	
Basic labour force estimate	0.6	
Average earnings per annum	11.8	
Consumer prices	10.0	
Real personal disposable income	1.4	
	1978	1985
Employment (m)	24.8	24.3
Basic labour force estimate (m)	26.7	27.9
Registered unemployment − high (m) ⎱	1.4	3.0
− low (m) ⎰		2.6
Trade and balance of payments		
Balance of trade (% of GDP)	1.2	2.5
Balance of payments (% of GDP)	−	1.2
Imports as % domestic final demand	27.1	34.8
Exports as % domestic output	28.1	34.1
Public sector borrowing requirement		
PSBR (% of GDP)	5.5	2.5

Note: The high and low estimates for registered unemployment
        correspond to marginal propensities to register of 1.0 and 0.7
        (which equals the average propensity in 1978), respectively.
        See text for discussion.

averaging 1.8 per cent per annum and to a lesser extent by government consumption and total investment (see Table 3.5).[2] The net
trade position worsens in constant prices with exports rising at 4.1
per cent per annum and imports at 5.3 per cent per annum. Favourable terms of trade convert a constant price deficit, however, into a
substantial surplus of 2.5 per cent of current price GDP. The rate of

inflation as measured by the consumers' expenditure deflator, averages 10 per cent per annum. Real personal disposable income lags somewhat behind private consumption indicating a reduction in the savings ratio from 15 to 13 per cent. The PSBR falls from 5.5 to 2.5 per cent of current price GDP.

By present standards the economy in 1985 is operating well within its financial constraints and there is obviously some scope for reflation in order to achieve a better performance on the employment front. The latter is indeed disappointing with a loss of 600 thousand jobs over the period. Combined with a rising labour force the implications of this for the *direction* of impact upon unemployment are obvious. The *magnitude* of change is highly uncertain, however. With an exogenous treatment of the labour force and an assumption that the marginal propensity to register is close to unity, the level of registered unemployment doubles between 1978 and 1985, reaching 3 million. Unregistered unemployment (including the out-of-work sick) is then at its ceiling of about 600 thousand throughout the forecast period. Although the evidence on the determinants of labour supply in the UK is extremely limited and hardly bears at all upon the sort of labour market situation portrayed in the pre-Budget simulation, the 3.7 million estimate of *total* unemployment is best regarded as an upper bound to what would be observed in practice. At such levels the *discouraged worker* phenomenon would probably be very strong and *short-run* excess supply would be significantly below 3.7 million. Without legislation to extend the period for which unemployment and other benefits were paid there would also be an increase in the number of people exhausting their rights to those benefits for which eligibility involves an obligation to register as unemployed. The marginal propensity to register would then fall and this would supplement the tendency of the discouraged-worker effect to mitigate the rise in registered unemployment. Of course any major extension of special employment and training measures in these circumstances would also reduce the marginal propensity to register amongst those unable to find 'conventional' jobs because participants in these schemes are excluded from the count of registered unemployed. Our estimate of the *average* propensity to register in 1978 is 71 per cent and applying this to the results for 1985 yields a level of registered unemployment of about 2.6 million. On balance this figure is probably the best guide we can offer to the lowest level of *registered* unemployment likely to be observed in practice, should employment fall as shown in the pre-Budget simulation and the long-run trend in labour supply follow that implied by our basic labour force estimates. Further comment is postponed until dealing more fully with the structure of employment under the standard (post-Budget) view.

Although substantial improvement is projected up to 1985, it is worth noting the compositional changes taking place in the current balance of payments and the PSBR. Both potential constraints on economic expansion are relaxed through the impact of North Sea oil but in such a way as to leave some cause for concern about the situation when oil production begins to decline towards the end of the 1980s.

The pre-Budget assessment for 1985 incorporates a current balance of payments surplus of £4 billion. Obviously, this is strongly influenced by the assumptions made about the world economic environment, the exchange rate and domestic wage inflation. Some equilibrating adjustments would be expected to come into play but this is not likely to be enough to offset the surplus which is due mainly to the £20 billion contribution from oil and natural gas production. The surplus from services reaches £7 billion in 1985 but the non-oil visibles account moves deeply into deficit, cutting the balance of trade back to £9 billion. The growth in government transfers abroad and the effects of remitted profits from North Sea operations cause the net balance on transfers and factor payments abroad to deteriorate.

The PSBR gradually declines over the period to 2½ per cent of GDP. By 1985 petroleum revenue tax contributes £5½ billion to the government account, amounting to 4 per cent of the total income of public authorities. At the same time, however, £7 billion is being paid out as unemployment benefit.

3.2 Change of Course

> 'The truth is that our troubles are very largely home-made. If we tackle them ourselves we can pull our own economy round even in a world of slow growth. If we do nothing to change course, nothing that happens beyond these shores can help us.'
>
> – The Chancellor of the Exchequer
> Budget Speech, 12 June 1979

Despite the attention given to analysing the short-term effects of the June Budget upon inflation, output and employment, the new government's strategy is, essentially, a long-term one, concerned with the supply side of the economy and should be judged primarily from that point of view. Remarking upon the experience of 1978 in which consumer spending increased in percentage terms by seven times as much as manufacturing output, the Chancellor concluded that: 'Though demand was rising strongly, and unemployment remained high, the economy was almost unable to increase supply.' The philosophy behind the new policy to deal with this problem was put most succinctly in the Queen's Speech :

> 'My Government will give priority in economic policy to controlling inflation through the pursuit of firm monetary and fiscal policies. By reducing the burden of direct taxation and restricting the claims of the public sector on the nation's resources they will start to restore incentives, encourage efficiency and create a climate in which commerce and industry can flourish. In this way they will lay a secure basis for investment, productivity and increased employment in all parts of the United Kingdom.'
> –Queen's Speech to Parliament, 15 May 1979

The purpose of this section is to set out our interpretation of Government policy as it affects the treatment of taxation and expenditure in the model and certain other exogenous variables which might be expected to respond to the new circumstances. More general comment on the strategy itself and its probable impact will be left for later sections.

The Chancellor began his policy of increasing incentives, through reducing taxes on income, by cutting tax rates and raising thresholds at all levels. The basic rate was reduced from 33 to 30 per cent and the top rate from 83 to 60 per cent. Increases in personal allowances provided for in the 'caretaker' Finance Act passed in April 1979 were doubled.

In order to finance these tax cuts, not only has public expenditure been reduced but indirect taxes have been increased. This reflects the difficulty of achieving very large cuts in expenditure in the short term but also the belief that the relationship between direct and indirect tax revenues has got out of balance in recent years and some further shifting of the burden of taxation on to indirect taxes is appropriate (over and above that which would occur as a result of reductions in income tax *per se)*. The revenue change arising from increases in VAT to a single rate of 15 per cent will pay for the direct tax reliefs in a full financial year so that increases in excise duties on oil will lead to the overall effect of the tax changes being slightly deflationary. In financial year 1979–80 VAT receipts will increase by only half that of a full year and indirect tax revenues will offset only £2.4 billion of the £3.6 billion of direct tax reliefs. However, the reflationary bias of the short-run effect of changes in taxes is reversed by reductions in various components of public expenditure for 1979–80, amounting to some £2¹/₂ billion.

Some of the short-term reductions in public expenditure appear to be no more than reflections of the likely shortfall, as mentioned in the previous section, and allowance is already made for this effect. The major changes anticipated in *actual* public expenditure expressed in 1970 prices and by economic category, are shown in Table 3.6. Omitting the effects of the shortfall, the specific cuts introduced in the Budget amount to less than ¹/₂ per cent of the pre-Budget levels of expenditure expected for 1979–80. The most important reductions in real terms follow from the application of the cash limits announced by the previous government in April 1979, without adjusting for price rises higher than those allowed for and with only a limited accommodation for higher pay rises.[3] In total the effects of specific cuts and cash limits are estimated to reduce current expenditure by 2 per cent in 1979 and 2¹/₂ per cent in 1980: education and other local government programmes are particularly affected.

The cuts in social capital formation are small once allowance is made for the likely shortfall in public housing. There are also reductions in current transfers, capital grants and subsidies (mainly employment subsidies) but the overall changes in public expenditure are dominated by those affecting current expenditure.

The Budget speech also gives guidance on the longer-term aims of the Government. Stating that the tax changes represented 'only the first stage of a major reduction in the burden of direct taxation that we are determined to make', the Chancellor indicated that he wished ultimately to reduce the basic rate to no more than 25 per cent and, having reduced the top rate to the European average, referred obliquely to the possibility of further reductions in higher rates.

Bearing in mind the financial situation projected under the pre-Budget scenario, we have made further cuts in the basic rate, to 28

Table 3.6 Reductions in Public Expenditure: the 1979 Budget Measures and Beyond

(a) Current expenditure on goods and services

| | | | | | | | £m 1970 prices |
	1979	1980	1981	1982	1983	1984	1985
Military defence	31	24	6	–	–	–	–
Health	53	47	8	–	–	–	–
Other central government	26	75	90	132	181	186	192
Education	59	87	69	90	120	122	124
Other local government	68	74	73	96	128	130	132
Total	237	307	246(1)	318	429	438	448
Total as % of planned	(2.1)	(2.6)	(2.1)	(2.7)	(3.6)	(3.6)	(3.6)

(b) Social capital formation

| | | | £m 1970 prices |
	1979	1980	1981–85
Education	1	4	–
Health	–	–	–
Roads	–	2	–
Other	6	15	–
Dwellings	6	14	–
Total	13	35	–

(c) Transfers and subsidies

| | | | £m 1970 prices |
	1979	1980	1981–85
Current transfers	16	34	–
Capital grants	18	37	–
Subsidies	11	19	–
Total	45	72	–

Sources: *Financial Statement and Budget Report;* MRG estimates.

Note: (1) This drop reflects the assumption that cash limits will be consistent with our wage inflation assumptions from 1981 onwards, so no cut in real spending arises from this source in 1981 in contrast to 1979–80.

per cent in 1980, 26 per cent in 1981 and 25 per cent by April 1982. Higher tax rates are also reduced accordingly, leaving the top rate at 50 per cent in 1982. This may be somewhat faster progress towards the Chancellor's 'long-term' aim than he intended but we would argue that the reductions in expenditure which are now being seriously considered by Government are large enough to warrant such changes if the fall in public sector demand for goods and services is to be offset by an increase in that of the private sector. Tax allowances are indexed for inflation as before. Over the medium term we again assume that specific rates are changed to keep pace with inflation even though this has not been the case in recent years. VAT is held at its new rate of 15 per cent throughout the period. This means we believe that no further stiffening of the indirect tax system is intended by the Government, beyond indexation.

As for public expenditure over the medium term, it is becoming apparent that the reductions announced in the Budget were only part of the overall strategy of reducing the size of the public sector. At the time of writing no public announcement has yet been made of the likely scale of future changes, although press reports suggest that they may be substantial. For present purposes it is enough, however, to get some estimate of their broad magnitude. Our reading of Government intentions is that current expenditure on defence and the National Health Service will be unaffected in the main but there could well be reductions in other central government spending rising from 5 per cent in 1981 to 10 per cent in 1983 and thereafter and reductions in education and other local government spending building up to 5 per cent in 1983 and thereafter. These changes from the pre-Budget view are shown in Table 3.6.

The restraint on future growth of public expenditure is evidently intended not only to finance income tax cuts but also to enable the Government to bring down its borrowing requirement. Reporting that the new measures would reduce the PSBR from 5$^{1}/_{2}$ per cent of GDP in 1978–79 to 4$^{1}/_{2}$ per cent in 1979–80 and achieve corresponding reductions in the public sector deficit, the Chancellor remarked (Budget speech, June 1979) that: 'These are important steps in the right direction. I intend to continue along that path in the years ahead.' Thus it would seem appropriate to expect the Government to manage its budget so as to continue the reduction in the PSBR as a percentage of GDP, perhaps reaching 2 or 3 per cent in the middle 1980s depending on the state of the economy.

The purpose of reducing the borrowing requirement is obviously to cut the rate of growth of money supply without undue restraint on the activities of the private sector. The adoption of 'firm monetary discipline and fiscal policies' consistent with that objective reflects the view that policies on the supply side of the economy, such as reducing direct taxes, 'will not themselves be enough unless we also squeeze inflation out of the system'.

This brings us to one of the most controversial aspects of evaluating the new approach to economic management: the estimation of the impact of monetary and fiscal restraint upon the rate of wage increases. We expect that wage bargains will be less influenced by the effects of cuts in direct taxes upon real incomes than by the prospect of a higher rate of price inflation arising from the higher rate of VAT. Any actual or expected rise in unemployment following the reduction in output caused by Government policy is assumed to have a negligible influence upon the progress of wage settlements during 1979–80. Accordingly we have increased wage inflation by about 1 percentage point in 1979 and 2 percentage points in 1980, obtaining 16 and 17 per cent respectively in these years. No change is made to the profile of wage inflation beyond 1980.

The deflationary effects of the Budget measures will tend to lower imports and so improve the trade balance but the wage response to the Budget will reduce export price competitiveness and we have assumed that the exchange rate will be about 1 per cent lower than in the pre-Budget view from 1980 onwards. In addition the interest rate has been raised by $1^1/_2$ percentage points in the short-term falling to 1 percentage point by 1985.

Finally we note that one of the aims of the new policy stance is to improve productivity and enterprise through providing higher incentives. No special adjustment is made for this aspect largely because there is little empirical evidence to support a link between the types of direct tax change introduced and changes in productivity or innovative activity. We shall return to this question later in this chapter and in Chapter 9.

3.3 The Medium-Term Implications of Current Policy

The changes introduced above were intended to cover the main elements of the Government's strategy but we should emphasise the difficulties of capturing the spirit in which the new Government plans to conduct its management of the economy. This is particularly the case when it would seem that such high levels of unemployment as given in the pre-Budget view are not anticipated and the reaction of the Government to a build-up of unemployment on this scale is highly uncertain. The standard view of economic change up to 1985 is presented below starting with the macroeconomic situation and then dealing in turn with trade, gross output and employment at the industry group level.

3.3.1 The macroeconomic situation

Under the standard view, the results of which are summarised in Table 3.7 (with annual profiles shown in Table 3.13), GDP grows at 1.1. per cent per annum between 1978 and 1985. Consumers' expenditure provides the main stimulus as in the pre-Budget view. Although the Budget itself was quite strongly deflationary, our interpretation of Government policy on further reductions in direct taxes and cuts in public expenditure over the medium run leads to only a small decline of about $\frac{1}{2}$ per cent in consumers' expenditure in 1985. The short-run effect is a fall in expenditure of 2 per cent in 1980 after which the overall impact of the policy change is gradually reduced, largely because the rate of VAT is held constant at 15 per cent whilst the basic rate of income tax falls to 25 per cent by 1982 and thereafter. The large reduction in the planned rate of growth of public expenditure is insufficient to neutralise the tax stimulus injected into the economy after 1980. In the short run the cash limit effects of higher money wages granted in the pay bargaining following the Budget are in fact more important sources of restraint upon public spending in real terms than are the planned cuts themselves. From 1981 the cuts introduced in our standard view, relative to the pre-Budget position, build up from 2 to $3\frac{3}{4}$ per cent by 1983 and thereafter. Gross fixed capital formation is reduced sharply in the short run, being 4 per cent below the pre-Budget view in 1980; after some further decline to almost 5 per cent below in 1982, the recovery of real incomes and output begins to influence investment. By 1985, however, it is still 3 per cent below the pre-Budget view. Growth rates for general government consumption and aggregate investment under our standard view are therefore more affected than is the case for private consumption and both are about 1 per cent per annum, close to the growth rate for GDP. The trade response is determined in part by our assumptions about the wage effects of the Budget strategy and the behaviour of the exchange rate. Both have been discussed earlier – a small loss of competitiveness arises

Table 3.7 Macroeconomic Summary of Standard View

GDP and its components	1978–85 % p.a. 1970 pr.	1975 pr.	1985 % change from pre-Budget scenario
GDP at market prices	1.1	1.0	−1.6
Consumers' expenditure	1.7	1.7	−0.6
General government final consumption	1.1	1.3	−3.7
Gross fixed capital formation	1.2	0.1	−2.7
Export of goods and services	3.9	4.1	−1.8
Imports of goods and services	5.1	4.9	−1.4
Labour market, prices and incomes			
Employment	−0.6		−1.6
Basic labour force estimate	0.6		−
Average earnings per annum	12.2		2.6
Consumer prices	10.9		5.5
Real personal disposable income	1.3		0.4

	1978	1985	1985: absolute change from pre-Budget scenario [1]
Employment (m)	24.8	23.9	−0.4
Basic labour force estimate (m)	26.7	27.9	−
Registered unemployment			
– high (m)[2]	1.4	3.5	0.4
– low (m)		2.9	0.4
Trade and balance of payments			
Balance of trade (% of GDP)	1.2	2.7	0.2
Balance of payments (% of GDP)	−	1.4	0.2
Imports as % domestic final demand	27.1	34.8	−
Exports as % domestic output	28.1	34.0	0.3
Public sector borrowing requirement			
PSBR (% of GDP)	5.5	2.8	0.3

Notes: (1) Units are those indicated.

          (2) The high and low estimates correspond to marginal propensities to register of 1.0 and 0.7 (which equals the average propensity in 1978), respectively.

in 1979–80, relative to that already occurring in the pre-Budget simulation. This feeds through to export volumes but its effect on export values is more than offset by the impact of higher prices. Imports fall to 3 per cent below the pre-Budget view in 1980 and then
recover gradually as private consumption gains ground. By 1981–82
exports and imports have both been reduced by 2 per cent but thereafter imports rise a little more so that by 1985 they are about 1½ per
cent below the pre-Budget view.

The standard view simulation, not surprisingly, leads to lower
employment. The loss of jobs quickly reaches 350 thousand in 1980
and rises to 400 thousand by 1982 and then remains at about that level. Health, education and public administration account for about
40 per cent of this reduction. Employment thus falls by 0.6 per cent
per annum in the standard view and registered unemployment is
likely to be in the region of 2.9 million by 1985 if the lower propensity to register is adopted (see below).

As one would expect from our discussion of the pre-Budget simulation, the balance of payments in the standard view records a surplus of £5 billion or 1.4 per cent of GDP. The additional £1 billion,
when compared with the pre-Budget view, is a consequence of the
trade volume responses and the terms of trade effects described
above, supplemented slightly by a fall in net factor payments
remitted abroad and offset by a small rise in net current transfers.

The borrowing requirement, on the other hand, also increases in
spite of the overall deflationary impact of the change of policy as reflected in the standard view and reaches £10 billion or 2.8 per cent
of GDP in 1985. Whereas the short-run effect of the changes in taxation and expenditure upon GDP is accompanied by a tiny reduction
in the PSBR as a percentage of GDP, the medium-run effect as VAT
remains at a constant rate is to increase the need to finance public
spending by about ½ per cent of GDP on average during 1981–85.
There are four major compositional changes which give rise to this
feature of our standard simulation when compared with the pre-
Budget view. First, by 1983 the tax changes cancel out on the income side of the government account: the reduction in taxes on income during 1981–83 is sufficient to exhaust the net gain arising
from the relative changes in taxes on income and expenditure
during 1979–80, *taking into account the fall in output and employment.* The second change follows from the fall in employment,
namely a large increase in social security payments amounting to

about £2 billion in 1985. The third change is the increase of £1 billion in expenditure on social capital formation in terms of current prices, due entirely to higher prices in the standard view. When set against the fourth item, which is the reduction in government consumption amounting to £2 billion, it seems that the fall in activity engendered by the medium-term policy stance, represented by our standard view, leads to perverse results. This is due to the fact that a shift in the structure of demand accompanies the deflationary package and this favours consumer's expenditure where the marginal propensity to import is relatively high. Thus imports do not fall enough, domestic output suffers disproportionately and the employment consequences undermine the restraint on public borrowing. Slowing down the reduction in direct taxes would cut the PSBR but would also raise unemployment.

3.3.2 Trade

Implicit in the projection is a worsening of the balance of payments after 1985 as North Sea oil production begins to slow down. The deterioration in the non-oil trade balance during 1978–85 partly reflects the 13 per cent decline in export price competitiveness that occurs as domestic prices grow faster than foreign prices, albeit to a smaller extent as we approach 1985, and the fact that the overall surplus on trade prevents the exchange rate from falling by more than the 12 per cent assumed. Certainly the trade balances in value terms for food etc. and some services do increase but these are exceptions to the general picture.

Table 3.8 gives import and export shares for SAM industry groups in the standard view. The main change is in mining where the import share, already lowered by the impact of North Sea oil, is fairly stable whilst the export share rises strongly between 1978 and 1981 to reach about 25 per cent. Within manufacturing, textiles and clothing continue to experience a declining export share and rising import share with inevitable consequences for output and employment. Only chemicals and food etc. achieve significant increases in export shares. The further loss of domestic markets by the engineering sector matches that of textiles and clothing: both these industry groups experience import shares of about a third by 1985. Manufacturing as a whole therefore records a marked worsening of its trade performance with the net export share falling from 1.2 to –3.1 per

cent of total supply between 1978 and 1985. For most of the manufacturing groups, UK export prices grow by some 4 per cent per annum faster than world prices and a similar situation holds for relative import prices. Only the impact of North Sea oil enables the
economy to retain precarious control of its overall trade position in
volume terms as indicated by the all industry ratios for imports and
exports of about 20 per cent by 1985.

Table 3.8   Import and Export Shares for Industry Groups : Standard View

SAM groups	Import share			Export share		
	1978	1981	1985	1978	1981	1985
Agriculture	17.9	19.8	18.7	3.7	4.4	4.9
Mining	23.6	20.5	22.3	10.4	24.5	23.6
Food, drink & tobacco	12.0	11.7	11.7	11.0	13.2	16.6
Chemicals etc.	18.1	19.1	19.2	26.7	32.4	35.4
Metals	17.5	19.3	24.4	12.3	12.9	13.2
Engineering	21.5	26.3	34.0	28.3	29.1	30.1
Textiles & clothing	22.2	26.1	31.3	19.0	15.8	13.6
Manufacturing n.e.s.	10.8	12.2	14.5	12.3	11.8	11.1
Construction	–	–	–	0.5	0.6	0.7
Public utilities	–	–	–	–	–	–
Transport & communication	20.2	23.4	28.5	23.7	26.4	30.1
Distribution	1.3	1.5	1.5	3.0	3.5	4.2
Professional services	3.4	6.1	5.5	12.1	12.3	13.4
Miscellaneous services	0.8	1.0	1.0	4.3	4.3	4.5
Manufacturing	17.2	19.8	23.8	18.4	19.5	20.7
Services	7.3	10.5	11.5	13.9	15.1	16.7
All industries	15.2	17.2	19.7	16.3	17.6	19.2

Note: Import and export shares are expressed as percentages of total
supply (i.e. output plus imports).

3.3.3 Output and productivity

The poor trade performance described above foreshadows the
development of a serious situation for industrial output and employment, the roots of which will be discussed more fully in Chapter

4. Output in metals, engineering and textiles and clothing falls by over $1/2$ per cent per annum between 1978 and 1985, as shown in Table 3.9. Only in chemicals is there evidence of firm growth underpinned by its export performance but even this is well below its historical trend. Manufacturing output as a whole increases by about $1/4$ per cent per annum. Gross output for all industries, excluding North Sea oil and gas, increases somewhat faster by virtue of the growth experienced in professional and miscellaneous services: the addition of the North Sea component contributes barely 0.1 per cent per annum to the all industry growth rate for gross output but, if expressed in 1975 prices and given the very high ratio of value added to gross output in this sector, the contribution rises to about 0.3 per cent per annum in terms of net industrial output or total GDP.

Realised productivity generally fails to close the gap with optimal productivity observed for 1978 (Table 3.1). Manufacturing productivity is still 9 per cent below optimal in 1985 and there remain substantial differences for mining, construction, public utilities and miscellaneous services. In aggregate, there is little change from the position in 1978, indicating that during the projection period we anticipate a recovery of productivity growth towards its long-run trend of about $2^1/2$ per cent per annum up to 1974 but starting from a low base. The slow-down to 1 per cent per annum between 1974 and 1978 is not reversed but, in effect, we take the view that during the last few years there has been some re-structuring of capital stock in order to save labour eventually. This tendency will continue and will increasingly make itself felt in the medium term as employers gradually manage to adjust employment levels to match their expectations of growth in demand. *Potentially,* this could lead to realised levels of productivity closer to those implied by our optimal levels. However, the slow growth in output will frustrate such a development and we would expect to forgo the additional 1 per cent or so per annum growth in productivity which might otherwise have been achieved had the economy reached peak efficiency in the course of a boom at the end of the period. Thus under the standard view of current economic policy, the slow growth in industrial output is a consequence of further losses of competitiveness, a depressed world economy and deflationary policies at home. Productivity growth recovers relative to the experience of 1974–78 but not sufficiently to offset the adverse effects of other determinants of competitiveness. The outlook is one in which the shift towards investment which replaces existing capital stock to save labour (with relatively small

Table 3.9   Output and Productivity in the Standard View

% p.a. 1978–85

SAM groups	Gross output	Gross output per man-hour	Gross output per man 1985 as % below optimal	
Agriculture	0.4	4.6	3.1	13
Mining[1]	−1.2	3.8	3.0	16
Food, drink & tobacco	1.4	3.6	2.5	3
Chemicals etc.	1.9	5.2	4.3	12
Metals	−0.6	2.3	1.7	14
Engineering	−0.9	3.3	2.3	8
Textiles & clothing	−0.7	4.2	3.4	9
Manufacturing n.e.s.	0.9	2.8	2.2	10
Construction	1.0	0.6	0.1	24
Public utilities	1.1	5.0	3.9	20
Transport & communication	−0.2	3.0	2.3	6
Distribution	1.1	3.6	2.0	0
Professional services	2.0	1.8	0.3	6
Miscellaneous services	1.5	1.1	−0.2	16
Manufacturing	0.3	3.7	2.9	9
Services	1.1	1.9	0.9	7
All industries [1]	0.6	2.4	1.6	12

Other measures of productivity	
All industries : gross output per man	1.7
All industries : net output per man	1.7
Gross expenditure per man in public services	0.5
GDP per man[1]	1.6

Note: (1) Excludes oil and natural gas production.

provision for increasing total output) is likely to intensify. In the following section we shall consider whether or not a major stimulus to the investment process might create conditions in which the demand for domestically produced commodities is increased enough to raise the demand for labour despite increasing productivity at the same time. Meanwhile, it is time to examine the employment situation implied by the standard view.

3.3.4 Employment and unemployment

Our discussion of the employment changes in the pre-Budget scenario raised the problem of interpreting their implications for unemployment, given the difficulties of defining and projecting labour supply. Obviously errors of only 1 per cent in the estimates of employment and labour supply in 1985 could easily reinforce each other to under-estimate or over-estimate unemployment by half a million or so. Related to this is the problem of estimating *registered* unemployment. Differences between the two estimates given for this politically sensitive indicator amount to about half a million simply according to the choice of the marginal propensity to register. For the purpose of exposition we shall normally refer to the lower estimate, partly because there are grounds for believing that the marginal propensity is unlikely to reach its maximum value of unity under the very high levels of unemployment being projected and partly because the discouraged worker effect is likely to become stronger in these circumstances and will reduce the size of the labour force. So although labour supply has not been endogenised with respect to unemployment or other variables such as wages, the state of demand has influenced our choice of the marginal propensity to register *with respect to the difference between the basic labour force estimate and projected employment.*

The profile of changes in the basic labour force, employment and registered unemployment are given in Table 3.10. The figures shown are rounded to the nearest 100 thousand to emphasise the degree of approximation in this sort of exercise. The labour force rises most strongly in 1981 and the three years following, slowing down in 1985. Employment falls markedly at the beginning of the projection period but the distribution of this reduction over the 1980–81 period is not precisely determined in a model based on annual observations and designed to track medium-term rather than short-term fluctuations in the economy.

The initial drop in employment is dominated by the impact of the Budget measures although the effects of this overlay the pre-Budget changes recorded for 1981–83 when further reductions in employment were already expected. Between 1983 and 1985 employment stabilises at about 23.8 million. Unemployment therefore rises sharply at the beginning of the projection period because of the fall in labour demand, continues to rise in the middle of the period because of large increases in labour supply supplemented by

Table 3.10   Employment and Unemployment : Standard View

Millions (1978 level and annual changes to 1985)

	Basic labour force estimate	Employment	Registered unemployment estimates	
			high	low
1978	26.7	24.8	1.4	
1979	0.1	−0.2	0.2	0.1
1980	0.1	−0.4	0.6	0.4
1981	0.2	−0.1	0.4	0.3
1982	0.2	−0.2	0.3	0.2
1983	0.2	−0.1	0.3	0.2
1984	0.2	−	0.2	0.2
1985	0.1	−	0.1	0.1
1978−85	1.2	−1.0	2.0	1.5

Note: Annual changes may not sum to those given for 1978−85 due to rounding. The high unemployment estimate is obtained by allow-ing the marginal propensity to reach unity; the low estimate is obtained by restricting its value to equal the average propensity in 1978 (equal to 0.7).

continuing reductions in demand, and slows down towards 1985 as the growth in labour supply moderates and employment reaches a plateau.

The industrial composition of changes in employment over the full period is shown in Table 3.11. Major reductions take place in engineering, textiles and clothing, transport and communications and distribution. Employment increases in construction, profession-al and miscellaneous services, and in the public services. The struc-ture of these large absolute changes provides us with no confidence that the necessary adjustment will be accomplished easily. Their oc-cupational and more detailed industrial composition is discussed in Chapter 4. It is worth noting at this stage that large groups of skilled or semi-skilled manual workers, seeking full-time employment which constitutes the main source of family income, face worsening job prospects. The implications for registered unemploy-ment are that those groups most likely to register when unemployed are amongst those most likely to become unemployed and that this will be compounded by increases in labour supply among so-called primary workers who dominate the supply to these occupations. In addition, it seems that the areas where employment is likely to increase, at least over the medium term, are those having relatively large concentrations of female workers, often working part-time. Thus the groups with the lower propensity to register as unemployed and the higher tendency to withdraw from the labour force under the discouraged worker effect face the most promising outlook. The main exceptions to this pattern are people employed in construction trades, managers and highly qualified technical manpower, where employment is dominated by prime-age males and is

Table 3.11 Employment by SAM Groups

	1978	1978–85	
	(thousands)	(thousands)	(% p.a.)
Agriculture	662	−111	−2.6
Mining	350	−89	−4.2
Food, drink & tobacco	732	−52	−1.1
Chemicals etc.	468	−72	−2.4
Metals	477	−68	−2.3
Engineering	3,357	−666	−3.1
Textiles & clothing	971	−231	−3.9
Manufacturing n.e.s.	1,480	−124	−1.2
Construction	1,591	104	0.9
Public utilities	350	−61	−2.7
Transport & communication	1,524	−246	−2.5
Distribution	3,161	−195	−0.9
Professional services	1,728	216	1.7
Miscellaneous services	2,683	337	1.7
Manufacturing	7,484	−1,213	2.5
Services	9,096	112	0.4
All industries	19,533	−1,259	−1.0
Health & education	3,484	202	0.8
Public administration etc.	1,956	85	0.6
Whole economy	24,973	−972	−0.6

Note: Employment figures are in terms of jobs, not persons employed as appear in the macroeconomic summary tables and elsewhere.

expected to increase. A further exception would be *older* male workers (including the skilled or semi-skilled) who may elect to retire earlier than usual if threatened with redundancy in a period of very high unemployment.

On balance, then, our treatment of the registration propensity in order to produce the lower benchmark for registered unemployment would not seem to be unduly pessimistic, bearing in mind the structure of employment changes examined in the standard view.

3.3.5 Equilibrating forces – the significance of omitted feedbacks

Both the pre-Budget scenario and the standard view were derived from assumptions not only about the structure of the economy as embodied in the macroeconomic model but also about the values of important economic variables which are exogenous (see section 3.1 and, more generally, Appendix A). When the rate of growth of domestic wage inflation and movements in the exchange rate are treated in this way it reflects considerable uncertainty about the major determinants of these variables over the medium term. Nevertheless it is important to consider to what extent those forces which some claim to be important would modify the projected outcome if they were to influence future changes.

Taking the average wage first, its progress over the period is in fact consistent with the form of 'real wage' equation estimated by Henry *et al.* (1976). This explanation of wages owes little to changes in excess demand, a finding common to recent empirical work on wage determination. The substantial increase in unemployment envisaged over the next few years does not therefore stem the pace of wage inflation.

Were we to support a wage equation in which increasing unemployment did have a moderating effect, the level of unemployment would be reduced by the order of 225–250 thousand in 1985, other things being equal. This assumes that a simple Phillips curve equation such as estimated by Lipsey and Parkin (1972), where the coefficient on the unemployment rate is negative and close to unity, were still valid. The implied reduction of money wages would be of the order of 10 per cent and, in the absence of accompanying changes in the exchange rate, real incomes would *fall* slightly as the increase in employment associated with higher export demand (given lower UK costs of production) does not quite offset the effect of a drop in the average money wage.[4] Consumers' expenditure is virtually unaffected as a result; imports then rise mainly because of the import content of production for exports.

As regards the exchange rate, each of the two simulations presented includes a large surplus on the balance of trade and on the current account of the balance of payments. This might be expected to lead to compensating exchange rate changes. On the other hand the trade surplus, for example, should be seen in perspective. Its four-fold increase in current prices is halved when expressed as a percentage of GDP. Moreover before we can conclude that such a position would lead to an increase in the exchange rate, it is important to consider other factors.[5] First, the behaviour of the capital account in the 1980s will be influenced strongly by the fact that the schedule of capital repayments of government and other public sector foreign borrowing is particularly heavy during 1980–84, averaging $2.4 billion per year, as well as by the (uncertain) effects of removing exchange controls.[6] In addition the North Sea capital account will probably move into deficit in 1981 when the net capital inflow gives way to a net outflow as debt repayments dominate further inflows of finance for oil and gas related investment.[7] Second, the deterioration in the non-oil trade account reflects worsening export price competitiveness despite a closing of the gap between domestic and overseas inflation rates during the period. If purchasing power parity is the prime long-run determinant of exchange rate movements, one would expect this divergence to have depressed the rate below that assumed in the projections of the standard view. This assumes, realistically enough, that the exchange rate in 1978–79 was not *under*valued.

Ignoring the fact that constant competitiveness would imply a lower exchange rate than has been assumed, and leaving aside the influence of other variables such as relative interest rates, let us assume that any *deviation* in wage inflation from the standard view will be accompanied by a movement in the rate such as to keep UK export prices constant relative to those of our competitors when expressed in terms of common currency. A fall in wage inflation would lead to a rise in the exchange rate, the results of which would be a fall in output through the decline in export demand (keeping the rate of wage inflation constant). The ensuing fall in import prices would feed through to real incomes in spite of the fall in employment. Consumers' expenditure would rise but not by enough to compensate for the drop in exports.

For a 10 per cent reduction in the average wage (which is the decline implied by the alternative simple Phillips curve referred to earlier) the level of unemployment in the standard view would fall by a little under 200 thousand. Putting together the first round effects of this money wage reduction and the accommodating exchange rate change which keeps relative export prices constant, some small gain in employment of less than 100 thousand might result. Allowing the complete cycle to work through does not materially affect this position.

A recent comparison of the properties of the three main short-term models of the U.K. economy (Laury *et al.,1978*) indicates that there are significant differences in their simulations of the employment consequences of changes in earnings with an endogenous exchange rate (and fixed interest rates) and *vice versa.* The London Business School model would predict little change in employment as a result of the sequence followed above, whereas the Treasury and the National Institute models would expect increases in employment of about 200 thousand six years after a once and for all reduction in money wages and somewhat less if the reduction was achieved gradually. The point at issue, however, is that these feedback effects are marginal relative to the decline in employment anticipated in the standard view. Even if wages were quite strongly influenced by variations in the level of unemployment, the anomalous exchange rate situation in the medium term means that the employment benefits from this response would be relatively small. Moreover, if exchange rate movements began to be more sensitive to changes in competitiveness in the middle 1980s, our conclusion would be the same. Only by arguing for a very much larger reduction in the exchange rate than has been assumed in the standard view, could employment be substantially higher in 1985 and, *for this effect to work, wages would have to be unaffected.*

Finally, if the real wage explanation of wage determination is preferred to the Phillips curve and its derivatives, then the cycle of adjustments to our standard view considered above would not even be initiated and the prospects of higher employment would fade.

3.4 Fiscal and Structural Alternatives

3.4.1 Reflation through fiscal policy

If the high level of unemployment in the standard view begins to be approached, one would expect policy to change. One obvious possibility would be for the Government to re-think its attitude to reducing the PSBR as rapidly as would appear to be envisaged. In keeping with the general policy on public expenditure this would allow for further reductions in direct taxes and perhaps some increase in transfers to persons: pensions, educational grants and social security benefits. The last of these includes payments of unemployment benefit, the level of which is regarded by the Government's main spokesmen as a factor which contributes significantly to the present high level of unemployment. Most economists would probably agree that this effect may be significant but it is not large and the improvements in benefits during the last decade have perhaps added 150 thousand to the level of registered unemployment, mainly by lowering the propensity to *leave* unemployment rather than by increasing the propensity to *become* unemployed.[8]

The policy simulation discussed below reduces the PSBR constraint on further expansion, bearing in mind that the balance of payments is comfortably in surplus under the standard view. As a percentage of GDP the PSBR is allowed to stay at about 5 per cent which is the average expected for financial years 1978–79 and 1979–80. The public expenditure cuts are maintained which means that reflation through fiscal policy is being conducted by measures which are most expensive in terms of changes to the PSBR and balance of payments for a given stimulus to employment.[9]

The results for the fiscal stimulus summarised in Table 3.12 are obtained by a reduction in the standard rate of tax to 20 per cent in three equal stages between 1981 and 1983, increases in transfers by 3, 6 and 10 per cent in the same three years (child benefits rise by 7 1/2, 16 and 25 per cent respectively), and reductions in the rates of national insurance contributions from employers and employees by 5 per cent in 1981 and 10 per cent in 1982. Although these changes all boost net earnings (as well as other incomes) no cut in the assumed rate of wage inflation has been made for this simulation. The cut in employers contributions will lead to some reduction in home unit costs and hence consumer prices and export prices.

The effects of the policy on output build up to a peak in 1983 when the final stage of the fiscal injection is reached and then decline a little (see Table 3.13). In 1983 GDP is nearly 2 per cent higher than in the standard view falling to 1 1/2 per cent by 1985. The profile of GDP growth between 1983 and 1985 is largely influenced by the cycle in fixed investment and stockbuilding. Most of the extra growth in GDP however is due to higher real incomes and consumption.

Table 3.12   Macroeconomic Summary of Alternative Policies

	Fiscal stimulus	Structural change
GDP and its components	*1978–85 % p.a. (1970 prices)*	
GDP at market prices	1.3	1.5
Consumers' expenditure	2.2	2.4
General government final consumption	1.1	1.1
Gross fixed capital formation	1.3	3.0
Export of goods and services	3.9	5.7
Imports of goods and services	5.6	8.0
Labour market, prices and incomes		
Employment	−0.4	−0.3
Basic labour force estimate	0.6	0.6
Average earnings	12.2	12.2
Consumer prices	10.8	9.9
Real personal disposable income	2.1	2.3
Exchange rate	−1.8	1.3

	1978	1985	
Employment (m)	24.8	24.1	24.2
Basic Labour force (m)	26.7	27.9	27.9
Registered unemployment (m)	1.4	2.7	2.6
Trade and balance of payments			
Balance of trade (% of GDP)	1.2	1.7	2.3
Balance of payments (% of GDP)	–	0.4	0.6
Imports as % domestic final demand	27.1	35.0	39.7
Exports as % domestic output	28.1	33.6	37.2
Public sector borrowing requirement			
PSBR (% of GDP)	5.5	4.8	3.8

Note: The registered unemployment estimate given is the lower one, obtained by assuming a marginal propensity to register equal to the average propensity in 1978.

Employment growth reaches a peak in 1984, a year after the peak in output, by which time another 240 thousand people are employed. The balance of payments deteriorates by about 1 per cent of GDP as the higher level of final demand induces a rise of 3 per cent in import volumes by 1985 and the public sector borrowing requirement increases by 2 per cent of GDP as intended.

The small employment response in relation to the size of the fiscal stimulus is a result which we observed in Lindley (1978, pp. 80–3). Over two-thirds of it occurs in the service sector and employment is only 50 thousand higher in manufacturing by 1985. Within the service sector, distribution and miscellaneous services provide the bulk of the increase in employment, accounting for 50 thousand and 90 thousand respectively by 1985 (Table 3.14).

Our main comment on the implications of these findings for future policy is that other measures must be found to work instead of or in conjunction with any relaxation of the fiscal stance through increasing real net incomes. ·

3.4.2 Major structural change

In our previous study[10] the industrial strategy of the then Labour government was characterised in terms of a boost to investment over the medium term, financed largely through the government account; and accompanied by, first, an increase in productivity in those industries stimulated directly and, second, a more modest increase in productivity elsewhere in the economy. The impact upon demand came from the additional investment and the effects of price reductions following the fall in labour costs resulting from higher productivity. The underlying relationships in the economy were unaffected and, in particular, the trade responses occurred through volume and price functions in the model whose parameters were unchanged. The employment consequences were accordingly disappointing. Indeed employment fell because the improved net trade position did not raise domestic output sufficiently to offset the impact of the increase in productivity. This followed partly from the pricing policies of firms in certain industries by which the reduction in costs was mainly taken as higher profit and the stimulus to exports through lower UK prices was relatively small. This suggested that an industrial strategy in which higher productivity was to play

Table 3.13   Profiles of Economic Change

	Standard view						Fiscal stimulus					Structural change				
	1980	1981	1982	1983	1984	1985	1981	1982	1983	1984	1985	1981	1982	1983	1984	1985
	Percentage change year-on-year						*Percentage change from standard view*					*Percentage change from standard view*				
GDP	−2.0	1.9	1.6	1.2	2.5	1.4	0.7	1.2	1.9	1.6	1.5	1.5	2.2	3.3	3.0	2.9
CE	−2.1	2.1	2.4	1.7	2.5	2.1	1.5	2.6	4.1	3.7	3.5	2.2	3.3	4.3	5.0	5.3
GC	1.2	1.8	0.3	1.1	2.1	2.0	−	−	−	−	−	−	−	−	−	−
GFCF	−3.0	0.7	1.2	3.9	4.9	1.8	0.5	1.0	1.7	1.6	1.0	8.6	12.9	13.8	13.6	13.6
X	4.6	5.6	4.3	2.8	4.0	4.0	0.1	0.2	0.2	0.2	0.1	1.9	5.2	11.7	12.0	12.7
M	1.7	7.6	5.7	4.4	7.0	5.7	1.5	2.5	4.0	3.2	3.1	6.9	12.5	18.7	19.8	20.6
EMP	−1.8	−0.5	−0.7	−0.4	0.2	−	0.3	0.6	0.9	1.0	1.0	0.7	1.1	1.7	1.7	1.7
W	17.0	14.0	12.0	10.0	9.0	8.0	−	−	−	−	−	−	−	−	−	−
CP	18.9	11.5	9.9	9.0	7.4	6.9	−0.3	−0.5	−0.7	−0.4	−0.2	−2.4	−3.6	−4.8	−5.6	−6.2
RPDI	−1.8	1.7	2.1	1.1	2.0	1.6	1.8	3.4	5.4	5.1	4.8	2.3	3.9	5.1	6.0	6.4
ER	−5.5	−4.5	−2.6	−1.5	−2.1	−0.4	−	−	−	−	−	8.0	12.9	16.7	21.4	24.1
	Annual values						*Absolute change from standard view*					*Absolute change from standard view*				
BOT	3.4	3.3	3.7	3.5	2.8	2.7	−0.5	−0.8	−1.2	−1.0	−1.0	−0.6	−0.9	−0.3	−0.4	−0.4
BOP	2.0	2.1	2.4	2.3	1.5	1.4	−0.5	−0.7	−1.2	−1.0	−1.0	−0.8	−1.1	−0.6	−0.7	−0.8
PSBR	4.5	4.6	4.1	3.6	3.2	2.8	0.6	1.2	2.0	2.0	2.0	1.0	1.5	1.2	1.4	1.6
EMPL	24.2	24.1	23.9	23.8	23.8	23.9	−	0.1	0.2	0.2	0.2	0.1	0.3	0.4	0.4	0.4
RU	2.0	2.2	2.5	2.7	2.8	2.9	−0.1	−0.1	−0.2	−0.1	−0.2	−0.1	−0.2	−0.3	−0.3	−0.3

Key to abbreviations: GDP – GDP (market prices), CE – consumers' expenditure, GC – general government final consumption, GFCF – gross fixed capital formation, X and M – exports and imports (goods and services) respectively, EMP – employment, W – average earnings, CP – consumer prices, RPDI – real personal disposable income, ER – $ exchange rate, BOT – balance of trade, BOP – balance of payments, PSBR – public sector borrowing requirement, EMPL – level of employment, RU – registered unemployment assuming the marginal propensity to register equals the average propensity in 1978.

Note: For the standard view, BOT, BOP, PSBR and EMPL and RU are expressed as percentages of GDP, and EMPL and RU are in millions of persons: figures for these items are the values recorded in each year concerned – not the year-on-year percentage changes. For the fiscal stimulus and structural change simulations, the differences from the standard view for BOT, BOP, PSBR, EMPL and RU are given as *absolute* differences in either per cent of GDP or millions of persons, as appropriate.

the major role would have to be supported by aggressive trade measures – import controls or devaluation – and these were not without technical and diplomatic problems of implementation.

Advocates of the significance of non-price competitiveness might well have emphasised that the industrial strategy was not primarily about raising productivity but concerned the whole approach to trade performance, including product quality and marketing policy. Our scepticism of the impact of the industrial strategy *per se* upon these factors, important as they most certainly are, led us to the conclusion that the mechanism by which the strategy would affect trade would in fact be mainly through raising productivity.

In present circumstances we would be reluctant to give too much ground for optimism about the potential for improving the so-called 'non-price' aspects of selling products abroad. On the other hand, it is conceivable that manufacturing investment on a much higher scale than envisaged in the standard view would generate benefits other than reduced costs. In particular, providing suitable technologies are adopted, the resulting industrial structure should be more responsive to evolving patterns of demand and be able to concentrate effectively on supplying growing markets for income-elastic commodities.

The relationships between investment and output per man and between investment and export performance are only mildly supported by the empirical evidence. The simulation results discussed below are simply illustrative of the type of mechanism whereby improved capital equipment might enhance labour productivity and the UK's ability to compete in world markets.

Industrial details of the simulation are given in Chapter 4. Investment is boosted by different amounts in nine of the SAM industries (chemicals, mechanical, instrument and electrical engineering, motor vehicles, metal goods, textiles n.e.s., paper and board, and manufactures n.e.s.), building up to nearly £1 billion (1970 prices) in aggregate by 1982 and thereafter. This is equivalent to about one-third of total manufacturing investment in the absence of the stimulus. One-third of the full impact is felt in 1980 and two-thirds in 1981.

The extra investment is estimated to increase optimal productivity with a lag of one-year according to parameters estimated from relationships between the cumulated level of investment and peak-to-

Table 3.14 Industrial Structure under Alternative Policies(1)

1978–85 % p.a. or thousands

	Chemicals etc.	Metals	Engineering	Textiles & clothing	Manufacturing n.e.s.	Construction	Distribution	Miscellaneous services	Manufacturing	Services(2)	All industries
Output growth											
Standard view	1.9	−0.6	−0.9	−0.7	0.9	1.0	1.1	1.5	0.3	1.5	0.7
Fiscal stimulus	2.0	−0.5	−0.8	−0.3	1.1	1.2	1.5	2.2	0.4	1.9	0.9
Structural change	2.5	−0.4	1.4	−1.3	1.0	1.5	1.6	2.2	1.1	1.9	1.2
Growth in output per man											
Standard view	4.3	1.7	2.3	3.4	2.2	0.1	2.0	−0.2	2.9	0.9	1.7
Fiscal stimulus	4.4	1.7	2.3	3.4	2.2	0.2	2.1	0.1	2.9	1.0	1.7
Structural change	5.1	1.7	3.4	3.6	2.4	0.4	2.2	0.1	3.3	1.0	1.8
Employment growth											
Standard view	−2.4	−2.3	−3.1	−3.9	−1.2	0.9	−0.9	1.7	−2.5	0.7	−1.0
Fiscal stimulus	−2.3	−2.2	−3.0	−3.6	−1.1	−1.0	−0.7	2.1	−2.4	0.9	−0.8
Structural change	−2.4	−2.1	−1.9	−4.7	−1.3	1.1	−0.6	2.1	−2.1	0.9	−0.7
Absolute employment change											
Standard view	−72	−68	−666	−231	−123	104	−195	337	−1,213	112	−1,256
Fiscal stimulus	−71	−67	−654	−213	−109	112	−146	427	−1,162	280	−1,022
Structural change	−75	−63	−422	−268	−133	130	−132	429	−1,013	270	−871

Notes: (1) The industries shown are those SAM groups recording the main changes in output and/or employment between the three simulations. A more detailed analysis of the standard view and structural change simulation is given in Chapter 4.

(2) Excludes transport and communication.

peak productivity. In addition the higher investment-output ratios are assumed to raise the corresponding export demand elasticities with an elasticity of unity (a value derived from an international comparison of manufacturing investment-output ratios and export demand elasticities).

The separate increases in productivity range from 4 per cent to 24 per cent in their full impact by 1985 and manufacturing productivity is increased by 0.4 per cent p.a. (the figure for all industries is just under 0.2 per cent p.a.).

The export demand elasticity for visible exports gradually rises from the value of 0.65 in the standard view to 1.03 by 1985. In particular the elasticities for export groups, metal manufacture, mechanical engineering and electrical engineering are doubled.

The strategy outlined above leads to an increase in the volume of exports for two reasons: higher productivity reduces export prices and higher export demand elasticities increase export volumes for any given level of world demand. In the standard view there is already a substantial balance of payments surplus so that the exchange rate is likely to be higher under this strategy than in the standard view. We have assumed that the exchange rate would rise between 1978 and 1985 to a level of $2.1, or 24 per cent higher than in the standard view. This then reverses some of the competitiveness gain from structural change but even so sterling export prices are 13 per cent lower by 1985 and export volumes almost 13 per cent higher. Import volumes are 20 per cent higher due to higher domestic demand and to lower import prices but the price reduction is only 18 per cent, so the balance of trade worsens by just over £1.5 billion (0.4 per cent of GDP), nearly all of which results from the higher value of imports.

There is an additional increase in investment induced by the rise in demand but this is concentrated in dwellings and construction. The extra investment demand in manufacturing is modest and there is little further improvement in productivity and export performance. So the stimulus does not generate a self-sustaining improvement in the efficiency of Britain's manufacturing industry.

Consumers' expenditure increases partly through the effect of higher employment but mainly because of lower import prices and the net result of the resource changes on GDP is to increase the growth rate to 1½ per cent per annum leaving it nearly 3 per cent higher at the end of the period than in the standard view.

The net impact of higher export demand, higher productivity and higher import demand upon output is greatest in chemicals, mechanical engineering and metal goods and employment in manufacturing increases by nearly 200 thousand. There is also a stimulus to output and employment in the service sector, particularly in distribution and miscellaneous services, adding 150 thousand to employment which for the economy as a whole rises by about 400 thousand.

The employment gain produced by a major investment strategy of this kind is rather disappointing compared with the level of unemployment being projected in the standard view. We have assumed that the government has in effect, financed the strategy, a notion which is inimical to the present policy of disengagement from industrial planning and subsidisation. Alternative provision on the scale assumed would hardly be forthcoming in the world economic climate anticipated over the next few years, even if the government were to adopt a more expansionist approach. Expectations about changes in product demand dominate investment behaviour and it is unrealistic to hope for economic recovery through an investment-led initiative from the private sector. The size of the stimulus chosen partly reflects our judgement about the capacity available to manage an injection of investment capital on a large scale together with a wish to restrict the PSBR effects whilst leaving some room for increasing incentives to the corporate-sector through other channels (an additional 1 per cent of GDP would be available for this if the overall stance adopted was the same as in the fiscal simulation). More significant though, for the purposes of exposition, is the interpretation of the simulation results in relation to the presence of North Sea oil. If there were no oil then this strategy would transform the underlying balance of payments position from deficit into balance without the adverse effects of an increase in the exchange rate relative to the standard view. Moreover the visible trade account (excluding oil) would also just be in balance. The investment strategy does leave UK manufacturing industry in a stronger competitive position which might make the rundown in oil production after 1985 less painful. However, it is clear that, even without the exchange rate appreciation adopted in this strategy, the grounds for expecting a virtuous circle of improving productivity and export performance are weak since the extent of further augmentation of the capital stock as the private sector takes over from government is likely to be moderate if historical relationships continue to hold.

Wages and the exchange rate under structural change

In the above simulation the exchange rate has been allowed to appreciate by almost 25 per cent relative to the standard view, leading to lower import prices and a reduction of 6 per cent in consumer prices but without any change to average money wages. We might expect some increase in wages at least in those industries gaining so much from higher productivity. Obviously, this would dampen down the beneficial impact of the whole policy. Leaving this possibility aside, proponents of a real wage explanation of wage inflation would expect wage settlements to be lower in view of the lower consumer prices. The possibility of entering a virtuous circle involving reinforcing reductions in wages and increases in the exchange rate then opens up. Whether such a process would be self-perpetuating depends on the models of wage and exchange rate determination adopted. Having made the point that both in general have performed badly in the past and might be expected to do even worse in the future under very different conditions, an estimate of the effects of endogenising wages as well as the exchange rate is discussed briefly below.

With a real wage model of wage inflation such as that of Henry *et al.* (1976), the assumption that exchange rates move in response to changes in price competitiveness leads one to expect a continuously changing inflationary process if the price coefficient in the model is unity. If it were less than unity, a rise in the exchange rate, reducing import prices, would cause a fall in the rate of wage inflation but one which was not continuous. Most types of real wage equation are in this last category with price coefficients well below unity. For example, adopting the model estimated by Henry *et al.* (1976, Table 10) it is possible to calculate the employment benefit which would be tied up with the limited response to lower import prices under the simulation of major structural change. We estimate that the average money wage would be 12 per cent lower than the exogenous level assumed whilst the exchange rate would appreciate by about the same amount (Table 3.15). Employment would be boosted by lower wage inflation but reduced by the higher exchange rate and the net effect is somewhat below 100 thousand by 1985.

Once again, therefore, the fact of having treated wages exogenously does not mean that a substantial employment generating adjustment process has been ignored. It would improve the employment position only a little relative to the situation being projected if we were to incorporate the real wage response.

Per cent

Table 3.15 The Impact of Endogenous Wages upon the Structural Simulation

	Money wages	Consumer prices	Real wages	Competitiveness	Employment (thousands)
(a) Impact from the higher exchange rate	–	–6.2	+ 6.4	–11.0	–470
(b) First round response of wages to lower prices and higher real incomes	–6.3	–5.0	–0.6	+ 2.7	157
(c) Exchange rate response to improved competitiveness under (b)	–	–1.4	+ 0.6	–2.7	–115
(d) Net effect of further wage and exchange rate changes	–5.6	–5.5	–	–	41
Total effect due to wage and exchange rate responses (= b + c + d)	–11.9	–11.9	–	–	83

Source: See text.

3.5 The Policy Dilemma

'...... over the last five years the economy has grown on average by less than one per cent a year. Given the worsening prospects for the world economy generally, then unless we can dramatically improve our own performance on productivity, external trade and inflation we cannot count on even that meagre growth in the years immediately ahead.'

The Chancellor of the Exchequer,
Financial Times Conference, London, 23 July 1979.

Our analysis shows that the Chancellor's fears are undoubtedly justified. In this chapter we have tried to shed some light on the extent to which the proposed changes in economic policy will improve or worsen the unemployment situation. In addition, the impact of alternative measures to those envisaged by the Government has been considered, mainly from the point of view of economic growth and employment over the medium term. Our general conclusions are that, in the absence of changes in policy, unemployment will rise above the levels anticipated by the Chancellor and that alternative ways of manipulating the conventional instruments of fiscal and monetary control *within the limits prescribed by the Government's economic philosophy* will not serve to alter this view significantly. In part, this is because the underlying position is one in which unemployment is likely to rise substantially in any case but it also reflects the fact that the Government has chosen to support a policy which is more costly, in terms of both the balance of payments and the borrowing requirement, in its promotion of employment over the short and medium term.

However, the policy is not intended to promote employment in the short term. Indeed, it is preoccupied with the need to control inflation and, because of the problems of adjusting expectations, the Government would not be surprised to see unemployment rising over the first few years. In the long term, however, the Government claims that unemployment will benefit from the responsible behaviour engendered by facing economic reality. What is at issue relates to the employment consequences over the medium term and to whether or not the basis for an industrial revival will in fact be prepared by means of the measures being taken in the meantime. It is possible, for example, that not only will unemployment remain high for much longer than anticipated, thereby putting the single-mindedness of the Government to test, but the effects of the policy upon investment, productivity and trade performance will be very slow to materialise. In these circumstances we would expect the unemployment situation itself to begin to undermine the long-term strategy by souring the bargaining environment. Even if wage inflation were reduced, this might be at the expense of any hoped-for improvement in labour market flexibility.

On the other hand, the Government recognises that the raising of incentives in order to begin a more purposeful period of economic change is a crucial part of the strategy. The problem is to assess the degree to which the measures chosen will bring about the desired effects. Our simulation results derive from relationships between economic variables for which there is at least a semblance of empirical support. The uncertainty surrounding the impact of income tax reductions upon for example, productivity, is very great and we have made no special provision for this aspect. Nor are we alone in sticking to our model, as is made clear in the Treasury commentary on the forecasts accompanying the Budget.

> 'Although the economy is modelled in such a way as to take account as far as possible of the effects of policy changes, it remains a possibility that large changes in policy will affect the economy in ways which are not foreseen. It is particularly difficult to take account of possible changes in confidence and expectations or, for the slightly longer term, of the effects of incentives on supply side relationships.'

> *Economic Progress Report,*
> June 1979, p.5

This is a distinct handicap when a government is as determined to change expectations and attitudes as is the present one, but the simulation results *do* suggest how much hangs on this element of policy as opposed to those elements which work through more conventional channels. Taking into account the simulation of major structural change, our findings imply that current policy depends for its success upon some very intangible responses. Without these, unemployment will reach a critical level. This position would seem to resemble that of the Bank of England which, perhaps emphasising its point rather more strongly than the Government would like, stated recently:

'The relative industrial decline of this country is now widely seen as a matter of grave concern. If allowed to continue, it would seem only too likely to lead to growing impoverishment and unemployment in years to come. To get the economy back to a healthier state – to re-establish stability and regain the conditions for resumed expansion – will require, not only continued firmness in monetary policy, but changes in attitude in the country generally. The more fully this is recognised the earlier economic recovery is likely to be.'

Bank of England Quarterly Bulletin, September 1979

Government statements certainly refer to the need to change attitudes but we get the impression that the mechanisms by which this will take place are already believed to exist. Through strong monetary policy a set of adjustments to the expectations of wage negotiators will be set in train which will moderate wage inflation. Through increasing incentives, productivity and entrepreneurial activity will be stimulated. If neither outcome occurs to the satisfaction of the Government and unemployment rises substantially, the errors of judgement will apparently belong to employers and trade unions for refusing to co-operate, rather than to the Government for calling into play parts of the economic system which, by their own argument, have been left unused for too long and therefore might be unable to function properly without more direct attention.

This raises particularly fundamental questions about the stance of policy towards the labour market and these will be discussed in Chapter 9. More generally, basic changes in the structure of the economy are required in order to raise output and employment through improving our trade performance in the medium and long term. If this is to be achieved as much as possible through the market mechanism then the Government will need to phase its withdrawal from economic 'management' at the same time as promoting the development of those parts of the economic system on which it seeks to rely. Finally we would emphasise once again the great uncertainties attached to projections of unemployment. Having noted that registered unemployment is likely to rise above 2 million in the early 1980s and remain high thereafter, attention should be focussed on the structure of the decline in employment and the extent to which it might be affected by alternative policies.

Notes

1   The prices of goods and services imported into the UK and of those ex-
    ported by the UK are influenced by other factors as well as world prices
    and domestic costs. Some discussion of this is given in Chapter 4.

2   Throughout this book, the analysis of past and future economic change
    is conducted in 1970 prices but, in tables which summarise the macroe-
    conomic results, growth rates are also given in 1975 prices to simplify
    comparison with other sources. In principle, we should have preferred
    to use the new price base adopted for the national accounts but too little
    time has elapsed since the appearance of the 1978 Blue Book and, more
    importantly, the release of corresponding disaggregate statistical series
    for us to have made the many adjustments required in time for publica-
    tion. Note that most of the disaggregate estimates for 1978 were pre-
    pared by the MRG using information available in the first half of 1979.
    They are, therefore, highly provisional and this will affect the growth
    rates calculated from 1978 as the initial year.

3   Note that the cuts are expressed relative to the planned levels as repre-
    sented in the pre-Budget simulation. An alternative treatment of short-
    fall, cash limits, etc. in deriving this 'no policy change' view from
    Cmnd.7439 would obviously lead to different (probably larger) esti-
    mates of the cuts, even if the *levels* of expenditure for the post-Budget
    simulation were chosen to be the same.

4   See Lindley (1978), Chapter 6, for further discussion of this effect.

5   See Batchelor (1977) for a study of the determinants of exchange rate
    fluctuations during 1951–76.

6   *Bank of England Quarterly Bulletin* (1979), 19, no. 3, statistical annex,
    Table 16.

7   See Tempest and Walton (1979). Indeed, despite approaching self-
    sufficiency, these authors expect the overall balance on oil and gas pay-
    ments to be in net deficit until the mid-1980s because of the effects of
    payments of interest etc. to foreign oil companies and repayment of ca-
    pital.

8   See Nickell (1979).

9   See Lindley (1978), Chapter 6.

10 See the discussion of simulation D in Lindley (1978), Chapter 6.

References

Batchelor, R.A. (1977). 'Sterling Exchange Rates 1951–1976: A Casselian Analysis'. *National Institute Economic Review,* 81 (August) 45–66.

Henry, S.G.B., M.C. Sawyer and P. Smith (1976). 'Models of Inflation in the United Kingdom: An Evaluation'. *National Institute Economic Review* 77 (August), 60–71.

Laury, J.S.E., G.R. Lewis and P.A. Ormerod (1978). 'Properties of Macroeconomic Models of the UK Economy: A Comparative Study'. *National Institute Economic Review,* 83 (February), 52–72.

Lindley, R.M. (1978). (ed.). *Britain's Medium-Term Employment Prospects.* Coventry: Manpower Research Group, University of Warwick.

Lipsey, R.G. and M. Parkin (1972). 'Incomes Policy: A reappraisal'. *Incomes Policy and Inflation,* eds. M. Parkin and M.T. Sumner. Manchester: Manchester University Press, 85–111.

Nickell, S.J. (1979). 'The effect of unemployment and related benefits on the duration of unemployment'. *Economic Journal.* 89, 353, 34–49.

Tempest, L.P. and R.J. Walton (1979). 'North Sea oil and gas in the UK balance of payments since 1970'. *Bank of England Quarterly Bulletin,* 19, 3, 283–89.

4 Industrial and Occupational Change

J.D. WHITLEY, R.A. WILSON AND D.J.E. SMITH

This chapter reviews historical trends in industrial and occupational employment and provides a more detailed analysis of the projections to 1985 discussed in the previous chapter. Section 4.1 classifies manufacturing industries into broad groups depending on their respective trade and employment performance and examines the relative importance of trade and domestic demand in employment generation. Section 4.2 looks at the various factors underlying trade performance, particularly changes in price competitiveness. The section goes on to consider the mechanism whereby investment may directly influence trade performance and deals more thoroughly with the simulation of major structural change summarised in Chapter 3. Section 4.3 then completes the link between trade and employment by analysing the growth of productivity and employment, dealing with manufacturing industries, which provides the focus for sections 4.1 and 4.2, and other sectors of the economy. Section 4.4 is concerned with changes in occupational employment throughout the economy and considers employment prospects for different skills. Section 4.5 summarises the findings of the chapter and draws out some of the implications for economic policy.

4.1 Trade and Employment in Manufacturing Industries

In our previous assessment (Lindley, 1978) manufacturing industries (SAMs 11–30) were classified into one of four groups, depending on their trade and employment performance over the period 1956–74.[1] These groups were:

(a) trade and employment gainers;
(b) trade gainers, employment losers;
(c) trade losers, employment gainers;
(d) trade and employment losers.

Table 4.1 extends the historical grouping to include the more recent experience of 1974–78. This period has been notable for the continuation of general employment decline in the manufacturing sector; only vehicles n.e.s. shows a (marginal) increase in employment. Most of the industries fall into either group (b) or group (d). Out of the nine industries which are both trade *and* employment losers two had previously been industries with decreasing employment but an improving trade balance; one (motor vehicles) had previously increased employment but experienced a worsening trade balance; and two industries (textile fibres and rubber) had previously gained on both employment and trade fronts.

In absolute terms motor vehicles was the biggest trade loser during 1974–78, whilst the largest trade gainer was the metal goods industry. Electrical engineering suffered the largest employment loss (nearly 100 thousand jobs).

Perhaps one of the most notable points, however, is the diversity of experience of the various industries over the entire period 1956–78. This is illustrated by the fact that only textiles n.e.s. remains in the same group throughout.

The results from our standard view of 1985 (see Table 4.1) continue the trends evident from the period up to 1978. Only timber and furniture is an employment gainer with an increase of 5 thousand jobs. Most of the industries become both trade and employment losers. The decline in the number of trade gainers is quite marked compared with the experience prior to 1978. There are only three trade gainers in our projection period: chemicals, mechanical engineering and instrument engineering, the first two of which have been trade gainers consistently since 1956.

Aggregate net trade deteriorates by nearly £4 billion, considerably larger than the figures recorded for the past. The most common feature of the adverse trend in net trade is the substantial rise in imports accompanied by only a modest increase in export volumes. The position is most marked in the cases of electrical engineering, motor vehicles, and leather, clothing etc. where the trade changes are £1.1 billion, £0.5 billion, and £0.4 billion respectively. The main causes of these results are the modest growth assumed for world demand coupled with the general adverse trends in competitiveness.

The relationship between trade changes and employment changes has many links. The fact that a substantial number of industries fall into groups (b) and (c) shows how difficult it is to make simple deductions about one from the other. Of major importance is the role of domestic demand which together with net trade determines changes in domestic output. The two are not independent however.

Table 4.1 Manufacturing Industries by Trade and Employment Performance

1956–65	1965–74	1974–78	1978–85
(a) Trade gainers, employment gainers			
11. Chemicals	22. Textile fibres		
12. Iron & steel	26. Timber & furniture		
14. Mechanical engineering	29. Rubber		
16. Electrical engineering			
18. Motor vehicles			
28. Printing & publishing			
29. Rubber			
(b) Trade gainers, employment losers			
17. Shipbuilding	11. Chemicals	11. Chemicals	11. Chemicals
20. Vehicles n.e.s.	14. Mechanical engineering	12. Iron & steel	14. Mechanical engineering
	15. Instrument engineering	14. Mechanical engineering	15. Instrument engineering
	19. Aerospace equipment	16. Electrical engineering	
	25. Bricks	21. Metal goods	
	28. Printing & publishing	24. Leather, clothing etc.	
		25. Bricks	
		26. Timber & furniture	
		28. Paper & board	
		30. Manufactures n.e.s.	
(c) Trade losers, employment gainers			
13. Non-ferrous metals	16. Electrical engineering	20. Vehicles n.e.s.	13. Non-ferrous metals
15. Instrument engineering	18. Motor vehicles		26. Timber & furniture
21. Metal goods	30. Manufactures n.e.s.		

22. Textile fibres
25. Bricks
27. Paper & board
30. Manufactures n.e.s.

19. Aerospace equipment
23. Textiles n.e.s.
24. Leather, clothing etc.
26. Timber & furniture

(d) Trade losers, employment losers

12. Iron & steel
13. Non-ferrous metals
17. Shipbuilding
20. Vehicles n.e.s.
21. Metal goods
23. Textiles n.e.s.
24. Leather, clothing etc.
27. Paper & board

13. Non-ferrous metals
15. Instrument engineering
17. Shipbuilding
18. Motor vehicles
19. Aerospace equipment
22. Textile fibres
23. Textiles n.e.s.
27. Paper & board
29. Rubber

12. Iron & steel
16. Electrical engineering
17. Shipbuilding
18. Motor vehicles
19. Aerospace equipment
20. Vehicles n.e.s.
21. Metal goods
22. Textile fibres
23. Textiles n.e.s.
24. Leather, clothing etc.
25. Bricks
27. Paper & board
28. Printing & publishing
29. Rubber
30. Manufactures n.e.s.

Source: MRG estimates: figures for 1978–85 taken from the standard view.

Poor trade performance will influence domestic demand not only through the familiar multiplier effect but also through its implications for government policy. The relative contributions of trade and domestic demand to employment creation are now discussed before we move on to an examination of the various factors underlying trade performance.

4.1.1. The relative importance of trade performance and domestic demand

In general, domestic demand has been the dominant influence on domestic output since 1956 but trade performance has become relatively more important in the very recent past. There has been a tendency for changes in domestic demand and in net trade to offset rather than to reinforce each other. This applies with most force to the period 1974–78 as shown in Table 4.2.

In the first sub-period, 1956–65, only the output of textiles n.e.s. was dominated by changes in the trade balance. For the subsequent period to 1974 there were no such cases but during 1974–78 trade was of prime importance for six industries: chemicals, shipbuilding, motor vehicles, textiles n.e.s., paper and board, and manufactures n.e.s. Not all these trade changes were adverse as in two of these industries, chemicals and manufactures n.e.s., the trade changes increased output and reinforced changes in domestic demand.

Up to 1974 the movement of domestic demand was generally beneficial towards employment, the exceptions being shipbuilding, non-ferrous metals and vehicles n.e.s. The main problem was that the scale of changes in domestic demand over this period was not great enough to offset the effect of improvements in productivity on employment. However, after 1974, in the wake of the oil price rises and in the slump in the world economy, even the positive effect of domestic demand waned, declining for eleven out of the twenty manufacturing industries under the influence of a restrictive fiscal policy. This behaviour is in sharp contrast to that of the trade balance which turned round during this period, and where improvements modified the deterioration in domestic demand for seven of these eleven industries although not enough to result in an increase in output. Industries most severely affected by the fall in domestic demand were iron and steel, mechanical engineering, electrical engineering and metal goods.

Table 4.2 Changes in Net Trade and Domestic Demand 1956–1985

£m 1970 prices

	Changes in net trade				Changes in domestic demand			
SAM industry	1956-65	1965-74	1974-78	1978-85	1956-65	1965-74	1974-78	1978-85
11. Chemicals	100	187	190	646	895	1,680	50	-191
12. Iron & steel	101	-142	156	-376	406	-292	-509	75
13. Non-ferrous metals	-15	-19	-9	-199	368	-50	-155	362
14. Mechanical engineering	70	13	81	83	956	862	-561	-328
15. Instrument engineering	-52	96	-56	2	252	127	85	-102
16. Electrical engineering	2	-395	147	-1,153	1,008	1,841	-213	1,471
17. Shipbuilding	1	-242	-163	-351	-187	275	102	279
18. Motor vehicles	199	-156	-285	-525	1,354	282	158	393
19. Aerospace equipment	-93	111	-37	-199	103	169	163	-35
20. Vehicles n.e.s.	1	-5	-8	-13	-116	-104	-13	-10
21. Metal goods	-50	-30	314	-409	638	57	-516	-14
22. Textile fibres	-2	15	-10	-86	113	192	-5	55
23. Textiles n.e.s.	-266	-15	-115	-375	236	22	-74	311
24. Leather, clothing etc	-21	-46	18	-428	233	154	57	321
25. Bricks	-24	7	48	-63	403	283	-126	365
26. Timber & furniture	-4	1	28	-66	319	171	-43	267
27. Paper & board	-76	-121	-72	-106	220	135	43	53
28. Printing & publishing	18	23	62	-121	640	443	-132	213
29. Rubber	1	15	-12	-12	156	51	75	-96
30. Manufactures n.e.s.	-24	-37	22	-90	300	446	9	145
Total	-134	-740	299	-3,841	8,297	6,744	-1,605	3,534

Source: MRG estimates; figures for the 1978-85 are taken from the standard view.

Nearly all the industries experienced large changes in both imports and exports over the period and this may represent the increasing degree of specialisation in international trade. However, industries which have been trade gainers have generally achieved this end by an increase in exports rather than by a reduction of imports whereas trade losers have usually experienced a strong growth in imports accompanied by a weaker growth of export demand. The main exceptions to this rule are among the trade gainers. Here imports of iron and steel and mechanical engineering fell between 1974 and 1978 and largely explain the subsequent improvement in net trade for these industries.

In order to assess the impact of trade performance on the economy, an attempt has been made to estimate the effect on the domestic economy had there been no change in the net trade balance in each of the three sub-periods. Such an exercise is not without its difficulties. For any given industry it is possible to calculate the impact on output of given assumptions about the trade balance. To attempt this for several industries simultaneously is more complicated since large multiplier effects on output could be induced by the overall change in the level of economic activity. A second problem is that this type of exercise does not take into account induced changes in government policy. For example, a major deterioration in the trade balance took place between 1965 and 1974. Without the worsening of the trade balance in this period, the level of economic activity may have become high enough to require measures to restrict domestic demand in order to avoid hitting capacity constraints. The degree of policy reaction would be influenced by the extent to which growth had been constrained initially by the balance of payments position.

Table 4.3 shows the direct employment implications in different industries of assuming a zero change in net trade in each of the three sub-periods, given the actual labour-output ratios at the end of the period. These results are subject to the qualifications noted above and are calculated to show the *diversity of behaviour of different industries rather than to show aggregate influences.*

By 1965 employment in textiles n.e.s. would have been 81 thousand jobs higher given no change in net trade but employment in motor vehicles would have been 35 thousand lower. After 1965 however, the absence of deterioration in trade performance would have left employment *higher* in motor vehicles, and between 1965 and 1974 employment in electrical engineering and shipbuilding

Table 4.3   Employment Implications of a Zero Change in the Trade Balance

Thousands

	SAM industry	1956–65	1965–74	1974–78	1978–85
11.	Chemicals	−17	−18	−17	−45
12.	Iron & Steel	−17	21	−25	55
13.	Non-ferrous metals	2	2	1	17
14.	Mechanical engineering	−20	−3	−18	−15
15.	Instrument engineering	21	−25	13	0
16.	Electrical engineering	−1	81	−27	179
17.	Shipbuilding	0	77	57	105
18.	Motor vehicles	−35	27	51	88
19.	Aerospace equipment	25	−27	11	56
20.	Vehicles n.e.s.	0	2	3	5
21.	Metal goods	11	7	−70	83
22.	Textile fibres	0	−2	1	6
23.	Textiles n.e.s.	81	3	24	59
24.	Leather, clothing etc.	9	15	−5	99
25.	Bricks	7	−1	−9	10
26.	Timber & furniture	1	0	−6	13
27.	Paper & board	13	16	9	12
28.	Printing & publishing	−5	−5	−12	21
29.	Rubber	0	−3	2	2
30.	Manufactures n.e.s.	7	8	−5	15
	Total	82	175	−22	765

Source: MRG estimates; figures for 1978–85 are taken from the standard view.

Note: See text for interpretation of figures.

would have benefited considerably. In the period up to 1978 some industries would have increased and some decreased their employment levels if no net trade changes had taken place but in our standard view of 1978–85 most would have benefited, the exceptions being chemicals and mechanical engineering. Electrical engineering, shipbuilding and motor vehicles are projected to be major trade and employment losers as they have been in the recent past; these industries are joined by metal goods and leather, clothing etc. The latter had experienced neither substantial employment

gains nor losses from trade in the past whereas the trade performance of metal goods was strongly beneficial to employment before
1978 as opposed to the deterioration shown between 1978–85.

The overall tendency of trade performance to depress employment between 1978–85 is not offset by the behaviour of domestic
demand. Although Table 4.2 shows that, in aggregate, domestic demand is projected to increase after the decline experienced between
1974 and 1978 the stimulus is much less than that between 1965
and 1974. The overall trend in output between 1978 and 1985 is
therefore downward with only eight industries showing an increase. These are chemicals, non-ferrous metals, electrical engineering, textiles n.e.s., bricks, timber and furniture, printing and publishing, and manufactures n.e.s.

Output in the chemicals industry grows at an annual rate of nearly 2 per cent as the positive effect of trade more than compensates
for the decline in domestic demand. The other seven industries face
worsening trade positions so that increases in gross output recorded
(which range from almost no growth for textiles n.e.s. to 3 per cent
per annum for bricks) rely heavily on the outlook for domestic demand. The main sources of domestic demand underlying the
growth of output in electrical engineering (1 1/4 per cent per annum)
are consumers' expenditure on durable goods and the pattern of industrial investment in plant and machinery.

In the remaining twelve industries gross output declines. In four
instances trade declines are augmented by the behaviour of domestic
demand. Industries affected in this way are aerospace equipment,
vehicles n.e.s., metal goods and rubber. The lack of domestic demand reflects the low level of intermediate demand which is due to
both technical changes in input requirements and to the general low
level of economic activity projected between 1978 and 1985.

This leaves eight industries where gross output declines as a result
of trade and domestic demand effects which oppose each other. In
the cases of mechanical engineering and instrument engineering the
trade influence is positive and the domestic demand influence is negative (largely due to low investment demand). In the rest, domestic
demand provides the positive stimulus to output growth. For most
of these industries the difference between domestic demand and net
trade is small so that there is only a modest decline in output (usually less than 1 per cent per annum) but for iron and steel and for
shipbuilding output declines by 1 3/4 and 2 per cent per annum respectively.

In the case of the major structural change simulation (which is discussed in detail later) the main differences from the standard view are that there are large improvements in trade for mechanical engineering following higher export growth, whilst the net trade position of iron and steel worsens as import penetration increases.

In the following section trade performance is analysed into its constituent parts and the rationale for the major structural change simulation is also described.

4.2 Price Competitiveness and Trade Performance

In this section the impact of changing price competitiveness on employment is estimated along with calculations of the effects of changes in the exchange rate. Discussion then moves on to consider the role of other factors, such as demand, capacity utilisation and non-price competitiveness, on trade and employment performance over the period 1956-85.

4.2.1 Competitiveness and employment

Productivity has two distinct influences on employment. One role of productivity is in its effect on domestic costs and prices which together with foreign prices and the size of import and export price elasticities explains some of the change in net trade and hence output and employment – this might be termed the *indirect effect* or *competitiveness effect*. The second role is in the impact of productivity on employment for a given level of output – this may be termed the *direct effect*. In this section we are solely concerned with the analysis of the competitiveness effect on trade. The relative impact of the direct and indirect effects on employment is discussed in section 4.3.

The link between productivity and net trade changes through the competitiveness effect is quite complex. First, improvements in productivity may be reflected in lower unit costs which can be passed on to the consumer (domestic or foreign) in the form of reduced prices or retained by the producer in the form of higher factor incomes (wages and profits). However, labour costs make up only a proportion of total unit costs so that the relationship between labour productivity and prices is not likely to be equi-proportional. This is

supported by very weak cross-sectional relationships within manufacturing between observed annual percentage changes in industrial
prices and percentage changes in output per man with a coefficient
of less than unity for each sub-period. The coefficient moves closer
to unity over the longer period but the association is still rather
weak ($R^2 = 0.24$). The positive relationship between export price
changes and changes in unit wage costs is more robust; again it is less
than equi-proportionate across industries for each sub-period, becoming almost so in the long run. Second, trade performance depends *ceteris paribus* upon *relative* prices. Domestic productivity
growth affects domestic prices but not the foreign price which will
be a function of productivity performance in the rest of the world.
Various studies, such as those by Ray (1978) and Brown and Sheriff
(1979), suggest that in general the UK has failed to achieve the same
rates of productivity growth as its competitors across most industries
including those experiencing relatively rapid growth in productivity. Thus, even if productivity improvements are reflected by reductions in home prices rather than higher factor incomes, competitiveness may not be improved correspondingly if productivity growth
is faster in the rest of the world.

In order to evaluate the changes in relative prices on domestic
output and employment, some measure of the size of import and export price elasticities is required. Barker (1976) gives a description
of the basic nature of the import and export functions used in the
earlier static version of the macroeconomic model and estimates of
the relevant elasticities are taken from the current dynamic model
which is used in the present projections. Using these estimates,
changes in trade due purely to relative price changes over the period
in question have been isolated.

Estimates of the price elasticities are presented in Table 4.4. The
export price elasticities range from –0.3 for iron and steel to –2.7 for
leather and clothing, with a weighted average of –1.1. The import
price elasticities have a larger range, from zero for textile fibres to
–3.7 for iron and steel with a weighted average of –1.2. The closen-
ess of the aggregate price elasticities is somewhat misleading since in
fourteen out of the twenty industries considered, the export price
elasticity is greater than the corresponding import price elasticity.
Whether aggregate competitiveness effects on the volume of net
trade are dominated by exports or imports will depend on two factors: first, which relative price varies most (for imports the relative
price is the world price in sterling relative to the domestic output

price while for exports it is the world price relative to the UK export price); second, on the compositional effects of changes in relative prices. The estimated competitiveness effects (in terms of employment) are shown in Table 4.5. Over the three sub-periods relative price changes have had varying effects on the volume of net trade. Between 1956 and 1965 relative prices produced a small reduction of £321 million (1970 prices) on the trade balance and 100 thousand in employment terms whereas in the following period, 1965–74, the effect of relative prices was to boost net trade by nearly £2 billion and employment by nearly 400 thousand jobs. Between 1974 and

Table 4.4 Price and Demand Elasticities for Imports and Exports

SAM industry	Exports [1]		Imports	
	Demand	Price	Demand	Price
11. Chemicals	0.36	−0.60	2.27	−0.58
12. Iron and steel	0.76	−0.26	0	−3.70
13. Non-ferrous metals	0.42	−0.63	0	−1.69
14. Mechanical engineering	0.87	−0.82	1.88	−0.23
15. Instrument engineering	0.36	−1.11	3.39	−1.62
16. Electrical engineering	0.77	−0.95	2.14	−0.89
17. Shipbuilding	0.58	−1.43	0.33	0.96
18. Motor vehicles	0.54	−1.56	2.22	−1.10
19. Aerospace equipment	0.62	−1.29	0	−0.78
20. Vehicles n.e.s.	0.52	−1.63	0	−2.52
21. Metal goods	0.98	−1.34	0.88	−0.13
22. Textile fibres	0.21	−0.79	3.21	0
23. Textiles n.e.s.	1.28	−2.18	0.37	−2.55
24. Leather, clothing etc.	1.25	−2.71	0.89	−1.94
25. Bricks	0.59	−1.42	1.48	−0.31
26. Timber, furniture	0.65	−1.53	0	−0.90
27. Paper & board	0.65	−1.53	2.15	−2.46
28. Printing & publishing	0.54	−1.45	1.49	−0.14
29. Rubber	0.80	−1.80	1.66	−0.92
30. Manufactures n.e.s.	0.51	−1.41	2.29	−0.68
Average	0.61	−1.14	1.80	−1.15

Source: Winters (1976); Barker (1977); MRG estimates.

Note: (1) Calculated from the area and commodity elasticities given in Winter (1976).

Table 4.5 **Employment Effects of Changes in Competitiveness**

	SAM industry	1956–65	1965–74	1974–78	*Thousands* 1978–85
11.	Chemicals	−9	19	−4	−17
12.	Iron & steel	−7	9	−20	−28
13.	Non-ferrous metals	3	3	−1	−9
14.	Mechanical engineering	−30	28	−50	−66
15.	Instrument engineering	−18	75	−28	−11
16.	Electrical engineering	19	23	−18	−117
17.	Shipbuilding	2	−10	−21	11
18.	Motor vehicles	34	56	−28	−130
19.	Aerospace equipment	−22	34	−34	−45
20.	Vehicles n.e.s.	4	5	5	−23
21.	Metal goods	−20	12	−11	−45
22.	Textile fibres	1	3	−2	−3
23.	Textiles n.e.s.	−39	12	−16	−80
24.	Leather, clothing etc.	4	73	7	−119
25.	Bricks	−4	5	−4	−12
26.	Timber & furniture	−2	1	7	−11
27.	Paper & board	−3	27	2	−26
28.	Printing & publishing	−2	6	−9	−17
29.	Rubber	−4	9	−3	−20
30.	Manufactures n.e.s.	−7	6	−11	−21
	Total	−100	396	−239	−789

Source: MRG estimates; see text for details.

1978 this trend was reversed, leading to a reduction of over £1 billion in the trade balance and an employment decline of nearly 240
thousand jobs. In the standard view, the employment loss is nearly
800 thousand jobs between 1978 and 1985.

The pattern for individual industries generally reflects the aggregate picture. There are of course exceptions. In the period 1956–65
it is estimated that competitiveness increased output in non-ferrous
metals, electrical engineering, shipbuilding, motor vehicles,
vehicles n.e.s., and textile fibres, and leather, clothing etc. Between 1965
and 1974 shipbuilding goes against the general trend, as do four

industries in 1974–78, including vehicles n.e.s. and leather, clothing etc. Industries which suffer particularly in the standard view to 1985 are mechanical engineering, electrical engineering, motor vehicles, textiles n.e.s. and leather, clothing etc. Only shipbuilding gains by changes in competitiveness.

The importance of the fact that import and export relative prices can move in different ways (see the discussion above) is shown by the existence of reinforcing import and export effects in only eight industries for 1956–65. In the following two periods this occurs for fourteen and ten industries respectively. The impact of changes in price competitiveness on the volume of exports exceeds the effect on the volume of imports for just over half of the industries, with the proportion a little higher in 1956–65 than in the later periods.

Not surprisingly, individual industries tend to have the dominant effect determined by the relative size of export and import price elasticities. Iron and steel and non-ferrous metals have relatively large import price elasticities and are accordingly import dominated. Mechanical engineering, electrical engineering, motor vehicles, metal goods, textile fibres, bricks, printing and publishing, and manufactures n.e.s. have relatively large export elasticities and net trade is dominated by export price changes. Leather, clothing etc. and timber and furniture are exceptions to this rule since they show larger relative price changes for imports than for exports, which offsets the effect of the higher export price elasticity. The remaining industries are sometimes dominated by import changes, sometimes by exports.

4.2.2 The role of exchange rate changes

We turn now to the effects on the volumes of imports and exports of the impact of devaluation on relative prices, ignoring any second round effects due to the possible repercussions of higher wages on domestic costs, the impact of the higher cost of imported components on export prices, and the general macroeconomic effects of devaluation (for example, higher consumer prices).

To evaluate the effects of devaluation, the link between changes in the exchange rate and changes in import and export prices must be incorporated before estimating the impact of relative price changes on the volumes of imports and exports.

Since we observe significant differences in prices of similar goods over fairly long periods, the general hypothesis that UK exporters are price-takers in the world market (often referred to as the law of one price) is implicitly rejected.[2] Our view of world markets incorporates the phenomenon where, according to Posner (1979), foreign markets are highly homogeneous but only imperfectly competitive. The exporter has a choice of selling at a higher or a lower price and the relative price will depend partly on UK costs. The fear of oligopolistic reaction by competitors suggests that exchange rate changes may just lead to higher profits rather than changes in the foreign currency price of exports. To the extent that this occurs then the impact of devaluation on export volumes through the mechanisms of relative price changes is weakened. In order to evaluate devaluation effects, the set of long-run export price parameters from the macroeconomic model has been used. The overall weight of home cost/prices in UK export prices is approximately 0.7 whilst the weight of foreign prices is 0.3. Different industries face different world market conditions however. Chemicals and mechanical engineering are to a large extent price-takers in world markets whilst electrical engineering and motor vehicles are largely price-makers. It should be noted however that it is difficult to define industries uniquely as pricemakers or price-takers on statistical grounds.

In the case of imports, the position is less complicated. The import price parameters in the model do not imply a one-to-one correspondence between changes in exchange rates and UK sterling import prices, but the average elasticity is of the order of 0.8 and only non-ferrous metals, textiles n.e.s. and shipbuilding have values of less than 0.6, the latter having a zero elasticity.

Table 4.6 presents the result of the effects of exchange rate changes over the periods 1965–74 and 1974–78 on the volume of imports and exports, given our assumptions about the elasticities involved (there were no changes before 1965). During 1965–74, the dollar exchange rate fell by $16^{1/2}$ per cent, the bulk of the decline occurring in 1967. The reduction between 1974 and 1978 was even sharper, being nearly 20 per cent, most of which occurred in 1976 after which the rate has drifted steadily upwards.

Devaluation would seem to have increased the volume of net trade through its impact on relative prices by just over £1 billion during 1965–74 and by nearly £2 billion during 1974–78. These figures should be compared with the full effects of relative price changes of £2 billion and –£1 billion respectively. In employment terms the relevant figures are 205 thousand and 363 thousand for devaluation compared with 396 thousand and −239 thousand for relative price changes due to all influences. Thus for the period 1965–74 devaluation accounts for about half of the total trade gain due to competitiveness whilst for 1974–78 the results imply that relative price changes would have had a substantially worse impact on net trade if there had been no devaluation. Of course, to some extent devaluation can be considered a reaction to changes in competitiveness either through policy responses under a fixed exchange system or through an automatic response under floating rates. Thus changes in relative prices due to devaluation are not independent of those due to underlying factors. However what the results do show is

Table 4.6 Employment Effects of Changes in the Exchange Rate

Thousands

	SAM industry	1965–74	1974–78
11.	Chemicals	9	15
12.	Iron & steel	42	83
13.	Non-ferrous metals	2	3
14.	Mechanical engineering	31	48
15.	Instrument engineering	15	22
16.	Electrical engineering	21	39
17.	Shipbuilding	2	3
18.	Motor vehicles	12	27
19.	Aerospace equipment	11	25
20.	Vehicles n.e.s.	3	9
21.	Metal goods	1	2
22.	Textile fibres	0	0
23.	Textiles n.e.s.	17	27
24.	Leather, clothing etc.	23	38
25.	Bricks	1	1
26.	Timber & furniture	1	2
27.	Paper & board	10	15
28.	Printing & publishing	1	1
29.	Rubber	2	2
30.	Manufactures n.e.s.	1	1
	Total	205	363

Source: MRG estimates; see text for details.

that exchange rate changes do not exactly compensate for underlying relative price changes.

Three quarters of the devaluation effects in general come from imports rather than exports but for chemicals, mechanical engineering, motor vehicles and aerospace equipment the export effect is stronger. Over one third of the import volume response to devaluation occurs in one industry, iron and steel, where the import price elasticity is very large. The responses of chemicals and mechanical engineering dominate the export reaction. Up to 1974 six industries seem to have had favourable underlying relative price trends which were boosted further by devaluation. These industries were chemicals, instrument engineering, motor vehicles, aerospace equipment, leather, clothing etc. and paper and board. The underlying trends of relative prices in other industries were much less favourable. After 1974 only four industries had healthy underlying relative price trends: these were chemicals, mechanical engineering, rubber and manufactures n.e.s. Trends in the remaining industries were much more unfavourable than they had been previously.

The basic conclusion that we can draw from this section is that devaluation has been an important tool in either promoting price competitiveness or in moderating adverse trends. It appears over-simplistic on the basis of the evidence presented here to regard the exchange rate mechanism as ensuring the equality of prices internationally.

Perhaps even more important is the difference in the estimated impact of devaluation on individual industries. The concern with devaluation as a macroeconomic tool can too easily distract attention from the important structural impact. We have already noted this conclusion in the context of full macroeconomic simulations (see Lindley, 1978 chapter 6) using a model similar to the one described in this volume.

It is important to emphasise finally that these results depend on the estimates adopted for the elasticities. It would have been useful to have repeated the exercise with alternative sets but to our knowledge there are no comparable disaggregated elasticities. The weighted averages of those used here do, however, correspond quite closely with other UK estimates at the macro-level (see for example, Posner, 1979).

4.2.3 Changes in net trade due to relative price effects compared with other factors

Having considered the relative importance of price competitiveness, consideration is now given to the question of whether the aggregate effect of changing relative prices has been significant from the point of view of the overall changes in net trade.

In the import functions used in the macroeconomic model, the main variables are total final demand, relative prices, capacity utilisation effects and a time trend, whilst for exports, world production, relative prices and capacity utilisation are the major elements. To begin with we shall treat effects other than those due to relative prices as a residual; the breakdown of this residual into its constituent parts, including the effect of non-price competitiveness is then discussed.

For the period 1956–65 we estimate the price competitiveness effect on net trade as –£321 million and the residual influence as £187 million. For 1965–74 the respective figures are £1,952 million and –£2,692 million, and for 1974–78 the price effect is –£1,157 million with a residual effect of £1,456 million (all figures are at 1970 prices).

Two points are worth noting. The first is that the two effects do not generally reinforce each other. The second is that, at the net trade level, competitiveness effects are significant in relation to the overall net trade change. At first sight this conclusion seems to contradict the findings of Fetherston *et al.* (1977) who argue that changes in price competitiveness could explain little of the declining share of UK exports between 1960 and 1976. However, estimates of the competitiveness effect presented here reflect the fact that, although for imports and exports separately changes in price competitiveness account for a minor part of the total trade change, the large residual effects for imports and exports tend to offset one another whereas the competitiveness effects are reinforcing. For example, between 1965 and 1974 exports increased by some £4 billion (1970 prices) of which only £1 billion can be attributed to changing price competitiveness, leaving £3 billion due to residual elements. Imports increased by about £4½ billion but in this case competitiveness lowered the import bill by £1 billion (i.e. it worked in the same direction as changing export competitiveness) so that the residual effect for imports was over £5½, resulting in a change in net trade of about –£½ billion. The competitiveness effects sum to

£2 billion while the *net* figure for residual changes is –£2¹/₂ billion.

In conclusion, although the share of manufactured exports in world trade has been declining until recently, the volume of exports has been increasing as has the volume of imports. The impact of changes in price competitiveness on imports and exports, taken separately, are small in relation to gross trade flows, but they have acted in concert and are much more important when viewed in terms of changes in net trade.

Separate industries do not seem to be dominated by the same effect in all sub-periods – this occurs for only six industries. Further, there does not appear to be any direct relationship between the sum of relative price elasticities for an industry and whether its trade change is price dominated. If anything, the tendency is rather that industries with high price elasticities also have large trade changes due to residual effects. In the standard view, there are substantial residual influences for iron and steel, electrical engineering, shipbuilding and metal goods.

4.2.4 Non-price factors and net trade changes

So far, an attempt has been made to isolate the influence of relative price changes upon net trade changes. This leaves a residual which can be explained by the following elements: demand factors; capacity utilisation; and unmeasured influences such as changes in non-price competitiveness. To the extent that price changes reflect variations in the last of these (e.g. quality changes) the estimated price elasticities will be downward biased, but to the extent that quality changes and price changes are substitutes the elasticities will be biased upwards.

The demand variable in the export equations used in the model is world industrial production and in the import equations it is domestic final demand. One of the general features of these demand elasticities is that many of the import elasticities exceed the corresponding export elasticities. This feature of the UK economy has also been noted by Thirlwall (1978).

This implies that for a balanced growth of domestic demand and world output the UK will inevitably run into balance of payments problems since import volumes will rise faster than export volumes. In the sets of import and export equations used in the macroeconomic model there are nine cases where the export demand elasticities exceed the import demand elasticities. However, the other eleven industries have substantially larger import elasticities so that on average the import elasticity is about 1.8 whereas the export demand elasticity is only one third of this. Chemicals, instrument and electrical engineering, motor vehicles, paper and board, and manufactures n.e.s. all have import demand elasticities with a value greater than 2.

The import and export functions used in the model and referred to above imply very little role for capacity utilisation effects. In the case of imports only seven industries have non-zero capacity utilisation influences and these have a high raw material content e.g. iron and steel, non-ferrous metals and metal goods. Hughes and Thirlwall (1977, 1979) argue that there are significant capacity influences on imports and that they largely reflect labour shortages. These results have been criticised by Whitley and Wilson (1979) who conclude that the evidence for both hypotheses is weak and that demand and relative price variables leave little room for capacity utilisation effects in most industries. Indeed, the fact that capacity effects are more easily found for metal manufacturing industries suggests that the underlying cause of pressure on capacity is more likely to be either raw materials or plant than labour shortages. Further support for this view is provided by the fact that alternative measures of capacity constraints work just as well as the vacancies-unemployment ratio used by Hughes and Thirlwall. Clearly, unless there is some permanent 'ratchet' effect on imports, cyclical variations will produce no lasting change in the trend in imports. Hughes and Thirlwall (1977) claim to find some evidence for 'ratchet' effects at the MLH level of disaggregation but this has been disputed by Whitley and Wilson (1979). Winters (1976) shows that the effects of domestic demand pressure on the volume of UK exports is also small.

This now leaves us with the vexed question of non-price competitiveness. There are two main problems here. One concerns what exactly is meant by non-price competitiveness. The second relates to problems of empirical measurement. In general, non-price competitiveness tends to be defined as an umbrella of all those elements which might possibly influence trade but which are not explicitly incorporated via relative prices, demand or capacity utilisation effects. The list of possible non-price elements comprises product superiority, after-sales service, delivery performance and marketing. It is difficult to disentangle non-price effects from estimated import and export relationships. To the extent that price indices do not measure quality changes then conventional price elasticities may be biased. The position can be complicated since changes in price competitiveness can either encourage non-price competitiveness or diminish it by shielding UK producers. Stout (1977) suggests that the latter may have occurred as producers have moved into low-quality goods as indicated by low unit values of exports of UK goods compared to those of German and French competitors, particularly in the mechanical engineering industries. It is possible to take the other view however and argue that price competitiveness stimulates effort into non-price activities. Some evidence on the importance of price and non-price competitiveness is given by Kravis and Lipsey (1971) who give the results of a survey into the relative importance of factors affecting US exports. These show that for the chemicals industries 56 per cent of the sample quoted relative prices as being most important whereas only 18 per cent and 14 per cent did so for finished manufactures and transport and machinery equipment respectively. The most important factors affecting non-price competitiveness reflected either product superiority, faster delivery or after-sales service.

The results of our earlier analysis suggest that changes in relative prices have usually explained a minor part of movements in import and export volumes. However, this does not mean that all of the residual element can be equated with non-price competitiveness in the sense that we have defined it. In particular, it is almost impossible to disentangle pure demand effects from those elements of non-price competitiveness which might be strongly trended. When the demand elasticities reflect variations in the growth of demand rather than the trend in the level of demand it would be reasonable to equate the former to demand rather than to non-price competitiveness. There are of course pure time trends in the import and export equations and these could be attributed to non-price competitiveness. We estimate that about one quarter to one third of the total non-price change in imports over the period 1956–78 is due to the pure time trend. Time trend elements are particularly important for iron and steel, non-ferrous metals and aerospace equipment. However, these are not cases where non-price competitiveness effects would be expected to be most significant. There are also time trend effects in the export equations but these are in aggregate less important than for imports.

In conclusion it may be said that the residual effect after allowing for changes in price competitiveness has been important in explaining trade flows at the industry level. However, this effect includes the role of changes in demand and capacity utilisation. Excluding these elements leaves the time trend effect. As noted above this may be interpreted as being due to non-price competitiveness but it may also be due to other factors (e.g. increasing specialisation). The time trend is much less important than demand in explaining trade flows and is approximately on a par with price competitiveness. It has been most important (from the import side) for metal manufactures and aerospace equipment industries rather than for machinery or transport equipment where non-price competitiveness has often been alleged to be extremely important.

4.2.5 Investment, productivity growth and trade performance

Neo-classical growth theory invariably concludes that, given the level of employment, the level of output per man is determined by the share of investment in the national product, and the growth rate of output per man by changes in technology. Detailed empirical work by Denison (1967) and others has produced much evidence to contradict this view and to suggest that the speed of diffusion of innovations and factor reallocation (and hence both the level and growth of output per man) depends upon the growth of, and fluctuations in, aggregate demand.

A simple expression of these ideas is found in Verdoorn's law which relates the growth in output per man to the growth in output. A regression across industries for each of our sub-periods reveals a significant positive but less than equi-proportionate relationship between these two variables ($R^2 = 0.7$). Various commentators have suggested that the level of investment is a crucial determinant of growth in output per man since this reflects the speed of diffusion of new technology as a result of growth in demand. However, the addition of a variable measuring the cumulative investment carried out in each industry in proportion to its level of output adds very little to our ability to explain the change in output per man in the sample.

It has also been suggested (Barker, 1979) that high ratios of investment to output are a critical factor in maintaining non-price competitiveness. The relationship of exports to investment is held to be primarily technological, with up-to-date capital enabling a country to offer better products which embody the latest techniques resulting in greater responsiveness to changes in taste. In consequence foreign demand for goods becomes more income-elastic. Barker finds some international evidence to support these ideas at an aggregate level.

We have made a similar international comparison but looking directly at manufacturing investment-output ratios and the corresponding export *and* import demand elasticities (the latter are taken from the studies of Houthakker and Magee (1969), Goldstein and Kahn (1978), and Basevi (1973)).[3] Unfortunately, it is not possible to test the relationship between trade elasticities and investment at a more disaggregated level due to the lack of a set of consistent trade elasticities. Our international cross-sectional regression results do not support the hypothesis of a significant relationship between import demand elasticities and investment but support the existence of a positive relationship between export demand elasticities and investment ratios as found by Barker. Using export demand elasticities from two of the studies we obtained a coefficient of approximately unity; from the third, a value of 0.6.

An elasticity of unity has been used to simulate the impact on the income elasticity of demand for UK exports when investment is boosted between 1980 and 1985 in our simulation of major structural change (the results of which have been summarised already in Chapter 3). Investment is increased by an amount totalling nearly

Table 4.7   Increased Investment in the Structural Change Simulation

		Changes from the standard view			
		Additional investment £m 1970 prices			Increase in investment-output ratio per cent
	SAM industry	1980	1981	1983-5 p.a.	1983-5
11.	Chemicals	66	133	200	53.5
14.	Mechanical engineering	50	100	150	106.4
15.	Instrument engineering	7	13	20	166.7
16.	Electrical engineering	52	107	160	128.0
18.	Motor vehicles	40	80	120	85.1
21.	Metal goods	33	67	100	109.9
23.	Textiles n.e.s.	17	33	50	50.5
27.	Paper and board	33	67	100	277.8
30.	Manufactures n.e.s.	20	40	60	80.0
	Total	318	640	960	

£1 billion at 1970 prices or one third of manufacturing investment by 1985. The industries chosen are shown in Table 4.7 and are similar to those selected in Lindley (1978, p. 126). One third of the investment increase occurs in 1980, two thirds in 1981 and the full impact takes effect from 1982 onwards.

Investment is assumed to increase optimal productivity with a one year lag using parameters estimated by observation of peak to peak growth in productivity and cumulated levels of investment, and by regression analysis. The changes in productivity and export elasticities are shown in Table 4.8 and 4.9. In aggregate, the export demand elasticity for goods increases from 0.65 in the standard view for 1985 to 1.03. Optimal productivity is increased by an average of about 10 per cent by 1985 in the industries selected.

Table 4.8 Productivity in the Structural Change Simulation

Per cent

SAM industry		Changes from the standard view				
		1981	1982	1983	1984	1985
11.	Chemicals	0.7	2.0	3.9	5.7	7.3
14.	Mechanical engineering	0.8	2.4	4.6	6.7	8.7
15.	Instrument engineering	1.0	3.0	5.5	7.9	10.1
16.	Electrical engineering	1.2	3.6	6.9	10.7	13.7
18.	Motor vehicles	0.5	1.5	3.0	4.4	5.8
21.	Metal goods	0.5	1.4	2.7	4.0	5.4
23.	Textiles n.e.s.	0.4	1.2	2.3	3.4	4.4
27.	Paper and board	2.2	6.5	12.7	18.6	24.4
30.	Manufactures n.e.s.	1.5	4.3	8.3	12.1	15.7

Since one of the main effects of this simulation is to improve the balance of trade which is already in surplus in the standard view the exchange rate appreciates by 9 per cent by 1985 as against the 16 per cent depreciation assumed in the standard view. This increase in the exchange rate then reduces a substantial part of the boost given to competitiveness under this simulation although by 1985 export prices in aggregate are over 13 per cent lower than in the standard view.

Productivity in manufacturing grows by nearly ¹/₂ per cent per annum faster and this results in lower prices and higher real incomes

Table 4.9 Revised Export Elasticities for the Structural Change Simulation

Export groups	1978-80	1981	1982	1983-5
6. Chemicals	.40	.46	.53	.60
7. Textiles	1.38	1.57	1.76	1.95
8. Iron & steel	.96	.96	.96	.96
9. Non-ferrous metals	.69	.69	.69	.69
10. Metal manufacture	1.02	1.37	1.74	2.10
11. Mechanical engineering	.84	1.09	1.35	1.60
12. Electrical engineering	.79	1.12	1.46	1.80
13. Transport equipment	.49	.58	.68	.78
14. Instruments	.30	.42	.56	.69
15. Clothing, footwear	1.32	1.37	1.43	1.48
16. Rest of manufactures	.65	.75	.85	.95

so that domestic demand rises because of higher consumption as well as the initial investment impetus. On the other hand, net trade is worse as the combined positive effects on imports from lower import prices and higher economic activity are greater than the effects on exports where higher productivity and larger demand elasticities are beneficial to export volumes but the higher exchange rate is not.

In principle, the higher trade surplus could be removed by fiscal expansion rather than by exchange rate appreciation thus providing employment opportunities elsewhere in the economy. However, the room for such expansion given likely government financial constraints is not great. The potential for employment increases outside manufacturing is considered in section 4.3.

It should be noted that the empirical evidence supporting the relationships between investment, productivity and trade performance is not particularly robust. In particular, the link between investment and productivity changes appears to be not very well-founded as we have noted earlier. Consequently, the strategy of major structural change should be regarded as an illustrative example of this type of mechanism at work rather than as showing the sort of results that one would be confident of appearing in practice.

From the analysis in this section it is clear that both price and non-price factors have had a very important part to play in determining UK trade performance. We have also discussed the link between productivity growth and the growth in demand of which the trade balance makes up a considerable part. Our analysis has therefore highlighted the circle of cause and effect. Trade performance depends on competitiveness, both price and non-price. Competitiveness depends upon productivity growth and non-price aspects of product improvement; these in turn depend upon the growth in investment which via expectations and confidence is primarily a function of aggregate demand, a major part of which is the trade balance. Poor performance in one area soon feeds through to others, generating the by now familiar vicious circle often associated with lesser developed countries. However, the reverse effect or virtuous circle appears not to be so easily realised. The extra imposed industrial investment in the structural change simulation does induce further increases in investment but most of this is in construction and dwellings and does not have a self-sustaining effect on productivity.

The productivity implications of the higher level of investment together with the improved export demand performance do lead to a gain in the balance of trade and hence employment but with a floating exchange rate the higher trade surplus is likely to lead to an appreciation of the exchange rate so that a large part of the competitiveness gain is reversed.

4.3 Productivity Change and Employment

From our discussions in the previous section it is clear that productivity growth is not independent of the growth in output. On the one hand, improvements in productivity are a necessary step to maintaining competitiveness and hence demand for a country's output in the rest of the world. On the other hand, output growth itself may be an important factor affecting the rate of improvement in productivity as reflected by Verdoorn's law.

Given any change in output the faster output per man grows the slower will be the growth (or faster the decline) in employment. This is the view of productivity change often emphasised by trade unions wishing to minimise the disruptive effects on their members. On the other hand improvements in the productivity will have a beneficial effect on employment due to the increase in demand for domestic output. This conflict between the employment displacement and creation effects of productivity improvements is but one aspect of the continuous impact of technological change and competition on employment. Most neo-classical theories suggest that in the long run the creation and displacement effects will balance out, and certainly this has been the broad pattern observed over the last century. However, this has not prevented very large and long-lasting periods of unemployment being experienced.

4.3.1 Productivity performance in manufacturing

In Table 4.10 we summarise the pattern of productivity growth in manufacturing as measured by gross output per man over the three sub-periods. Since changes in hours have affected all industries to much the same extent, a similar picture emerges if productivity is measured as output per man-hour.

Manufacturing has been divided into industries which have experienced relatively fast and relatively slow productivity growth. The ranking of industries over time tends to remain stable: industries such as mineral oil refining, chemicals, instrument engineering and textile fibres have experienced the most rapid growth while tobacco manufacture and coke ovens have generally experienced very slow growth. Up until 1974 most industries increased productivity by between 1 and 3 per cent per annum, the average for all manufacturing industries being 2.9 per cent per annum. Between 1956–65 and 1965–74 there was a significant acceleration for most industries although some important sectors such as motor vehicles, vehicles n.e.s. and metal goods were exceptions. Productivity growth in motor vehicles in particular slumped from over 5 per cent per annum to less than 1 per cent between the two sub-periods and after 1974 fell further as the economy moved into the recent recession. Productivity growth for all manufacturing industries was 2.8 per cent per annum over the period 1956–65, 3.0 per cent per annum from 1965–74 and only 1.0 per cent per annum between 1974 and 1978. Excluding those exceptions already noted, this pattern was reflected by the individual industries. Many industries in fact experienced a fall in productivity in the most recent sub-period.

Table 4.10 also illustrates how each manufacturing industry fares in our projections of output per man in the standard view. Our exogenous assumptions with respect to optimal productivity and hours have been discussed in Chapter 3. As noted there, although optimal productivity is exogenously determined, our employment model is specified in such a way that for most industries a version of Verdoorn's law applies and faster growth of actual output results in faster realised productivity growth. The realised growth in output per man for some of the SAM groups in the standard view was presented in Table 3.14 together with the rates of growth achieved in the structural change simulation.

Output per man in manufacturing industry grows at a rate of 2.9 per cent per annum between 1978 and 1985. This is roughly equal to the trend rate of increase observed in the period up to 1974. Since the 1978 figure was well below trend, this implies that growth over the period 1974–85 is projected to be well below trend (about 2.2 per cent per annum). With a continued fall in hours worked, output per man-hour grows at about 3.7 per cent per annum between 1978 and 1985.

Within manufacturing the fastest rates of productivity growth are in mineral oil refining and textile fibres. Motor vehicles and coke ovens continue to experience very small improvements in productivity, output per man growing at less than 1 per cent per annum. Most industries again fall into the category of growth in output per man of between 1 and 3 per cent per annum.

Productivity growth accelerates in the second half of the period from a rate of 2.6 per cent up to 1981 to 3.0 per cent from 1981 to 1985. Individual industries within manufacturing do not all follow this pattern. Notable exceptions are the metal producing industries, mechanical engineering and several industries in the vehicles and textile groups.

With one or two exceptions, productivity in industries within manufacturing also grows between 1978 and 1985 at about the trend rate of growth experienced over the period 1956–74 (or just below that rate). The most notable exceptions are mineral oil refining, non-ferrous metals, shipbuilding, textiles n.e.s. and printing and publishing where productivity growth is around 0.5 per cent per annum higher than the trend rate of increase. As a consequence, in the great majority of industries, productivity growth is insufficient to remove any of the gap between realised and optimal productivity that exists in the base year. In aggregate, manufacturing productivity was some 9 per cent below the optimal level in 1978. By 1985 in our standard view it is still 8.5 per cent below the optimal level. Although the difference between the actual and realised levels differs between individual industries within manufacturing, this overall pattern is repeated with the exception of those noted above, where actual productivity moves closer towards the optimal level, and in motor vehicles and electrical engineering, which fall some 5 per cent further below the optimal level by 1985. Productivity is very close to the optimal level throughout the period in only food, drink

Table 4.10 Manufacturing Industries by Productivity Performance

1956–65	1965–74	1974–78	1978–85
5.0% per annum or greater			
10. Mineral oil refining	7. Drink		10. Mineral oil refining
15. Instrument engineering	10. Mineral oil refining		22. Textile fibres
18. Motor vehicles	11. Chemicals		
22. Textile fibres	15. Instrument engineering		
	22. Textile fibres		
3.0% to 4.9% per annum			
7. Drink	14. Mechanical engineering	5. Cereal processing	7. Drink
11. Chemicals	16. Electrical engineering	8. Tobacco manufacture	11. Chemicals
24. Leather, clothing etc.	23. Textiles n.e.s.	15. Instrument engineering	15. Instrument engineering
25. Bricks	24. Leather, clothing etc.	22. Textile fibres	23. Textiles n.e.s.
26. Timber & furniture	25. Bricks	24. Leather, clothing etc.	25. Bricks
30. Manufactures n.e.s.	27. Paper & board	29. Rubber	30. Manufactures n.e.s.
	30. Manufactures n.e.s.		
1.0% to 2.9% per annum			
5. Cereal processing	5. Cereal processing	6. Food processing nes	5. Cereal processing
6. Food, processing n.e.s	6. Food processing n.e.s.	7. Drink	6. Food processing n.e.s.
12. Iron & Steel	8. Tobacco manufacture	9. Coke ovens	8. Tobacco manufacture
13. Non-ferrous metals	13. Non-ferrous metals	11. Chemicals	12. Iron & steel
14. Mechanical engineering	17. Shipbuilding	16. Electrical engineering	13. Non-ferrous metals
16. Electrical engineering	19. Aerospace equipment	23. Textiles n.e.s.	14. Mechanical engineering
19. Aerospace equipment	26. Timber & furniture	25. Bricks	16. Electrical engineering

20. Vehicles n.e.s.	28. Printing & publishing	27. Paper & board	17. Shipbuilding
21. Metal goods	29. Rubber	28. Printing & publishing	20. Vehicles n.e.s.
23. Textiles n.e.s.		30. Manufactures n.e.s.	21. Metal goods
27. Paper & board			24. Leather, clothing etc.
28. Printing & publishing			26. Timber & furniture
29. Rubber			27. Paper & board
			28. Printing & publishing

less than 1.0% per annum

8. Tobacco manufacture	9. Coke ovens	10. Mineral oil refining	9. Coke ovens
9. Coke ovens	12. Iron & steel	12. Iron & steel	18. Motor vehicles
17. Shipbuilding	18. Motor vehicles	13. Non-ferrous metals	19. Aerospace equipment
	20. Vehicles n.e.s.	14. Mechanical engineering	29. Rubber
	21. Metal goods	17. Shipbuilding	
		18. Motor vehicles	
		19. Aerospace equipment	
		20. Vehicles n.e.s.	
		21. Metal goods	
		26. Timber & furniture	

Source: MRG estimates; changes for 1978-85 are taken from the standard view.
Note: Productivity is measured as output per man.

and tobacco and certain industries within the SAM group manufacturing n.e.s. This implies that there is considerable scope for faster improvements in productivity within the remainder of the manufacturing sector if only productivity could move nearer to its optimal value by 1985.

In our structural change simulation optimal productivity growth in manufacturing is accelerated by a substantial boost to industrial investment, as noted in Table 4.7. As a result, actual productivity growth increases for these industries as shown in Table 3.14. The growth in output per man in manufacturing in total accelerates from 2.9 to 3.3 per cent per annum compared with the standard view. There is some improvement compared with the standard view in industries other than those directly effected, but these are of minor significance. The major impact is on the chemicals and engineering groups and in manufacturing n.e.s. Despite the faster growth in realised productivity, it still remains well below the new optimal level by 1985. Within manufacturing instrument engineering is the only additional industry which achieves sufficient growth to reach an optimal level of output per man by 1985. In the cases of electrical engineering and motor vehicles, despite faster growth in actual productivity, they are further below the optimal level in 1985 than in our standard view. We return to this issue of the potential for a faster growth of realised productivity after discussing the implications for employment growth in manufacturing.

4.3.2 Employment in manufacturing

A detailed summary of the changes in gross output and employment for manufacturing industries is given in Tables 4.11 and 4.12. These tables follow Table 4.10 in dividing industries up according to their experience in each of the sub-periods. Despite the improvements in productivity experienced in the 1950s and early 1960s, manufacturing employment in aggregate rose by about 350 thousand from 1956 to 1965. This was due to growth in domestic output which was in turn a reflection of the growth in world trade. Employment grew in many industries during this period but was particularly strong in electrical engineering and motor vehicles where output growth was high.

During 1965–74, this pattern altered. Productivity growth accelerated as we have already noted but UK output grew less rapidly resulting in a fall in employment in many industries; only manufactures n.e.s. experienced a significant rise over this period. The picture since 1974 has been one of stagnant output growth, much slower productivity growth and falling employment in all manufacturing industries except vehicles n.e.s.

This pattern is projected to continue in the future in our standard view. Employment is not expected to grow in any SAM groups within manufacturing. Manufacturing employment is projected to fall at about 3 per cent per annum between 1978 and 1981, slowing to 2 per cent per annum from 1981 to 1985. This decline occurs in both the standard view and in the structural change simulation as indicated by the results presented in Tables 3.11 and 3.14. From these results it is clear that the decline is most rapid in textiles and clothing as a result of continued effects of foreign competition on domestic output. The picture in the engineering sector is almost as bad. These two groups account for over three quarters of the 1.2 million jobs lost in manufacturing between 1978 and 1985.

Employment in the engineering group declines at a rate of 3.1 per cent per annum. Within this group the fall in employment is least for electrical engineering and motor vehicles but even in these two industries averages 1.5 per cent per annum. The only industries within manufacturing which are projected to grow between 1978 and 1985 are drink, and timber and furniture. Employment in food proceessing, coke ovens, non-ferrous metals and bricks shows little or no change. The most buoyant areas of employment are those for which output is projected to rise, the main exception to this being chemicals etc. where above average productivity growth converts an almost 2 per cent per annum output growth rate into a 2.4 per cent per annum rate of decline in employment.

In our structural change simulation the main beneficiary of higher employment within manufacturing is the engineering group where employment now falls by only 1.9 per cent per annum. Mechanical engineering, instrument engineering and metal goods account for 230 thousand of the additional 243 thousand jobs in this group. Electrical engineering and motor vehicles fare much worse, the latter actually experiencing a small fall in employment compared with the standard view.

4.3.3. The scope for increasing manufacturing employment

As noted above, our view of the UK economy in the 1980s envisages productivity within manufacturing remaining some 9 per cent below its optimal level throughout the forecast period. In other

Table 4.11 Output Growth in Manufacturing

1956–65	1965–74	1974–78	1978–85
5.0% per annum or greater			
7. Drink	7. Drink		7. Drink
10. Mineral oil refining	10. Mineral oil refining		
11. Chemicals	11. Chemicals		
15. Instrument engineering	22. Textile fibres		
16. Electrical engineering	30. Manufactures n.e.s.		
18. Motor vehicles			
22. Textile fibres			
30. Manufactures n.e.s.			
3.0 to 4.9% per annum			
13. Non-ferrous metals	15. Instrument engineering		10. Mineral oil refining
14. Mechanical engineering	16. Electrical engineering		
25. Bricks			
26. Timber & furniture			
27. Paper & board			
28. Printing & publishing			
29. Rubber			
1.0 to 2.9% per annum			
5. Cereal processing	6. Food processing n.e.s.	5. Cereal processing	6. Food processing n.e.s.
6. Food processing n.e.s.	8. Tobacco manufacture	7. Drink	11. Chemicals
12. Iron & steel	14. Mechanical engineering	11. Chemicals	13. Non-ferrous metals

21. Metal goods
24. Leather, clothing etc.
25. Bricks
26. Timber & furniture
28. Printing & publishing
29. Rubber
15. Instrument engineering
24. Leather, clothing etc.
29. Rubber
16. Electrical engineering
25. Bricks
26. Timber & furniture

−1.0 to 0.9% per annum

8. Tobacco manufacture
19. Aerospace equipment
23. Textiles n.e.s.
5. Cereal processing
13. Non-ferrous metals
17. Shipbuilding
18. Motor vehicles
19. Aerospace equipment
21. Metal goods
23. Textiles n.e.s.
24. Leather, clothing etc.
27. Paper & board
6. Food processing n.e.s.
8. Tobacco manufacture
9. Coke ovens
16. Electrical engineering
22. Textile fibres
26. Timber & furniture
28. Printing & publishing
30. Manufactures n.e.s.
9. Coke ovens
14. Mechanical engineering
18. Motor vehicles
23. Textiles n.e.s.
24. Leather, clothing etc.
28. Printing & publishing
30. Manufactures n.e.s.

−7.0 to −1.1% per annum

9. Coke ovens
17. Shipbuilding
20. Vehicles n.e.s
9. Coke ovens
12. Iron & steel
20. Vehicles n.e.s.
10. Mineral oil refining
12. Iron & steel
13. Non-ferrous metals
14. Mechanical engineering
17. Shipbuilding
18. Motor vehicles
19. Aerospace equipment
20. Vehicles n.e.s.
21. Metal goods
23. Textiles n.e.s.
25. Bricks
27. Paper & board
5. Cereal processing
8. Tobacco manufacture
12. Iron & steel
15. Instrument engineering
17. Shipbuilding
19. Aerospace equipment
20. Vehicles n.e.s.
21. Metal goods
22. Textile fibres
27. Paper & board
29. Rubber

Table 4.12 Growth of Employment in Manufacturing Industries

1956–65	1965–74	1974–78	1978–85
3.0% per annum or greater			
16. Electrical engineering			
18. Motor Vehicles			
1.0% to 2.9% per annum			
14. Mechanical engineering	30. Manufactures n.e.s.		7. Drink
15. Instrument engineering			
21. Metal goods			
22. Textile fibres			
27. Paper & board			
28. Printing & publishing			
29. Rubber			
30. Manufactures n.e.s.			
−1.0% to 0.9% per annum			
5. Cereal processing	6. Food processing n.e.s.	7. Drink	6. Food processing n.e.s.
6. Food processing n.e.s.	7. Drink	11. Chemicals	9. Coke ovens
7. Drink	8. Tobacco manufacture	17. Shipbuilding	13. Non-ferrous metals
8. Tobacco manufacture	10. Mineral oil refining	18. Motor vehicles	25. Bricks
11. Chemicals	11. Chemicals	20. Vehicles n.e.s.	26. Timber & furniture
12. Iron & steel	15. Instrument engineering		
13. Non-ferrous metals	16. Electrical engineering		
25. Bricks	18. Motor vehicles		
26. Timber & furniture	21. Metal goods		
	22. Textile fibres		

−7.0 to 1.1% per annum

26. Timber & furniture	5. Cereal processing	5. Cereal processing	5. Cereal processing
28. Printing & publishing	9. Coke ovens	6. Food processing n.e.s.	8. Tobacco manufacture
29. Rubber	12. Iron & steel	8. Tobacco manufacture	10. Mineral oil refining
	13. Non-ferrous metals	9. Coke ovens	11. Chemicals
9. Coke ovens	14. Mechanical engineering	10. Mineral oil refining	12. Iron & steel
10. Mineral oil refining	17. Shipbuilding	12. Iron & steel	14. Mechanical engineering
17. Shipbuilding	19. Aerospace equipment	13. Non-ferrous metals	15. Instrument engineering
19. Aerospace equipment	20. Vehicles n.e.s.	14. Mechanical engineering	16. Electrical engineering
20. Vehicles n.e.s.	23. Textiles n.e.s.	15. Instrument engineering	17. Shipbuilding
23. Textiles n.e.s.	24. Leather, clothing etc.	16. Electrical engineering	18. Motor vehicles
24. Leather, clothing etc.	25. Bricks	19. Aerospace equipment	19. Aerospace equipment
	27. Paper & board	21. Metal goods	20. Vehicles n.e.s.
		22. Textile fibres	21. Metal goods
		23. Textiles nes	22. Textile fibres
		24. Leather, clothing etc.	23. Textiles n.e.s.
		25. Bricks	24. Leather, clothing etc.
		26. Timber & furniture	27. Paper & board
		27. Paper & board	28. Printing & publishing
		28. Printing & publishing	29. Rubber
		29. Rubber	30. Manufactures n.e.s.
		30. Manufactures n.e.s.	

Source: MRG estimates; figures for 1978–85 taken from the standard view.

words, in both our standard view and in our structural change simulation, the economy never regains the loss in productivity it experienced as a result of the slow-down in its rate of growth after 1973.

If productivity in manufacturing were to grow at a much faster rate so as to place the economy back on trend by 1985, this would have two main effects. The direct effect would be to reduce employment overall by about 9 per cent (or some 550 thousand jobs), assuming hours only decline by around 5 per cent as in our standard view. This displacement effect would be spread fairly evenly throughout the manufacturing sector, with the exception of those industries noted earlier in which productivity is already close to its optimal level. The displacement effect would primarily affect engineering because of its size, with a loss of an additional 250 thousand jobs compared with our standard view. This direct effect would of course be offset by the indirect impact of improved competitiveness on the trade balance and hence domestic output. Assuming the productivity improvement were translated into improvements in competitiveness, and using similar assumptions about trade demand elasticities as used in section 4.2, domestic output in manufacturing might be expected to increase by about £1.7 billion in 1970 prices. Using the employment-output relationships embedded in the macroeconomic model, this would translate into about 240 thousand jobs.

Thus the overall impact of a realised rate of productivity growth which increases sufficiently to reach the optimal levels given by long-term trends by 1985 might be to reduce manufacturing employment by an additional 300 thousand jobs. This pattern would appear to apply to virtually all the industries within manufacturing and, notably, to electrical engineering and motor vehicles which have in the past been areas of employment growth. In section 4.1.1 it was estimated that in the standard view trade changes lead to a loss of 179 thousand and 88 thousand jobs respectively in these industries and that changes in competitiveness are responsible for most of this loss. Given that output per man is some 5 per cent below optimal in 1985, some of this loss in competitiveness could be reversed if this gap were removed. Using the same assumptions as above the effect of productivity on competitiveness might stimulate output and employment in electrical engineering by £120 million and 24 thousand jobs respectively (the corresponding estimates for motor vehicles being £70 million and 10 thousand jobs). The direct effect of productivity on employment, on the other hand, would be to cause a loss of 37 thousand and 25 thousand jobs respectively (all these comparisons being made with respect to output and employment levels in the standard view). The net effect is therefore a further loss of 13 thousand jobs in electrical engineering and 15 thousand in motor vehicles. These results provide further evidence of the difficulty, given historical relationships between productivity, competitiveness, trade and employment, of achieving a virtuous circle. The analysis suggests that, even with a significant improvement in the underlying performance of the manufacturing sector in terms of output and trade, it will remain a job loser over the forecast period.

4.3.4 Employment outside the manufacturing sector

Detailed results for productivity, output and employment growth outside the manufacturing sector are summarised in Tables 4.13 to 4.15 respectively. These tables are in the same format as those presented earlier for manufacturing industries. The performance of the whole manufacturing sector is also included in this set of tables for comparison.

In Table 4.16 we contrast the past and projected employment growth of the manufacturing sector with that of other employing activities. The experience of manufacturing has been discussed in detail above. In total manufacturing employment grew by about 350 thousand between 1956 and 1965, fell by 700 thousand from 1965 to 1974 and by a further 575 thousand by 1978. Over the whole period 1956–78 there was therefore a loss of some 920 thousand jobs. In our standard view this decline is projected to accelerate, there being a loss of a further 1,200 thousand jobs by 1985. Table 4.16 indicates the extent to which the jobs lost in manufacturing have been replaced elsewhere in the economy.

In this table we have grouped the industries outside manufacturing into three categories. 'Non-manufacturing industries' includes agriculture, mining, construction and the public utilities. 'Services' incorporates transport and communications, distribution, professional services and miscellaneous services and finally, 'Institutional employment' covers employment in government and non-profit-making bodies.

Dealing with these categories in turn, the first has experienced a fairly steady decline throughout the period 1956–78 as shown in Tables 4.15 and 4.16. Employment in agriculture has fallen despite

Table 4.13 Productivity Growth in Non-Manufacturing

	1956–65	1965–74	1974–78	1978–85
5.0% per annum or greater				
	1. Agriculture	1. Agriculture	3. Oil & natural gas	3. Oil & natural gas
	3. Oil & natural gas	3. Oil & natural gas	36. Communications	32. Gas
	4. Mining n.e.s.	4. Mining n.e.s.		
	33. Electricity	32. Gas		
		33. Electricity		
3.0 to 4.9% per annum				
	35. Transport	35. Transport	32. Gas	1. Agriculture
		36. Communications	33. Electricity	4. Mining n.e.s.
			35. Transport	33. Electricity
			39. Professional services	
1.0 to 2.9% per annum				
	2. Coal mining	34. Water	2. Coal mining	2. Coal mining
	31. Construction	37. Distribution	31. Construction	34. Water
	32. Gas	38. Insurance	38. Insurance	35. Transport
	36. Communications	All Manufacturing	All Manufacturing	36. Communications
	37. Distribution			37. Distribution
	38. Insurance			All Manufacturing
	40. Miscellaneous services			
	All Manufacturing			

34. Water
39. Professional Services

−1.0 to 0.9% per annum

2. Coal mining
31. Construction
39. Professional services
40. Miscellaneous services

1. Agriculture
4. Mining n.e.s.
37. Distribution

31. Construction
38. Insurance
39. Professional services
40. Miscellaneous services

−6.0 to −1.1% per annum

34. Water
40. Miscellaneous services

Table 4.14 Output Growth in Non-Manufacturing

	1956–65	1965–74	1974–78	1978–85
5.0% per annum or greater				
	3. Oil & natural gas	3. Oil & natural gas	3. Oil & natural gas	3. Oil & natural gas
	33. Electricity	32. Gas		
	38. Insurance	36. Communications		
		38. Insurance		
3.0 to 4.9% per annum				
	4. Mining n.e.s.	4. Mining n.e.s.	32. Gas	
	31. Construction	33. Electricity	36. Communications	
	36. Communications	39. Professional services	39. Professional services	
	37. Distribution			
	39. Professional services			
	All manufacturing			
1.0 to 2.9% per annum				
	1. Agriculture	1. Agriculture	33. Electricity	4. Mining n.e.s.
	34. Water	34. Water	34. Water	31. Construction
	35. Transport	35. Transport	35. Transport	32. Gas
	40. Miscellaneous services	37. Distribution	38. Insurance	37. Distribution
		All manufacturing	40. Miscellaneous services	38. Insurance
				39. Professional services
				40. Miscellaneous services

−1.0 to 0.9% per annum

−8.0 to −1.1% per annum

32. Gas

31. Construction
40. Miscellaneous services

2. Coal mining
37. Distribution
All manufacturing

1. Agriculture
33. Electricity
34. Water
35. Transport
36. Communications
All manufacturing

2. Coal mining

1. Agriculture
4. Mining n.e.s.
31. Construction

2. Coal mining

2. Coal mining

Table 4.15 Employment Growth in Non-Manufacturing

1956–65	1965–74	1974–78	1978–85
		5.0% per annum or greater	
	44. Education		
38. Insurance, 39. Professional service	3. Oil & natural gas, 38. Insurance, 42. National Health Service	3. Oil & natural gas, 34. Water, 42. National Health Service	
		1.0 to 2.9% per annum	
31. Construction, 33. Electricity, 34. Water, 36. Communications, 37. Distribution, 40. Miscellaneous services	36. Communications, 39. Professional services, 43. Other central government, 45. Other local government	40. Miscellaneous services, 43. Other central government, 44. Education, 46-48. Private non-profit making bodies,	38. Insurance, 39. Professional services, 40. Miscellaneous services, 42. National Health Service, 45. Other local government, 46-48. Private non-profit making bodies
		−1.0 to 0.9% per annum	
4. Mining n.e.s., 35. Transport, All Manufacturing	31. Construction, 34. Water, 37. Distribution, 40. Miscellaneous services, 46-48. Private non-profit making bodies, All Manufacturing	2. Coal mining, 4. Mining n.e.s., 32. Gas, 35. Transport, 37. Distribution, 38. Insurance, 39. Professional services, 41. Defence, 45. Other local government	31. Construction, 37. Distribution, 41. Defence, 43. Other central government, 44. Education, All Manufacturing

less than – 1.0% per annum

1. Agriculture	1. Agriculture	1. Agriculture	1. Agriculture
2. Coal mining	2. Coal mining	31. Construction	2. Coal mining
3. Oil & natural gas	4. Mining n.e.s.	33. Electricity	3. Oil & natural gas
32. Gas	32. Gas	36. Communications	4. Mining n.e.s.
	33. Electricity	49. Private domestic service	32. Gas
	35. Transport	All Manufacturing	33. Electricity
	41. Defence		34. Water
	49. Private domestic service		35. Transport
			36. Communications
			49. Private domestic service

Note: Estimates of employment are not available for the earlier period on a consistent basis for Sams 41-49.

Table 4.16 Sectoral Breakdown of Employment Change 1956–85

Thousands

	SAM industry	1956–65	1965–74	1974–78	1978–81	1981–85	1978–85
5–30	Manufacturing	357	–701	–576	–655	–558	–1,213
1–4, 31–34	Non-manufacturing industries	–159	–680	–197	–102	56	–158
35–40	Services	821	248	217	–100	212	112
41–49	Institutional	227[1]	829	243	113	174	287
1–40	All industries	1,013	–1,133	–554	–857	–402	–1,259
1–49	Whole economy	1,240[1]	–304	–312	–744	–228	–972

Source: MRG estimates; figures for 1978–85 and sub-periods are taken from the standard view.

Note: (1) Excluding private domestic service.

a steady rise in output as a result of relatively fast productivity growth. Mining, on the other hand, has experienced a substantial loss of jobs primarily due to declining output in coal mining. These two industries have lost about 500 thousand jobs each over this period. Employment in construction and public utilities has been more stable (construction gained 300 thousand jobs up to 1965 only to lose them again by 1978). In our standard view, further falls of about 100 thousand are projected for both agriculture and mining resulting from stagnant output growth but modest improvements in productivity. This decline is partly offset by a 100 thousand rise in construction due to very slow improvements in productivity combined with a modest rise in output. There is a further decline of about 50 thousand in public utilities. In total non-manufacturing industries experience an overall loss of some 160 thousand jobs between 1978 and 1985.

Up to 1965, employment in 'services' grew rapidly by some 820 thousand. Since then this group of industries has expanded more slowly. Employment in transport and communications and in distribution actually fell between 1965 and 1978 by about 200 thousand in each case. In part, this was offset by rapid growth in professional services and in miscellaneous services. Between 1978 and 1985 employment in 'services' is expected to grow by only 110 thousand. Declines of 250 thousand and 200 thousand are expected, respectively, in transport and communications and distribution, which offset in part the growth anticipated in the other two industry groups.

'Institutional employment' was one of the faster growth areas in the period up to 1974. Employment in public health and educational services grew particularly rapidly, adding about 240 thousand and 540 thousand jobs respectively between 1965 and 1974. After 1974 this growth slowed with the imposition of stricter limits on government expenditure, the total rise between 1974 and 1978 falling to 245 thousand jobs. In our standard view this pattern of much slower growth is expected to continue particularly for government administration. Employment in the health and education services is only projected to grow by about 200 thousand with a rise of less than 100 thousand jobs in other government employment.

As noted above, the forces of technological advance and competition can be regarded as resulting in a continual conflict between job creation and job displacement. After 1965, displacement effects became predominant in the manufacturing sector but, as we have noted, new jobs were created to offset the losses here (and in other production industries) by expansion in services. At least this was the case up until 1974 when the economic recession considerably worsened the employment picture, and despite further displacement of labour in the manufacturing sector, there has been little or no creation of new jobs to replace those lost. This gloomy picture is forecast to continue up to 1985 in our standard view. The prospects for world trade and hence domestic output growth give little scope for the creation of new jobs either within manufacturing or the previously buoyant service sector.

The structural change simulation and our estimation above of the implication of achieving a return to the long-run trend in optimal productivity reinforce this gloomy picture. Such scenarios imply even more job displacement in manufacturing without automatic creation of additional employment outside this sector. Employment changes very little between simulations for this group of industries. The one exception is miscellaneous services which responds to the higher overall level of economic activity and in particular to higher levels of consumer demand (see Table 3.14). However, there would be a significant improvement in the economy's underlying trade position in these scenarios which could provide considerable scope for the discretionary expansion of domestic demand, thus generating further employment both within manufacturing and in other areas, notably private and public services.

4.4 Occupational Change

Examination of the changing pattern of employment in the UK economy in both the past and the future is extended in this section to cover the occupational dimension. The section is in three parts: the first deals with occupational change since 1961, the second describes briefly our method of projecting occupational structure and the third discusses the results for 1985 and the extent to which supply constraints might arise even in a period of high unemployment.

Inevitably, our analysis of occupational change is restricted by the lack of consistent and regularly conducted surveys of occupational structure. The plethora of classifications used and their limited relevance for the study of labour markets, as opposed to social structure, places more than the usual demands upon the exercise of judgement in preparing projections.

4.4.1 Past trends in occupational employment

An analysis of shifts in occupational employment over the past and the extent to which they are dominated by sectoral shifts in industrial employment helps us to build up a picture of possible movements in job structure in the future. Trends in occupational employment resulting from industrial changes will only continue if trends in industrial employment remain similar. On the other hand, technological and organisational developments can result in changes in occupational employment even when the industrial distribution of employment remains stable.

In our previous study of Britain's employment prospects the occupational classification chosen was based on an aggregation of census of population occupations. This has now been modified to accommodate the outcome of recent discussion between the MSC and other manpower agencies in the UK. It remains a very imperfect vehicle for analysis but is the best we have to work with at present. The composition of the Warwick Occupational Categories (WOCs) is shown in Appendix C.

Table 4.17 shows employment in each of the Warwick Occupational Categories, expressed as a proportion of total employment for 1961, 1971 and 1978,[4] together with annual percentage changes in these proportions.

Total employment (excluding HM forces and family workers) fell by $1/4$ per cent per annum over the ten years 1961–71 and is estimated to have grown at roughly the same rate over the following seven years to 1978. Within the aggregate there has been a continued growth of non-manual jobs but this was not sufficient to offset the decline in manual jobs between 1961 and 1971. Non-manual jobs rose from just over one third of total employment in 1961 to nearly one half of employment in 1978. The general trends in manual and non-manual occupations have been echoed at a more detailed level. The exceptions have been employment of other professions and sales occupations which declined during 1961 to 1971 when employment in other non-manual occupations was increasing and engineering craftsmen, security occupations and personal service occupations which grew over the same period when manual jobs were decreasing.

Employment in particular occupational groups can change for two reasons: either because industries in which they are concentrated grow or decline, or because of changes in occupational structure

Warwick Occupational Category	1961 proportion	1971 proportion	1978(1) proportion	Changes 1961–1971	(% of change due to)		Changes 1971–1978	(% of change due to)	
				Annual % change	Industry effect	Occupation effect	Annual % change	Industry effect	Occupation effect
1. Managers and administrators	0.066	0.078	0.087	1.5	−6.0	106.0	1.8	20.0	80.0
2. Education professions	0.023	0.031	0.038	2.8	165.9	−65.9	3.1	96.8	3.2
3. Health professions etc.	0.025	0.032	0.038	2.3	86.3	13.7	3.0	76.8	23.2
4. Other professions	0.019	0.019	0.022	−0.1	187.2	−87.2	2.2	60.3	39.7
5. Literary, artistic & sports	0.012	0.014	0.017	1.1	−2.5	102.5	3.5	43.6	56.4
6. Engineers, scientists, etc.	0.017	0.021	0.024	1.7	−74.8	174.8	2.0	−2.7	102.7
7. Technicians, draughtsmen	0.018	0.021	0.024	1.6	−44.0	144.0	2.1	6.1	93.9
8. Clerical occupations, etc.	0.140	0.150	0.159	0.4	−35.3	64.7	1.1	53.1	46.9
9. Sales occupations	0.056	0.054	0.055	−0.5	107.4	−7.4	0.5	56.3	43.7
10. Supervisors, foremen(2)	0.007	0.005	0.004	−3.8	15.6	84.4	−1.5	−83.3	16.7
11. Engineering craftsmen	0.090	0.095	0.091	0.4	−86.3	186.3	−0.4	149.0	−49.0
12. Other transferable craftsmen	0.045	0.038	0.034	−1.9	18.6	81.4	−1.7	−1.9	101.9
13. Non-transferable craftsmen	0.062	0.042	0.035	−4.0	72.8	27.2	−3.0	71.9	28.1
14. Skilled operatives	0.032	0.031	0.027	−0.7	14.8	85.2	−1.5	55.5	44.5
15. Other operatives	0.229	0.204	0.185	−1.4	76.6	23.4	−1.2	67.2	32.8
16. Security occupations	0.010	0.013	0.012	1.6	70.6	29.4	−0.4	−167.5	267.5
17. Personal service occupations	0.089	0.105	0.112	1.4	63.0	47.0	1.3	142.5	−42.5
18. Other occupations	0.061	0.048	0.038	−2.6	9.4	90.6	3.4	12.4	87.6
1–9. Non-manual occupations	0.375	0.419	0.463	0.9	34.7	65.3	1.7	49.6	50.4
10–18. Manual occupations	0.625	0.581	0.537	−1.0	61.8	38.2	−0.9	27.7	72.3
1–18. Whole economy(3)	1.000	1.000	1.000	−0.2	100.0	0.0	0.2	100.0	0.0

Sources: OPCS *Census of Population* for relevant years; MRG estimates.
Notes: (1) 1978 is an estimate.
(2) Because of classification difficulties this group only covers supervisors and foremen in the engineering and transport industries.
(3) Excludes H.M. Forces.

within industries. The former we term the industrial effect, the latter
the occupational effect.[5] Both are shown in Table 4.17. The overall
changes observed are the result of a combination of these two effects.
Some occupations may experience growth despite an unfavourable
industrial employment effect and vice-versa. Thus we can classify
the occupational groups into four categories: first, those which experience favourable industrial and occupational effects; second,
those with a favourable industrial effect but an unfavourable occupational effect; third, those with an unfavourable industrial effect
but favourable occupational effect; and fourth, where both effects
are unfavourable to employment. In the first and last groups the
overall effect on occupational employment is unambiguous. In the
two middle groups the net outcome depends on the relative strength
of the two effects. These broad groupings are shown in Table 4.18.
Only three occupational groups had favourable industrial and occupational effects between 1961 and 1971. These were health professions etc., security occupations and personal service occupations.
The expansion in the government sector was a major factor in the
favourable industrial effect for these occupations. By 1978 however
security occupations experienced unfavourable industrial and occupational effects whilst the occupational effect became unfavourable
for personal service occupations.

Only one group, education professions, had a favourable industrial effect but an unfavourable occupational effect between 1961
and 1971. Overall, employment rose as the strong increase in government demand easily offset the impact of changing occupational
structure so that this group recorded the highest rate of growth of all
occupations over this period. In the subsequent period to 1978 the
occupational effect reversed direction so that employment growth
accelerated although it was no longer the fastest growing occupational group. Eight groups experienced an unfavourable industrial
effect with a favourable occupational effect during 1961–71. Only
one of these, engineering craftsmen, was a manual occupation in
which over 100 thousand jobs disappeared. Of the non-manual
groups, strong trends in occupational structure towards managers
and administrators, literary, artistic and sports occupations, engineers, scientists etc., and technicians and draughtsmen comfortably
offset the industrial impact. Industrial effects were dominant in
other professions and sales occupations so that employment declined but the balance between the two effects was narrower in clerical occupations etc. where employment rose moderately. All except

one of these non-manual occupations (engineers, scientists etc.) experienced a beneficial industrial effect in the subsequent period however. This reflected the strong growth in the service and government sectors of the economy whereas the industrial position of engineers, scientists, etc. as well as that of engineering craftsmen was dominated by the manufacturing sector.

The group consisting of occupations experiencing unfavourable industrial and occupational effects is wholly comprised of manual jobs between 1961 and 1971. In four cases (supervisors and foremen, other transferable craftsmen, skilled operatives and other occupations (mostly labourers), the overriding factor was falling occupational proportions. Some 200 thousand jobs in the category other transferable craftsmen and nearly 350 thousand jobs in the other occupations category were lost over this period. By 1978 the occupational trend was reversed for supervisors and foremen although not sufficiently to prevent a continuing fall in employment, whilst the industrial trend was reversed for other transferable craft occupations (including bricklayers, painters and decorators) but there was still a further loss of 100 thousand jobs. Continuing trends meant that employment in other occupations fell steeply between 1971 and 1978 with a loss of 250 thousand jobs.

Over 300 thousand non-transferable craft jobs disappeared between 1961 and 1971, with a further 200 thousand by 1978. Changes in industrial structure were dominant in this decline (mainly due to the shedding of manpower in the mining industry and the continued decline of textiles). The decline in employment of other operatives has also been due to industry-specific changes. Declines in the labour force in agriculture and transport have been largely responsible for a fall of 750 thousand by 1971 and a further loss of 400 thousand jobs by 1978, for this occupational group.

In summary, the underlying trend in occupational employment between 1961 and 1971 has been the continued growth in the proportion of non-manual occupations. Even where industry-specific changes have been unfavourable the changes in occupational structure have usually more than compensated for this effect. On the other hand the general decline in manufacturing employment has reinforced the occupation-specific effect for manual occupations and the loss has been too great to be absorbed by the growth in non-manual jobs. In particular, over 1 million craft jobs have been lost over the period.

Table 4.18 Occupational Employment: Grouping by Industry and Occupation Effects 1961–85

1961–71	1971–78	1978–85
Favourable industrial and occupational effects		
3. Health professions etc.	1. Managers and administrators	3. Health professions etc.
16. Security occupations	2. Education professions	4. Other professions
17. Personal service occupations	3. Health professions etc.	5. Literary, artistic & sports occupations
	4. Other professions	
	5. Literary, artistic & sports occupations	
	7. Technicians, draughtsmen	
	8. Clerical occupations, etc.	
	9. Sales occupations	
Favourable industrial effect, unfavourable occupational effect		
2. Education professions	12. Other transferable craftsmen	2. Education professions
	17. Personal service occupations	12. Other transferable craftsmen
		16. Security occupations
		17. Personal service occupations
Unfavourable industrial effect, favourable occupational effect		
4. Other professions	6. Engineers, scientists, etc.	1. Managers
5. Literary, artistic & sports occupations	10. Supervisors, foremen	6. Engineers, scientists, etc.
6. Engineers, scientists, etc.	11. Engineering craftsmen	7. Technicians, draughtsmen
7. Technicians, draughtsmen		8. Clerical occupations, etc.
8. Clerical occupations, etc		9. Sales occupations
9. Sales occupations		11. Engineering craftsmen
11. Engineering craftsmen		

Unfavourable industrial and occupational effects

1. Managers and administrators
10. Supervisors, foremen
12. Other transferable craftsmen
13. Non-transferable craftsmen
14. Skilled operatives
15. Other operatives
18. Other occupations

13. Non-transferable craftsmen
14. Skilled operatives
15. Other operatives
16. Security occupations
18. Other occupations

10. Supervisors, foremen
13. Non-transferable craftsmen
14. Skilled operatives
15. Other operatives
18. Other occupations

Source: MRG estimates; figures for 1978–85 are taken from the standard view.

Confirmation of this trend before 1961 is offered by the Manpower Research Unit (1967) of the Department of Employment in a study of changes in occupational employment between 1951 and 1961. They reported that the main trend had been a continuation of that revealed by an examination of the material from earlier censuses, namely, the shift from the manual to the administrative, clerical and technical or non-manual groups. Traditionally this shift has been associated with the expansion of the service sector and during the 1970s many non-manual occupations grew most rapidly in the services sector. However, the 1960s highlighted the increase of non-manual jobs in manufacturing. Most of the growth of managers and of engineers and scientists was provided from this declining sector.

The largest impact on occupational employment since 1961 was from government where employment expanded by some 850 thousand over the 1960s and by 680 thousand between 1971 and 1978. The dramatic growth of education and health professions was an aspect of this, but most other non-manual occupations benefited. Manual employment was also stimulated but to a smaller degree. Increases in security and personal service occupations during the earlier period were for the most part from government. To a lesser extent engineering craftsmen and skilled operatives expanded in the government sector. The implications for future job opportunities of this dependence on government will be discussed in due course.

4.4.2 Method of projecting occupational structure

In theory it would be possible to estimate a variety of occupational supply and demand functions. In practice, previous economy-wide forecasts of occupational structure have been simplistic in their approach and little more than extrapolations of past trends. For example, a study by Woodward (1975) used the censuses of population of 1961, 1966 and 1971 to construct industry by occupation matrices which were then projected to 1981 by fitting log linear trends through the occupational proportions for each industry. The projections were made separately for males and females. Previous work by the Manpower Research Group (Lindley, 1978) used the censuses of population to project occupational structure for 16 occupations and 45 industries to 1976 and 1982. The method of projection was an extrapolation of past trends tempered by reference to the movements of non-manual proportions in each industry between 1971 and 1976 together with information on specific occupations. Occupational structure in 1982 was converted to jobs through a vector of industrial employment. The projections were intended to highlight those medium-term occupational employment trends which were most likely on the basis of past data and to examine their consequences for the pattern of job opportunities, rather than being forecasts of economic demand as such. For further discussion of the interpretation of such projections see Lindley (1978, p.61).

In the United States the Bureau of Labor Statistics (BLS) often produces forecasts of occupational employment in conjunction with the Interagency Growth Project (e.g. BLS, 1978). These are based upon occupation by industry matrices for U.S. censuses of population and a projection of industrial employment. Bezdek (1974) who uses and extends the BLS projections, remarks that the projection of occupational coefficients in each industry is made by taking account of historical trends, technological change, changes in product mix and shifts in industrial organisation. In other words, past trends are predicted into the future unless marked changes are expected, in which case an attempt is made to identify the underlying factors and modify the projections if necessary. Where relevant, the results of detailed industrial and occupational studies are incorporated to modify the initial projection based upon the continuation of past trends. No specific consideration is given to the availability of workers with the required skills. In this respect the methodology of the BLS projections can be termed a manpower 'requirements' approach.

The methodology adopted here is similar to that in Lindley (1978). The initial projection of occupational structure to 1978 and 1985 is based on historical trends from the censuses of population of 1961, 1966 and 1971. This projection is constrained by 1978 observations together with forecasts for subsequent years of the non-manual proportion in each industry. For many industries, where the relative growth of non-manual employment was rapid over the 1960s but decelerating through the 1970s, this procedure is important. Unconstrained projections would, by continuing the earlier trend in non-manual proportions, generate severe over-estimation of these occupations in recent years and hence, probably, for the future. Finally, the constrained projections are modified to take account of more detailed information available for the engineering and construction sectors and for highly qualified manpower.

More explicitly, the stages involved in estimating occupational structure in 1978 and 1985 were as follows.

(i) Occupational coefficients in terms of persons employed for the 18 WOCs were estimated for each SAM industry for 1961, 1966 and 1971.

(ii) These occupational employment coefficients were then extrapolated to 1978 and scaled to sum to unity.

(iii) Estimates of the non-manual/manual split were made for 1978 and a projection made to 1985 for each SAM industry. These were based on census of population estimates for 1961, 1966 and 1971 and a combination of census of production and new earnings survey information for more recent years.

(iv) The 1978 projections of occupational coefficients were then adjusted to agree with the non-manual/manual split estimated in (iii).

(v) Further adjustments were made to individual occupational categories in the light of other *ad hoc* information.

(vi) The procedure outlined in (ii) – (v) was then repeated for 1985. Unlike the previous study (Lindley, 1978) no specific allowance for hours worked was made.

A major deficiency of this method arises when examining the impact on occupational employment of an alternative employment scenario in 1985. The occupational *structures* of each industry are fixed in 1985. They are insensitive to different levels of output and levels of industrial employment. The fixed coefficient nature of the projection is however common to Woodward (1975) and BLS (1978).

4.4.3 Occupational projections for 1985

Applying the projected occupational coefficients to industrial employment in the standard view of the economy gives estimates of occupational employment in 1985. This together with the projected industrial and occupational effects is shown in Table 4.19.

Total employment falls by about 1 million jobs between 1978 and 1985. The general picture is one of continuing growth in non-manual occupations and decline for manual occupations. The fastest growing occupational group between 1978 and 1985 is that of literary, artistic and sports occupations, where previous beneficial industrial and occupational effects continue. Two other groups which experience the same trends are health professions etc. and other professions. Growth in the former is strongly influenced by continued growth in the government sector (though this is moderate by historical standards).

Table 4.19 Occupational Employment in the Standard View *Thousands*

Warwick Occupational Category	1978 level	1978 proportion	1985 proportion	Absolute change 1978–1985	% of total change due to industry effect	% of total change due to occupation effect
1. Managers and administrators	2,146	0.087	0.096	122	-53	153
2. Education professions	933	0.038	0.040	14	213	-113
3. Health professions etc.	942	0.038	0.046	145	74	26
4. Other professions	536	0.022	0.025	62	52	48
5. Literary, artistic & sports occupations	432	0.017	0.022	86	31	69
6. Engineers, scientists, etc.	577	0.023	0.026	46	-65	165
7. Technicians, draughtsmen	591	0.024	0.027	42	-68	168
8. Clerical occupations, etc.	3,919	0.159	0.167	45	-66	166
9. Sales occupations	1,360	0.055	0.054	-75	102	-2
10. Supervisors, foremen	106	0.004	0.004	-24	63	37
11. Engineering craftsmen	2,250	0.091	0.087	-188	135	-35
12. Other transferable craftsmen	828	0.034	0.031	-88	-17	117
13. Non-transferable craftsmen	833	0.034	0.026	-223	73	27
14. Skilled operatives	669	0.027	0.023	-116	69	31
15. Other operatives	4,553	0.185	0.163	-690	76	24
16. Security occupations	297	0.012	0.013	1	1158	-1058
17. Personal service occupations	2,770	0.112	0.121	101	128	-28
18. Other occupations	921	0.037	0.029	-230	22	78
1–9. Non-manual occupations (1)	11,435	0.464	0.503	489	-7	107
10–18. Manual occupations(1)	13,228	0.536	0.497	-1457	64	36
1–18. Whole economy (2)	24,663	1.000	1.000	-969	100	0

Notes: (1) Components may not sum to totals due to rounding.
　　　　(2) Excludes H.M. Forces.

In all, eleven out of the eighteen occupational groups remain in the same broad classification according to industrial and occupational effects as they did prior to 1978. The exceptions are: education professions and supervisors, foremen n.e.s., where previously favourable trends in occupational structure are reversed and there is a small decline in employment in both occupations; security occupations, where industry-specific changes are expected to be favourable so that employment stabilises; and managers and administrators, technicians and draughtsmen, clerical occupations etc. and sales occupations, where previously favourable changes in industrial structure are reversed. However, favourable changes within industries (the occupational effects) are strong enough to ensure overall employment growth for these last four groups except in the case of sales occupations. Introduction of new office machinery embodying microprocessor technology may ultimately have an even larger impact on clerical occupations etc. Our present view is that such factors will not become of major importance until after 1985. In fact sales occupations are the only declining non-manual profession whereas only personal service occupations within manual occupations show any significant employment increase. Craft jobs continue to disappear. Nearly 200 thousand engineering craft jobs and slightly more non-transferable craft jobs are lost. Employment in other occupations continues to decline (again by roughly 200 thousand) and nearly 700 thousand jobs are lost in the group 'other operatives'.

Where favourable industrial effects exist they are usually as a result of expansion in the service and government sectors more than offsetting the decline in the primary and manufacturing sectors. Growth in the construction industry benefits managers and administrators, engineers and scientists etc. and technicians and draughtsmen but not by enough to counteract adverse trends in manufacturing industry. Within manufacturing, the decline in engineering employment obviously affects the engineering craft category adversely although some of the losses are offset by growth in construction and miscellaneous services. It also leads to a decline in the numbers of supervisors and foremen and accounts for some 14 per cent of the decline in sales occupations and 34 per cent of the fall in the number of skilled operatives.

Ignoring, for the moment, the problem mentioned earlier about the fixed coefficient nature of our method of projecting occupational structure, Table 4.20 summarises the differences between the pattern of occupational employment generated by the standard view and our simulation of major structural change.

Table 4.20 Occupational Employment in the Structural Simulation

Warwick Occupational Category	1985 (thousands)	Standard view 1978–1985 (%)	Structural relative to standard in 1985 (%)
1. Managers and administrators.	2,268	5.7	1.9
2. Education professions	947	1.6	0.2
3. Health professions etc.	1,087	15.4	0.4
4. Other professions	598	11.6	0.6
5. Literary, artistic & sports occupations	518	19.8	1.8
6. Engineers, scientists etc.	623	8.0	2.3
7. Technicians, draughtsmen	633	7.2	1.7
8. Clerical occupations etc.	3,964	1.1	1.3
9. Sales occupations	1,285	−5.5	2.2
10. Supervisors, foremen	82	−22.8	2.2
11. Engineering craftsmen	2,062	−8.4	4.7
12. Other transferable craftsmen	739	−10.7	1.7
13. Non-transferable craftsmen	610	−26.8	−1.6
14. Skilled operatives	553	−17.3	2.5
15. Other operatives	3,863	−15.2	1.3
16. Security occupations	298	0.3	0.3
17. Personal service occupations	2,871	3.6	1.5
18. Other occupations	692	−24.9	1.4
1–9. Non-manual occupations	11,924	4.3	1.4
10–18. Manual occupations	11,770	−11.0	1.9
1–18. Whole economy	23,694	−3.9	1.6

Total employment in the structural change simulation is 1.6 per cent higher in 1985 than in the standard view. Manual occupations benefit most with employment 1.9 per cent higher than in the standard view. The change in the structure of industrial employment in this simulation is insufficient, however, to generate growth between 1978 and 1985 in those occupations which are projected to decline in the standard view. The increase in industrial employment means that, in general, occupations which were already projected to grow in the standard view grow somewhat faster and previously declining industries decline more slowly. The exception is employment of non-transferable craftsmen which is now projected to fall more rapidly, primarily as a result of the faster decline in employment in textiles and clothing.

The different pattern of industrial growth responsible for the changing levels of occupational employment in 1985 was shown in Table 3.14. Comparing the structural change simulation with the standard view, the most notable features are the slowdown in the rate of decline in engineering and distribution, higher growth in miscellaneous services, and faster employment decline in textiles and clothing.

Engineering employment is 9 per cent above the standard view in the structural simulation and this results in an increase of 3.5 per cent in engineering craft jobs over the level attained in the standard view and, in total, there are 4.7 per cent more engineering craft jobs. Similarly the higher level of employment in the engineering industry accounts for 2 per cent of the 2.3 per cent increase in jobs of engineers, scientists, etc. Nearly all of the extra employment generated for technicians and draughtsmen is also from engineering.

The accelerated decline of textiles and clothing employment in this simulation reduces the number of non-transferable craft jobs, over 50 per cent of which were in this sector in the standard view. Higher employment in distribution is a boost to employment of managers and particularly of sales occupations. Distribution accounts for three-quarters of the 2.2 per cent improvement in employment in the latter group. Even so the extra industrial growth is not enough to create an increase in employment in sales occupations between 1978 and 1985. Similarly, miscellaneous services accounts for almost all of the 1.8 per cent increase in literary, artistic and sports occupations and the 1.5 per cent increase in personal service occupations over the standard view.

It is important to re-iterate that this comparison assumes no change in occupational structure within each industry between the structural change simulation and the standard view. This implies that the elasticity of employment with respect to changes in output between the two simulations is the same for each occupational group. It is well established that this elasticity is in fact higher for some groups such as craftsmen, than for others, such as professional occupations although this may reflect cyclical rather than long-term influences. This could lead to the impact on some groups being exaggerated while that on others is underestimated. However set against this is the fact that investment is also increased substantially in the structural change simulation and this may itself affect the employment of certain occupations directly. Thus the elasticity with respect to investment may be higher for some groups than for others. First, the introduction of new investment may be expected to lead to demand for various occupations, such as engineers, as indicated in Chapter 8. Second, once the investment is in place, the new technology might be expected to favour non-manual occupations in general and engineers, scientists, etc., and technicians and draughtsmen in particular rather than engineering craftsmen and all operatives. Any bias in our estimates of the overall impact on occupational employment of moving from the standard view to the structural change simulation will depend upon the relative size of these offsetting effects.

Occupational supply constraints

With registered unemployment in mid-1979 at the high level of 1.3 million many employers were still reporting severe shortages of certain types of skilled labour. Consequently the question of supply constraints or skill shortages in our standard view of 1985 still needs to be considered despite an even higher level of recorded unemployment. Undoubtedly many shortages occur at local labour market level. At the aggregate level these often cancel out because surpluses arise in other localities. Furthermore many shortages are short-term in nature. Our concern is with the medium-term outlook for broad categories of skill and the likelihood of major medium-term imbalances arising for these occupational groups into the 1980s. The projections of occupational employment to 1985 suggest, even in the standard view, that some occupations will be experiencing reasonable growth in the future and the rest of this section provides a very broad assessment of how these occupational demands might be met.

It is well know that vacancies-unemployment ratios are of doubtful validity especially for cross-occupational comparisons. However, relative trends in these ratios are informative and Table 4.21 shows how these ratios have moved from June 1973 to June 1978. Although 1973 is often regarded as the period of highest economic activity in recent times it is noticeable that the labour market

Table 4.21   Vacancies – Unemployment ratios by Occupation 1973 to 1978

Warwick Occupational Category	1973	1974	1975	1976	1977	1978
1. Managers and administrators	0.590	0.436	0.206	0.141	0.121	0.152
2. Education professions	0.204	0.143	0.116	0.050	0.035	0.039
3. Health professions etc.	2.506	2.755	1.483	0.384	0.308	0.435
4. Other professions	0.687	0.703	0.407	0.245	0.177	0.153
5. Literary, artistic & sports occupations	0.105	0.085	0.044	0.036	0.041	0.045
6. Engineers, scientists, etc.	0.989	0.866	0.523	0.339	0.201	0.215
7. Technicians, draughtsmen	1.098	1.311	0.509	0.250	0.265	0.351
8. Clerical occupations, etc.	0.607	0.688	0.226	0.125	0.145	0.201
9. Sales occupations	1.375	1.326	0.368	0.189	0.191	0.247
10. Supervisors, foremen	0.572	0.653	0.302	0.194	0.295	0.379
11. Engineering craftsmen	1.204	1.555	0.419	0.210	0.369	0.534
12. Other transferable craftsmen	1.661	0.740	0.126	0.109	0.137	0.257
13. Non-transferable craftsmen	2.407	2.925	0.979	0.445	0.625	0.620
14. Skilled operatives	1.662	1.819	0.597	0.280	0.339	0.415
15. Other operatives	0.956	0.815	0.169	0.094	0.132	0.185
16. Security occupations	1.284	2.816	1.168	0.522	0.658	0.774
17. Personal service occupations	2.506	2.893	1.087	0.449	0.456	0.658
18. Other occupations	0.100	0.137	0.020	0.013	0.019	0.025
1–9. Non-manual occupations	0.770	0.800	0.302	0.158	0.159	0.210
1–18. Manual occupations	0.562	0.627	0.170	0.095	0.130	0.180
1–18. Whole economy (1)	0.611	0.669	0.200	0.111	0.138	0.188

Source: DE *Gazette* for relevant years.

Note: (1) Excludes H.M. Forces.

appears to have tightened more by June 1974, both in terms of the level of registered unemployment and in the movement of the aggregate vacancies-unemployment ratio. This tightening was more pronounced in the manual occupations than in non-manual occupations although rising vacancies for technicians and draughtsmen brought about a marked increase in the V-U ratio in this occupation. Within the manual occupations, groups contributing most to the overall increase in the V-U ratio were engineering and non-transferable craftsmen (but not other transferable craftsmen where labour market pressures appear to have eased substantially), security occupations and personal service occupations.

From 1975 registered unemployment in the whole economy rose sharply until it stabilised in 1978. The overall vacancies-unemployment ratio fell significantly in 1975 and again in 1976 but then rose in 1977 and 1978 by which time it had almost recovered to the 1975 level. This decline in labour market pressure was shared fairly equally between manual and non-manual occupations in 1975 and 1976 but in 1977 the rise in the aggregate V-U ratio was wholly due to an increase in vacancies in manual occupations.

By 1978 most manual occupations were at a situation comparable to 1975. The major exceptions were engineering and other transferable craftsmen where the labour market appears to have been slightly tighter than in 1975 (but less so than in 1974). However, for non-transferable craftsmen the opposite was true. Non-manual occupations in general faced a much slacker labour market in 1978 than in 1975. This conclusion is most marked for health professions etc., engineers, scientists etc. and technicians and draughtsmen. The implications of these changes for female employment are discussed in Chapter 6.

Identification of those WOCs experiencing high levels of vacancies in relation to unemployment in the upturn of 1973 does not necessarily imply that these will emerge as shortage occupations in the future. Since the experience of 1973 and 1974, much has been done by government and industry training boards to try to prevent such shortages recurring. Furthermore our standard view of the economy contains no tendency towards any marked expansion and the alternative simulation does not indicate anything like the low unemployment rates of the early 1970s.

In attempting to assess the supply and demand position for the occupational groups in 1985, paucity of data on potential sources of occupational supply makes firm conclusions very difficult. Informa-

Table 4.22 Past and Projected Net changes in Occupational Employment   *Thousands*

Warwick Occupational Category	Change in employment 1971–78	Employment 1978	Registered unemployment 1978	Change in employment 1978–85
1. Managers and administrators	256	2,146	26	122
2. Education professions	181	933	11	14
3. Health professions etc.	177	942	15	145
4. Other professions	76	536	13	62
5. Literary, artistic & sports occupations	91	432	11	86
6. Engineers, scientists, etc.	75	577	9	46
7. Technicians, draughtsmen	79	591	9	42
8. Clerical occupations, etc.	287	3,919	171	45
9. Sales occupations	45	1,360	67	–75
10. Supervisors, foremen	–12	106	16	–24
11. Engineering craftsmen	–62	2,250	57	–188
12. Other transferable craftsmen	–103	828	46	–88
13. Non-transferable craftsmen	–196	834	5	–223
14. Skilled operatives	–75	669	25	–116
15. Other operatives	–405	4,553	212	–690
16. Security occupations	–9	297	5	1
17. Personal service occupations	231	2,770	62	101
18. Other occupations	–251	921	443	–230
1–9. Non-manual occupations	1,268	11,435	332	489
10–18. Manual occupations	–881	13,228	870	–1457
1–18. Whole economy	386	24,663	1202	–969

Sources: OPCS *Census of Population* for relevant years; DE *Gazette* for relevant years; MRG estimates for 1978–85 are

tion which may act as a guide to making some tentative judgements is summarised in Table 4.22. The change in employment to 1985 reflects the demand expected for each category of skill. The change in employment from 1971 to 1978 indicates the size of changes in occupational employment that the economy has produced in the recent past. The levels of registered unemployment in 1978 do not identify the stocks of available manpower with the relevant skills since many workers with those skills may be working in other occupations (see Chapters 7 and 8). Nevertheless the unemployment levels do provide some guidance on supply relative to demand at the beginning of the period. Estimates of new entrants and returnees to the labour market by occupational category over the projection period are not available but in total the labour force is projected to increase by 1.2 million between 1978 and 1985.

The projected growth of jobs in non-manual occupations in no case exceeds the growth experienced over the period 1971 to 1978. But projected growth does exceed the unemployed stock of non-manual occupations except for clerical and sales occupations. A similar observation, however, would apply to comparisons between occupational unemployment in 1971 and changes in employment to 1978. Employment in sales occupations declines, so that prospects of shortages here are unlikely; the same would seem to apply to clerical occupations, etc. where the change in employment is considerably less than the level experienced over the recent past and is also substantially less than the level of registered unemployment in 1978. In no case does expected employment growth exceed that of the recent past although employment in health professions, etc. and literary, artistic and sports occupations comes closest to doing so. However, in these cases employment is heavily dominated by females who traditionally have a lower propensity to register as unemployed. For this reason the registered unemployed stock is an even cruder indicator than usual of the potential additional supply to these occupations. Other considerations which cast doubt on shortages arising in these occupations are the projected increase in the proportion of economically active females and the fact that there will be a substantial inflow of young entrants into the work force over this period, who, together with retrainees from those leaving declining manual craft occupations, could provide a very large source of potential additional supply. Together these effects probably add well over 1 million new entrants to the labour force *per annum* between 1978 and 1985. These considerations also apply to the technicians and draughtsmen group which in any case is only projected to grow at half of the rate experienced over the recent past. A more detailed analysis of the prospects for this group within engineering industries is contained in Chapter 7.

Amongst the manual occupations only security occupations and personal service occupations avoid significant reductions in employment. Growth in the former, however, is negligible, while that in the latter is half of the rate recorded between 1971 and 1978 and there is also a substantial level of registered unemployment in this occupation in 1978. Employment of other-transferable craftsmen does decline more slowly to 1985 than it has done in the past but once again this should be considered in relation to the stock of unemployment existing at the beginning of the period.

In conclusion, it can be said that the likelihood of significant skill shortages between 1978 and 1985 *at the level of aggregation adopted* here is remote given the overall low level of employment expected. This does not mean that more localised shortages will not appear however. On the other hand, although our general conclusion is not modified by the results from the structural change simulation, these do indicate a somewhat tighter market for craftsmen in particular.

4.4.4 Impact of microprocessors

In the results described in this chapter we have not explicitly incorporated the effects of the introduction of such technologies as the microprocessor. This is not because we feel that the effects are unimportant. Two general points are in order. First, it is likely that the impact of microprocessor technology will be slower and will take place more smoothly than many commentators are currently implying. Thus the bulk of the effects will probably not be felt until after 1985 – the end of our projection period.

Second, the effects of microprocessor technology require great care in modelling and in interpretation. Some studies such as Barron and Curnow (1979) deal only with the possible displacement effects which, they conclude, would result in an unemployment rate of 10–15 per cent for the UK. Others (e.g. Beenstock, 1979) tend to assume that, because job displacement and job creation effects have broadly averaged out over fairly long time spans, there will be no major unemployment problem in the future. Whether such a problem does arise depends on many factors: the speed with which UK manufacturers incorporate microprocessor technology into their industrial processes compared with the rate at which major competitors adapt; the impact of new technology on productivity and on prices and thus the level of real demand; and the balance of demand-induced employment gains against lower employment due to increases in productivity.

More work clearly needs to be done in this area. We confine ourselves here to indicating which industries and occupations are most likely to be affected by microprocessor technology. The Science Policy Research Unit has done a great deal of work into the possible implications of the new technology. Freeman (1977) and Pavitt (1978) examine the prospects for industrial performance while others have examined the implications for particular industries in some detail. This work suggests that while higher product demand is likely to result for certain parts of electrical and instrument engineering supplying the new technology, the long-term prospects are for very little growth in most parts of manufacturing with many previously rapidly growing industries such as chemicals, electrical engineering and motor vehicles facing saturated product markets. Even in services the long-term prospects are gloomy since most industries which provide auxiliary services to the market economy such as banking and insurance, and distribution are particularly vulnerable to the introduction of the new technology, one of their main activities being the handling of large quantities of simple information. The resulting impact on occupational employment is more difficult to assess. Clerical and sales occupations will certainly be affected, particularly in distribution, insurance and professional and miscellaneous services. In the engineering sector certain types of technicians and engineers may benefit directly from the impact of new technology while for most others the displacement effect is expected to dominate.

4.5 Summary and Conclusions

Chapter 3 has already pointed to the dilemma facing the British government in reconciling long-run objectives with the transitional problems which will confront it over the medium-term. The present chapter has examined in some detail a central feature of that situation, namely, the problem of our manufacturing trade performance, looking at the implications for output and employment in the years to 1985 and setting them against the experience of the last two decades.

The results of the analysis conducted in this chapter illustrate the diversity of behaviour of different industries in terms of trade, productivity and employment performance. Changes in price competitiveness have had both positive and negative effects on output in the past but are expected to lead to a large fall in output in the future. Output in electrical engineering, motor vehicles, metal goods, textiles n.e.s. and leather, clothing etc. is affected particularly strongly in this respect. Only chemicals, mechanical engineering and instrument engineering are expected to improve their trade performance between 1978 and 1985 and, of these industries, output increases only in chemicals as the decline in domestic demand otherwise offsets the trade improvement.

Output in electrical engineering grows during 1978–85 despite the major deterioration in trade performance but increases in domestic demand in motor vehicles and leather, clothing etc. are not strong enough to compensate for the worsening trade positions so that output falls in these industries whilst the drop in domestic demand augments the trade impact in metal goods.

There are very few instances of employment growth in manufacturing in the standard view projection to 1985 since productivity growth tends to more than offset growth in output. Major declines in employment are expected in mechanical engineering, electrical engineering, motor vehicles, metal goods, textiles n.e.s. and leather, clothing etc. In most of these industries productivity growth is projected to grow no faster than the period up to 1974 whilst for electrical engineering and motor vehicles output per man falls further below the optimal level by 1985. Consequently the employment projections are not the result of any assumed acceleration in the rate of productivity growth. The prospects for the last two industries do not appear to be easily remedied. The results of the structural change simulation suggest that even if export demand elasticities are changed substantially the increase in employment would not be very great. On the other hand, some industries do show a significant response to such a broad structural policy, for example, mechanical engineering, instrument engineering and metal goods.

Outside the manufacturing sector, employment grows only in some of the service and institutional sectors (but at a slower rate than in the past) and in construction. Employment declines in the primary sector, in public utilities and in transport and communication.

The industrial employment projections dominate most of the prospects for occupational employment with the exception of education professions and employment of supervisors and foremen where changes in occupational structure become unfavourable to employment. Most of the non-manual occupations are expected to grow in the future albeit less rapidly than in the past with the exception of sales occupations where employment is projected to fall by 75 thousand. Only personal service occupations show any substantial increase in employment among the manual occupations whilst the numbers of supervisors, skilled operatives, engineering and non-transferable craftsmen, and other occupations decline substantially. Where favourable trends in occupational employment do exist they are usually a result of expansion in the service and government sectors more than offsetting the decline in the primary and manufacturing sectors. Increases in employment in services and in the government sector are not strong enough to increase total employment between now and 1985 at a time when the labour force is expected to increase by 1.2 million people.

There are several possible reasons for the decline in the manufacturing sector but we might mention particularly: the competitive failure of manufacturing industry; shortages of skilled manpower; and the growth in the public sector. The decline in manufacturing employment, it must be noted, is not a problem confined to the UK, as other countries such as Belgium, Denmark, West Germany, Holland, the United States and Sweden have also experienced this phenomenon (but not, as yet, France, Ireland, Italy or Japan). Thus it is also relevant to consider to what extent this decline in employment is a reflection of the shift towards a 'post-industrial' society where employment moves out of manufacturing into services, in much the same way as it shifted out of agriculture at the beginning of the century, or whether it implies further substantial increases in unemployment.

In section 4.2 it was argued that the decline in manufacturing employment can only be blamed partly on the price competitiveness of UK industry. There are also other elements, notably the tendency of import demand elasticities to exceed the corresponding export demand elasticities, which are of major importance in producing the adverse changes in the net trade balance (and hence employment).

The second argument, that shortages of skilled labour are responsible for the continuing decline in manufacturing output and employment, is difficult to test directly. However, as we have argued elsewhere (Whitley and Wilson, 1979), there is little support for the thesis that labour shortages have been the cause of increased import penetration. Furthermore, the discussion of skill shortages in section 4.4, tentative as it is, indicates that if skill shortages have been a problem in the past, the outlook to 1985 suggests that such problems will not be widespread enough to jeopardise the growth of the economy.

A third theory, which is often associated with the work of Bacon and Eltis (1978), relies on public sector expansion squeezing out manufacturing employment either directly or through the financial implications of higher public spending. The evidence as we interpret it, however, shows that an increase in public sector employment in the early 1970s primarily affected female employment rather than the central core of the labour force. During the same period the level of unemployment of prime-age males was rising rapidly. It is therefore difficult to see how the public sector can have squeezed manufacturing employment directly. Such a possibility would seem to be even more unlikely in the future. It is more difficult to come to a conclusion on the indirect impact of higher public spending on the manufacturing sector since the predictions of the theory are also consistent with other explanations. We find the discrepancy between import and export demand elasticities to be a more plausible explanation than the Bacon and Eltis approach.

A general movement of employment from manufacturing towards service industries has occurred over the past and is expected to continue in the future. This has particularly important implications for occupational employment where jobs in non-manual occupations have increased rapidly (especially in education and health professions and clerical and personal service occupations) and jobs in the main manual occupations have declined. The most important question however, is why the service sector has been unable to absorb the reduction in manufacturing employment in spite of the lower growth of productivity in the service sector over the last decade. The answer lies in the role of trade. As the manufacturing sector has declined, so has its trade position worsened, but the improvement in trade in services has been inadequate to offset this decline so that equilibrium in the balance of payments could no longer be maintained at the satisfactory levels of employment and the exchange rate. The standard view for 1985 shows that the volume improvement in net trade of services is not expected to continue although there is still some benefit from improving terms of trade in services. If manufacturing productivity had grown sufficiently fast in relation to the UK's competitors, then manufacturing employment may have been able to decline over the past without being accompanied by a deteriorating trade position. This would have left more room for expansion of domestic demand which would then have induced an expansion of employment in the service and government sectors of the economy.

The simulation of major structural change is an attempt to see what might happen if the so-called vicious circle could be broken. The results, taken at face value, are not very encouraging since the gain in competitiveness in the manufacturing sector is soon eroded by an appreciating exchange rate. In part, these effects are due to the presence of North Sea oil; without the effect of the latter the structural change simulation would result in the removal of a trade deficit without the need for devaluation (which would have adverse effects on domestic inflation). Thus the economy in 1985 under this simulation is in a stronger position to face the consequences of declining oil production in subsequent years. New capital equipment would have been installed which would have put UK manufacturing industry in a stronger underlying competitive position in terms of both productivity growth and in the ability of UK manufacturers to take advantage of future increases in world trade, as well as producing other benefits such as higher real incomes.

In any case there appears to be no real alternative to introducing new technology since it is highly likely that it will be adopted by the UK's major competitors and, consequently, unless the UK follows suit its position will be substantially weakened, with even worse implications for employment.

In general, higher productivity growth which improves trade performance in the manufacturing sector provides policy makers with the room to expand employment in other sectors of the economy. However, in the specific example of the structural change simulation, a substantial amount of public finance is used to stimulate higher investment, and hence productivity, and therefore there would be little room to stimulate the economy further by fiscal means.

We therefore take the view that some form of structural policy is necessary if we are to overcome the problems inherent in the observed gap between import and export demand elasticities. However, the structural change simulation indicates that increases in investment *by themselves* would be insufficient to enable the manufacturing sector to generate a self-sustaining improvement in output and employment. Changes in the underlying trade relationships are necessary in order to remove this gap. Even if a structural policy were to be adopted, it would not be able to return the economy to a full employment path given the modest growth expected for world demand and, as noted above, the scope for increasing non-manufacturing employment is contrained by the PSBR. Nevertheless, a structural policy would avoid some of the difficulties inherent in the vicious circle of trade, productivity and employment that we have identified and thus moderate the employment decline that might otherwise occur. A general strategy to return to 1978 levels of unemployment by the 1980s would however require expansionary action by other governments as well as that of the UK.

Notes

1 Trade is defined in volume terms (here measured at 1970 prices). Thus a trade gainer is an industry where export volumes have increased more rapidly than the corresponding volumes of imports.

2 This conclusion is supported by evidence given in Kravis and Lipsey (1977) and Isard (1977).

3 The countries chosen were United States, Canada, Japan, France, West Germany, United Kingdom, Italy and Sweden.

4 1978 is a projection.

5 The two effects sum to 100 per cent. The industrial effect is obtained by applying the occupational proportions for each industry in the earlier year (say 1961) to the industrial employment levels in the later year (say 1971). Aggregating over all SAMs the changes in occupational employment implied relative to 1961 are expressed as percentages of the actual changes. The occupational effect is the residual.

References

Bacon, R.W. and W.A. Eltis (1978). *Britain's Economic Problem: too few Producers.* London: Macmillan.

Barker, T.S. (1976). (ed.). *Economic Structure and Policy.* Cambridge Studies in Applied Econometrics no. 2. London: Chapman and Hall.

——(1977). 'Time Trends versus Activity Effects in the Explanation of Imports'. Cambridge Growth Project Paper no. 445. Cambridge: Department of Applied Economics. (mimeographed)

——(1979). 'Investment-led Growth in the U.K. 1980–90'. Paper presented to the Seventh International Conference on Input-Output Techniques, Innsbruck, Austria. Cambridge Growth Project Paper no. 472. Cambridge: Department of Applied Economics. (mimeographed)

Barron, I. and R. Curnow (1979). *The Future of Micro-Electronics.* London: Frances Pinter Ltd.

Basevi, G. (1973). 'Commodity Trade Equations in Project Link'. *The International Linkage of National Economic Models,* ed. R.J. Ball. Amsterdam: North Holland, 227–81.

Beenstock, M. (1979). 'Do U.K. Labour Markets Work?'. *Economic Outlook 1978–1982,* 3, nos. 9 and 10, 21–31.

Bezdek, R.H. (1974). 'Long-range Forecasting of Manpower Requirements –Theory and Applications'. Institute of Electrical and Electronic Engineers Manpower Mimeograph. New York: The Manpower Planning Committee.

Blackaby, F.T. (1979). (ed.). *De-industrialisation.* NIESR Economic Policy Papers 2. London: Heinemann.

Brown, C.J.F. and T.D. Sheriff (1979). 'De-industrialisation: a background paper', in Blackaby (ed.), 233–62.

Bureau of Labor Statistics (1978). 'Labor Force Projections to 1990: Three Possible Paths'. *Monthly Labor Review,* 101, no. 12, 25–35.

Denison, E.F. (1967). *Why Growth Rates Differ.* Washington: Brookings Institution.

Fetherston, M.B. Moore and J. Rhodes (1977). 'Manufacturing Export Shares and Cost Competitiveness of Advanced Industrial Countries'. *Economic Policy Review,* no. 3, 62–70.

Freeman, C. (1977). 'Technical Change and Unemployment'. Paper presented to conference on 'Science, Technology and Public Policy: an International Perspective'. Sydney: University of New South Wales.

Goldstein, M. and M.S. Kahn (1978). 'The Supply and Demand for Exports: A Simultaneous Approach'. *Review of Economics and Statistics,* 60, no. 2, 175–86.

Houthakker, H.S. and S.P. Magee (1969). 'Income and Price Elasticities in World Trade'. *Review of Economics and Statistics,* 51, no. 2, 111–25.

Hughes, J.J. and A.P. Thirlwall (1977). 'Trends and Cycles in Import Penetration in the U.K.'. *Oxford Bulletin of Economics and Statistics,* 39, no. 4, 301–17.

——(1979). 'Imports and Labour Market Bottlenecks: A Disaggregated Study for the U.K.'. *Applied Economics,* 11, no. 1, 77–94.

Isard, P. (1977). 'How Far Can One Push the Law of One Price?'. *American Economic Review,* 67, no. 5, 942–48.

Kravis, I. and R.E. Lipsey (1977). 'Export Prices and the Transmission of Inflation'. *American Economic Association Papers and Proceedings,* 67, no. 1, 155–62.

Lindley, R.M. (1978). (ed.). *Britain's Medium-Term Employment Prospects.* Coventry: Manpower Research Group, University of Warwick.

Manpower Research Unit (1967). 'Occupational Changes 1951–61'. Manpower Studies no. 6. London: Ministry of Labour.

Pavitt, K. (1978). 'Technical Change: The Prospects for Manufacturing Industry'. *Futures,* 10, no. 4, 283–92.

Posner, M.V. and A. Steer (1979). 'Price Competitiveness and Performance of Manufacturing Industry', in Blackaby (ed.), 141–65.

Ray, G.F. (1978). 'UK Productivity and Employment in 1991'. *Futures,* 10, no.2, 91–108.

Stout, D.K. (1977). *International Price Competitiveness, Non-Price Factors and Export Performance.* London: National Economic Development Office.

Whitley, J.D. and R.A. Wilson (1979). 'Trends and Cycles in Import Penetration in the U.K. Comment'. *Oxford Bulletin of Economics and Statistics,* 41, no. 1, 69–77.

Winters, L.A. (1976). 'Exports', in Barker (ed.), 131–61.

Woodward, V.H. (1975). 'A View of Occupational Employment in 1981'. D.E. *Gazette,* LXXXIII, no. 7, 619–22.

5 Regional Employment Prospects

G.T. KEOGH AND PETER ELIAS

5.1 Introduction

The previous chapters have been concerned with medium-term economic prospects at the national level. Using the macroeconomic model, alternative economic outcomes have been projected under different policy assumptions. These projections embody demands for labour which have been analysed in terms of industrial and occupational structure. However, the analysis so far has been non-spatial. Thus, employment levels have been projected for each industry group and occupational category but nothing has been said about where within the UK these demands will occur. Similarly, the projections of the labour force have been made for the nation as a whole. There are several reasons why it is important to introduce a spatial dimension into the analysis. First, spatial mismatching of demands for and supplies of labour may be an important aspect of unemployment and may cause considerable wastage of labour resources. It is, therefore, important to know whether the projected demands for labour will occur at locations where the availability of labour enables them to be satisfied. Second, spatial disparities remain a contentious issue. One would, therefore, wish to make some comment on spatial differences in employment opportunities. Third, it is at the local level that much employment policy must be implemented. Demand-deficient unemployment can perhaps be tackled by broad national policies to stimulate the economy, but structural unemployment must be tackled locally by providing appropriate aid to retraining or relocation.

In this chapter a spatial dimension is added to the projected employment levels by industry order. Labour supply and demand are forecast for the eleven standard planning regions of the UK.[1] This only goes part-way towards describing the spatial distribution of employment. The regions are large and considerable geographical mismatching of workers and jobs will be disguised within the projections. From a policy point of view it is also necessary to face the fact that spatial disparities within each region could exceed the

141

differences between regions. However, the disaggregation of employment projections at the regional level provides forecasts that can be more readily assessed by those with specialist knowledge of particular regions.

Section 5.2 examines recent trends in regional employment, unemployment and regional policy. The regional projections of employment and the labour force to 1985 are discussed in sections 5.3 and 5.4 respectively. The demand and supply projections are brought together in section 5.5 to provide a tentative assessment of the prospects for regional unemployment. The concluding section 5.6 provides an overview of regional employment prospects. This section discusses the validity of the projections, their limitations and their value as part of a prescriptive policy-making process.

5.2 Recent Trends in Regional Performance

It is useful, prior to examining the regional employment projections, to look briefly at the relative performance of the regions over recent years. This provides a context within which the results can be assessed and helps in understanding the forces that underly the projections. The projection model, at this stage in our work, is based on past trends in employment[2] and therefore depends for its validity on the continuation of these relationships. For this reason, the fortunes of the regions over the period 1965–76, which is the data base of the projection model, are particularly important.

Several indicators have been used in attempts to assess the relative economic performance of the regions. Prominent amongst these have been unemployment, employment, incomes and productivity, although there are many other potentially useful economic and social measures of regional disparity. Following convention, discussion is concentrated on questions of employment and unemployment. However, this is a pragmatic choice and is not meant to suggest that other regional indicators are of no importance.

Regional employment trends

Over the period 1965–76, employee jobs in the U.K. declined by 2.4 per cent. Table 5.1 gives the region by industry order distribution of this change in employees in employment. The region by industry data on employees, from which the table is derived, form the basis of the employees projection model described in section 5.3. It is of particular interest, therefore, to note that this data set embraces

Table 5.1 Change in Employees by Industry Order and Region 1965–76

Per cent of 1965 employees

Industry order	SE	EA	SW	WM	EM	YH	NW	N	Wa	Sc	NI	UK
1. Agriculture	−37	−37	−34	−33	−34	−33	−37	−32	−33	−38	−20	−35
2. Mining	−21	25	−25	−41	−34	−33	−56	−58	−56	−42	−23	−44
3. Food, drink & tobacco	−27	19	−3	−13	5	1	−11	5	−10	−6	−7	−10
4. Petroleum products	−18	0	0	−25	−23	−23	−29	−10	10	−7	0	−15
5. Chemicals	−12	50	22	−5	14	−3	−7	−9	25	−8	15	−5
6. Metals	−39	130	−3	−24	−17	−28	−45	−29	−23	−26	0	−27
7. Mechanical engineering	−21	11	0	−14	−9	−15	−19	9	21	−22	−12	−14
8. Instrument engineering	−22	83	111	−9	−43	20	−23	63	−10	16	−5	−8
9. Electrical engineering	−15	11	9	−17	5	−5	−22	3	8	22	−16	−10
10. Shipbuilding etc.	−8	20	−12	0	60	−7	−18	−20	−68	−17	−26	−14
11. Vehicles	−24	27	−8	−21	−4	−7	3	1	17	−23	5	−14
12. Metals goods n.e.s.	−17	63	−4	−24	27	−11	−15	14	−3	−9	0	−13
13. Textiles	−39	0	−23	−19	−14	−42	−42	−2	−5	−39	−31	−33
14. +15. Clothing	−47	−26	−20	−24	−20	−14	−28	−5	−3	8	−30	−26
16. Bricks etc.	−35	−20	−31	−15	−8	−17	−30	−18	−20	−28	12	−23
17. Timber etc.	−26	9	13	−13	14	8	2	−7	43	−19	−4	−10
18. Paper etc.	−20	23	0	−9	14	−8	−7	37	1	−23	−13	−12
19. Other manufacturing	−16	56	28	4	26	55	−17	23	35	−3	177	3
20. Construction	−29	−14	−24	−24	−15	−18	−24	2	−5	−5	−5	−19
21. Public utilities	−24	−1	−8	−10	−9	−17	−22	−14	−13	−14	29	−16
22. Transport & communication	−3	23	−18	−11	−9	−12	−20	−25	−19	−17	−15	−11
23. Distribution	−3	0	−5	−5	11	−4	−15	−5	−15	−16	−15	−6
24. Insurance & finance	34	71	63	42	77	32	18	41	16	58	44	37
25. Professional, scientific services	45	65	39	51	60	45	49	44	42	44	84	48
26. Miscellaneous services	0	21	26	12	14	18	14	29	26*	26	30	12
27. Public administration etc.	11	18	16	9	36	20	30	34	6	29	53	18
Total	−3	14	4	−6	3	−5	−7	−1	−3	−2	7	−2

Sources: DE *Gazette* (August 1976 and December 1977).

Note: Unabbreviated regional names appear in Table 5.10.

periods of growth and decline in employment. To differing degrees, the regions all reflect cyclical changes in employment at the national level. East Anglia and Northern Ireland both show a strong upward trend in employees in employment over the period and the South West and East Midlands also exhibit a higher level of employment by the end of the period. The South East and Scotland closely mirror the UK. With the exception of the North, the remaining regions suffer greater percentage losses than the nation as a whole. Of particular interest is the West Midlands, a traditionally prosperous manufacturing region, which lost over 6 per cent of its 1965 employment. For the purpose of the projection model, it is important to ask whether the particularly strong performance of East Anglia and Northern Ireland or the weak performance of the North West and West Midlands is likely to continue into the projection period.

The profile of total regional employment of employees obscures changes in the industrial structure of employment in the regions. The final column of Table 5.1 shows that the overall national employment fall of 2.4 per cent between 1965 and 1976 is composed of percentage employment changes that vary widely between industries.[3] To generalise, the primary and manufacturing sectors show employment losses which are offset by gains in service sector employment. Clearly then, the employment performance of the regions will depend on their industrial structure. Taking manufacturing employees alone, the national trend is strongly downwards over the period 1965–76, alleviated only slightly in 1968–70 and 1972–74 (see Figure 5.1). Nationally, manufacturing employment fell by over 15 per cent during the period and most regions reflected the cyclical variations. However, the degree of responsiveness of regional manufacturing employment to changes in the national total differed widely. The South West, the North and Wales all fared much better than the UK with employment losses of less than 5 per cent. East Anglia must be singled out for special comment since it showed a strong *upward* trend in manufacturing employees which resulted in a 16 per cent increase between 1965 and 1976. In contrast with manufacturing, employment in the service sectors showed a strong upward trend at the national level, increasing by 14 per cent over the period (see Figure 5.2). The regions all tended to follow the national trend but East Anglia, the East Midlands and Northern Ireland showed particularly large gains in service employment.

A re-examination of Table 5.1 shows that, not only do individual industry groups vary widely in terms of employment change, but within each industry order there are also very marked differences in regional employment change. These variations may be due to the fact that disaggregation to industry orders is not sufficient to allow the structural differences in regional employment to be identified. Alternatively, they could be due to specifically regional growth characteristics.[4] However, Table 5.1 provides an indication of the extent to which region by industry employment may be expected to vary about the average rate of change at industrial, regional and national levels.

Regional unemployment

The key indicator of regional performance has traditionally been registered unemployment both because of the availability of data and because of its obvious significance for regional welfare. Table 5.2 shows the registered mid-year unemployment rates for males over the period 1966–78. The regional ranking of these rates is remarkably constant even though the registered unemployment rate for males in the UK has risen over the period from 1.5 per cent to 7.1 per cent.[5] However, as Armstrong and Taylor (1978) show, there is some variation between regions in the sensitivity of their unemployment rates to the UK rate. Between 1951 and 1974 the South East proved to be remarkably insensitive to national changes, while the North and North West showed considerable cyclical sensitivity.[6] There was some sign that historical patterns were changing between 1974 and 1976 when the traditionally low unemployment regions, i.e. the South East, East Anglia and the West Midlands, responded strongly to the sharp increase in national unemployment, whereas unemployment rates in the North, Wales and Scotland, regions of high relative unemployment, increased much more slowly than the national average. The effect of this was to cause regional rates to converge although no major reordering occurred. (Scotland was an exception here, moving from ninth to seventh in the unemployment ranking.) This apparent convergence was halted after 1976 as the unemployment position of the traditionally high unemployment regions again started to worsen in relation to the rest.

There are many factors which might influence the stability of regional ranking with respect to unemployment rates. It is well recognised that the propensity to register as unemployed, the willingness

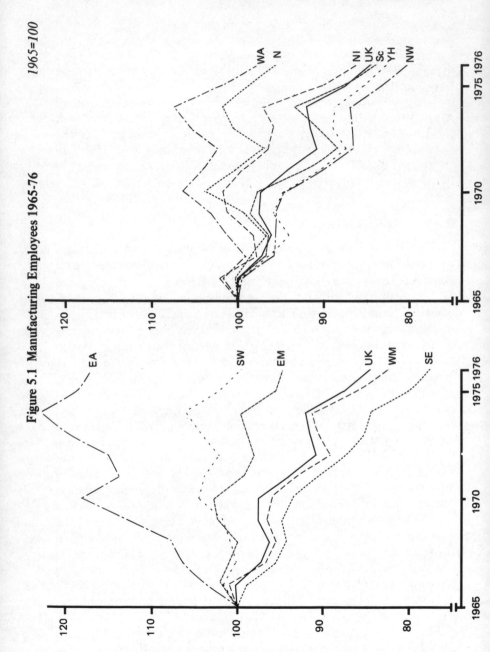

Figure 5.1 Manufacturing Employees 1965-76

1965=100

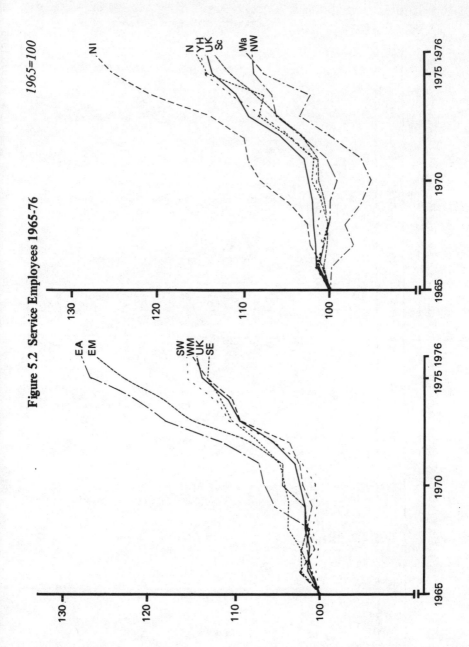

Figure 5.2 Service Employees 1965-76

Economic Change and Employment Policy

Table 5.2 Male Registered Unemployment Rates by Region and Regional Rankings 1966–78

Per cent

	1966	1967	1968	1969	1970	1971	1972	1973	1974	1975	1976	1977	1978
SE	0.9 (2)	2.0 (1)	2.1 (1)	2.0 (1)	2.0 (1)	2.6 (1)	2.7 (1)	1.9 (1)	2.0 (1)	3.4 (1)	5.4 (1)	5.6 (1)	5.1 (1)
EA	1.3 (5)	2.2 (3)	2.4 (3)	2.3 (2)	2.6 (2)	3.8 (2)	3.4 (2)	2.3 (2)	2.4 (2)	4.3 (2)	6.3 (3)	6.6 (4)	6.0 (2)
SW	1.6 (7)	2.6 (5)	2.8 (5)	3.0 (5)	3.2 (4)	4.0 (3)	4.2 (4)	3.0 (5)	3.1 (5)	5.6 (6)	8.0 (6)	8.3 (6)	7.6 (6)
WM	0.8 (1)	2.7 (6)	2.7 (4)	2.5 (4)	3.3 (5)	4.4 (5)	5.0 (5)	2.6 (3)	2.6 (3)	4.6 (4)	6.9 (4)	6.4 (3)	6.1 (4)
EM	1.0 (3)	2.0 (1)	2.3 (2)	2.4 (3)	3.0 (3)	4.0 (3)	4.0 (3)	2.7 (4)	2.7 (4)	4.3 (2)	6.1 (2)	6.2 (2)	6.0 (2)
YH	1.1 (4)	2.4 (4)	3.2 (7)	3.1 (6)	3.6 (7)	5.0 (6)	5.2 (6)	3.5 (6)	3.2 (6)	4.7 (5)	7.0 (5)	6.7 (5)	6.8 (5)
NW	1.5 (6)	2.9 (7)	3.1 (6)	3.1 (6)	3.5 (6)	5.0 (6)	6.6 (8)	4.7 (8)	4.3 (8)	6.8 (9)	9.1 (9)	9.1 (8)	8.8 (7)
N	2.4 (8)	4.6 (10)	5.6 (10)	5.8 (10)	5.7 (10)	7.1 (9)	7.7 (9)	5.8 (10)	5.5 (10)	7.1 (10)	9.4 (10)	9.7 (9)	10.0 (10)

Wa	2.4 (8)	4.1 (8)	4.4 (8)	4.4 (8)	4.2 (8)	5.3 (8)	5.8 (7)	4.2 (7)	4.2 (7)	6.3 (8)	8.7 (8)	8.7 (7)	9.0 (8)
Sc	2.8 (10)	4.2 (9)	4.6 (9)	4.5 (9)	5.1 (9)	7.5 (10)	7.9 (10)	5.6 (9)	4.9 (9)	6.0 (7)	8.2 (7)	9.8 (10)	9.4 (9)
NI	7.3 (11)	8.5 (11)	8.4 (11)	8.5 (11)	7.7 (11)	9.1 (11)	9.0 (11)	6.9 (11)	6.5 (11)	8.7 (11)	11.7 (11)	13.0 (11)	13.7 (11)
UK	1.5	2.8	3.1	3.1	3.4	4.5	4.9	3.3	3.2	5.0	7.1	7.4	7.1

Source: DE *Gazette* for relevant years.

Notes: Prior to 1973, the registered unemployment figures include persons temporarily stopped from work. No adjustments have been made for the change in regional boundaries affecting certain regions following the reorganisation of local government on April 1, 1974.

of unemployed persons to sustain longer periods of job search and the level of inter-regional migration of labour may vary between regions and over time. Caution must therefore be exercised in interpreting the rankings. However, this historical resilience of the unemployment ranking over a period in which there have been considerable changes in both the structure of employment and the absolute levels of unemployment provides a basis for assessing regional unemployment rankings implied by the regional projection model.

Regional policy

In trying to assess regional economic performance as background to the projections that follow, it is important to consider the effects of government policy. Regional policy has been used to enhance the relative attractiveness of specific areas as sites for industrial expansion or relocation and this should affect patterns of regional employment and unemployment. The employment projections assume that any trends in regional policy or its effectiveness over the data period will be continued to the projection year.

To generalise, regional policy has been comprised of positive inducements to encourage factor mobility and negative controls on industrial or office development.[7] Such policies have existed for over fifty years although the measures used and the degree of commitment on the part of government have varied widely. It is generally agreed that the 1950s represent a hiatus in regional policy due to low levels of unemployment and to central government opposition to restrictions on industrial location (McCallum, 1979). Moore and Rhodes (1973) show that changes in manufacturing employment in the Development Areas between 1950 and 1963 could be accounted for almost entirely by the industrial structure of those regions. They argue that regional policy became more active again from 1960, with 1963 representing a major turning point. The Local Employment Act of that year introduced standard investment and building grants in the assisted areas and the resulting increase in expenditure on regional policy was boosted further by the investment grants offered under the Industrial Development Act of 1966 and by the introduction of the Regional Employment Premium. McCallum (1979, Table 1.5) quantifies the funds devoted to all aspects of regional policy between 1962/3 and 1977/8. His estimates of total expenditure are reproduced here as Figure 5.3. They show a steep increase throughout the 1960s to a peak in 1970 of £324m.[8] Between

1971 and 1974 expenditure on regional policy fell by almost one third but was restored in 1974/75 following the change in government. Since 1976, expenditure has once again fallen due, it seems, partly to the exigency of recession and partly to a change in emphasis in industrial policy. The implied strength of commitment to

Figure 5.3 Indicators of Regional Policy 1950–78

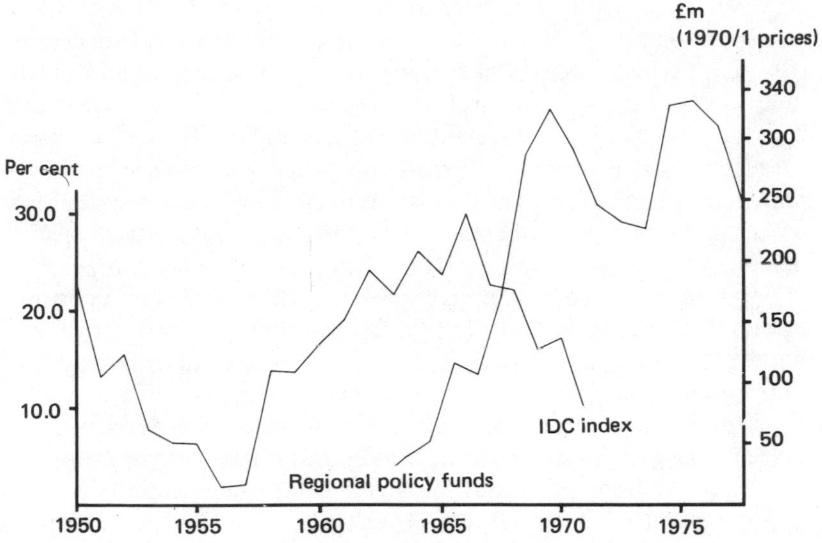

Sources: Moore & Rhodes (1976, Table A2); McCallum (1979, Table 1.5).

regional policy is reflected in the use of Industrial Development Certificates (IDCs) as a negative control on industrial location. Moore and Rhodes (1976) produced an index of the strength of IDC policy over the period 1950–71 based on the ratio of estimated employment loss from IDC refusals in the Midlands and South East to estimated employment associated with total IDC applications in these areas. The index showed that location controls, weak from 1953 to 1957, were strengthened throughout the period from 1958 to 1966 and were subsequently relaxed considerably. By 1971 their index shows that IDC policy was exerting no more control than existed during the mid-fifties. In 1972 the government raised the exemption limits for IDCs and these have remained broadly unchanged. It seems unlikely, therefore, that the strength of IDC policy would have increased subsequent to 1971.

Opinions vary concerning the effectiveness of the overall regional package and its policy components. However, there appears to be general agreement that it has been effective in generating employment in the assisted areas. Moore and Rhodes (1973) estimate that about 220 thousand jobs generated in the Development Areas in the period 1963–70 were due to the effects of regional policy. In a later paper (Moore and Rhodes, 1976) they estimate that some 165 thousand manufacturing jobs accrued to the Development Areas between 1960 and 1971 as a result of the movement of manufacturing firms under the stimulus of regional policy. The largest part of this employment growth was attributed to IDC controls. Ashcroft and Taylor (1977 and 1979) argue that the Moore and Rhodes model of industrial movement is incorrectly specified and overestimates induced employment. Nevertheless, they estimate that regional policy generated industrial movement to the Development Areas involving between 90 thousand and 100 thousand jobs in the period 1961–71. They find both location controls and capital subsidies to be important with the greatest contribution to employment coming from the latter. It seems, then, that regional policy has been an important determinant of the spatial distribution of employment.

The data base of the regional employment model embraces a period of strong commitment to regional policy (1965–70) and a period in which the financial and ideological commitment fluctuated. It is arguable that the employment projections presented in section 5.3 may be boosted for the assisted areas at the expense of the rest of the nation because the effects of a strong regional policy will be built into the underlying employment data. However, that data will also reflect the varying commitment to regional policy during the early 1970s, to some extent offsetting any tendency to over-predict employment in the assisted areas. It is difficult to assess the possible strength of regional policy over the projection period. The industrial strategy introduced in 1976 was intended to create a shift in emphasis away from assistance to specific areas and towards the stimulation of those sectors which indicated favourable growth prospects. Cameron (1979) shows that the goal of sectoral stimulus could conflict with regional development. An increased willingness to assist industry purely on a sectoral basis will increase the propensity of firms to grow at or near their existing locations. It certainly seems unlikely that regional incentives will be offered on anything like the previous scale, but the degree to which the government can extricate itself from regional policy will depend on the performance of the assisted areas in relation to the rest of the UK. The likely lower emphasis on regional incentives should be borne in mind in interpreting the employment projections.

5.3 Projections of Regional Employment

This section describes the projections of regional employment which are derived from the national employment projections discussed in Chapter 3. The regional projections are developed from a model which is similar to that described in Keogh and Elias (1979), except that the level of industrial disaggregation has been increased to distinguish industry orders and the model now incorporates information on region by industry trends in the ratio of male to female employment.

Table 5.3. and 5.4 show the projected levels of total employment (employees adjusted for double-jobbing, self-employed, HM Forces, private domestic service and family workers) by standard planning region and industry order for 1978[9] and 1985 derived from the standard view as described in Chapter 3. Table 5.5 shows the change in employment by region and industry order between 1978 and 1985 as a percentage of 1978 employment. The final row of the table indicates the regional distribution of the 3.9 per cent decline in total employment projected for the UK. In the South East, West Midlands and North West the decline in employment is much more severe than at the national level, while the South West and East Midlands exhibit modest employment growth. In East Anglia, the smallest region in terms of numbers employed, employment is projected to grow by 7 per cent.

Nearly all industry orders in the South East experience a decline in employment, the exceptions being construction, insurance and finance, professional and scientific services and miscellaneous services. Even in these industries though, the increase in employment is considerably less than at the national level. Within the manufacturing sector in the South East, employment in food, drink and tobacco declines by 36 thousand, proportionately a much larger decline than for the UK. Employment in metal manufacture is expected to decline by 15 thousand between 1978 and 1985, a decrease of

Table 5.3　Projected Total Employment(1) by Industry Order and Region, June 1978

Thousands

Industry order	SE	EA	SW	WM	EM	YH	NW	N	Wa	Sc	NI	UK
1. Agriculture	105	53	92	51	55	54	35	29	53	73	47	647
2. Mining	11	2	12	27	69	81	15	48	39	36	2	341
3. Food, drink & tobacco	150	41	59	55	50	83	109	33	19	95	25	718
4. Petroleum products	10	0	0	1	3	5	6	3	6	3	0	36
5. Chemicals	125	11	17	19	29	34	93	52	18	28	2	428
6. Metals	27	2	8	114	38	90	19	45	74	39	1	455
7. Mechanical engineering	223	29	63	123	83	90	119	71	27	98	11	937
8. Instrument engineering	69	5	19	7	4	5	11	6	4	17	2	149
9. Electrical engineering	280	20	44	96	41	28	94	49	32	50	11	744
10. Shipbuilding etc.	40	4	20	3	2	7	9	46	2	42	11	184
11. Vehicles	196	21	59	187	50	49	119	12	26	37	11	767
12. Metal goods n.e.s.	124	8	20	166	34	73	49	17	22	30	12	548
13. Textiles	20	0	12	26	107	94	112	22	14	56	33	495
14. +15. Clothing	84	11	25	23	63	49	71	34	18	39	18	434
16. Bricks etc.	48	6	12	68	22	30	35	14	11	17	6	269
17. Timber etc.	107	11	23	22	20	32	41	14	11	22	5	309
18. Paper etc.	236	20	38	30	30	33	75	24	12	44	6	548
19. Other manufacturing	96	14	23	50	24	22	44	15	24	16	9	336
20. Construction	466	60	126	128	95	131	165	107	82	180	44	1,582
21. Public utilities	103	10	31	29	25	33	37	20	19	28	11	347
22. Transport & communication	628	46	85	100	76	112	171	67	60	138	22	1,505
23. Distribution	1,094	103	245	273	199	274	369	168	121	262	60	3,166
24. Insurance & finance	633	31	74	78	45	64	107	33	27	83	17	1,191
25. Professional, scientific services	1,315	125	272	314	215	321	424	188	165	367	101	3,808
26. Miscellaneous services	1,005	98	262	228	151	246	325	152	134	279	57	2,936
27. Public administration etc.	682	49	162	128	115	124	172	92	87	168	64	1,932(2)
Total	7,876	779	1,801	2,345	1,645	2,162	2,825	1,361	1,105	2,245	578	24,811

Source:　See text.

Notes:　(1)　Total employment consists of employees in employment (adjusted for double jobbing), employers and self-employed, H.M. Forces private domestic service and family workers.

　　　　(2)　The UK total for public administration and defence (order 27) includes an estimated 90 thousand H.M. Forces serving abroad.

Table 5.4 Projected Total Employment[1] by Industry Order and Region 1985

Thousands

Industry order	SE	EA	SW	WM	EM	YH	NW	N	Wa	Sc	NI	UK
1. Agriculture	81	35	83	43	45	46	33	26	41	56	48	537
2. Mining	9	2	11	22	54	68	9	26	19	30	1	253
3. Food, drink & tobacco	114	42	53	50	49	84	104	33	19	94	24	666
4. Petroleum products	8	0	0	1	3	5	3	3	6	3	0	31
5. Chemicals	97	13	19	13	26	31	84	37	15	25	1	362
6. Metals	12	3	9	101	34	82	10	40	62	34	0	387
7. Mechanical engineering	157	25	55	97	63	73	75	70	22	84	7	728
8. Instrument engineering	38	4	21	1	4	2	5	7	0	11	3	95
9. Electrical engineering	237	18	46	78	48	28	82	47	32	45	10	670
10. Shipbuilding etc.	31	5	7	3	5	5	9	31	0	34	6	135
11. Vehicles	149	22	53	134	44	40	113	11	23	23	14	625
12. Metal goods n.e.s.	94	9	17	115	32	58	35	16	17	22	2	417
13. Textiles	13	0	11	23	96	50	78	21	10	35	25	360
14. +15. Clothing	32	10	23	20	55	45	58	30	20	41	9	341
16. Bricks etc.	38	7	13	65	22	32	35	15	14	15	6	262
17. Timber etc.	104	11	27	21	21	36	45	13	12	19	5	314
18. Paper etc.	185	22	36	29	31	31	70	28	10	35	5	481
19. Other manufacturing	63	14	24	41	26	27	30	15	23	12	8	282
20. Construction	471	69	128	133	109	148	173	130	83	198	42	1,685
21. Public utilities	75	10	30	26	22	30	29	17	18	18	13	287
22. Transport & communication	500	58	67	89	95	88	128	51	47	122	19	1,262
23. Distribution	1,048	103	240	258	204	264	310	165	106	220	49	2,967
24. Insurance & finance	706	42	96	91	54	72	111	38	28	101	20	1,358
25. Professional, scientific services	1,362	151	296	340	230	374	473	208	167	394	118	4,112
26. Miscellaneous services	1,034	110	300	248	163	278	367	173	161	320	64	3,219
27. Public administration etc.	664	51	168	132	139	135	189	101	90	183	75	2,016[2]
Total	7,320	834	1,834	2,172	1,675	2,129	2,657	1,351	1,044	2,172	575	23,852

Source: See text.

Note: See Table 5.3.

Table 5.5 Projected Change in Total Employment by Industry Order and Region 1978-85.

Per cent of 1978 employment

Industry order	SE	EA	SW	WM	EM	YH	NW	N	Wa	Sc	NI	UK
1. Agriculture	-23	-33	-11	-17	-17	-14	-6	-12	-23	-23	3	-17
2. Mining	-23	0	-9	-17	-21	-16	-37	-46	-50	-17	-37	-26
3. Food, drink & tobacco	-24	3	-9	-9	-1	2	-5	-2	-1	-1	-2	-7
4. Petroleum products	-23	0	81	-41	10	-1	-55	2	8	8	81	-14
5. Chemicals	-22	20	12	-32	-9	-10	-10	-29	-15	-11	-42	-16
6. Metals	-55	17	21	-21	-11	-9	-46	-10	-16	-12	-42	-15
7. Mechanical engineering	-30	-14	-13	-21	-24	-19	-37	-2	-19	-15	-37	-22
8. Instrument engineering	-45	-19	11	-90	-12	-63	-57	18	-100	-36	61	-36
9. Electrical engineering	-15	-9	5	-19	17	-1	-12	-5	0	-10	-6	-10
10. Shipbuilding etc.	-22	39	-64	-2	165	-32	-4	-33	-100	-18	-43	-27
11. Vehicles	-24	1	-9	-29	-11	-17	-5	-10	-14	-37	17	-19
12. Metal goods	-24	20	-18	-31	-8	-21	-29	-7	-22	-27	-40	-24
13. Textiles	-34	0	-14	-10	-11	-47	-31	-7	-27	-38	-25	-27
14. +15. Clothing	-62	-15	-11	-14	-12	-9	-18	-11	9	7	-50	-21
16. Bricks etc.	-20	15	13	-4	-1	6	-2	5	29	-13	5	-3
17. Timber etc.	-3	-1	16	-4	3	14	9	-3	8	-14	0	2
18. Paper etc.	-22	8	-7	-5	5	-8	-6	20	-13	-21	-14	-12
19. Other manufacturing	-34	-1	5	-17	7	22	-31	-1	-4	-28	-11	-16
20. Construction	1	17	2	4	15	13	5	21	1	10	-4	7
21. Public utilities	-27	-4	-2	-10	-13	-10	-24	-13	-8	-38	15	-17
22. Transport & communication	-20	25	-21	-11	24	-22	-25	-24	-21	-12	-15	-16
23. Distribution	-4	0	-2	-6	3	-4	-16	-2	-12	-16	-18	-6
24. Insurance & finance	11	35	31	17	21	12	4	15	5	22	18	14
25. Professional, scientific services	4	21	9	8	7	16	11	11	1	7	16	8
26. Miscellaneous services	3	12	15	9	8	13	13	14	20	15	14	10
27. Public administration etc.	-3	4	4	3	21	9	10	11	3	9	17	4
Total	-7	7	2	-7	2	-2	-6	-1	-6	-3	-1	-4

Sources: Tables 5.3 and 5.4.

nearly 55 per cent in this period. Clothing industries lose 52 thousand persons and bricks etc. lose 10 thousand persons from employment. Other larger than average declines are forecast for paper etc. and other manufacturing which together account for a drop of nearly 84 thousand in the South East. Employment in public administration in the South East is expected to decline, even though employment in the UK is forecast to rise by 4.3 per cent in this sector.

East Anglia shows either a greater than average rate of growth or a smaller than average rate of decline in employment in all industry orders in the manufacturing and service sectors with the exception of timber etc. and public administration. This performance is offset to some extent by a decline of 17 thousand in employment in agriculture. Those industry orders which perform particularly well in East Anglia are chemicals, metal goods n.e.s., construction, transport and communication, insurance and finance and professional and scientific services.

The South West is expected to gain employment by about 32 thousand between 1978 and 1985 and these gains are concentrated in the service sector. In proportional terms, employment grows at a particularly rapid rate in insurance and finance. Professional and scientific services and miscellaneous services show an employment gain of 62 thousand. Within the manufacturing sector, chemicals, instrument engineering, electrical engineering and timber etc. display strong employment growth. The shipbuilding industry in this region is expected to decline rapidly, losing almost 13 thousand jobs by 1985.

The decline in the manufacturing sector has a depressing effect upon the West Midlands economy. Employment in vehicles and metal goods falls by about 50 thousand in each case. Instrument engineering loses 6 thousand, as does the chemicals industry. With a projected decline in total employment of 173 thousand, the West Midlands displays a larger proportional decrease than any other region of the UK.

In contrast, employment in the East Midlands grows by 30 thousand. In proportional terms, the largest employment gains are found in the electrical engineering industries with an increase of 7 thousand, construction which increases by 14 thousand and transport and communication, distribution and public administration which add 48 thousand in total. These gains are offset by employment losses in the primary sector and the rest of the engineering sector.

In Yorkshire and Humberside the decline in textiles is felt strongly. The decrease of 44 thousand projected over the seven year period represents a reduction of over half in the industry's work force in the region. Employment in transport and communication also falls by nearly 25 thousand. Offsetting these employment losses are proportionately large increases in employment in other manufacturing, construction and professional and scientific services.

The North West suffers a large decline in employment, its work force contracting by 6 per cent. Notable reductions are expected in mechanical engineering, textiles, transport and communications and distribution. These four industry orders show a total fall in employment of 179 thousand. Metals and other manufacturing also show proportionately large decreases in employment when compared with the national average, although in absolute terms the fall in employment in these two industry orders is only 22 thousand.

The North exhibits a lower than average rate of decline in employment of 0.7 per cent. The projected decline in mining and quarrying, chemicals, shipbuilding and transport and communication is offset by increases in paper etc., construction and service sector employment. Also the national decline in employment in mechanical engineering of 22 per cent is not evident in this region.

Wales is strongly affected by the projected national decline in mining where employment falls by 19 thousand. Against this must be placed the modest increase in employment of about 6 thousand from coal and petroleum products, clothing, bricks etc. and timber etc. Employment in miscellaneous services is expected to grow strongly whereas other service industries grow at a lower rate or decline at a faster rate than for the UK.

In Scotland, as in the West Midlands, the national decline in the motor vehicle industry has a particularly severe impact upon the regional economy, resulting in a loss of nearly 14 thousand jobs. Further proportionately large declines are forecast for textiles, bricks etc., timber etc., paper etc., other manufacturing, public utilities and distribution.

Employment prospects in aggregate for the Northern Ireland economy are expected to be somewhat better than average. Employment losses in absolute terms are most severe in textiles, clothing and distribution which show a combined fall in employment of 28 thousand. Proportionately large losses are also projected for shipbuilding and construction. These declines are offset by the increases in employment projected for most service industries in Northern

Ireland. Employment growth is expected to be particularly strong in professional and scientific services and public administration, which yield nearly 28 thousand additional jobs in the province.

Turning next to the distribution of labour demand between males and females, Table 5.6 shows the change in the proportion of females in employment, by region, between 1978 and 1985.[10] For each industry order within a region, the proportion of females in employment relative to the national industry sex ratio has been projected along a simple trend. Generally speaking, the changing industrial structure of employment within a region has more impact upon the projected ratio of males to females than region-specific trends in the sex ratio. The share of females in total employment is projected to increase in all regions. The largest increases occur in Scotland and the North, reflecting both the decline of heavy manufacturing industries which employ predominantly male labour, and the

Table 5.6 Change in the Proportion of Females in Employment by Region 1978–85

	Proportion of females in employment		Change in proportion of females in employment as % of 1978 proportion
	1978	1985	
SE	40.8	43.0	5.4
EA	38.2	40.0	4.7
SW	39.0	41.6	6.7
WM	39.0	41.8	7.2
EM	39.2	40.4	3.1
YH	39.4	42.2	7.1
NW	41.1	44.0	7.1
N	39.2	42.3	7.9
Wa	37.7	41.2	9.3
Sc	41.5	44.2	6.5
NI	37.6	39.7	5.6
UK	39.8	42.3	6.3

Source: See text.

expansion of miscellaneous services, in which females represent a large proportion of the labour force. The changing industrial structure of the East Midlands favours male employment, with the proportion of females growing by only 3.1 per cent compared with the national average of 6.3 per cent.

Regional employment projections relating to the *structural simulation* described in Chapters 3 and 4 have also been prepared. For this simulation, the decline in UK employment between 1978 and 1985 is only 2.3 per cent, compared with 3.9 per cent in the standard view. The effects of this 1.6 per cent reduction in the rate of decline of employment vary across the regions. Those regions which particularly benefit from the structural effects are the North West, which shows a 2.3 per cent gain over the standard view, Scotland (2.2 per cent), the North (1.8 per cent) and the West Midlands (1.8 per cent). In the first two regions it is the better than average growth of employment in miscellaneous services which yields the result. The improvement in employment prospects in mechanical engineering has most impact upon the North and Scotland, while the benefits of the improved prospects for instrument engineering and metal goods n.e.s. are also felt strongly in the North. The West Midlands economy benefits because of its reliance upon employment in the engineering sector generally. In contrast, the South East and Northern Ireland gain the least in terms of the improvement in employment prospects compared with the structural simulation. The South East responds poorly to the employment gains in miscellaneous services with a gain of only 1.2 per cent over the standard view, while it is the further decline in employment in clothing which offsets employment gains in Northern Ireland. In the latter region the relative gain in employment is only 0.7 per cent.

A regional analysis of female employment prospects from the structural simulation indicates that it is the regional trends in the growth of miscellaneous services and the decline in employment in clothing which have most impact upon the regional sex ratios. Not surprisingly then, the North West shows the greatest proportional increase in female employment prospects over the standard view, with a gain of 1.9 per cent against 1.6 per cent for the UK, and Northern Ireland shows the smallest increase of 0.5 per cent.

In absolute terms, these differences are very small and do not affect the regional rankings with respect to the unemployment rates derived in section 5.5.

5.4 Trends in Regional Population and Labour Force

This section comprises three parts. The first examines trends in inter-regional migration and the regional distribution of the population while the second brings together recent OPCS projections of the regional population and DE forecasts of regional labour force participation to yield projections of the regional distribution of the labour force. However, the levels of migration and labour force participation which are embodied in any projections of the regional labour force are likely to be related to employment growth and unemployment in the regions. For this reason the third part considers the UK evidence for these relationships.

Regional distribution of the home population and inter-regional migration

Changes in the regional distribution of the home (resident) population of Great Britain between 1966 and 1976 are summarised in Table 5.7. In this table changes in the regional populations in the periods 1966–71 and 1971–76 are broken into a component which measures the excess of births over deaths in the region (natural increase) and a balancing item which approximates to net civilian migration into the region. During 1966–71 the natural increase in the population of Great Britain was 2.6 per cent. Regionally, there was substantial variation in this component, ranging from 1.5 per cent in Wales and the South West to 3.9 per cent in the West Midlands, mainly resulting from the different age structure of the regional populations. The regional differences in migration are much more pronounced. While there was a net outward migration of 0.6 per cent for Great Britain between 1966 and 1971, regional migration varied between net in-migration to East Anglia of 4.5 per cent and net out-migration from Scotland of 2.6 per cent. This overall pattern of migration reflects long-term trends in the redistribution of the home population from northern to southern regions and, within central and southern England, from the South East to East Anglia, the East Midlands and the South West. This pattern of redistribution should be compared with that which occurred between 1971 and 1976. The regional differences in fertility and mortality are virtually unchanged, the decline in the birth rate affecting all regions in proportion to their populations. The changes in regional population due to migration are similar to those observed in the previous five year period, with a few notable exceptions. Wales has become a net

Table 5.7 Changes in the Regional Home Population 1966–76

	Home population 1966 (thousands)	1966-1971 as % of 1966			1971-1976 as % of 1971			Home population 1976(3) (thousands)
		Natural increase(1)	Other(2)	Total	Natural increase	Others	Total	
SE	16,719	2.7	-1.0	1.6	0.9	-1.4	-0.6	16,894
EA	1,575	2.6	4.5	7.0	1.3	5.7	6.9	1,803
SW	3,920	1.5	2.7	4.3	-0.1	4.2	4.1	4,254
WM	4,946	3.9	-0.3	3.5	1.7	-0.8	0.9	5,165
EM	3,497	3.1	0.8	3.9	1.3	1.4	2.7	3,733
Y & H	4,809	2.6	-1.4	1.2	0.7	-0.2	0.5	4,892
NW	6,539	2.2	-1.3	1.0	0.5	-1.2	-0.7	6,554
N	3,125	2.2	-1.8	0.4	0.4	-0.9	-0.5	3,122
Wa	2,694	1.5	-0.4	1.1	0.2	1.4	1.6	2,767
Sc	5,201	2.9	-2.6	0.3	0.9	-1.1	-0.2	5,205
GB	53,025	2.6	-0.6	2.0	0.8	-0.2	0.6	54,390

Source: OPCS *Demographic Review 1977* (DR No. 1), Table 6.3.

Notes: (1) Excess of births over deaths.
         (2) Net civilian migration, changes in armed forces, and balancing adjustments.
         (3) Provisional estimates.

gainer of population through migration in marked contrast to its net loss due to migration throughout the previous two decades. East Anglia, the East Midlands and the South West have increased their rates of net in-migration whereas Scotland, the North and Yorkshire and Humberside have more than halved the rates at which their populations fell due to net out-migration.

The changes in the rates of net migration depend upon a variety of factors, both social and economic, and mask quite large variations from year to year and within the regions. Table 5.8 indicates the more recent annual net migration levels experienced by the regions. This table shows estimates of annual net migration for each country of the United Kingdom for the period 1971/2 to 1975/6, and for the regions of England for the period 1971/2 to 1974/5. Also shown are the projected levels of net migration used in the 1975-based and 1977-based regional population projections, developed by the Department of the Environment in collaboration with the Office of Population Censuses and Surveys. Projections of net migration for each country of the United Kingdom, made by the Government Actuary's Department, are disaggregated into regions and, ultimately, local authority areas.

In most regions, the levels of net migration have been reduced in the later projections, significant reductions having been made in the projected levels of net in-migration to East Anglia, the South West, the East Midlands and Wales. With the exception of the North, the remaining regions of the UK have had reductions made to their levels of net out-migration. In other words, inter-regional net migration for all regions except the North has been brought closer to a position of no net change, reflecting general reductions in the gross flows of migrants between regions resulting from the major depression commencing in late 1974. The projected national economic environment is bound to have an impact upon migrant flows through a reduction in labour turnover. The possibility that this might be specific to a particular region's economic fortunes or misfortunes is an issue which is considered in the last part of this section.

Regional labour force projections

Previous work by the authors (Keogh and Elias, 1978) and by the Department of Employment (DE *Gazette,* September 1978) has

Table 5.8 Net Migration by Region and Country of the United Kingdom 1971/2 – 1984/5

Thousands

	1971/2	1972/3	1973/4	1974/5	1975/6	1976/7	1977/8	1978/9	1979/80	1980/1	1981/2	1982/85 per annum
SE	−35	−42	−75	−47	.. (−36)	(−36)	−34 (−36)	−34 (−36)	−35 (−37)	−37 (−37)	−34 (−38)	−35 (−38)
EA	17	26	15	19	.. (19)	(19)	14 (19)	14 (19)	14 (19)	14 (18)	10 (16)	10 (16)
SW	32	50	29	28	.. (28)	(28)	23 (28)	23 (28)	23 (28)	23 (27)	22 (28)	22 (28)
WM	0	−9	−1	−14	.. (−8)	(−8)	−8 (−8)	−8 (−8)	−8 (−8)	−8 (−9)	−7 (−9)	−8 (−9)
EM	12	22	9	6	.. (11)	(11)	8 (10)	8 (10)	8 (10)	8 (10)	4 (9)	4 (9)
Y & H	−3	−5	1	−3	.. (−4)	(−4)	−1 (−4)	−1 (−4)	−2 (−4)	−2 (−4)	−2 (−4)	−3 (−4)
NW	−15	−18	−22	−17	.. (−14)	(−14)	−13 (−15)	−13 (−15)	−14 (−15)	−14 (−15)	−11 (−14)	−12 (−14)
N	−9	−9	−6	−4	.. (−4)	(−4)	−5 (−5)	−5 (−5)	−5 (−5)	−5 (5)	−5 (−4)	−5 (−4)
Eng	−11	8	−72	−50	−19.7 (−8)	(−8)	−15 (−11)	−15 (−12)	−18 (−13)	−21 (−15)	−24 (−16)	−25 (−16)
Wales	6	11	7	6	4.7 (6)	(6)	4 (6)	4 (6)	4 (6)	4 (6)	4 (6)	4 (6)
Scot	−28	−11	−2	−19	−4.8 (−8)	(−8)	−10 (−10)	−10 (−10)	−10 (−10)	−10 (−10)	−10 (−10)	−10 (−10)
NI	−12	−13	−10	−9	−8.9 (−12)	(−12)	−9 (−12)	−9 (−12)	−9 (−12)	−9 (−12)	−9 (−12)	−9 (−12)
UK	−44	−5	−77	−72	−28.7 (−22)	(−22)	−30 (−27)	−30 (−28)	−33 (−29)	−36 (−31)	−39 (−32)	−40

Sources: OPCS (unpublished tabulations); GAD (unpublished tabulations).

Notes: Projections in parentheses are those used in the 1975–based regional population projection.
Migration projections for 1977/8 to 1984/5 not in parentheses are those used in the 1977 based regional population projection.
Migration estimates for 1971/2 to 1975/6 not in parentheses are estimates prepared by OPCS.

shown that, between 1966 and 1975, regional labour force participation rates for males and females were moving towards the average
rates for Great Britain. The convergence probably results from a
variety of factors, principal amongst which must be the strong
growth of employment in regions such as East Anglia and the South
West and the reduction in the regional dispersion of earnings (DE
Gazette, April 1979).

The DE projections of the relationship between regional and national rates of labour force participation (the regional relativities)
have been adopted as the basis for projecting the regional civilian labour force. By applying these regional relativities to projections of
labour force participation in Great Britain, regional labour force
participation rates have been obtained. These have been applied, in
turn, to the 1977-based regional home population projection (which
is the latest available) to yield projections of the regional civilian labour force by sex for each year, 1977–85.

Table 5.9 shows the change in the projected regional civilian labour force by sex, between 1978 and 1985. By holding activity rates
at their 1978 level, the change in the labour force which would result solely from the changing distribution of regional population can
be derived. The column headed 'activity effect' measures the change
in the regional labour force which results from the change in labour
force participation rates between 1978 and 1985. Over the seven
year period the male civilian labour force of Great Britain is expected to grow by just over half a million and the female labour force to
grow by nearly 700 thousand. The increase in males is mainly due
to the growing size of the population of working age. This large 'population effect' is offset by a smaller 'activity effect' resulting from
the decline in the labour force participation of older males. Within
the regions, variations in the rate of growth of the labour force are
mainly due to differences in the net migration assumptions for the
regions: East Anglia and the South West show a higher than average
rate of growth of the male labour force. For females, the general increase in labour force participation projected for Great Britain generates a large 'activity effect' in the change in the regional labour
force. In Wales and the South West this is reinforced by the tendency for female labour force participation rates to catch up with
the average for Great Britain. In addition there is a general increase
in the female population of working age in all regions, with high
rates of growth in the female labour force as the overall result. As for
males, net migration gains for East Anglia, the South West and the

Table 5.9 Projected Change in the Regional Labour Force between
1978 and 1985   *Thousands*

	Labour force 1978	Labour force 1985	$\Delta LF^{(1)}$ 1978-85 (%)		Population effect (2)	Activity effect (3)
Males						
SE	4,936	5,008	72	(1)	112	−40
EA	538	588	50	(9)	50	0
SW	1,222	1,303	81	(7)	83	−2
WM	1 573	1,643	70	(4)	67	3
EM	1,104	1,157	53	(5)	65	−12
YH	1,406	1,444	38	(3)	52	−14
NW	1,846	1,872	26	(1)	55	−29
N	903	926	23	(3)	24	−1
Wa	790	825	35	(4)	36	−1
Sc	1,452	1,484	32	(2)	50	−18
GB	15,858	16,339	481	(3)	602	−121
Females						
SE	3,274	3,400	126	(4)	55	71
EA	334	390	56	(17)	26	30
SW	740	827	87	(12)	37	50
WM	967	1,013	46	(5)	36	10
EM	694	758	64	(9)	35	29
YH	909	974	65	(7)	27	38
NW	1,280	1,356	76	(6)	23	53
N	556	598	42	(8)	13	29
Wa	475	518	43	(9)	21	22
Sc	971	1,033	62	(6)	25	37
GB	10,200	10,868	668	(7)	303	365

Sources: OPCS: unpublished tabulations of the 1977-based home population projection for regions of England.
GAD: unpublished tabulations of the 1977-based total population projection for countries of United Kingdom.
DE *Gazette* (September 1978), p.1042.

Notes: (1) ΔLF refers to the change in the labour force.
(2)   'Population effect' gives the change in the labour force
resulting from a change in the home (resident) population
only, holding activity rates constant at their 1978 values.
(3)   'Activity effect' gives the change in labour force resulting
from the change in activity rates only, holding the home
population constant at its 1985 level.

East Midlands give labour force growth rates for these regions which are above the national average.

Projection of the regional labour force as described in this section depends principally upon two factors. First, trends in regional migration embodied in the home population projections are assumed to be unaffected by the state of the regional economies. Second, it is implicitly assumed that the projected increase in the labour force participation of females will develop within all regions independent of the level of aggregate demand in each region. These assumptions are difficult to sustain in practice, for reasons outlined below. It must be stressed, therefore, that the labour force projections presented here are intended as a 'benchmark', indicating the regional distribution of the labour force given a continuation of present trends.

The relationship between migration, labour force participation, employment and unemployment

The projections of the regional labour force presented above do not take account of the forecast changes in projected employment or unemployment, except in so far as any historical relationship is built into the past trends from which the projections are derived. This means that the regional labour force will remain unchanged under different regional employment simulations. In practice this seems unrealistic. Net migration between regions is likely to respond to changes in regional employment and unemployment and this will affect labour force participation rates as well as the size of regional populations. Participation rates may also be expected to vary with the level of unemployment, the demand for labour and the industrial composition of that demand. It would, for example, be very surprising if there existed no relationship between the high rate of growth of employment, the high rate of net in-migration and the increase in the female labour force participation rates experienced in East Anglia and the South West.

Some research has already been conducted on these relationships. For example, Weeden (1973) has investigated the association between the variability of gross migrant flows and certain economic factors, including employment growth, regional unemployment rates and income.[11] In general he finds little statistical association between employment growth, the income variables and migrant flows. However, the unemployment rate does appear to be related to these flows. In a review of Weeden's results, Brown (1972) assesses the impact that a difference of 1 percentage point between a region's registered male unemployment rate and the average for the rest of the country would have on the rate of net migration between the region and the rest of Great Britain. An unemployment differential of this size would result in a difference of between 0.2 and 0.5 per cent[12] in the rate of annual net in–or out–migration of economically active males. Between 1977 and 1985, the projected rates of net migration of males aged between 15 and 65 years, as a percentage of males of working age in the region, vary from 0.8 per cent per annum for East Anglia to –0.2 per cent in the North, South East and North West. The implication of Weeden's results is that an increase of 1 percentage point between a region's unemployment rate and that for the rest of Great Britain could significantly affect the *direction* of net migration.

Gordon (1975) finds support for the hypothesis that net migration levels depend more upon the rate of employment growth than upon inter-regional differences in unemployment. This contradicts Weeden's findings and he argues that Weeden's model is incorrectly specified, failing to distinguish between migration for 'housing' reasons as opposed to migration related to employment change. However, Gordon supports the broad hypothesis that migration is related to the economic climate of the regions.

Turning now to labour force participation, there is evidence to suggest that the female participation rate in a region rises as the unemployment rate falls. Corry and Roberts (1970 and 1974) show that after allowing for trend growth in rates of female labour force participation, this inverse relationship is strongest in the South East, East Anglia[13] and the South West. Their results should be viewed with caution. By defining an activity rate which excludes the unregistered unemployed they incorporate the cyclical variation in the registration propensity into their estimate of the cyclical elasticity of labour force participation. However, they do indicate that there is considerable regional variation in these elasticities. In a cross-sectional sub-regional analysis, Gordon (1970) finds that this effect is strongest for women over 35 years of age. Moseley and Darby (1978) conducted a cross-sectional analysis at the parish level for the county of Norfolk and again concluded that local unemployment rates have a significant negative impact upon female labour force participation.

So far little work has been done on the interrelated issues of migration, participation, employment and unemployment. Galambos (1967) notes that regions which exhibit high levels of in-migration are also those in which female labour force participation has been growing rapidly, and this is consistent with the research findings reported above.

This evidence suggests that independent projection of the regional labour force, ignoring the forecast changes in employment, will yield poor estimates of regional unemployment. The following section confronts the employment projection described in section 5.3 with this exogenous forecast of the regional labour force and attempts to show how sensitive the resulting unemployment estimates are to different assumptions about the migration and labour force participation rates built into the labour supply projection.

5.5 Regional Unemployment and Labour Supply Changes

This section discusses the regional unemployment projections which are obtained if the employment forecasts described in section 5.3 are compared with the projected labour force given in section 5.4. An attempt is made to develop regional estimates of *registered* unemployment (as opposed to total unemployment, which includes unregistered unemployment) and the section concludes with a discussion of the likely response of the regional labour force to the projected levels of labour demand.

In Chapter 3 it was emphasised that the medium-term trends incorporated in the labour supply projection will be modified by a 'discouraged worker' response to the high levels of unemployment. To derive a benchmark for the projected level of registered unemployment, the marginal propensity to register as unemployed between 1978 and 1985 was set equal to the 1978 estimate of the average propensity to register, yielding a figure of about 3 million registered unemployed in 1985. On present trends in sex ratios (see Chapter 6), the male registered unemployment rate would be 16 per cent and the corresponding female rate would be 6 per cent. This disparity in itself suggests that there might well be repercussions upon the pattern of employment of males and females, leading to a lowering of female representation in their traditional occupations. The main issues involved will be discussed more fully in Chapter 6 but meanwhile separate estimates of male and female registered unemployment rates are required in order to explore the potential impact of migration and labour force participation responses. So far.

these have been ignored in projecting the regional distribution of the labour force. Thus the exceptionally high rates of male unemployment indicated below for certain regions are used in order to calculate very rough orders of magnitude for the effects of the male migration response upon the final unemployment outcome.

By assuming that the relative pattern of registration propensities across the regions is similar to that which is indicated in the 1971 *Census of Population,* the regional projections of total unemployment, obtained by subtracting regional employment forecasts from the projected regional labour force, are converted to a set of estimates of registered unemployment which are consistent with the national rates of 16 and 6 per cent for males and females respectively. Table 5.10 indicates the regional distribution of registered unemployment. Part of the regional variation in these rates is attributable to regional differences in the propensity to register as unemployed. In the traditionally low unemployment areas like the South East, the propensity to register as unemployed is much lower than in high unemployment areas such as Northern Ireland.

The regional projections of registered unemployment in 1985 should be compared with the actual registered unemployment rates by region in 1978 shown in Table 5.10. The final column of this table shows the regional distribution of the change in registered unemployment between 1978 and 1985. If these changes are to be believed, they imply some major reversals in the regional rankings shown in Table 5.2. For example, male registered unemployment in the West Midlands increases by 14 percentage points, taking the region from fourth place in the regional ranking in 1978 to ninth place in 1985. Wales shows an increase in male registered unemployment of 12 percentage points, whereas the North shows only a small increase of 5 percentage points, lifting it from tenth place to fifth. Female registered unemployment in East Anglia, Wales and Northern Ireland increases by much more than the national average of 1 per cent, whereas in the North, the registered unemployment of females is shown to be in *decline.* It was shown in Table 5.2 that the ranking of regions with respect to their registered unemployment rates has been remarkably constant through time. This, in itself, is not sufficient reason to reject the projections of registered unemployment, for it is quite reasonable to suppose that a major decline in employment in those industries specific to a region will have a pronounced effect upon the region's registered unemployment rate. A good example might be the decline of the engineering sector and its effect

Table 5.10   Regional Unemployment Rates by Sex 1978 and 1985

	Males		Females		Males plus Females	
	1978	1985	1978	1985	1978	1985
South East	5	13	3	3	4	9
East Anglia	6	15	4	10	5	13
South West	8	18	5	5	6	13
West Midlands	6	20	4	6	5	15
East Midlands	6	13	4	7	5	11
Yorkshire & Humberside	7	14	4	5	6	11
North West	9	18	6	8	8	14
North	10	15	7	3	9	11
Wales	9	21	6	14	8	18
Scotland	9	18	7	7	8	13
Northern Ireland	14	22	9	20	12	21
United Kingdom	7	16	5	6	6	12

Sources: DE *Gazette* (July 1978); MRG estimates.

upon employment in the West Midlands. However, some evidence was presented in the previous section on the relationship between the regional labour force and registered unemployment. It is the extent of these influences and their resulting effect upon the regional labour force and unemployment which remains to be considered.

The migration levels embodied in the labour force projections are described in Table 5.8. Using Weeden's estimate, that a difference of 1 percentage point between a region's male registered unemployment rate and the national rate will yield a change in net migration of 2 per thousand of the regional male population aged between 16 and 64 years, the regional registered unemployment differentials shown in Table 5.10 can be used to derive an indication of the possible effect that these differentials may have on the labour force. This exercise is no more than a guide to the possible order of magnitude of the effects, given that the parameters are estimated from migration flow statistics which relate to a period of relatively low unemployment. Taking as an exteme case the projected increase in male unemployment in the West Midlands, the differential between the region's registered unemployment rate and that for the UK would lead to an estimated increase in net out-migration of 14 thousand males per annum on Weeden's analysis. While this figure is large in relation to the level of net out-migration of 8 thousand males and females per annum embodied in the labour force projection, the effect on the registered unemployment rate is only of the order of a 0.75 percentage point reduction. Similarly for Wales, if one considers the migration response to the projected increased in male registered unemployment, Weeden's results point to a reduction in male unemployment of only 1 percentage point.

Unfortunately, there is no information pertaining to the migration response of females, although it will probably be related to the male unemployment differentials, given that married women usually move with their husbands. If it is assumed that the variations in female migration matches the male response, the overall effect upon female registered unemployment is still very small. However, it is probably the regional variation in the discouraged worker effect which has the largest influence upon the female labour supply estimates. Although an element of regional variation had already been built into the registered unemployment projections via the regional differences in the propensity to register, there remains the distinct possibility that these effects will become more pronounced within those regions which show the largest increases in registered unemployment. Corry and Roberts' estimates of the effect of changes in registered unemployment on female labour force participation are used as a guide in determining the likely impact of the projected unemployment rates on regional labour supply.[14] As emphasised earlier, their results are only indicative of regional variation in the discouraged worker effect, for they do not distinguish between variations in the propensity to register and the cyclical sensitivity of the labour force. Given that a degree of regional variation in the propensity to register has already been built into the registered unemployment rates shown in Table 5.10, the following analysis probably overestimates the additional impact of regional unemployment on female labour supply. The projected increase in unemployment in the South East and East Anglia could lead to a reduction in the labour force in these two regions of 106 thousand in 1985. If, for example, 12 thousand of this reduction occurs in East Anglia, this would result in a 3 percentage point decrease in registered unemployment in that region. Similarly, the forecast of an 8 percentage point increase in female registered unemployment in Wales would

yield a reduction of 45 thousand in the female labour force, representing a 9 percentage point reduction in female registered unemployment. A change of this magnitude would yield a registered unemployment rate for females in Wales *lower* than the national average. Clearly then, there is a need to consider the regional projection
of registered female unemployment rates with a degree of circum-
spection. There is no reason to assume that the DE projection of a
convergence of regional labour force participation towards the national average is likely to persist in the face of changing regional employment prospects. Those regions in which this trend has been
most marked over the 1966–75 period are regions in which female
employment has been growing rapidly. In Wales and Northern Ireland the scope for further improvement in female employment prospects appears limited. One must, therefore, seriously question the
projected relative increase in female labour force participation in
these regions.

While the lack of endogeneity in the migration projection may
not have a great impact upon the regional unemployment rates, the
neglect of the link between labour force participation and local employment prospects appears to be very significant. The crude calculations presented in this section represent a 'first round' estimate of
what is essentially an iterative process. Further work in this area can
only proceed by making this link endogenous both within the national macroeconomic model and the regional employment submodel. At this stage it is only possible to conclude that it is the regional projection of *female* registered unemployment that is likely
to be most seriously affected by this omission. This implies that
the disparity between male and female registered unemployment
rates could even be *greater* than that discussed above and whilst regional rates in aggregate would be lower than those shown in Table
5.10, there remains the major problem of anticipating consequential
changes in employment ratios for males and females.

5.6 Summary

This chapter began with an examination of recent trends in employment and unemployment at the regional level and then de-
scibed a series of projections for employment, the labour force and
unemployment over the period to 1985. This concluding section reviews the findings set out above and considers the usefulness of the
projections in analysing regional employment prospects.

In section 5.2 it was shown that there was wide regional variation in employment change within each industry order over the period 1965–76. The employment projections by industry presented in section 5.3 also show considerable variation across the regions up to 1985. However, despite the changing industrial structure of total employment and the regional differences in employment change within each industry, the pattern of change in *total* regional employment relative to that of the UK remains largely unaltered. East Anglia, the East Midlands and the South West show overall employment growth between 1978 and 1985 while employment prospects are poor for the West Midlands, South East, North West and Wales. In the case of East Anglia the strong projected employment growth should perhaps be queried. It reflects the sharp employment increase in both manufacturing and service employment in the region between 1965 and 1976. A more detailed study of the reasons for the strong performance is required to justify a continuation of these trends. It is also interesting to note the better than average employment performance of most northern regions at the expense of the South East and the West Midlands. It is possible, as indicated in section 5.2, that the influence of regional policy during the data period 1965 to 1976 has imposed an upward influence on projected employment in the assisted areas which might not be continued into the projection period. Evidence suggests that regional policy has been effective in redirecting jobs towards the assisted areas. However, the scale of this influence appears to be very small when compared with the underlying trends in employment growth and decline at the regional level.

The structural simulation yields broadly similar changes in regional employment between 1978 and 1985. However, when comparing the 1985 regional employment projections from the standard view with the structural simulation, some minor differences emerge. This simulation has a more favourable impact upon employment in the North West, Scotland, the North and West Midlands and the least effect, when compared with the changes projected from the standard view, upon employment in the South East and Northern Ireland.

Section 5.4 was devoted to an analysis of past trends in regional labour supply and the generation of regional labour force projections to 1985. These were then compared with employment forecasts to derive projected regional unemployment rates in section 5.5.

The evidence cited in section 5.4 indicates that labour force participation and migration are likely to be related to regional employment and unemployment. In section 5.5 an attempt was made to develop a set of regional *registered* unemployment rates and to assess the likely impact of these relationships upon the regional distribution of registered unemployment. On the basis of the scant evidence available, it was concluded that the lack of endogeneity in the migration response is unlikely to have a major effect on regional unemployment. More important is the effect of regional employment prospects on female labour supply. For this reason the regional estimates of female registered unemployment are probably the least reliable. It should be stressed, however, that the projected disparity between male and female unemployment rates follows from assumptions about continuing trends in employment sex ratios. We have suspended our judgement on this matter, which is dealt with in the following chapter, but any convergence of male and female unemployment rates compared with those used in order to estimate migration and labour force participation responses here will tend to strengthen our conclusion about the relative and absolute importance of these responses in relation to the projection of the regional distribution of the labour force.

Two further qualifications of the results presented in this chapter should be noted. First, the analysis has only limited spatial content. The projection model treats the regions as a series of point economies without taking account of the spatial characteristics of economic activity within each region or the spatial linkages between regions. Thus, the possibility of geographical mismatch between the demand for and supply of labour within the regions is not taken into account. This could be an important cause of increased regional unemployment. Second, the projections of labour demand are disaggregated by industry order but not by occupation. This is an important deficiency, since no insight is gained into occupational mismatch within the regions, but one which is difficult to overcome given the lack of employment data by occupation and region.

Notwithstanding these limitations, we would stress the following features of the results presented in this chapter. The regional employment projections are determined by changes in industrial structure at the national level and region-specific trends. The changes in industrial structure are derived from a consistent set of projections provided through a national macroeconomic model and utilise the high level of industrial disaggregation in which the national forecasts are prepared. These changes are significant and their regional repercussions are developed quite clearly within the regional submodel. Region-specific trends are generated from the regional performance of industries over an eleven year period. It is the strength of these structural and region-specific trends which should be of immediate interest to planners concerned with structural change and the underlying shifts in regional employment. The time scale of the model is such that it enables the implications of the continuation of these trends to be examined more fully. If these implications are to be avoided, the procedure helps to direct attention to those trends which need to be broken. As such, the modelling exercise provides policy makers with a consistent set of regional projections which can form the basis for the introduction of additional statistical information and special knowledge pertaining to particular industries and geographical areas.

Notes

1. 'Regions' refers to the eleven Economic Planning Regions of the UK as defined on and after the 1 April 1974.

2. See Keogh and Elias (1979) for a detailed description of the projection model for regional employment and Elias and Keogh (1979) for a summary of the current equation structure of the model.

3. The industrial breakdown follows the twenty-seven industry orders of the 1968 Standard Industrial Classification. The primary sectors are agriculture and mining (order 1 and 2: SAMs 1–4), manufacturing industries are orders 3–19 (SAMs 5–30) and the service sector comprises transport, distribution and all other private and public sector services (orders 22–27: SAMs 35–48).

4. The work of Weeden (1974) and Buck and Atkins (1976) shows that differential regional growth in employment is only partly explained by industrial structure. There is a region-specific growth effect which should also be taken into account.

5. Female registered unemployment rates have been omitted because they provide a poor indication of regional economic conditions. However, a similar stability exists in their regional ranking.

6. The degree of cyclical sensitivity varies depending on whether the dependent variable is taken to be absolute changes in unemployment levels or proportionate changes. Elias (1978) argues that the elasticity of regional unemployment rates with respect to the national rate is higher in low unemployment regions and lower in regions of high unemployment.

7. A chronology of regional policy measures is given in Armstrong and Taylor (1978, Appendix C). The development of regional policy is discussed at length in McCrone (1969) and McCallum (1979).

8. See also Begg *et al.* (1975).

9. The 1978 region by industry order employment matrix is described as a projection because it is derived from the regional model using provisional estimates of UK employment by industry order as input data. Provisional employment estimates by region are not available at this level of industrial disaggregation.

10. Employment estimates by sex and region can be obtained by applying these percentages to the total regional employment figures shown in Tables 5.3 and 5.4.

11. Weeden excludes the South East, East Anglia and the South West from his multi-regional analysis of gross migrant flows. These regions he investigates separately because the net flows are away from the South East towards East Anglia and the South West, the opposite direction to that which would be predicted by his model.

12. The higher estimate is derived from the 1961 data. The lower estimate relates to 1966.

13. Due to reorganisation of regional boundaries, Corry and Roberts merge data for the South East with that for East Anglia.

14. For males, Corry and Roberts found that the regional variation in the response of labour force participation and the registration propensity to changes in registered unemployment was much less marked than for females.

References

Armstrong, Harvey and Jim Taylor (1978). *Regional Economic Policy and its Analysis.* Oxford: Philip Allan.

Ashcroft, Brian and Jim Taylor (1977). 'The Movement of Manufacturing Industry and the Effect of Regional Policy'. *Oxford Economic Papers,* 29, no.1, 84–101.

——(1979). 'The Effect of Regional Policy on the Movement of Industry in Great Britain', in Maclennan and Parr (eds.), 43–64.

Begg, H.M., C.M. Lythe, A. Sorley and D.R. MacDonald (1975). 'Annual expenditure on special regional assistance to industry in Great Britain 1960/1 – 1972/3: A Note'. *Economic Journal,* 85, no.4, 884–87.

Brown, A.J. (1972). *The Framework of Regional Economics in the United Kingdom.* Cambridge: Cambridge University Press.

Buck, T.W. and M.H. Atkins (1976). 'The Impact of British Regional Policies on Employment Growth'. *Oxford Economic Papers,* 28, no.1, 118–32.

Cameron, Gordon C. (1979). 'The National Industrial Strategy and Regional Policy', in MacLennan and Parr (eds.), 297–322.

Corry, B.A. and J.A. Roberts (1970). 'Activity Rates and Unemployment: The Experience in the United Kingdom 1951–66'. *Applied Economics,* 2, no.3, 179–201.

——(1974). 'Activity Rates and Unemployment. The U.K. Experience: Some Further Results.' *Applied Economics,* 6, no.4, 1–21.

Elias, D. Peter B. (1978). 'Regional Unemployment Elasticities: Further Evidence'. *Scottish Journal of Political Economy,* 25, no.1, 89–96.

Elias, D.P.B. and G.T. Keogh (1979). 'Structural Change in Regional Employment in the UK, 1965–1985'. Manpower Research Group Discussion Paper no.6. Coventry: University of Warwick. (mimeographed)

Galambos, P. (1967). 'Activity Rates of the Population of Great Britain, 1951–1964'. *Scottish Journal of Political Economy,* 14, no. 1, 48–69.

Gordon, I.R. (1970). 'Activity Rates: Regional and Sub-regional Differentials'. *Regional Studies,* 4, no.4, 411–24.

——(1975). 'Employment and Housing Streams in British Inter-regional Migration'. *Scottish Journal of Political Economy,* 22, no.2, 161–78.

Keogh, G.T. and D.P.B. Elias (1978). 'A Model for Projecting Regional Employment in the UK'. Manpower Research Group Discussion Paper no.1. Coventry: University of Warwick. (mimeographed)

——(1979) 'A Model for Projecting Regional Employment in the UK'. *Regional Studies,* 13, no. 5.

McCallum, J.D. (1979). 'The Development of British Regional Policy', in MacLennan and Parr (eds.), 3–42.

McCrone, Gavin (1969). *Regional Policy in Britain.* London: George Allen and Unwin.

Maclennan, Duncan and John B. Parr (1979). (eds.). *Regional Policy: Past Experiences and New Directions.* Oxford: Martin Robertson.

Moore, Barry and John Rhodes (1973). 'Evaluating the Effects of British Regional Economic Policy'. *Economic Journal,* 83, 87–110.

——(1976). Regional Economic Policy and the Movement of Manufacturing Firms to Development Areas'. *Economica,* 43, no. 169, 17–31.

Moseley, M.J. and Jane Darby (1978). 'The Determinants of Female Activity Rates in Rural Areas: an analysis of Norfolk Parishes'. *Regional Studies,* 12, no.3, 297–309.

Weeden, R. (1973). 'Interregional Migration Models and their Application to Great Britain'. *NIESR Regional Papers II.* London: Cambridge University Press.

——(1974). 'Regional Rates of Growth of Employment: An Analysis of Variance Treatment'. *NIESR Regional Papers III.* London: Cambridge University Press.

6 Labour Supply and Employment Opportunities for Women

PETER ELIAS

6.1 Introduction

Over the past two decades female employment has expanded at a steady and relatively rapid rate. By 1978 women held over two-fifths of the employee jobs in the UK. This contrasts sharply with the slow growth and recent downward trend in male employment. This chapter examines these trends in detail and develops labour force and employment projections by sex.

The last five years have seen the introduction of more legislation affecting female employment prospects than in any other period since the Second World War. One purpose of this chapter is to examine these changes and to consider their implications for female employment. In paticular, little is known about the effects of 'equal pay' and anti-discrimination legislation on the employment of women. These are exceedingly complex issues and a thorough analysis is not attempted in this chapter. Instead, recent information on trends in employment is brought together with a review of the possible impact that this legislation could have upon future trends. A two-sided approach to this task has been adopted. The second section brings together some pertinent information related to trends in labour force participation and develops a view of the projected growth in the female labour force between 1978 and 1985. The third section examines female employment in industrial detail, concentrating upon the occupational structure of employment and trends in part-time working. The trends in occupational structure and hours of work are used to develop a model of employment by sex. Finally, the projections of the labour force and employment are confronted to yield forecasts of unemployment by sex. The chapter concludes with a discussion of the plausibility of these unemployment forecasts and re-examines the potential impact of the recent legislation on female employment in the light of these projected trends. This work must be viewed cautiously, simply because the most difficult aspects of employment forecasting lie in those areas

180

where the social and economic environment has been changing rapidly.

The remainder of this introduction summarises past changes in female labour force participation, employment and unemployment and reviews recent legislation intended to influence the position of women in the economy.

Table 6.1 indicates the scale of the increase in the labour force participation of married women in the post-Second World War period. For males and unmarried females under 24 years old, increases in educational participation have reduced the labour force participation rates by about 10 per cent between 1951 and 1975. For males in higher age groups, the rate of labour force participation has been high and constant, with the exception of men over the state retirement age who now participate to a much lesser extent in the labour force. For married women, the pattern of change is quite different. For all age groups, including the under-24s and women over the state retirement age, participation in the labour force has increased dramatically throughout this period. The participation rate of married women in their reproductive age range (15–44 years) has doubled between 1951 and 1975. For married women in their post-reproductive, pre-retirement years the rate has nearly trebled.

Tables 6.2 and 6.3 indicate the more recent changes that have occurred in the male and female labour force, in terms of employment and unemployment changes. In Table 6.2 the annual percentage change in the male labour force between 1971 and 1978 is disaggregated into changes in full-time and part-time employment, self-employment and unemployment. The last row of this table shows that there has been a small decline in the male labour force in this period, principally due to the raising of the school leaving age in 1973. The increased educational participation of young males and the decreased economic activity of men over the state retirement age have offset the increase in the population of young males resulting from the 'baby boom' of the 1950s and early 1960s. An almost continual decline in full-time employment (both male employees and self-employed) is noticeable, most of which is reflected in the rise in registered unemployment. The part-time employment of males grew steadily throughout this period, but not on a scale large enough to have an offsetting influence upon the decline in full-time employment. For females, changes in the labour force and employment contrast sharply with those for males. Table 6.3 shows the high rate of growth of the labour force (1.6 per cent per annum on average) as-

Table 6.1   Economic Activity Rates by Age Group and Sex: Great Britain

Per cent

	1951	1961	1966	1971	1975
Males					
Under 20	83.8	74.6	70.6	69.7	65.8
20–24	94.9	91.9	92.6	89.9	88.9
25–44	98.3	98.2	98.2	97.9	97.7
45–64	95.2	97.6	95.1	94.5	94.0
65+	31.1	24.4	23.5	19.4	15.3
All ages	87.6	86.0	84.0	82.6	80.6
All Females					
Under 20	78.9	71.1	66.5	63.0	59.4
20–24	65.4	62.0	61.6	60.1	64.1
25–44	36.1	40.8	47.1	50.6	58.4
45–64	28.7	37.1	46.1	50.2	53.7
65+	5.3	5.4	6.7	6.4	4.8
All ages	34.7	37.4	42.2	43.0	45.7
Married women					
Under 20	38.1	41.0	43.6	42.4	51.9
20–24	36.5	41.3	43.5	46.7	54.3
25–44	25.1	33.6	41.8	47.1	55.1
45–64	19.0	29.6	41.4	47.6	52.4
65+	2.7	3.3	5.5	6.5	5.2
All ages	21.7	29.7	38.1	42.3	47.9
Males and females					
All ages	59.6	60.5	62.1	61.9	62.4

Sources: OPCS *Census of Population* 1951, 1961, 1966 and 1971; DE *Gazette* (June 1977).

Note: Before 1975 the age group 'under 20' consists of 15–19 year olds, except for married women for whom it is 16–19 years. For 1975 the age group consists of 16–19 year olds.

sociated with the rapid increase in the labour force participation of married females. Female full-time employment displays the same general overall pattern of decline as male full-time employment, whereas the growth in female part-time employment has absorbed the major part of the increase in the labour force. Female registered unemployment quadrupled between 1971 and 1978 and the year-on-year pattern of change is similar to that for males. This increase is examined in more detail in Table 6.4.

In almost 30 years the proportion of females in the labour force has risen from about 30 to 40 per cent and the proportion of married women from 12 to 25 per cent. The increase in labour force participation is not confined to an increase in employment. The General Household Survey indicates that females comprised nearly half of the unemployed in 1978. The fifth row of Table 6.4 shows that the proportion of unemployed females who register as unemployed (the average propensity to register) has been increasing quite rapidly since 1974. The proportion of females in registered unemployment was quite high during the 1950s, falling to very low levels in the 1960s and early 1970s. Between 1974 and 1978, male registered unemployment more than doubled, increasing from 460 thousand to 1,023 thousand. Female registered unemployment increased more than five-fold in this same period, from 82 thousand to 423 thousand. Approximately 120 thousand of this increase may be attributed to the rise in the registration propensity. Part of this rise follows from the large increase between 1975 and 1976 in the proportion of unemployed female school leavers in the registered unemployed. This group has a high propensity to register as unemployed, given the present nature of the social security benefit system. However, Table 6.4 also indicates that the proportion of married women in the registered unemployed has doubled between 1974 and 1978, reflecting a general increase in the numbers of married women, both registered and unregistered, who are seeking employment.

Against this broad examination of the changes that have occurred in the female labour force, employment and unemployment, consideration is now given to recent legislation which is aimed at improving the role of women in the economy. The four major pieces of legislation to be discussed are:

   a) Equal Pay Act (1970),
   b) Social Security Pensions Act (1975),
   c) Sex Discrimination Act (1975), and
   d) Employment Protection Act (1975).

Table 6.2   Annual Change in the Composition of the Male Labour Force: United Kingdom 1971–78

Component of labour force		June 1971 (thousands)	Change to each mid-year as % of labour force							June 1978 (thousands)
			71/72	72/73	73/74	74/75	75/76	76/77	77/78	
Employees in employment(1)	FT	13,116	-0.7	0.6	-0.8	-0.8	-0.9	-0.2	-0.3	12,602
	PT	597	0.1	0.4	0.2	0.1	0.0	0.1	0.2	752
Self-employed(2)		1,534	-0.1	0.3	-0.1	-0.2	-0.3	-0.3	-0.1	1,404
Registered unemployed(3)		618	0.3	-1.2	-0.1	1.5	1.9	0.3	-0.2	1,023
Unregistered unemployed(4)		286	0.1	0.1	-0.2	0.0	0.0	0.2	0.0	291
Adjustments(5)		294	-0.3	0.5	-0.6	0.0	-0.1	-0.5	0.6	211
Labour force(6)		16,446	-0.6	0.7	-1.8	0.5	0.5	-0.4	0.2	16,283

Notes:
(1) 1971-76 from Census of Employment; 1977, 1978 are provisional estimates (FT/PT split estimated by MRG).
(2) 1971-75 from DE *Gazette* (various issues); 1976-78 estimated by MRG.
(3) June count of registered unemployed (exc. adult students), DE *Gazette* (July each year).
(4) 1971-76 estimates from DE *Gazette* (June 1977) with estimate of unregistered unemployed in N. Ireland; 1977, 1978 estimated by MRG.
(5) Family workers; HM Forces; private domestic service workers; adjustments for workers with two or more jobs; residual balancing adjustment.
(6) 1971-76 from DE *Gazette* (June 1977) plus estimated labour force for N. Ireland; 1977, 1978 and MRG estimates.

Table 6.3   Annual Change in the Composition of the Female Labour Force: United Kingdom 1971–78

Component of labour force	June 1971 (thousands)	Change to each mid-year as % of labour force							June 1978 (thousands)
		71/72	72/73	73/74	74/75	75/76	76/77	77/78	
Employees in employment[1] FT	5,616	−0.2	0.9	−0.3	−0.9	−0.6	−0.3	−0.7	5,408
PT	2,791	1.3	3.1	2.7	1.4	0.4	1.6	1.4	3,948
Self-employed[2]	375	0.0	0.0	0.0	0.0	0.0	0.0	0.0	372
Registered unemployed[3]	106	0.2	−0.4	−0.1	0.8	1.6	0.8	0.2	423
Unregistered unemployed[4]	343	−0.6	−0.2	−0.1	−0.1	0.3	0.2	0.1	309
Adjustments [5]	198	−0.3	1.1	−1.5	−0.3	−0.1	−0.9	0.1	−6
Labour force [6]	9,430	0.4	4.5	0.7	0.8	1.6	1.3	1.1	10,454

Notes: See Table 6.2.

The Equal Pay Act of 1970 was not fully implemented until 1975, making that year a legislative 'watershed' in terms of the new legislation affecting female employment. Equal pay for the purpose of the Act is defined as equal treatment as regards the terms and conditions of employment of men and women on 'like work' and on work 'rated as equivalent'. 'Like work' is defined as work for which the differences (if any) between the things a man does and the things a women does are not of practical importance in relation to the terms and conditions of employment. Work 'rated as equivalent' is defined as work given an equal value under various headings (for instance, effort, skill and decision) on a job evaluation or work study scheme.[1] The Social Security Pensions Act of 1975 introduced the State Earnings-Related Pension Scheme and provided legislation for the gradual abolition, from April 1978, of 'opted-out married women', a mechanism whereby married women could elect to pay a reduced national insurance contribution in exchange for the forefeit of certain state benefits and pensions (principally unemployment, sickness and maternity benefit and a state retirement pension). The Sex Discrimination Act of 1975 extended the anti-discrimination legislation of the Equal Pay Act to declare as unlawful, discrimination by an employer against women in hiring and firing policies and procedures and in the way in which the employer affords access to training, promotion and transfer within the organisation. The legal definition of discrimination is extended to include not just the less favourable treatment of a woman on the grounds of her sex, but the imposition of a requirement or condition which satisfies all of the following. It must be to her detriment; it must be such that the proportion of women who can comply with it is considerably smaller than the proportion of men who can comply with it[2]; and it must be such that the employer cannot justify it irrespective of the sex of the person to whom it is applied. The Employment Protection Act of 1975 established a legal minimum requirement by employers to make maternity payments for six weeks at 90 per cent of full pay and established the right for a women to return to work with her original employer at any time before the end of a period of 29 weeks after her confinement. It also established the right for her to return to the job 'in which she was employed under her original contract of employment and on terms and conditions no less favourable than those which would have been applicable to her if she had not been so absent'.[3] The provisions of the Act relating to statutory maternity leave were implemented in April 1977.

This body of legislation has only been in operation for four years or less, so it is perhaps premature to attempt an overall assessment of its impact.[4] The equal pay legislation could have had an impact upon male-female wage differentials although the requirement that jobs should be 'rated as equal' by a work evaluation scheme limits the scope of the Act considerably, given that the employer is not required to carry out such an evaluation. The phasing out of the married woman's option will increase the deduction from a married woman's gross pay by as much as 4 per cent, and will probably increase the propensity of married women to register on becoming unemployed. More important possibly are the provisions of the Sex Discrimination and Employment Protection Acts which could lead to the development of better career prospects for a woman throughout her working life. This would contrast with the typical pattern of full-time employment until the birth of her first child, a period of absence from the labour market for five to ten years, followed by part-time employment in which her promotional prospects are limited by age, occupation and lack of experience. However, as will be shown in the second and third sections of this chapter, such developments are limited by the inadequate provision of child-care and education for the under-fives and the poor employment prospects in many sectors of the economy apart from those providing traditionally 'female' jobs.

6.2 Women in the Labour Force

This section is in two main parts. The first considers those factors which could have influenced the medium-term trends shown in the labour force participation rates of married women. The second part explains the labour force projections presented in Chapter 3 in more detail, paying particular attention to the medium-term influences affecting female labour force participation. Also included in this part is additional information on possible cyclical influences on these labour force participation rates.

6.2.1 Medium-term trends in the labour force participation of married women

There are a variety of factors which could have had an impact upon the labour force participation of married women in the medium-term. Unfortunately, the dearth of time-series information on

Table 6.4 Females in the Labour Force and Unemployment: Great Britain 1951–78

Per cent

	April 1951	April 1961	April 1966	June 1971	June 1972	June 1973	June 1974	June 1975	June 1976	June 1977	June 1978
Females (labour force)	30.8	32.4	35.7	36.4	36.7	37.5	38.1	38.2	38.5	38.9	39.1
Married females (labour force)	11.8	16.3	20.4	23.2	23.6	24.9	25.8	25.8	26.0	24.8	24.8
Females (total unemployed) [1]	28.5	39.6	39.0	33.3	29.6	31.1	31.6	29.5	32.2	34.2	35.8
Females (total unemployed) [2]	..	..	..	32.3	27.1	32.2	37.6	36.0	38.1	41.1	44.7
Females, registered unemployed (total female unemployed)	63.4	47.4	26.5	22.7	30.2	24.4	23.1	38.0	52.7	57.1	57.8
Females (registered unemployed)	34.9	28.2	21.7	14.3	15.5	15.4	14.6	18.0	23.9	27.4	29.3
Female school leavers (registered unemployed)	..	..	0.1	0.2	0.3	0.2	0.3	0.9	4.1	4.7	4.6
Married women (registered unemployed)	..	..	10.2	5.0	5.5	5.8	4.9	6.7	8.0	9.9	11.1
Males and females (registered unemployment rate)	1.2	1.5	1.3	3.2	3.4	2.4	2.3	3.6	5.5	6.0	5.9

Females (registered unemployment rate)	1.2	1.2	0.8	1.2	1.4	1.0	0.8	1.6	3.3	4.2	4.4

Sources: OPCS *Census of Population* (1951, 1961, 1966, 1971); DE *Gazette* for relevant years; OPCS *General House-hold Survey* (1971–78).

Notes:

(1) Total unemployment consists of registered and unregistered unemployment. Unregistered unemployment includes persons who would be seeking work but for temporary sickness. Information on unregistered unemployment is derived from Censuses of Population (1951–71). Department of Employment estimates (*Gazette*, June, 1977) and MRG estimates for 1977 and 1978.

(2) The ratio of unemployed females (registered plus unregistered) to all unemployed in General Household Survey.

labour force participation rates makes the search for statistical relationships difficult. Some information on the probable determinants
of these medium-term trends is considered below, namely, trends in
fertility, the provision of child care and education for the under-
fives, domestic technology, trends in the education of young women
and the influence of rising real earnings. From this study it is concluded that, over the next five years or so, trends in family formation, the provision of child care and the change in real earnings will
probably have more influence on labour force participation than the
other variables which are considered.

Trends in fertility, family structure and formation

Between 1964 and 1977 the number of live births in Great Britain
declined from a peak of 980 thousand to approximately 630 thousand per annum. This decline is indicative of some major changes
that have been taking place since the mid-1960s in family building
patterns.

Part of the decline in the number of births per annum is related to
the rapid decline in the first marriage rate. This decline is most
marked for women in the 20–24 range, although it is prevalent
amongst all age groups under 30 years. Recent demographic work
(Leete, 1979) indicates that the decline in marriage levels is not sufficient to explain the fall in fertility. A trend towards the reduction
or deferment of child-bearing within marriage began in the 1960s
and has continued through the 1970s, levelling out in 1977 and
1978. However, from the perspective of married women within the
labour force, it is not this overall reduction in fertility which is important, but the fact that fertility has fallen most at the shorter and
longer durations of marriage. Table 6.5 expresses the 1976 age-specific fertility rates of married women at selected durations of first
marriage as a percentage of the corresponding rates in 1966.[5] Over
this decade it can be seen that there has been a general reduction in
fertility within first marriage but, from about the third year of marriage to the seventh year the decline in fertility is less steep than outside this period. In other words, there has been a compression of
childbearing towards the period from the third to the seventh year of
marriage. This shorter period will inevitably yield potentially longer spells of labour force participation for women.

Now that the majority of couples in this country use some form
of birth control and exercise more control over ultimate family size,

Table 6.5   Fertility Rates by Age and Duration of Marriage: Great Britain
1966–76

1976 as % of 1966

Age of mother at birth of child	Duration of current marriage (completed years)					
	1	3	5	7	9	10–14
Under 20	72	101				
20–24	56	75	72	56		
25–34	69	81	85	74	56	41
35–44	75	72	70	59	51	37
All ages under 45	61	77	83	73	53	43

Source: OPCS *1977 Demographic Review*, Table 3.11.

any decision to postpone births from one period to the next can have marked changes upon the birth rate. While such changes might have little impact upon the overall level of female labour force participation, they could affect the participation rates of various age groups. Some US economists (Wachter 1977, Easterlin 1978) have suggested that changes in the age structure of the male population could have an effect upon income aspirations and expectations of young men, leading to the bringing forward or postponement of family formation. This, in turn, affects the degree of labour force participation of younger versus older women. On the basis of their hypothesis, the continued rise up to the mid-1980s in the ratio of younger to older males in the economy, resulting from the baby-boom of the 1950s and early 1960s will depress the employment and income prospects for young people. According to their theory, such a reduction in employment opportunity will lead to a further fall in the birth rate due to the postponement of family formation and an increase in the labour force participation rates of young married women in order to supplement family income.

Figure 6.1 portrays the change in the total period fertility rate (TPFR)[6] and the proportion of males aged 40–64 to males aged 15–39 in the total population of England and Wales for the period 1931–91.[7] The peak in fertility in 1964 surpasses the immediate post-war baby-boom in magnitude. This rise in fertility and the subsequent fall does correspond with the increase in the proportion of older males in the working age population. The figure shows that

the GAD project an upturn in fertility between 1980 and 1981.
Recent information from OPCS indicates that a sharp upturn com-
menced in 1979, one or two years earlier than anticipated by GAD
in their 1977-based population projection. However, this recent rise
in fertility rates *precedes* the up-turn in the male population ratio by
seven years. The GAD projection of the total period fertility rate assumes that the upward trend in fertility will continue through the
mid-1980s, levelling off just above the replacement level for the population.

**Figure 6.1 Total Fertility Rate (TPFR) and Male Population Ratio:
England and Wales 1931–91**

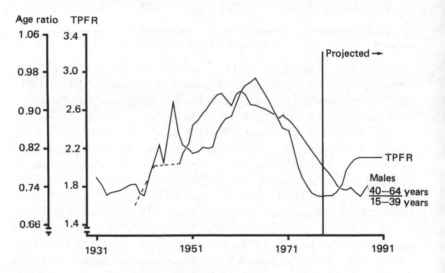

Sources: OPCS Summary Series FMI; Registrar General's *Annual Statistical Review for England and Wales;* GAD 1977-based population projection (unpublished).

If a causal relationship does exist between male population ratios
and fertility rates, then one might be able to make use of this link to
relate female labour force participation to fertility via the age structure of the population. Given the present lack of long-run time-
series information on labour force participation rates, this is as yet
infeasible. If fertility continues to increase as projected, this will obviously have some impact upon the participation of women in the
younger age groups.

Trends in the provision of child care and education for the under-fives

There are two issues which need to be considered with respect to the provision of care and education for the children of working mothers. First, has such provision improved over the last two decades to the extent that it could have contributed to the rise in the labour force participation of married women? Second, does a lack of such provision remain a constraint upon the decision to participate in paid work by the mothers of young children? The available evidence on these issues indicates that the increase in the provision of care and education for the under-fives has probably had a considerable part to play in the growth of female labour force participation, but that the lack of adequate provision remains a major factor in preventing many mothers from working when they would otherwise do so.

Between 1961 and 1977 the provision of nursery school or primary education for the 3 and 4 year olds in the UK rose from 16 per cent of all children in the age cohort to 36 per cent. Although the cohort has been declining in size quite rapidly recently, the improvement in absolute terms is still substantial, from 255 thousand to 569 thousand pupils. However, there is plenty of evidence from the General Household Survey to indicate that the lack of adequate provision for the young children of working mothers depresses economic activity rates of mothers below their desired levels. Between 1971 and 1976, one third of the economically inactive mothers in the survey who had stated an intention to work in the future, were asked if they would work earlier than intended if suitable arrangements were available for the care of their children. Approximately one third again of this group responded positively to this question. It is not known whether the provision of child care and education facilities by local authorities or employers, possibly at some financial cost to the family, would be considered 'suitable' by these women in the GHS, nor is the phrase 'earlier than intended' quantified. However, if it is assumed that 'suitable arrangements' could be found this would represent a 7 per cent increase in the size of the female labour force. Under the further assumption that the age distribution of these women is the same as the distribution of all women with dependent children, whether working or not, this 7 per cent addition to the female labour force breaks down into a 6 percentage point increase in the labour force participation rate for

women aged 16–24, a 9 per cent addition for women in the age
groups between 25 and 44 and a 4 per cent addition to the female labour force aged between 45 and 59 years. These calculations are obviously crude, but give some indication of the large unsatisfied desire for child care and education.

Table 6.6 indicates the extent of the provision of full-time and
part-time care for children under 5 in 1976. From the table it can be
seen that the provision of day nursery care is extremely low. The
statistics on child-minding cover only registered child-minding. The
geographical distribution of this child care is varied. Day nursery
provision in Camden in Inner London in 1976 was at a level equivalent to nearly one child in ten of the under-fives in that area. In War-
wickshire this provision was non-existent. Playgroups are fairly
evenly distributed, but only offer part-time care on a limited basis.
Nursery schools and classes are well provided in Inner London, the
West Midlands and South Yorkshire, but in other areas local authorities have excluded the rising-fives from early access to the education system. Unregistered child-minding and care provided within
the family remain as the major forms of provision for the under-
fives.

Some attempt is being made to meet the demand for child care
provision and to improve the quality of that which already exists, as
indicated in the joint DES/DHSS circular to local authorities on the
co-ordination of provision for the under-fives,[8] but progress is likely
to be limited by the financial stringencies under which local
authorities are presently operating.

Trends in domestic technology

The development of labour-saving devices in the home has facilitated the participation of married women in the labour market by
increasing the productivity of domestic work. While such developments must have had a long-term impact upon the choice between
market and domestic work, they are probably not a major contribu-
tory factor to the recent strong upward trend in married women's
participation rates.

Table 6.7 shows the growth in the proportion of households in the
Family Expenditure Survey possessing certain amenities. The considerable growth in the possession of washing machines, refrigera-
tors and central heating is indicative of the general increase in labour-saving devices in the home. The growth in access to the

Table 6.6   Provision for Children Under Five: Great Britain 1976

	Places				Pupils	
	Local authority day nurseries	Private day nurseries	Registered child minders	Registered playgroups	Nursery schools and classes (inc. rising 5s)	Primary schools (non-nursery classes inc. rising 5s)
Number	33,859(1)	27,433	84,827(2)	415,304(3)	234,375(2)	277,826
Rate per 1,000 under-fives	9	8	24	115	65	77

Source: *Services for Young Children with Working Mothers.* Report by the Central Policy Review Staff (1978).

Notes:
(1)   Includes 3,376 part-time places.
(2)   Full-time and part-time.
(3)   Part-time.

telephone system has improved communication, thereby helping jobseekers in particular and increasing economic efficiency general-ly. The growth in car ownership, to the extent that cars are made available to married women, increases the area in which a woman can seek and obtain employment. However, there is a causal prob-lem when considering such trends, for it is not known whether the ownership of consumer durables has increased as a result of the in-crease in family income when the wife takes a job.[9] It seems reason-able to assume though that such trends have facilitated market work by married women through the increase in the productivity of domestic work. There is plenty of scope for such productivity gains to continue in the medium-term.

Trends in education

There has been a steady increase in the post-war period in the number of women undertaking non-compulsory full-time educa-tion. One would expect investment in education prior to marriage and family formation to increase the likelihood that a women re-turns to work after child-bearing. Thus, there is a long-term link between the rise in the educational participation of single women and the increased labour force participation of married women.

Table 6.8 indicates the recent trends in the composition of full-time students in non-compulsory education by sex and institution. These figures indicate that, in total, men and women are participat-ing in the education system in almost equal proportions, given that there are 5 per cent more males than females in the 16–24 year age group throughout the period covered in this table. The institutional disaggregation shows that, in higher education, women are concen-trated in the former teacher training establishments and men are over-represented in universities. Any trend towards a more even distribution of the sexes in the various institutions of higher educa-tion will result in a higher proportion of women obtaining a univer-sity education. Coupled with the recent decline in teaching jobs, a redistribution of educational opportunity can only improve career prospects for women. Such an improvement depends upon the will-ingness of schools and universities to co-operate in providing more university places for qualified women to pursue study in the sciences, engineering and other technological subjects and in per-suading more women to follow these non-traditional career paths. In the medium-term this would serve to increase the labour force

Table 6.7   Proportion of Households Possessing Certain Amenities 1959-78

Amenity	1959	1960	1964	1965	1966	1967	1968	1969	1970	1971	1972	1973	1974	1975	1976	1977	1978
Washing machine	34	36	53	57	62	..	..	63	65	64	65	67	69	72	72	..	75
Refrigerator	15	21	34	41	45	..	..	60	66	69	74	78	82	85	88	..	91
Central heating (full or partial)	..	..	7	9	13	..	..	25	30	32	37	38	43	47	47	51	52
Telephone	..	..	22	23	25	26	29	32	35	38	42	43	49	52	53	..	57
Car[1]	24	25	37	40	44	45	48	51	52	51	53	54	56	57	55	56	57

Sources: DE *Family Expenditure Survey* (1959–76). United Kingdom.
OPCS *General Household Survey* (1977–78). Great Britain.

Note: (1) For 1959–66 the figures are based on physical possession; for 1967 onwards on payment of Road Tax.

Table 6.8   **Female Students as a Percentage of All Students Beyond Compulsory School Age: United Kingdom 1968/69–1975/76**

Establishment	1969	1970	1971	1972	1973	1974	1975	1976
Schools	47.4	47.6	47.6	47.8	48.0	47.9	48.3	48.1
Further Education								
Non-advanced	46.2	44.6	42.4	46.6	47.4	49.4	50.3	51.9
Advanced	25.1	24.9	25.4	27.0	27.7	29.3	30.8	50.0[1]
Colleges of education	73.0	72.4	72.6	71.6	70.5	70.2	72.0	
Universities	28.3	28.2	29.0	29.8	30.9	32.0	33.1	33.7
Total	45.7	45.1	45.0	45.7	46.0	45.8	46.3	46.5

Source: DES *Education Statistics for the United Kingdom* (1968-76).

Note: Figures relate to January of each year for schools and autumn of preceding year for other establishments. Before 1973 overseas students are excluded from figures for Further education, Colleges of education and Universities.

    (1) From 1976 separate figures for Colleges of Education cannot be shown because of the reorganisation of teacher training institutions in England and Wales.

participation rates of married women. It is unlikely, though, that any major effect will be felt over the next ten years, given the present general lack of commitment to such a policy and the long training lead-time it involves.

Trends in real earnings

Studies of cross-sectional information in both the US and the UK (see for example, Mincer (1962), Cain (1966), Bowen and Finegan (1969) and, for the UK, Greenhalgh (1977)) have shown that changes in earnings have a significant impact upon the labour force participation decisions of married women. For most married women, domestic work is their major responsibility. One would expect, therefore to find a strong substitution effect away from domestic work towards market work with real increases in market wages and earnings. For the family though, a general rise in household income resulting, perhaps, from the increase in real earnings of the husband, might increase leisure amongst all family members, reducing both market and domestic work for the wife.

Table 6.9 shows real average gross hourly earnings for male full-time manual employees (over 21 years) and female full-time manual employees (over 18 years) from 1952 to 1978 and the ratio of female to male earnings for these groups of workers. There are certain interesting features in these data. First, real average gross earnings for full-time manual male employees have grown fairly steadily at about 2.5 per cent per annum throughout this period, never falling more than 1 per cent between any two years, until 1975–77 when there was a fall of 8 per cent. For full-time female manual employees the corresponding reduction was only 6 per cent over a shorter period, because of the implementation of equal pay legislation. Second, the ratio of female to male earnings held remarkably constant for two decades at approximately 60 per cent, increasing between 1973 and 1976 to 70 per cent. The available information indicates that this represents a new stable differential, showing that equal pay legislation has had a once-and-for-all impact upon levels of female earnings.

This information is inadequate in many respects. It relates only to women working full-time. While many such women will be married, it was shown in Table 6.3 that the major increases in employment have come from married women in part-time jobs. Furthermore, it indicates little about the 'trade-offs' available within the

Table 6.9 **Real Average Gross Hourly Earnings for Full-time Workers and Earnings Relativities 1952–78**

£ per hour – 1975 prices

	1952	1953	1954	1955	1956	1957	1958	1959	1960
Manual men	0.60	0.62	0.64	0.68	0.69	0.69	0.70	0.73	0.77
Manual women	0.37	0.38	0.40	0.41	0.41	0.42	0.42	0.44	0.47
Manual women as % of manual men	62	62	62	61	60	61	61	61	60

	1961	1962	1963	1964	1965	1966	1967	1968	1969
Manual men	0.81	0.80	0.82	0.86	0.88	0.93	0.92	0.96	0.96
Manual women	0.49	0.48	0.49	0.52	0.52	0.55	0.55	0.56	0.56
Manual women as % of manual men	61	60	60	60	59	59	60	59	59

	1970	1971	1972	1973	1974	1975	1976	1977	1978
Manual men	1.02	1.04	1.09	1.14	1.14	1.22	1.21	1.12	1.16
Manual women	0.60	0.62	0.66	0.70	0.72	0.81	0.85	0.80	0.83
Manual women as % of manual men	59	60	60	61	63	66	70	71	71
Non-manual men	1.61	1.61	1.69	1.70	1.70	1.77	1.78	1.63	1.71
Non-manual women	0.85	0.86	0.94	0.93	0.95	1.08	1.11	1.03	1.05
Non-manual women as % of non-manual men	53	53	54	54	56	61	62	63	61

Sources: 1952–1968; DE *British Labour Statistics, Historical Abstract 1886–1968,* 1971, Tables 47 and 48.
1969: DE *British Labour Statistics Year Book 1973,* 1975, Table 26.
1970-1978: DE *New Earnings Survey* (annual).
All earnings data deflated by Retail Price Index (April 1975 = 100). 1952-69 refer to United Kingdom, 1970-78 refer to Great Britain.

household concerning the husband's earnings, the wife's earnings and non-labour household income. Nor does it provide any information about the effect of unemployment on household earnings and the wife's decision to work. Some of these deficiencies can be overcome by building up time-series observations of such variables from a continuous household survey. Table 6.10 gives annual estimates of selected characteristics of households in which a married couple is present from the Family Expenditure Survey (FES), 1968–75.[10] This table shows that the percentage of economically active wives (whose husbands were present) in the FES rose from 44 per cent in 1968 to 54 per cent by 1975. During this seven-year period their unemployment rates rose by only about ¹/₂ per cent and their self-employment rate remained constant, indicating that the increase in participation was mainly absorbed through an increase in employee jobs. With such low unemployment rates one would expect the 'discouraged worker' effect to be small or non-existent. A further examination of this data set uncovers evidence about the possible strengths of the various factors which could be associated with the increase in the labour force participation of wives in the FES. For example, the unemployment rate of the husbands of these wives rose by only about one percentage point in the seven-year period, suggesting that the 'additional worker' effect of the husband's unemployment on the labour force participation of the wife is likely to be small in relation to the increase in wives' participation rates. The pattern of family formation has been changing within this period. For households with young children, the average number of children in the 0–1 and 2–4 year age groups has declined only slightly, whereas nearly 4 per cent more households had no children in the 0–1 age group and nearly 3 per cent more households had no children in the 2–4 year age group. The decline in the birthrate in this period is shown clearly as a decrease in the number of couples with children under school age rather than as an increase in the spacing of children. It is interesting to note that the percentage of households without children at state secondary schools declined by more than 3 per cent. This decline may be attributed to the rise in the birth rate through the 1950s and early 1960s. These children will be entering the labour market between now and 1982, after which year the rate of labour force entry will commence to fall.

Over this short period, the average net real earnings of married women grew by 3.4 per cent per annum while their husbands' net earnings grew by only 1.7 per cent. For both husbands and wives

Table 6.10 Selected Characteristics of Family Expenditure Survey Households with Married Couples: United Kingdom 1968–75.

		1968	1969	1970	1971	1972	1973	1974	1975
% economic activity rate	wives	44.4	46.5	49.1	48.5	50.1	52.6	52.8	53.8
% unemployment rate	wives	0.3	0.2	0.3	0.3	0.8	0.4	0.6	0.7
	husbands	1.3	1.6	1.3	1.9	3.5	2.5	2.2	2.7
Average no. of children per houshold with children in specified age range	0–1 years	1.07	1.05	1.07	1.05	1.05	1.05	1.04	1.05
	2–4 years	1.18	1.17	1.17	1.16	1.16	1.15	1.15	1.14
% of households without children in specified age range.	0–1 years	86.0	86.4	86.6	87.1	87.1	88.4	89.2	89.7
	2–4 years	80.2	80.5	81.9	81.7	82.3	83.0	82.5	82.9
% of households without children at state secondary school		82.2	81.2	80.5	81.5	80.2	80.1	80.7	78.8
Average normal hours worked per week as employee in main occupation	wives	27.6	27.4	26.8	27.4	27.3	26.4	26.6	26.6
	husbands	44.3	44.7	44.3	43.5	43.6	43.5	43.7	43.5
Average normal net real hourly earnings (£ per hour)	wives	0.49	0.51	0.52	0.55	0.57	0.60	0.62	0.62
	husbands	0.81	0.82	0.85	0.88	0.92	0.96	0.94	0.91
Average non-labour real household income (£ per week)		8.64	9.60	9.51	9.18	9.65	10.97	11.39	11.09
No. of households in sample		5,289	5,173	4,677	5,154	5,131	5,066	4,729	5,050

Source: DE, Family Expenditure Survey Base Tapes (1968–75).

Notes: All data are annual averages from a subset of the Family Expenditure Survey, consisting of all married women whose husbands are present in the household. Hourly earnings and non-labour household income are deflated by Retail Price Index (Jan. 1975 = 100).

there was a similar decline in average hours of employees worked per week of about 0.5 per cent per annum. Household income from all non-labour sources[11] grew by an average of 3.6 per cent per annum in real terms over this same period. This income category constituted about 15 per cent of total household income (both labour and non-labour income) in 1975, although this average will probably vary considerably according to the ages of the married couple.

Using this source of information, a set of equations was estimated for eight age groups, relating the variations in real net earnings of wives and husbands to variations in the labour force participation of married women. The equations were based upon a similar model developed by Wachter (1972). Further details are given in Elias (1980). Variables were included to account for the effect of young children on the labour force participation of their mothers and to capture transitory influences upon the married women's labour supply decision. These short-run influences will be discussed in the second part of this section. Apart from the obvious trend correlation between the rise in real earnings and the labour force participation of married women, this work suggests that the changing pattern of family formation appears to have had a significant impact upon the labour force participation of married women over 35 years old, particularly the increase in the proportion of households in this category without very young children. It must be stressed, however, that these results are derived from the analysis of household data over a short time period. Further work needs to be conducted over a longer time span before any conclusive results are obtained.

6.2.2 Projecting the female labour force

After examining recent trends in female labour force participation, this sub-section deals with the evidence of cyclical influences upon participation. Finally, a projection of the female labour force is made taking together these short-run influences with possible medium-term trends described in the first part of this section.

Recent trends in female labour force participation

Because of the differences in labour force attachment, the female labour force is usually subdivided into married women and non-married women, the latter category consisting of single, widowed, separated and divorced women. Labour force participation rates for non-married women are higher than for married women and have shown a very gradual decline through the 1970s. The slow decline is thought to be associated with the increase in the divorce rate by mothers with dependent children, increasing the proportion of economically inactive women in the non-married population (OPCS 1977, p. 50). Table 6.11 shows the labour force participation rates for non-married women from 1971–78, together with the rates for 1985 as projected by the Department of Employment (DE *Gazette,* April 1978). An inspection of these participation rates suggests that the projected rates for 35–54 year old non-married women are perhaps too high, although the GHS has recorded considerable variation in the participation rates of these age groups, part of which may be attributed to the small size of the sample. The projected rate for 60–64 year olds appears to be inconsistent with the sharp fall in participation rates for this age group which occurred between 1975 and 1976.

The prime focus of attention is upon the recent behaviour of participation rates for married females, because these have been displaying the greatest change, leading to potentially large margins of error in prediction. To gain some understanding of the effect that the growth in the labour force participation rates of married women has had upon official projections, Table 6.12 gives an example of the variation in rates of economic activity of married women projected by the DE over the last thirteen years. Apart from differences of definition noted in the table, it is clear that the Department of Employment has continually found it necessary to revise the projected participation rates for 25–54 year old married women in an upward direction. Participation rates for older married women were revised upwards until the January 1974 projection, the first projection to utilise the 1971 *Census of Population,* since when they have been revised downwards. In the light of this information it would not be surprising to find that participation rates for the younger age groups are still underestimated, and, for the older age groups, overestimated by the Department of Employment.

Table 6.13 shows the DE estimates of labour force participation of married women for 1971–75, together with their projections for 1976–78 and 1985. This information is compared with estimates from the General Household Survey (GHS), Family Expenditure Survey (FES) and the EEC Labour Force Surveys (LFS). It can be seen that the DE has projected major increases in participation in the 35–59 year age groups. For the 35–44 year age group, the DE projects a 9 percentage point increase in labour force participation

Table 6.11 Non-married Females in the Labour Force: Great Britain 1971–78 and 1985

Per cent

Age group	Non-married females economically active in each age group									Non-married females as % of labour force in each age-group	
	1971	1972	1973	1974	1975	1976	1977	1978	1985	1978	1985
16–24	68	68	74	67	70	71	67	69	65	31	31
25–34	78	76	82	76	76	74	74	73	77	9	11
35–44	80	76	76	76	75	72	78	69	78	6	7
45–54	78	78	74	79	77	72	72	71	77	8	8
55–59	68	68	69	65	62	61	69	62	65	11	11
60–64	30	33	34	35	34	27	27	27	30	10	8
65+	7	7	6	7	6	6	5	4	4	20	23
Total	45	44	45	42	42	41	41	40	42	13	14

Sources: OPCS *General Household Survey* (1971–78); DE *Gazette* (April 1978).
Note: GHS estimates 1971–78 : DE projection for 1985.

Table 6.12　Comparison of Successive Forecasts of Economic Activity Rates for Married Women in 1981 with MRG Projected Rates: Great Britain

Per cent

Age group	Department of Employment Forecasts of Activity Rates for Married Women in 1981					MRG Projections
	November 1966(2)	March 1969(2)	August 1971(2)	January 1974	June 1977	
25-34	31.6	34.9	38.4	41.7	49.6	49.6
35-44	54.0	55.5	56.8	63.3	70.3	69.7
45-54	58.5	60.2	66.8	68.2	70.9	70.6
55-59	52.0	54.5	58.0	56.5	54.8	54.8
60-64	26.0	26.0	33.0	31.6	29.1	26.2
65+	9.5	8.0	11.0	8.5	6.1	6.1

Source: DE *Gazette* (month and year indicated in table). (Formerly Department of Employment and Productivity; formerly Ministry of Labour.)

Notes: (1) Official forecasts have, in some cases, been aggregated from different age groupings. Where aggregation has occurred, the population weights are derived from the 1977 – based total population projection for 1981.

(2) These projections exclude the unregistered unemployed. The rates will therefore be slightly lower than projections made in subsequent years.

Table 6.13 Comparison of Female Economic Activity Rates from Various
Sources 1971–78

	1971	1972	1973	1974	1975	1976	1977	1978	1985
DE Estimates (1971-75) and Projections: married women (all women) GB									
20-24	47	48	51(63)	54	54(64)	55	55(65)	55	56
25-34	38	39	44(49)	47	47(52)	48	49(54)	49	51
35-44	55	55	60(62)	64	64(66)	66	68(69)	69	73
45-54	57	58	63(65)	64	64(66)	66	68(70)	69	75
55-59	46	46	48(53)	49	49(53)	50	51(55)	52	58
60-64	25	25	26(28)	26	26(28)	27	27(29)	28	30
65 +	7	6	6(6)	5	5(5)	5	6(5)	6	7
General Household Survey: married women GB									
18-24	46	46	50	49	54	53	55	61	..
25-34	40	42	44	50	52	49	52	52	..
35-44	58	57	64	64	66	67	68	70	..
45-54	57	62	63	64	67	65	68	69	..
55-59	47	45	48	50	49	53	50	52	..
60-64	26	25	25	30	26	28	26	24	..
65+	5	7	8	7	6	6	6	5	..
Family Expenditure Survey: married women, husbands present UK									
20-24	51	56	58	59	63	..	..	..	..
25-34	51	52	56	56	56	..	..	..	..
35-44	62	64	68	66	71	..	..	..	..
45-54	63	60	66	66	69	..	..	..	..
55-59	47	50	50	53	52	..	..	..	..
60-64	25	28	27	31	25	..	..	..	..
65+	7	7	7	7	5	..	..	..	..
EEC Labour Force Survey: all women UK									
20-24	..	..	60	..	66	..	68	..	..
25-34	..	..	45	..	51	..	52	..	..
35-44	..	..	57	..	65	..	65	..	..
45-54	..	..	60	..	66	..	65	..	..
55-59	..	..	49	..	53	..	57	..	..
60-64	..	..	29	..	30	..	27	..	..
65+	..	..	5	..	5	..	5	..	..

Sources: DE *Gazette* (June 1979); OPCS *General Household Survey* (1971-
78); DE Family Expenditure Survey tapes (1971-75); SOEC
Labour Force Survey (1973, 1975 and 1977).

between 1975 and 1985. For 45–54 year old married women, an increase of 11 percentage points is forecast. In the 55–59 year age category, evidence from the LFS suggests that participation rates continue to rise rapidly but this information is contradicted by evidence from the GHS. The 60–64 year age group is projected as increasing by 4 percentage points between 1975 and 1985. However, the FES, GHS and LFS all indicate a continued fall in participation for this age group.

Further information on recent trends in female labour force participation is given in Table 6.14. The age-specific labour force participation rates for all women shown in the table are derived from the 1977 EEC Labour Force Survey, with modifications to make allowance for differences in definition, timing and coverage.[12] These modified activity rates are compared with the DE projections for 1977. The final column of this table indicates that the DE projection for 35–44 year old women is an *overestimate* of possibly more

Table 6.14   **Female Economic Activity Rates : A Comparison of DE Projections for 1977 with results derived from EEC Labour Force Survey**

Age group	DE[1]	EEC LFS[2]	Difference
20 – 24	64.7	65.8	1.1
25 – 34	53.6	53.3	−0.3
35 – 44	69.3	66.6	−2.7
45 – 54	69.7	65.7	−4.0
55 – 59	54.6	56.8	2.2
60 – 64	28.7	24.5	−4.2
65 +	4.9	4.6	−0.3

Sources: DE *Gazette,* June 1977; SOEC *Labour Force Sample Survey,* 1977.

Notes: (1)   Latest official projection for Great Britain, mid-1977.
         (2)   EEC Labour Force Survey 1977, adjusted for differences in definition, timing and coverage.

than 2.5 percentage points. For 45–54 year old women the degree of overestimation appears to be much higher, as is the case for 60–64 year old women.

Clearly, the DE projections of female labour force participation are in need of some revision. Some of the medium-term influences upon participation are likely to develop over the next six years in a manner which was not expected at the time the DE projection was prepared. The upturn in fertility, cuts in the planned provision of education for under-fives and the outlook for the growth of real earnings are recent factors which need to be taken into account. However, there are certain short-run influences which also have to be considered. Before describing the labour force projection, some information on such influences is presented.

Short-term variations in female labour force participation rates

Most researchers who have investigated the variation in female labour force participation rates have found a significant inverse statistical relationship between female participation in the labour force and unemployment rates. In other words, at lower levels of unemployment and higher levels of labour demand, more women are drawn into the labour force. The UK research on this issue is not as highly developed as the US research, mainly due to the lack of long-run time-series data and the lack of 'longitudinal' survey information on labour force participation. The UK research falls into two major categories: cross-sectional and time-series. Each category will be considered in turn.

Cross-section studies

In her study of the variation in the labour force participation of married women in 106 towns and cities in Great Britain using census of population data, Greenhalgh (1977) includes both the male unemployment rate within the town or city and the difference between the regional unemployment rate and the regional unemployment rate at 'full' employment as explanatory variables. Her results indicate that a 1 per cent increase in local unemployment (not matched by variation in regional 'deficient demand') would have a net effect of discouraging participation by 0.75 per cent. This result was also found in her age-disaggregated analysis.

Grice (1978), using a similar data base to Greenhalgh, develops a model for forecasting activity rates by age group, sex, and (for females) by marital status. The preferred equations for forecasting the labour force participation of married women show a negative relationship between the unemployment rate and the participation rate, with a 1 percentage point increase in the unemployment rate yielding a 0.4 percentage point decrease in the participation of married women in the 25–44 age groups and a lesser response for older age groups.

McNabb (1977) finds a larger response, his results suggesting that a 1 percentage point increase in the female unemployment rate will yield a 2.5 percentage point decrease in the labour force participation of married females. No disaggregated analysis by age-groups is presented.

Time-series studies

Corry and Roberts (1970, 1974) analyse the cyclical variation in activity rates derived from the Department of Employment's *working population* series. No distinction is made in this data between married and non-married females. They consider the relationships between female activity rates (which exclude the unregistered unemployed) and male and female registered unemployment rates. They find an inverse relationship between female activity rates and female unemployment. After taking account of the general upward trend in female activity rates, a 1 percentage point increase in registered female unemployment leads to a 0.7 percentage point decrease in female labour force participation. These results are replicated by Berg and Dalton (1977)[13] who also investigate the relationships between female participation rates and trends in real wages, real wages relative to the trend and unemployment, postulated by Wachter (1972). Again, the inverse relationship between unemployment and female labour force participation arises. In an analysis of FES data described in the previous subsection, the author has also found a significant negative relationship between the unemployment rate of husbands in the FES sample and the labour force participation rates of their wives, for the 25–44 year age groups.

Transitory changes in real earnings could also have an impact upon the choice between market and domestic work for married women. Quarterly observations from the FES sample on the deviation of wives' real net earnings from trend were found to be negatively related to their labour force participation rates. This confirms the findings of Berg and Dalton for the UK and Wachter for the US. Wachter suggests that this indicates a desire to supplement family income when present real earnings are low relative to the long-run trend.

This evidence, both time-series and cross-sectional, is overwhelmingly in favour of an inverse relationship between unemployment rates (whether male or female, registered or registered plus unregistered) and the labour force participation rates of married women, particularly in the 25–44 year age groups. Given that unemployment rates in the medium-term are expected to be significantly higher than in the late 1960s and early 1970s, this suggests that the labour force participation rates of married women will be depressed below their long-term trend values.

The projected labour force

As was shown in Table 6.11, labour force participation rates for non-married women have been declining slowly throughout the 1970s. However, there is considerable variation about this trend for most age groups, with the exception of the 60–64 year age group. The DE projection of labour force participation for this age group is 30 per cent in 1985. This rate has been revised down to 25 per cent, with pro-rata adjustments made to projections for earlier years. Overall this represents a small adjustment to the projected labour force. Non-married women form only one third of the total female labour force and, as can be seen from the final columns of Table 6.11, those aged 60–64 form only 10 per cent of non-married economically active females.

For married women, revisions have been made to the projected activity rates in the 35–54 and 60–64 age ranges. For the 35–44 year age group, it was noted earlier that the DE projects a 9 percentage point increase in labour force participation between 1975 and 1985. An upturn in fertility amongst the younger age groups might reduce the participation of younger women, in turn making more jobs available for women who are past their peak reproductive years, but an increase of this magnitude is not thought likely, given the forecast higher levels of unemployment. Again, in the 45–54 year age group, the DE projects a rise of 11 percentage points between 1975 and 1985. For similar reasons this projection seems on the high side. For the 55–59 year age group it was noted in Table 6.13 that the LFS and GHS provide contradictory evidence on the trend in their labour force participation. The DE projection for this age group has been retained, therefore, on the grounds that recent information does not consistently refute it. The projected increase in the economic activity of 60–64 year old married women appears unlikely, given the consistent downward trend in participation recorded in the FES, GHS and LFS.

In the present study, therefore, the projected rates in 1985 for 35–54 year old married women have been reduced by 2 percentage points, from the DE projection, making pro-rata adjustments for earlier years. For 60–64 year old married and non-married women the projected labour force participation rates for 1985 have been reduced by 5 percentage points, again making pro-rata adjustments for earlier years. The revised projections of the labour force of the United Kingdom are shown in Table 6.15. The projected female labour force in 1985 based on DE activity rate forecasts has been revised down by nearly 200 thousand.

Table 6.15 Revised Labour Force Projections: United Kingdom 1978–85

	Labour force (DE projections)		Revisions to female labour force		*Thousands* Revised female labour force projections
	Males	Females	Married	Non-Married	
1978	16,283	10,502	−45	−3	10,454
1979	16,316	10,609	−54	−6	10,549
1980	16,368	10,714	−76	−9	10,629
1981	16,430	10,858	−54	−13	10,791
1982	16,524	10,946	−84	−16	10,846
1983	16,637	11,098	−115	−20	10,963
1984	16,746	11,244	−146	−24	11,074
1985	16,788	11,345	−168	−26	11,151

Sources: 1977-based total population projection; GAD (unpublished tabulations, 1978); DE *Gazette* (June 1977); MRG estimates of female labour force participation, 1978–85.

6.3 Women in Employment

This section studies the characteristics of the jobs in which women are employed, in terms of their occupations and hours of work. It is presented in three parts. The first examines occupational trends in female employment. The second part looks at the growth of part-time employment by industry. The third describes the model that has been developed which relates the proportion of females in an industry to trends in occupations and part-time working.

Before concentrating upon a more detailed analysis of these trends, it is worth noting the main developments occurring during the last two decades. In 1961, women held 35 per cent of employee jobs in the UK. By 1978 this had risen to an estimated 41 per cent. As was shown in Table 6.3, most of this growth has been concentrated in part-time jobs. In Chapter 4, occupational changes over the period 1961–78 were examined, indicating that rapid growth had occurred in occupations in which women are concentrated (e.g. health and education professions, clerical occupations etc., personal service occupations). Also, certain industries employ a much higher proportion of women than others. As these industries expand or contract, female employment prospects are likely to change accordingly. Table 6.16 shows the change in employment by sex in 39 industry groups[14] for the period 1971–78, and the breakdown of female employment changes into two components. The first is the change in female employment attributed to the change in industrial employment. This is obtained by applying the 1971 sex ratios for employees and self-employed to the change in employment by industry between 1971 and 1978. The second component measures the change in female employment which results from the change in the female sex ratio for employees and the self-employed between 1971 and 1978, applied to the 1978 employment estimates. The general pattern of change in industrial employment shown in the table will be familiar from Chapter 4. The decline in the primary and manufacturing sectors and increase in the service sector is quite apparent. In nearly all industries where total employment falls, female employment declines by much less. Where total employment rises, the rise in female employment accounts for the major part of the gain. From the breakdown of the change in female employment into its two components, it appears that about 60 per cent of the overall increase may be attributed to changes in industrial structure. The pattern across industries is extremely varied, but within the service

Table 6.16   Composition of Industrial Employment Changes for Women: United Kingdom 1971-78

	Total employment change	Female employment change		Breakdown of female employment change Due to industry		Due to sex ratio	
	(thousands)	(thousands)	% of total change	(thousands)	% of female employment change	(thousands)	% of female employment change
Agriculture	−79.7	−8.0	10.0	−14.2	178.0	6.2	−78.0
Coal mining	−52.6	−1.1	2.0	− 1.7	155.6	0.6	−55.6
Oil, natural gas, mining n.e.s.	0.9	0.9	99.2	0.1	6.9	0.8	93.1
Cereal processing	−39.6	−12.7	32.0	−14.7	116.1	2.0	−16.1
Food processing n.e.s.	− 7.4	1.7	−23.5	3.2	−183.1	4.9	283.1
Drink	0.3	0.9	302.7	0.1	8.2	0.8	91.8
Tobacco manufacture	− 4.8	−5.1	107.0	− 2.8	54.5	−2.3	45.5
Coke ovens	− 3.4	−0.5	13.9	− 0.2	42.1	−0.3	57.9
Mineral oil refining	− 4.6	−0.6	14.1	− 0.6	97.3	−0.0	2.7
Chemicals	− 5.8	−0.7	11.4	− 1.8	273.8	1.1	−173.8
Iron & steel	−77.0	−7.4	9.6	− 7.3	98.4	−0.1	1.6
Non-ferrous metals	−21.1	−4.8	22.7	− 3.8	79.9	−1.0	20.1
Mechanical engineering	−114.2	−19.7	17.3	−18.0	91.1	−1.7	8.9
Instrument engineering	−17.4	−5.9	33.9	− 6.1	102.8	0.2	− 2.8
Electrical engineering	−62.8	−34.2	54.5	−23.9	70.0	−10.3	30.0
Shipbuilding	− 7.8	1.7	−21.9	− 0.5	−32.0	2.3	132.0
Motor vehicles	−13.5	−9.4	69.3	− 7.1	17.9	− 7.7	82.1
Aerospace equipment	−18.6	−0.7	3.7	− 2.5	354.0	1.8	−254.0

Vehicles n.e.s.	-10.0	-1.4	14.3	-1.0	72.1	-0.4	27.9
Metal goods	-36.2	-19.2	53.1	-10.6	55.0	-8.7	45.0
Textile fibres	-8.0	-0.8	9.7	-1.1	136.0	0.3	-36.0
Textiles n.e.s.	-118.3	-64.3	54.3	-58.2	90.5	-6.1	9.5
Leather, clothing etc.	-80.9	-57.1	70.6	-58.2	101.9	1.1	-1.9
Bricks	-39.0	-3.7	9.5	-8.3	226.0	4.6	-126.0
Timber & furniture	5.8	1.2	21.3	-0.7	-59.8	2.0	159.8
Paper & board	-11.4	-3.2	28.3	-2.1	64.8	-1.1	35.2
Printing & publishing	-39.1	-12.5	32.0	-13.8	110.1	1.3	-10.1
Rubber	-5.2	-4.3	82.7	-1.3	29.7	-3.0	70.3
Manufactures n.e.s.	2.0	1.5	75.8	1.0	65.9	0.5	34.1
Construction	0.0	20.9	0.0	0.5	0.0	20.4	0.0
Gas	-17.1	3.2	-18.9	-3.3	-102.0	6.5	202.0
Electricity	-29.7	1.8	-6.2	-4.7	-254.3	6.5	354.3
Water	20.4	4.1	20.0	1.9	47.7	2.1	52.3
Transport & communication	-116.9	-1.8	1.5	-19.9	*	18.1	*
Distribution	70.0	93.7	133.9	51.7	55.2	42.0	44.8
Insurance & finance	179.3	101.0	56.3	90.3	89.4	10.7	10.6
Professional, scientific services	660.9	528.8	80.0	449.5	85.0	79.3	15.0
Miscellaneous services	393.6	324.5	82.4	203.7	62.8	120.8	37.2
Public administration etc.	73.1	125.6	171.8	24.2	19.3	101.4	80.7
Total	364.2	932.6	256.1	536.8	57.6	395.6	42.4

Source: DE *Gazette* (various issues).

Note: An asterisk denotes that the base for calculation of a percentage is too small to yield a meaningful result.

sector, where the major part of these changes is concentrated, the industrial effects predominate. An important exception is public administration, for which the major part of the increase in female employment between 1971 and 1978 was associated with the rise in the proportion of female employees.

While there are many other factors affecting the demand for female workers, it is the interplay of occupational change, industrial change and changes in hours of work which is used in this study to generate employment forecasts by sex. Alternative approaches suggest themselves, which acknowledge the influence of relative earnings by occupation and industry, but the opportunity for the development of such models, given the available data, is extremely limited. It will be seen later in this section that this lack of data poses problems even for this simple approach to modelling the sex ratio in employment forecasts.

6.3.1 Occupational trends and female employment

In an examination of information from censuses of population from 1911–71, Hakim (1978) has shown that the increased participation of women in the labour force has been associated with a decrease in the proportion of women in skilled manual jobs and with little change in the proportion of women in professional, technical and managerial occupations. Between 1961 and 1971 the proportions of females in the latter occupational categories did increase marginally, but the majority of women workers have been absorbed into clerical and sales jobs and into semi-skilled and unskilled manual occupations.

Table 6.17 shows the changes that occurred in the sex ratio by occupation and industry order between 1961 and 1971, together with the percentage of females in employment in 1971. Examination of the penultimate row of this table shows that there are certain occupational categories in which women are predominant. In the education professions (WOC 2), health professions (WOC 3), clerical occupations (WOC 8), sales occupations (WOC 9) and personal service occupations (WOC 17), women accounted for more than half of total employment in 1971. With the exception of the education professions and the personal service occupations these occupations also showed larger than average percentage increases in the proportion of females in employment between 1961 and 1971. In the managerial occupations (WOC 1), education professions (WOC 2), engineers and scientists etc. (WOC 6), engineering craftsmen (WOC 11) and other craftsmen with transferable skills (WOC 12) there was no change or even a decline in the proportion of females in employment between 1961 and 1971. The next to last column of this table indicates the proportions of females in employment in different industries. Across industries there is a much more even distribution of female employment than across occupations, although it is clear that the service sector (orders 21–27) employs proportionately more women than the manufacturing sector (orders 3–19). Certain small industry orders in the manufacturing sector employ a large proportion of women: for example, women constituted 70 per cent of employment in the clothing industry (orders 14 plus 15) and 47 per cent in the textile industry (order 13) in 1971. The proportions of females in employment in the manufacturing sector either declined, or rose only slightly, between 1961 and 1971.

Within the body of the table the proportion of females within an occupation is fairly uniform across industries. It is interesting to note that, in miscellaneous services (order 26) and public administration (order 27), the proportion of females has grown in almost every occupation between 1961 and 1971, with the exception of the education professions for miscellaneous services and sales occupations for public administration.

The results support Hakim's findings, and illustrate clearly the need to incorporate information on occupational trends by industry in any projection of employment by sex. Unfortunately, there is a severe lack of data on employment by occupation since that provided by the 1971 *Census of Population*. Information is available on the occupation by industry structure of employees in the *New Earnings Survey* (NES) sample, but the industrial detail is only reliable when the occupational information is aggregated to manual and non-manual categories. Trends in the proportion of non-manual employees in the NES between 1970 and 1978 are shown in Table 6.18. In most industry orders a slow growth is observed in the proportion of employees in non-manual occupations to all employees. Some industries in the manufacturing sector, for example, shipbuilding (order 10), vehicles (order 11) and clothing (orders 14 plus 15) indicate a slight downward trend in this proportion. In the service sector, particularly public administration (order 27), the growth in non-manual employment as a proportion of total employment has been quite rapid.

As the proportion of non-manual jobs in the economy increases,

Table 6.17   Female Employment Proportions by Occupati⊙

Industry order	Warwick Occupational Category (WOC)									
	1	2	3	4	5	6	7	8	9	1⊙
1.	8(4)	100(0)	86(86)	43(11)	27(27)	13(1)	20(−5)	83(8)	44(13)	0(⊙
2.	2(1)	2(2)	59(−3)	19(14)	1(0)	1(0)	19(2)	46(6)	3(3)	0(⊙
3.	8(2)	37(−12)	77(−10)	13(0)	40(3)	6(1)	39(−2)	73(6)	12(8)	0(⊙
4.	4(2)	11(11)	31(−40)	10(−1)	6(4)	2(0)	6(−7)	59(9)	2(0)	0(⊙
5	7(2)	23(23)	39(−14)	16(2)	24(3)	4(1)	25(1)	74(4)	8(4)	0(⊙
6.	2(0)	6(6)	65(11)	15(6)	12(−1)	1(0)	9(−1)	56(2)	3(2)	3(
7.	4(2)	4(−13)	63(0)	21(4)	16(0)	0(0)	5(0)	67(3)	3(−1)	7(⊙
8.	4(0)	10(−4)	35(−10)	33(11)	26(14)	1(0)	13(−2)	76(1)	3(1)	23(
9.	5(2)	32(26)	82(0)	15(−2)	21(1)	1(0)	13(0)	69(1)	11(1)	21(
10.	4(1)	0(0)	44(−8)	23(17)	8(5)	0(0)	5(−6)	51(9)	18(18)	0(⊙
11.	3(0)	5(4)	65(3)	12(−3)	9(0)	0(0)	4(−2)	53(1)	4(1)	4(⊙
12.	6(2)	11(2)	82(−9)	25(1)	24(1)	1(0)	9(0)	75(0)	4(2)	13(
13.	8(2)	51(−2)	95(3)	25(5)	29(9)	3(2)	29(−1)	76(4)	11(6)	9(
14.† 15.	18(2)	76(9)	87(−5)	31(7)	42(−10)	3(−8)	28(−4)	85(5)	28(14)	50(
16.	3(0)	25(25)	45(−21)	11(−8)	25(1)	1(0)	11(1)	66(4)	6(4)	0(
17.	5(0)	0(−32)	79(−8)	33(12)	16(−1)	1(0)	3(−1)	74(6)	8(4)	0(
18.	9(1)	22(0)	83(0)	28(11)	20(4)	1(0)	16(1)	71(6)	14(7)	0(
19.	8(1)	17(9)	79(−1)	25(7)	25(−3)	2(0)	14(0)	77(6)	7(3)	0(
20.	4(1)	0(0)	50(33)	28(4)	14(4)	0(0)	6(2)	72(11)	27(−1)	0(
21.	3(2)	3(3)	65(12)	11(5)	10(8)	1(0)	16(1)	53(14)	47(−3)	0(
22.	8(0)	11(−4)	46(13)	17(8)	33(9)	0(0)	7(4)	56(10)	31(−3)	2(
23.	31(2)	45(3)	34(9)	34(7)	56(3)	3(1)	22(−16)	84(6)	72(6)	2(
24.	10(3)	13(−38)	66(9)	12(4)	27(9)	1(1)	19(−2)	72(12)	34(−5)	0(
25.	27(7)	57(−1)	74(6)	12(5)	57(18)	5(1)	32(7)	85(9)	61(−12)	6(
26.	8(0)	64(−12)	72(12)	25(3)	34(5)	3(2)	21(5)	82(2)	49(3)	0(
27.	17(1)	16(1)	55(15)	34(1)	37(6)	3(1)	14(1)	67(12)	54(−45)	0(
Total	18(0)	55(−3)	71(7)	17(4)	37(8)	2 (0)	17(3)	72(8)	62(5)	7(
Total employed 1971 (thousands)	1,831	679	690	437	317	494	498	3,477	1,280	1⊙

Source: OPCS *Census of Population* (1961 and 1971); occupation by
          industry tables.

Notes: Occupational groups are the Warwick Occupational Categories
         (WOCS). For further details see Appendix C. Percentage point
         changes between 1961 and 1971 are shown in parentheses.
         Supervisors and foremen (WOC 10) are concentrated mainly in
         engineering and transport industries. For other industries they are
         allocated to the occupation which they are supervising.

nd Industry Order: Great Britain 1961–71.

	Warwick Occupational Category (WOC)								Total	Per cent Total employed, 1971 (thousands)
1	12	13	14	15	16	17	18			
(0)	0(0)	19(−17)	51(−5)	15(5)	6(3)	96(7)	28(9)	17(6)	641
(0)	0(0)	0(0)	5(0)	1(0)	0(0)	75(0)	2 0	4(1)	391
(0)	2(0)	57(6)	36(2)	45(0)	2(0)	86(−4)	26(−3)	39(1)	738
(0)	2(0)	0(−3)	0(−3)	2(0)	0(0)	83(3)	5(1)	13(1)	59
(0)	3(1)	64(37)	22(0)	24(0)	2(1)	89(−1)	20(1)	29(1)	459
(0)	2(0)	3(0)	17(2)	9(1)	2(2)	88(0)	3(0)	12(1)	551
(0)	3(0)	7(1)	22(−2)	18(−1)	1(1)	91(−1)	9(2)	17(0)	1,125
(7)	11(−8)	34(2)	37(0)	49(1)	0(0)	93(2)	35(3)	35(1)	145
(5)	13(0)	23(5)	53(3)	55(4)	1(0)	90(−2)	35(4)	38(2)	844
(0)	0(0)	5(3)	2(2)	2(1)	0(0)	84(−2)	4(2)	6(2)	180
(0)	2(0)	7(1)	14(0)	14(1)	1(0)	87(−1)	8(1)	13(0)	789
(−2)	21(−6)	12(−3)	37(0)	47(−7)	2(2)	92(−3)	15(−5)	29(−3)	586
(1)	5(4)	58(−6)	25(4)	44(−9)	0(0)	89(−4)	26(−3)	47(−7)	591
(6)	10(5)	86(0)	64(12)	52(4)	0(0)	77(0)	42(−11)	70(1)	523
(0)	3(2)	37(−4)	17(2)	14(0)	0(0)	86(−1)	9(0)	22(−2)	306
(0)	7(0)	41(0)	21(−4)	15(0)	0(0)	92(−2)	7(−1)	17(0)	302
(2)	11(9)	68(24)	24(0)	32(−6)	1(0)	90(0)	27(0)	32(−1)	612
(3)	26(1)	61(−10)	39(4)	39(−1)	1(1)	91(−1)	26(−3)	37(−1)	325
(0)	0(0)	2(1)	1(1)	0(0)	0(0)	78(−2)	1(0)	6(2)	1,669
(0)	0(0)	3(2)	8(6)	1(0)	0(0)	89(2)	7(6)	17(−7)	362
(0)	1(0)	4(1)	4(3)	5(0)	15(14)	37(11)	13(4)	17(3)	1,564
(1)	3(0)	64(−1)	13(2)	22(5)	20(11)	90(−1)	16(−2)	52(5)	3,016
(2)	1(0)	55(−12)	24(−14)	7(0)	6(4)	86(23)	42(21)	50(10)	952
(0)	1(0)	87(−2)	10(4)	13(5)	18(−9)	86(1)	47(4)	64(4)	2,901
(0)	1(0)	38(2)	22(0)	17(2)	3(1)	80(0)	45(17)	55(1)	2,357
(1)	0(0)	37(11)	13(−3)	5(2)	6(2)	75(8)	5(2)	29(9)	1,572
(0)	2(0)	44(5)	25(2)	21(1)	6(2)	81	14(2)	37(4)	
287	944	1,006	731	4,762	520	2,341	1,145		23,555

Table 6.18   Non-manual Employees as a Percentage of All Employees in *New Earnings Survey:* **Great Britain 1970–78**

Industry order	1970	1971	1972	1973	1974	1975	1976	1977	1978
1.	10.6	10.7	10.4	12.4	12.3	13.4	13.5	13.1	14.2
2.	12.1	11.6	11.1	12.9	13.3	15.5	15.0	15.2	16.5
3.	26.4	27.5	27.5	27.3	27.2	29.7	28.6	28.0	26.4
4.	39.7	35.0	27.3	32.4	29.5	43.0	44.9	42.8	40.9
5.	39.6	38.5	39.5	37.9	38.3	39.7	39.0	39.1	39.4
6.	20.5	20.6	22.6	20.9	22.2	22.5	23.4	21.7	21.5
7.	30.7	31.1	31.7	31.4	31.2	31.8	32.8	31.7	31.9
8.	36.1	35.6	37.1	35.5	38.1	37.3	39.7	40.6	41.6
9.	34.1	34.6	34.0	32.9	32.0	33.6	36.0	34.6	35.4
10.	16.1	18.6	16.9	15.7	13.4	15.2	14.5	15.2	15.8
11.	26.6	27.7	25.4	24.2	24.7	24.0	24.2	24.3	23.9
12.	20.8	21.6	21.2	21.8	22.0	23.5	24.0	23.7	23.1
13.	15.9	16.0	16.8	17.1	17.9	18.2	18.4	17.8	17.5
14.+ 15.	15.5	14.7	13.8	13.5	13.8	15.0	14.4	14.3	13.9
16.	19.5	19.3	21.0	20.5	20.5	23.5	25.1	23.7	22.7
17.	20.1	20.9	20.9	21.6	19.7	24.2	24.2	24.0	24.0
18.	31.3	31.2	31.2	34.4	34.3	34.5	36.5	36.2	36.0
19.	23.5	22.3	22.9	21.4	22.7	23.8	23.1	22.6	23.0
20.	18.3	18.0	18.1	19.7	21.0	23.9	24.3	24.4	24.8
21.	37.9	39.9	42.0	46.6	46.4	48.5	48.2	48.5	50.3
22.	31.1	31.7	32.2	33.8	34.4	33.9	33.7	32.7	36.9
23.	66.8	67.7	67.9	69.0	68.7	71.6	70.4	70.8	70.5
24.	85.3	83.7	84.8	86.5	86.8	88.7	88.6	88.6	89.7
25.	67.3	65.7	66.5	66.0	68.3	71.8	70.1	69.7	70.3
26.	33.1	33.4	32.7	34.5	35.3	39.0	38.4	36.9	37.3
27.	56.0	62.6	64.5	66.8	68.2	72.6	71.0	75.4	76.0
Total	40.2	41.1	41.8	42.5	42.8	45.6	46.5	46.5	47.2

Source: DE *New Earnings Survey* (1970–78).

one would expect this to favour the employment of women. However, as was indicated in Table 6.17, the effect depends upon the industry in which occupational structure is changing and upon the nature of the occupational changes. For example, the growth of non-manual occupations in service sector industries is probably associated with the increase in clerical, sales and personal service occupations, thereby providing a greater proportion of jobs for women than for men. The decline in the proportion of non-manual jobs in the vehicles industry (order 11) probably results from the growth of semi-skilled occupations. The consequences for female employment prospects in this industry are unclear. Without more detailed statistical analysis on the recent changes in occupational structure by industry and sex, much uncertainty surrounds the effect of changing occupational structure on female employment prospects.

This expansion of employment in the occupations in which women are concentrated is mirrored in the changing occupational structure of registered unemployment. Figures 6.2 and 6.3 show the broad occupational changes that have occurred within the registered unemployment and vacancies series between 1973 and 1979. Once again, it can be seen that, in both the manual and non-manual occupational categories, the rise in female registered unemployment is confined mainly to those occupations which contain a high proportion of women. In the three non-manual categories male registered unemployment has remained fairly steady or fallen since the end of 1977, while female unemployment has continued to rise. The registered unemployment of women in clerical and related occupations has nearly quadrupled since December 1972, whereas for males there has been no corresponding increase in unemployment. For manual occupations, it is principally within the unskilled category, general labourers, that female unemployment has risen rapidly compared with male unemployment.

The above information confirms that there is a definite relationship between the growth of female employment and the expansion of those occupations in which women are concentrated. However, this is not the only factor which has led to the growth of female employment. Within certain industries and particularly within the service sector, the rapid rise in female employment has been associated with a rise in part-time employment. While some occupations are linked to part-time working, this effect is considered separately.

6.3.2 Women and part-time jobs

It was shown in Table 6.3 that the major source of employment growth has been the part-time employment of women. The growth of part-time employment is not a general phenomenon, but is restricted to relatively few industries. Table 6.19 shows the proportion of part-time employees to all employees in the NES sample[15], by industry order for the period 1970–78. There are three major

Figure 6.2 Registered Unemployment by Sex and Vacancies: Non-manual Occupational Groups 1972–78   *December 1972 = 100*

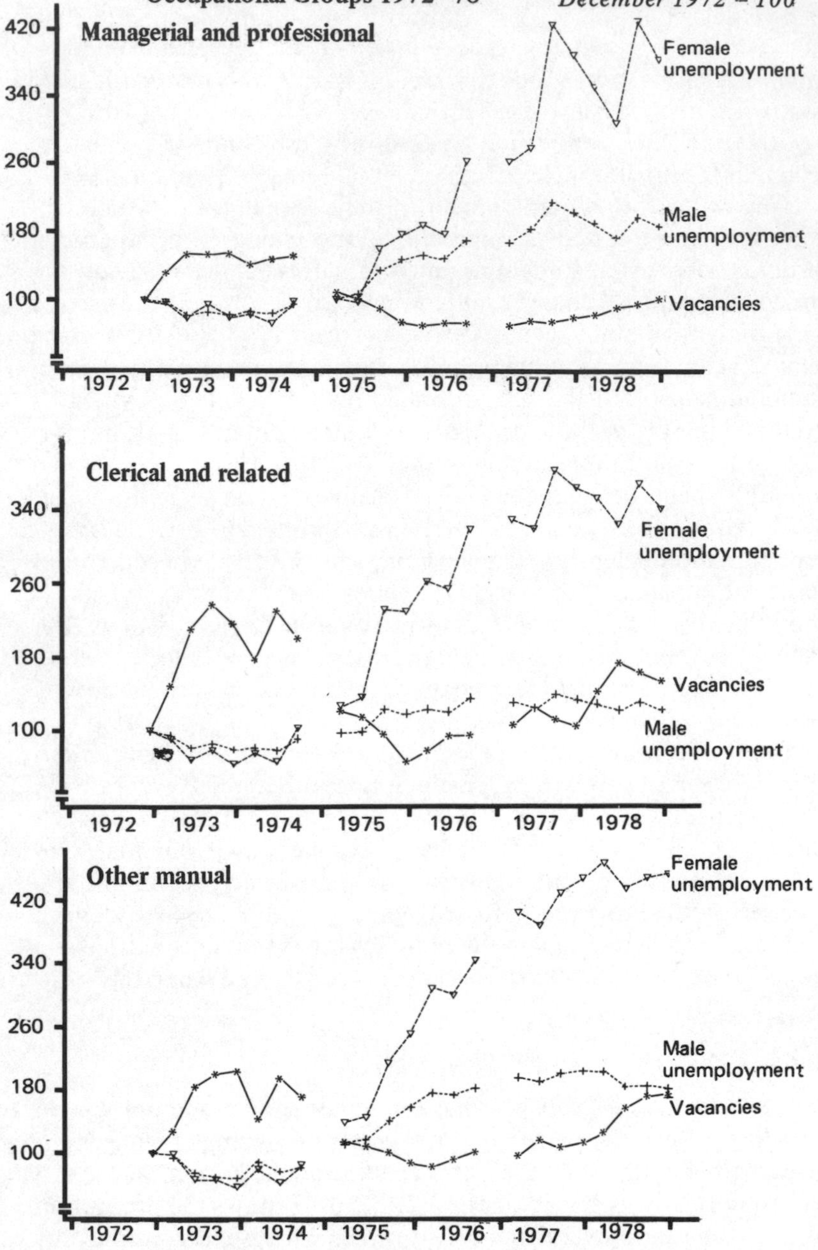

Sources: DE *Gazette* (various issues, 1973–79).

Notes: Unemployment and vacancy statistics for December 1974 and December 1976 were not collected by the Department of Employment.

Figure 6.3 Registered Unemployment by Sex and Vacancies: Manual Occupational Groups 1972–78

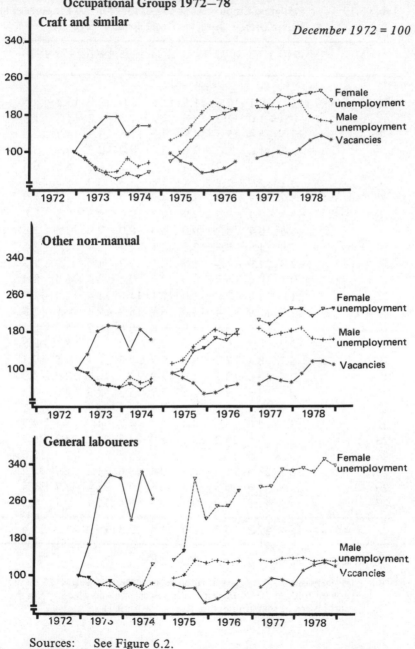

Sources: See Figure 6.2.

Notes: See Figure 6.2.

| Table 6.19 | | Part-time Employees as a Percentage of All Employees in *New Earnings Survey :* Great Britain 1970–78 | | | | | | | |

Industry order	1970	1971	1972	1973	1974	1975	1976	1977	1978
1.	11.3	10.1	10.3	11.6	12.5	12.0	12.9	13.3	13.5
2.	0.9	1.0	1.3	1.3	1.1	1.3	1.2	1.3	1.8
3.	15.5	15.4	15.5	14.9	17.5	15.6	14.9	15.7	15.5
4.	2.8	1.6	1.2	2.6	2.0	3.0	2.3	2.9	3.4
5.	6.2	6.5	5.7	6.4	7.5	6.2	6.0	5.8	6.4
6.	3.1	2.9	2.8	3.4	3.8	3.3	3.0	3.1	3.2
7.	3.9	3.7	3.8	3.8	4.5	4.3	4.0	3.7	4.0
8.	8.4	7.7	8.2	7.9	10.2	10.0	9.8	9.5	7.8
9.	8.6	8.7	8.1	9.0	10.4	10.0	7.9	7.8	7.8
10.	1.8	1.8	2.3	2.1	2.1	2.4	2.4	2.6	2.5
11.	2.3	1.9	1.9	1.9	2.1	1.7	1.6	1.9	1.7
12.	9.1	9.6	8.4	9.0	9.6	9.4	8.4	8.0	8.4
13.	11.8	11.6	9.9	11.0	12.1	11.6	11.4	11.4	11.0
14.+ 15.	12.7	12.9	13.4	14.0	16.9	18.9	17.1	16.8	15.9
16.	4.2	4.4	3.8	4.9	6.0	6.6	6.7	5.7	5.6
17.	5.9	6.8	6.4	6.6	7.3	7.3	6.9	8.1	8.5
18.	8.7	8.4	7.7	8.5	9.7	9.3	10.1	9.5	10.1
19.	9.7	10.6	10.1	11.0	12.9	12.6	10.9	10.7	9.9
20.	2.5	2.2	2.3	2.5	2.9	3.3	3.5	3.0	3.3
21.	3.0	3.2	3.6	3.9	5.3	4.7	4.7	4.6	4.1
22.	3.7	4.0	3.9	4.4	4.4	4.7	4.7	5.1	4.7
23.	22.3	23.5	24.2	25.7	27.2	24.5	24.2	24.2	24.7
24.	13.2	11.5	12.2	11.8	12.8	13.8	13.5	12.9	12.5
25.	26.3	28.5	29.0	30.4	30.4	28.6	31.4	32.7	33.2
26.	25.6	27.4	29.5	30.3	30.6	29.8	31.4	32.7	31.6
27.	14.2	11.3	9.9	9.2	9.5	9.4	11.1	9.1	9.3
Total	12.4	12.8	13.3	14.0	14.4	13.8	15.0	15.2	15.4

Source: DE *New Earnings Survey* (1970–78).

Note: A part-time employee is defined as an employee expected to work not more than 30 hours, excluding overtime and mealbreaks. For employees in teaching occupations the limit is 25 hours.

features to this table. First, the service industries contain a much higher proportion of part-time employees than the rest of industry and the proportion of part-timers has been growing significantly in this sector. Second, it appears that, in some industry orders, the part-time proportions are cyclically sensitive, rising to a peak in 1974. This is most evident in the food, drink and tobacco industry (order 3), the engineering sector (orders 7–12), textiles (order 13), clothing (orders 14 and 15), other manufacturing (order 19) and distribution (order 23). Finally, for most of the industries in which women are concentrated, the proportion of part-timers has been displaying an upward trend. This trend growth in part-time jobs, together with any cyclical influences upon the trend, will affect the opportunities for female employment, for women take the majority of part-time jobs. To the extent that the growth in part-time employment is demand-determined, then any projection of female employment opportunities should take account of these trends.

6.3.3 Projecting employment by sex

This subsection describes the model that has been developed for projecting the sex ratio within the forecasts of industry employment. After a brief description of the model there follows an analysis of the derived female employment projection.

From the information presented in the previous two sections, it is clear that changes in female employment are closely related to the changing occupational structure of industrial employment and the trends and variations in part-time employment. To incorporate the maximum industrial detail given limited consistent data, the estimation of relationships between female employment, non-manual employment and part-time employment[16] had to be restricted to the period 1971–76 and to very simple linear and non-linear regression equations. The industrial forecasts of employees in employment (Census of Employment definition), self-employed and registered unemployment described in Chapter 4 were used as inputs to the model. The forecast of registered unemployment was used to generate a part-time employment proportion which, when combined with an exogenous estimate of the non-manual employment proportion, yielded a forecast of the proportion of female employers to total employees. In this fashion the cyclical sensitivity of part-time employees in employment influences the sex composition of employees. The exogenous estimate of non-manual employees in employment is consistent with that used in the preparation of the occupational projection described in Chapter 4. Self-employment is disaggregated by sex using simple time-trend relationships.

The relationship between part-time working and unemployment is not strong but for 9 out of the 40 industries it is statistically significant. In all but four industry groups the relationship is negative. Presumably this represents a cost-saving approach adopted by employers in dealing with the cyclical adjustment of the labour force by altering the level of part-time employment. The effect is most marked in vehicles n.e.s. and public administration. Underlying the majority of these relationships is a significant upward trend, particularly in mechanical engineering, electrical engineering, metal goods, printing and publishing, distribution and miscellaneous services.

A priori, one would expect a positive relation between the non-manual proportions and the female employee ratio. In fact only four industries record a significant relationship, two of which have negative coefficients. Moreover, in a considerable number of industries, principally in the manufacturing sector, the coefficient on this variable is insignificant and negative. As was indicated earlier, this is probably a reflection of different occupational trends within the manual and non-manual categories having a varying impact upon female employment. Similarly, only seven industries have significant coefficients on the part-time variable and five industries have the 'wrong' sign (i.e. negative) on this coefficient, the most important of these being professional and scientific services. Nonetheless, these simple equations have been used to project, first, the part-time proportion and second, the female employment ratio, initially to 1978 and then to 1985 for the standard view. Comparing the projected sex ratios by industry for 1978 with those derived from the DE's provisional employment estimates, it was found that in only thirteen industry groups was the projected sex ratio more than half a percentage point different from the estimated ratio. For most of the industry groups involved, female employment is very low. The only significant exception was insurance and finance, in which the projected 1978 sex ratio was 2.1 percentage points below the estimate. For these thirteen industries a minor adjustment factor was incorporated into the model to correct for this under– or over–prediction.

Finally, consideration is given to the implications of the projected changing industrial structure of employment and the projected change in the female sex ratio within each industry for future levels of female employment.

Table 6.20 shows the employment projection for 1985 by sex and in industrial detail. Table 6.21 relates this 1985 projection to the DE's provisional estimate of employment in 1978. As in Table 6.16, the change in female employment is broken down into an industrial component (assuming a constant 1978 sex ratio for each industry) and a component which reflects changes in the sex ratio (assuming 1985 levels of employment throughout). Once again, this analysis shows that, in the primary and manufacturing sectors, it is principally the decline in industrial employment which has the major impact upon female employment. In many of these industries this decline is exacerbated by a deteriorating ratio of female to male employment. This is a result of the higher unemployment rate projected for 1985, resulting in a contraction or moderation in the rate of growth of part-time jobs. The effect is felt most severely in electrical engineering, motor vehicles and textiles n.e.s. Within most of the manufacturing industries the decline in female employment is smaller than the decline in male employment, with the important exception of the leather and clothing industry. This reflects the high proportion of women working in this industry.

The construction industry records a modest increase of 29 thousand in female employment, principally due to the improvement in the projected proportion of women in the industry.

The public utilities show little overall change in female employment, even though male employment declines by 61 thousand. The same effect is forecast for transport and communication for which the decline in female employment is only about 12 per cent of the overall employment decline. Within distribution the decline of 195 thousand in employment is expected to consist of 83 thousand women. Insurance and finance is expected to show a growth in employment of 169 thousand between 1978 and 1985, but only 40 thousand of this increase provides jobs for women and the proportion of women employed in this industry order declines. This may well be an underestimate of female employment growth, given the poor performance of the estimating equations in the industry described earlier in the section. The growth in employment in the remaining industry orders: professional, scientific services, miscellaneous services and public administration yields an additional 672 thousand jobs between 1978 and 1985. Female employment in these industries is expected to grow by 677 thousand in the same period.

Table 6.20 Industrial Employment by Sex: United Kingdom 1985

	Projected proportions (%)				Employment projection by sex (thousands)			
	Non-manual (1)	Part-time (2)	Female employees	Female self-employed	Female employees	Male employees	Female self-employed	Male self-employed
Agriculture	14.3	21.0	22.3	16.3	70.6	245.9	37.0	189.6
Coal mining	9.7	1.6	3.7	0.0	8.1	208.8	0.0	0.0
Oil, natural gas, mining n.e.s.	25.0	3.5	10.9	0.0	4.1	33.5	0.0	0.9
Cereal processing	17.0	20.9	37.5	25.1	56.1	93.7	1.0	3.0
Food processing n.e.s.	20.2	22.7	42.0	0.0	158.0	218.3	0.0	2.9
Drink	29.9	3.8	24.9	0.0	28.3	85.3	0.0	0.0
Tobacco manufacture	24.3	4.4	47.9	0.0	12.9	14.0	0.0	0.0
Coke ovens	16.0	0.6	2.1	0.0	0.2	10.1	0.0	0.0
Mineral oil refining	35.5	3.0	13.6	0.0	2.9	18.3	0.0	0.0
Chemicals	40.5	9.3	28.7	0.0	104.9	260.8	0.0	0.0
Iron & steel	27.0	2.7	9.4	0.0	25.9	250.4	0.0	0.9
Non-ferrous metals	26.4	6.1	16.7	0.0	19.2	95.3	0.0	0.0
Mechanical engineering	35.2	6.5	15.8	6.7	113.4	603.0	1.3	18.2
Instrument engineering	42.8	10.3	33.8	0.0	32.3	63.1	0.0	1.0
Electrical engineering	36.5	8.9	34.8	35.6	234.1	439.3	1.6	2.8
Shipbuilding	27.1	3.0	8.8	0.0	11.9	122.8	0.0	2.1
Motor vehicles	23.6	1.6	9.8	0.0	45.7	418.6	0.0	0.5
Aerospace equipment	51.5	2.2	15.1	0.0	18.7	105.4	0.0	0.0
Vehicles n.e.s.	20.6	1.5	8.9	0.0	3.8	39.2	0.0	0.0

Metal goods	26.8	10.0	26.5	8.4	106.7	295.9	1.6	18.0
Textile fibres	19.8	3.1	12.2	0.0	3.0	21.7	0.0	0.0
Textiles n.e.s.	20.0	12.0	45.3	40.0	151.7	183.2	1.8	2.8
Leather,clothing etc.	16.4	17.4	72.7	53.9	240.4	90.3	7.7	6.6
Bricks	26.8	7.9	24.7	0.0	64.6	196.7	0.0	3.6
Timber & furniture	26.9	8.9	20.4	1.8	53.2	208.1	1.0	55.0
Paper & board	25.6	3.8	15.3	0.0	7.7	42.5	0.0	0.0
Printing & publishing	39.6	16.9	34.5	39.3	145.4	275.6	6.0	9.3
Rubber	31.1	4.9	19.6	0.0	18.8	77.0	0.0	0.0
Manufactures n.e.s.	26.4	16.4	41.8	66.0	77.6	108.1	2.6	1.4
Construction	27.3	6.0	9.7	0.5	133.6	1248.8	1.7	313.3
Gas	65.7	6.9	32.1	0.0	27.4	57.8	0.0	0.0
Electricity	46.1	6.1	22.6	0.0	33.9	116.3	0.0	0.0
Water	52.0	2.9	15.7	0.0	8.5	45.6	0.0	0.0
Transport & communication	33.6	6.8	19.7	2.7	230.2	936.5	3.0	106.3
Distribution	74.6	44.6	56.8	33.4	1464.0	1112.6	128.7	257.0
Insurance & finance	91.3	18.8	47.3	51.6	620.6	692.1	31.0	29.0
Professional, scientific services	72.1	39.8	71.6	16.7	2837.0	1124.8	30.7	152.7
Miscellaneous services	39.7	55.4	62.8	39.7	1838.0	1040.2	132.9	202.1
Public administration etc.	81.1	10.3	42.1	0.0	735.7	1299.2	0.0	0.0
Total					9749.1	12,498.8	389.7	1378.9

Source: 1985 – standard view.

Notes: (1) *Census of Production* definition.
           (2) *Census of Employment* definition.

Table 6.21 Composition of Industrial Employment Changes for Women: United Kingdom 1978–85

	Total employment change	Female employment change		Breakdown of female employment change Due to industry		Due to sex ratio	
	(thousands)	(thousands)	% of total change	(thousands)	% of female employment change	(thousands)	% of female employment change
Agriculture	−111.5	−21.9	19.6	−22.9	104.5	1.0	−4.5
Coal mining	−76.4	−1.8	2.4	−2.6	*	0.8	*
Oil, natural gas, mining n.e.s.	−13.1	−0.6	4.5	−1.2	*	0.6	*
Cereal processing	−46.4	19.0	40.9	−17.8	93.6	−1.2	6.4
Food processing n.e.s.	−6.2	−11.2	180.4	−2.7	24.1	−8.5	75.9
Drink	−10.2	1.9	18.4	2.6	139.1	−0.7	−39.1
Tobacco manufacture	−9.8	−6.2	63.1	−5.1	82.3	−1.1	17.7
Coke ovens	0.0	−0.1	0.0	0.0	0.0	−0.1	0.0
Mineral oil refining	−4.9	−0.7	13.8	−0.7	98.8	−0.0	1.2
Chemicals	−67.0	−17.7	26.4	−18.6	105.2	0.9	−5.2
Iron & steel	−68.7	−6.7	9.7	−6.5	97.2	−0.2	2.8
Non-ferrous metals	0.3	−0.6	−188.7	0.1	−9.2	−0.6	109.2
Mechanical engineering	−211.5	−31.6	15.0	−33.4	105.5	1.7	−5.5
Instrument engineering	−54.2	−21.0	38.8	−19.2	91.2	−1.8	8.8
Electrical engineering	−75.0	−41.1	54.9	−27.6	67.0	−13.6	33.0
Shipbuilding	−49.2	−1.9	3.9	−3.7	*	1.8	*
Motor vehicles	−54.9	−15.4	28.1	−6.4	41.5	−9.0	58.5
Aerospace equipment	−75.0	−9.3	12.4	−10.5	113.7	1.3	−13.7

Vehicles n.e.s.	−13.9	−1.7	11.9	−1.3	80.4	−0.3	19.6
Metal goods	−132.2	−42.6	32.2	−37.6	88.4	−4.9	11.6
Textile fibres	−14.2	−2.4	17.0	−2.0	81.8	−0.4	18.2
Textile n.e.s.	−122.4	−67.1	54.8	−58.5	87.3	−8.5	12.7
Leather, clothing etc.	−94.0	−67.8	72.1	−67.9	100.2	0.1	−0.2
Bricks	−7.2	1.8	−24.5	−1.7	−96.7	3.5	196.7
Timber & furniture	5.1	1.7	33.5	−0.3	−18.5	2.0	118.5
Paper & board	−12.6	−2.7	21.4	−2.1	77.4	−0.6	22.6
Printing & publishing	−54.9	−18.1	32.9	−19.2	106.0	1.1	−6.0
Rubber	−20.9	−6.8	32.4	−4.6	67.6	−2.2	32.4
Manufactures n.e.s.	−33.3	−16.5	49.7	−14.3	86.7	−2.2	13.3
Construction	−103.6	29.1	28.1	9.1	31.4	20.0	68.6
Gas	−17.7	1.0	−5.9	−4.5	*	5.6	*
Electricity	−31.8	−1.1	3.5	−6.1	*	5.0	*
Water	−11.5	0.1	−1.0	−1.5	—	1.6	1405.4
Transport & communication	−246.0	−29.1	11.8	−49.3	169.4	20.2	−69.4
Distribution	−195.3	−82.8	42.4	−101.7	122.8	18.9	−22.8
Insurance & finance	168.8	39.7	23.5	83.6	210.6	−43.9	−110.6
Professional, scientific services	305.8	318.6	104.2	202.9	63.7	115.6	36.3
Miscellaneous services	281.4	277.7	98.7	153.7	55.3	124.0	44.7
Public administration etc.	84.6	81.1	95.9	30.8	38.0	50.3	62.0
Total	−971.9	207.2	−21.3	−68.7	−33.1	276.2	133.1

Notes: See Table 6.16.

Two-fifths of this increase is associated with the rise in the sex ratio, the remainder is derived from the overall growth in employment in these industries. Obviously, this does not imply that all *new* jobs created in these industries between 1978 and 1985 will fall to women, but it does indicate that the *net* gain in employment favours women.

In summary, this attempt to model female employment prospects indicates that the decline of just over 970 thousand jobs between 1978 and 1985 can be broken down into a decline in male employment of 1.2 million and an increase in female employment of about 200 thousand. The increase in female employment is composed of a decline of 540 thousand in all industries except construction, insurance and finance, professional, scientific services, miscellaneous services and public administration which, on the basis of past relationships, are expected to yield an additional 746 thousand jobs for women. Whether women will supply this labour and the effect of these changes on male and female unemployment rates are issues which are discussed in the next section.

6.4 Fair Shares of Unemployment

This section brings together the labour force projection by sex, discussed in the second section, with the employment projections by sex which are discussed in the previous section. Projections of both total unemployment (registered plus unregistered) and registered unemployment are presented for the simulations of the economy discussed in Chapter 3. This information provides an overall assessment of the likely trends in female unemployment. Further information on the regional distribution of female employment and unemployment has been provided in Chapter 5.

In section 6.2 it was argued that female labour force participation will not grow as rapidly as has been projected by the Department of Employment. Although the DE projection does not take explicit account of the effect of the rise in women's real earnings on the labour force participation of married women, it is anticipated that their earnings will not grow as rapidly as they have grown relative to men's real earnings over the last six years. It appears that the effect of the existing equal pay legislation has produced a new stable differential between men's and women's real earnings. Furthermore, the projected increases in fertility could suppress the rate of increase of labour force participation of married women in the 20–34 year age groups, but this might simply result in a slight change in the age structure of the female labour force as employers seek to hire older women to cover for women taking maternity leave. More important, though, could be the effect of the sustained high levels of unemployment which are embodied in the medium-term projections, compared with the low levels of unemployment prevailing throughout the period upon which the DE based their projection of female labour force participation rates. There is a substantial amount of evidence to indicate that female labour force participation is discouraged during periods of high unemployment.

In the medium-term, female employment will continue to grow fairly rapidly as a result of the continued expansion of service sector employment, the trend towards more part-time working and the changing occupational structure of employment in favour of occupations which have traditionally absorbed women. In the primary and manufacturing sectors, female employment is expected to decline by over 400 thousand jobs, compared with a decline in male employment in these sectors of more than 1 million jobs. In construction and the service sector industries, male employment is expected to decline by about 200 thousand, whereas female employment is expected to grow by 630 thousand. The major growth areas for female employment are professional and scientific services, which include the national health service, private health services and education, and miscellaneous services, which include recreation and tourist industries, catering, cleaning and community service industries.

By bringing together the labour force projection with the employment projection, a very tentative forecast of the sex composition of the unemployed has been made. Section 6.2 discussed the empirical evidence relating to the cyclical sensitivity of the female labour force. However, it is not only the female labour force which is cyclically sensitive, but also the proportion of total unemployment which is registered. Therefore, to derive registered unemployment, proportions for males and females need to be forecast. As was discussed in Chapter 3, the average propensity to register as unemployed has been held at its estimated 1978 level through to 1985. While there is some evidence to suggest that the *marginal* propensity to register rises as total unemployment increases, the projected high levels of unemployment will probably discourage increased registration rates. The average registration propensity for males is assumed to be 78 per cent in 1985. For females the rate is set at 58 per cent. The aggregate registration rate is 71 per cent.

Table 6.22 shows the projected total unemployment rates for 1985 by sex for the standard view and the structural change simulation, compared with the estimated 1978 total unemployment rates by sex. The bottom half of the table shows the projected changes in registered unemployment by sex. The doubling of the total unemployment rate between 1978 and 1985 in the standard view masks the larger increase in male unemployment. Female unemployment is not expected to rise to such an extent, given the projected increase in female employment. Male registered unemployment rises from 7 per cent in 1978 to 16 per cent in 1985. Female registered unemployment increases from 4 per cent to 6 per cent. The structural

Table 6.22 Unemployment Rates by Sex: United Kingdom 1978 and 1985

Per cent

	1978	1985 Standard view	Structural simulation
Total unemployment rate	8	15	13
Male total unemployment rate	8	18	17
Female total unemployment rate	7	9	8
Females in total unemployment	36	25	24
Registered unemployment rate	6	14	12
Male registered unemployment rate	7	16	15
Female registered unemployment rate	4	6	5
Females in registered unemployment	29	20	19

Sources: 1978: DE *Gazette* (July 1978); MRG estimates of unregistered unemployment.

simulation yields similar trends in unemployment by sex, although the forecast rates of unemployment are about one percentage point lower.

Inevitably, a comparison must be made between employment prospects for women and for men. Unemployment is expected to increase considerably over the next six years, but the increase in unemployment will be predominantly that of males. One consequence of this increasing disparity between male and female unemployment rates could be an increase in the numbers of men taking jobs which have traditionally gone to women. Over the next seven years, this is unlikely to have much effect upon the sex ratio in those occupations and industries which require substantial training, for example, the health occupations. It is possible that more men will obtain part-time work in personal service occupations, such as catering and cleaning, which are usually held by women. On balance, though, it is unlikely that the decline in full-time male employment in the manufacturing sector will be offset to much extent by inroads into those areas of employment traditionally held by women.

If the forecast disparity between male and female unemployment is realised, it will generate calls for a more equitable distribution of unemployment. Already, suggestions have been made to the MSC (Manpower Society, 1979) that married women be paid to stay at home or receive a lower tax allowance for working. However, as has been stressed throughout this chapter, unemployment statistics, particularly registered unemployment statistics, are no guide to policy formulation. As was suggested in Chapter 3, with such high levels of unemployment many persons will simply not bother to seek employment. The majority of such discouraged workers are likely to be married women. In a sense, they will simply 'disappear' from the labour force. Registered unemployment statistics cannot, therefore, be relied upon to indicate the extent of the welfare loss associated with low levels of labour demand. Furthermore, unemployment changes represent changes that are occurring at the margin of the labour force. This focus on unemployment draws attention away from the problems associated with the changing structure of employment. Women will probably continue to have lower rates of unemployment than men because they take more of the lower paid, lower status jobs with limited career prospects. Many women can only work part-time because of their role as providers of unpaid domestic and child care services. As the service sector of the economy expands, together with the occupations which are generally associated with female employment, the scope for further employment in lower paid, low status, part-time jobs increases. While this favours female employment, it cannot really be said to constitute a more equitable distribution of employment opportunity.

The process of occupational segregation begins at an early age. Women are under-represented in higher education, particularly in those institutions which can provide the engineers, scientists and other technologists equipped with the skills required for future development. Women also form a very small proportion of persons training as technicians and skilled workers and are under-represented in many supervisory and managerial positions. However, without a better redistribution within society and within the family of the domestic and child care responsibilities shouldered by most women, the return from an investment in training and education by women cannot be fully realised.

This chapter began by describing the various legislative influences that could have an impact upon women's employment prospects in the medium term. Viewed within the context of a general rise in unemployment, particularly of male unemployment, there exists the possibility that this legislation will be viewed as too favourable to women. Such a view is shortsighted, for the case for legislative action on equal opportunity for women rests not upon an analysis of unemployment, but upon the structure of female employment and the provision of education and training for women to enable them to enter non-traditional areas of employment. Given the degree of occupational segregation which exists within the labour market, the present legislation will probably remain virtually ineffective in creating a more equitable distribution of employment opportunities for women. What is required is a more embracing policy, linking affirmative action on the provision of such education and training for women with a commitment to increase the provision of child care and education for the children of mothers who want to work. Such a policy will not produce a more balanced distribution of registered unemployment between the sexes, but it is a necessary precondition for the creation of a more balanced life-time distribution of employment opportunity.

Notes

1 Equal Pay Act (1970), Chapter 41, section 1(4–5).

2 Sex Discrimination Act (1975), Chapter 65, section 1(1).

3 Employment Protection Act (1975), Chapter 71, section 48(1).

4 Research on the impact of this legislation is presently being conducted under the auspices of the Joint Panel on Equal Opportunities established by the Equal Opportunities Commission and Social Science Research Council in December, 1977.

5 As the figures relate only to women in their first marriage, the effect of the increase in divorce rates, subsequent remarriage rates, and thus of births to remarried women is excluded. However, the divorce rate for women in the 25–34 year age group stood at approximately 2 per cent of married men in this age group in 1977. Hence, the effect of excluding this group on the information presented in Table 6.5 is minimal.

6 The total period fertility rate for a particular year measures the average number of liveborn children per women that would result if women survived to the end of their reproductive period and throughout this period were subject to the age-specific fertility rates of that year.

7 The proportions for 1977–1991 are derived from the 1977–based total population projection for England and Wales.

8 Reproduced in *Services for Young Children with Working Mothers* (Central Policy Review Staff, 1978) pp. 71–80.

9 Variables measuring consumer durable ownership by households and access to the telephone system were introduced into the regression equations discussed in section 6.2.1 in terms of current and lagged values but these variables did not show any statistically significant relationship with the labour force participation of married women. However, these equations were only estimated for the period 1969–73.

10 The information presented in Table 6.10 is derived from the Family Expenditure Survey tapes. This information is only available three years following publication of FES results by the DE.

11 This variable includes the income accruing to all household members from investments, pensions and other social security benefits, plus income from sub-letting, imputed rent-free income and imputed income from owner occupation.

12 The adjustment was made by comparing the results of the 1975 EEC Labour Force Survey (SOEC 1976) with the 1975 labour force participation rates given in the DE *Gazette* (June 1977). The derived adjustment factors were applied in an additive fashion to the 1977 EEC Labour Force Survey.

13 Berg and Dalton estimate a logarithmic form of the relationship between female activity rates and unemployment, as do Corry and Roberts in both their 1970 and 1974 papers. All authors find the same elasticity between female activity and unemployment, approximately −0.03 to −0.04. Translated into linear terms, this implies that a 1 percentage point increase in unemployment would result in a 0.75 to 1 percentage point reduction in female activity (calculated at the means).

14 The 39 industries comprise SAMs 1–34 and industry orders 22–27. The lack of detailed information on the proportion of non-manual occupations in the service sector necessitated the aggregation to industry orders.

15 From 1975 onwards, selection of the sample of employees for the NES was related to PAYE information. This new procedure excludes persons whose earnings are below a certain low level. Examinations of the data shows that this could have imparted a small downward bias to the proportion of part-time female employees in industry orders 1, 23, 25 and 26 in the NES sample.

16 To obtain the fullest industrial detail on part-time employment, proportions derived from the *Census of Employment, 1971–76,* were utilised. At the industry order level, there is a very high correlation between these proportions and those listed in Table 6.19.

References

Berg, S.V. and T.R. Dalton (1977). 'United Kingdom labour force activity rates : Unemployment and real wages'. *Applied Economics,* 9, no. 3, 265–70.

Bowen, W.G. and T.A. Finegan (1969). *The Economics of Labor Force Participation.* Princeton: Princeton University Press.

Cain, G. (1966). *Married Women in the Labor Force.* Chicago: Chicago University Press.

Central Policy Review Staff (1978). *Services for Young Children with Working Mothers.* London: HMSO.

Corry, B.A. and J.A. Roberts (1970). 'Activity Rates and Unemployment : The Experience of the United Kingdom 1951–1966'. *Applied Economics,* 2, no. 3, 179–201.

——(1974). 'Activity Rates and Unemployment. The UK Experience : some further results'. *Applied Economics,* 6, no. 1, 1–21.

Easterlin, R.A. (1978). 'Fertility and Female Labor Force Participation in the United States : Recent Changes and Future Prospects'. Paper prepared for the International Union for the Scientific Study of Population Conference, Helsinki. (mimeographed)

Elias, D.P.B. (1980).' A Time-Series Analysis of the Labour Force Participation of Married Women in the UK, 1968–1975'. MRG Discussion
Paper, University of Warwick. (mimeographed)

Employment Protection Act (1975). c. 71.

Equal Pay Act (1970). c. 41.

Greenhalgh, C. (1977). 'A Labour Supply Function for Married Women in
Great Britain'. *Economica,* 44, no. 175, 249–65.

Grice, J.W. (1978). 'A Time Series Model for the Labour Supply'. Treasury
Working Paper AP(78) 11. (mimeographed)

Hakim, C (1978). 'Sexual divisions within the labour force : occupational
segregation'. Department of Employment *Gazette,* November,
1,264–68.

Leete, R. (1979). 'New Directions in Family Life'. *Population Trends,* no.
15, 4–9.

McNabb, R. (1977). 'The Labour Force Participation of Married Women'.
The Manchester School, 45, no.3, 221–35.

Manpower Society, The (1979). 'Comment on "MSC Review and Plan
1978" '. May. (mimeographed)

Mincer, J, (1962). 'Labor Force Participation of Married Women', in
Aspects of Labor Economics : A Conference of the Universities.
National Bureau of Economic Research Princeton : Princeton
University Press.

Office of Population Censuses and Surveys (1978). *1977 Demographic Review,* DR1. London: HMSO.

——(1978a). General Household Survey, 1976. London: HMSO.

Sex Discrimination Act (1975). c. 65.

Statistical Office of the European Communities (1976). *Labour Force Sample Survey, 1975.* Luxembourg.

——(1978). *Labour Force Sample Survey, 1977.* Luxembourg.

Wachter, M.L. (1972). 'A Labor Supply Model for Secondary Workers'.
Review of Economics and Statistics, 54, no. 2, 141–50.

——(1977). 'Intermediate Swings in Labor Force Participation', in Okun,
A.M. and G.L. Perry (eds.). *Brookings Papers on Economic Activity.*
2, 545–74.

7 Skilled Labour in Engineering and Construction

G. BRISCOE, P.A. DUTTON AND R.M. LINDLEY

7.1 Introduction

Prospects for the two major sectors discussed in this chapter provide something of a contrast. Employment in engineering is expected to fall substantially over the medium-term whereas in construction it is likely to rise. Both industries frequently claim that government attempts to regulate the economy impinge too much upon their activities, undermining product demand, making planning almost impossible and generally dissipating business confidence. Whether this exacerbates the cyclical fluctuations to which investment industries are in any case prone or simply slows down their average rates of growth or leads to both problems, the uncertainties about future demand in engineering and construction are usually considerable. These uncertainties and the relatively long lead-times required in training people for skilled trades combine to produce the classic situation with which 'active manpower policy' is intended to cope. Periodic labour shortages apparently occur, allegedly widespread and severely restricting the potential for higher output and employment.

On the face of it, however, there are some puzzling aspects to this situation. For more than a decade the employment of skilled and other manual workers in both engineering and construction has been falling. There is little evidence to suggest that this reflects a generally applicable labour supply constraint. One would expect cyclical manpower shortages to add *some* momentum to the introduction of labour-saving technologies but the way in which capital goods producing industries are organised does not make for a close relationship between the state of the labour market and the pattern of investment. Reports of labour shortages have persisted even as high levels of unemployment among skilled workers have emerged and government has intervened to stem the fall in industrial training.

240

As regards the narrowing of earnings differentials between crafts-men and less skilled workers, this may be seen either as an explana-tion of why shortages have continued or as grounds for doubting the reliability of the information about shortages. The conventional wisdom favours the first explanation but the problems of interpret-ing information about labour supply problems reported by firms suggest that the existence of inadequate differentials is only one con-tributory factor. The narrowing of differentials is normally attribut-ed to the effects of incomes policies imposed upon firms as a result of national negotiation between government, trade unions and, to a lesser extent, employers. On the other hand, the way in which these policies have operated in a period of high inflation suggests that had firms been particularly concerned to deal with the shortages of craftsmen by maintaining or even increasing differentials, then they had more scope for doing so than is generally appreciated. In fact, in engineering at least, it is in keeping with the practice of the earlier part of the post-war period that firms should not use relative earn-ings as a major device to control supply. This is largely because they are not sufficiently in control of the wage bargaining framework to ensure that they can actually carry through a policy of increasing the pay of craftsmen without leading to compensating changes for other employees, which would frustrate the object of the initial in-crease.

Under these circumstances, a study of the decision-making pro-cesses that give rise to the recruitment of craftsmen, the upgrading of semi-skilled employees and the recruitment of apprentices sheds considerable light on the extent to which the operation of the labour market is circumscribed by institutional factors. The conclusions from a review of this evidence for engineering are summarised be-low.[1]

(i)   If firms forecast their demands for craftsmen at all, it is rarely sufficiently far ahead for them to adjust the recruitment of appren-tices in accordance with expectations about demand conditions in the early part of the period when those apprentices begin to work as fully trained craftsmen.

(ii)   Current labour shortages appear to play a major role in deter-mining levels of apprentice recruitment. The ability of apprentices to contribute to production itself (depending on the ar-rangements for training) and the fact that a combination of apparently tight labour markets and high productive activity tends to create an environment in which training is seen as more profitable encourages recruitment. Moreover, at such times cash flow problems are less likely to be a constraint upon the rather vulnerable manpower budget.

(iii)   Trade union restrictions òn apprentice recruitment, upgrading of adult workers and the recruitment of dilutees do operate in certain localities but are not generally a significant constraint upon managements' prerogatives in this area.

(iv)   Upgrading occurs infrequently in response to short-run problems of labour supply largely because of a wage-structure somewhat favourable to semi-skilled workers (and a cause of downward occupational mobility among skilled workers) and the inability of training systems to train semi-skilled workers for craft jobs in the time required.

(v)   The internal supply of skilled workers, therefore, appears to be largely determined by the training of apprentices and the scope for increasing the supply in the short-run through upgrading is rather limited.

(vi)   Within engineering, wage structures produced by collective bargaining under successive incomes policies have probably led to a misallocation of the existing stock of skilled labour. This reflects not only the problem of intra-plant differentials but, probably more important, also the existence of inter-plant or inter-industrial differentials which are determined mainly by features of product markets rather than labour markets (and result in movement from skilled employment in one part of engineering to semi-skilled employment in another part).

(vii)   Differentials between engineering and other industries suggest that for a large part of the last decade or so engineering industries, except motor vehicles, paid their skilled and semi-skilled workers little more than average for these occupations and significantly less than did certain other manufacturing industries.

Not all the above conclusions will apply to construction. There has been much less analysis of this industry's labour market than that of engineering. However, one of the main differences between the two is the more competitive structure of major parts of construction and an apparently more aggressive use of the wage system by firms in search of skilled labour. The nature of its product market clearly affects the organisation of both employers and trade unions and the low degree of concentration and unionisation leads to a much greater use of the external labour market in satisfying the demand for skilled workers. At the same time the determinants of apprentice recruitment are similar to the factors found to be dominant in the case of engineering.[2]

Thus, there would seem to be some potentially very interesting contrasts between the ways in which policy might be designed to influence behaviour in these two labour markets and in the sorts of empirical models which could be constructed to represent them.

It is not difficult to see why labour shortages should arise under the situation described above (particularly for engineering) even against the background of a long-term decline in employment opportunities for craftsmen as already noted. Chapter 9 discusses the general questions raised by the way in which manpower policy has evolved during the 1960s and 1970s. One of the problems of the last five years has been to devise policies which discriminate sufficiently between those short-term and medium-term developments in the labour market which they are designed to influence. The purpose of the present chapter is to identify medium-term trends in the demand for craftsmen and to consider the fragments of evidence on the supply side. Our work on engineering and construction is at different stages and space does not allow us to discuss in detail the models used in this exercise or those being developed for implementation in future. The somewhat greater attention paid to contruction trades simply reflects the lack of previous published research into the pattern of employment in this sector.

Section 7.2 and 7.3 deal with engineering and construction respectively; each covers briefly the experience of the last decade, discusses the projections of output derived from the results given in Chapters 3 and 4 and presents an assessment of the demand for skilled workers over the medium-term. The main conclusions are stated in section 7.4.

7.2 Engineering Trades

Previous research at Warwick has provided a substantial amount of detailed analysis of past changes in the industrial and occupational structure of engineering employment. No attempt will be made here to review or update that work.[3] Our concern is with the industry's progress over the last decade and its prospects up to 1985 at a slightly more aggregate level, as represented by the individual SAM industries: mechanical, instrument and electrical engineering, motor vehicles, aerospace equipment, other vehicles and metal goods n.e.s.[4] This section will concentrate upon the consequences for the employment of engineering craftsmen and technicians of changes in past and future output which have already been discussed in Chapters 3 and 4.

7.2.1 Background

The early 1960s saw record rates of growth of output within engineering and was a period of increasing employment. The mid-1960s to the early 1970s experienced the 'labour shake-out' of 1967–68 and a considerable degree of rationalisation in major parts of the sector took place.[5] During 1964–73 output grew at an average of 2.6 per cent per annum. Since the oil crisis, engineering activity has yet to return to the level recorded in 1969–72 and is well below the peak reached in 1973 (figure 7.1). For 1964–78 as a whole, the rate of growth of output was only 1 per cent per annum.

Employment followed a downward trend averaging 0.7 per cent

Figure 7.1   Output and Employment in Engineering 1964–85

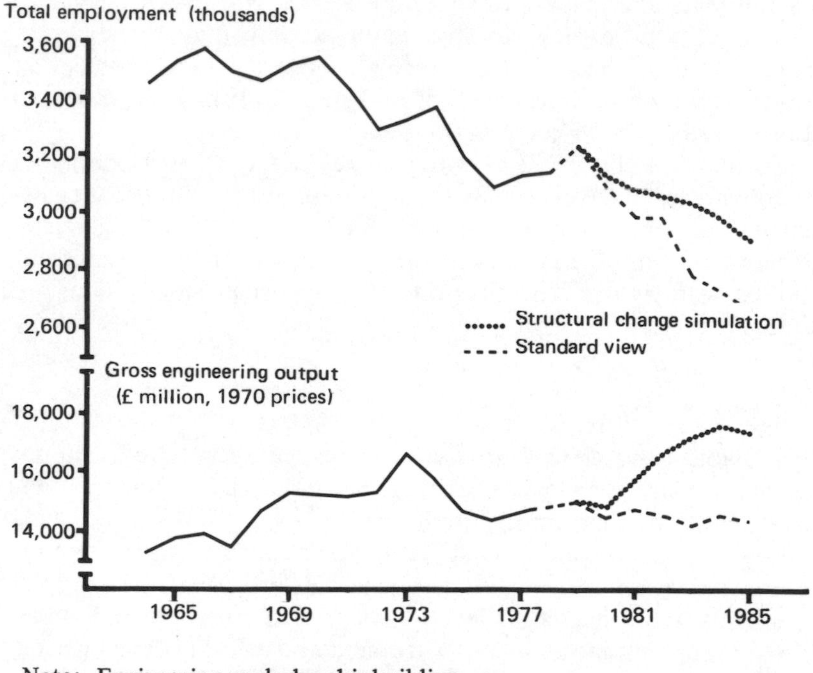

Note: Engineering excludes shipbuilding.

per annum during the same period but, in contrast to output, its cyclical pattern was disturbed only slightly in the course of the post-1973 recession. In the tentative recovery of 1976–77 employment increased in conjunction with output, breaking with the usual lag observed between the two over previous cycles. Before that, however, a rather more striking change had taken place which accounted for the relatively even cyclical profile of employment : productivity hardly rose at all after 1974 and thus took the burden of adjustment to the prolonged recession in output. Even so employment fell by almost half a million from the peak of 1966 to the trough of 1976.

Different parts of the sector are more distinguished by their growth records prior to the recession than the effects of the recession upon their performances (see Table 7.1). Whereas instrument and electrical engineering achieved growth rates exceeding 5 per cent per annum up to 1973 and mechanical engineering achieved 3 per cent per annum, all three subsequently experienced cuts in their growth rates of about 5 per cent, leaving only the relatively small instrument engineering industry with continued growth after 1973. Output in motor vehicles and aerospace equipment was similarly affected so that for a period of 5 years up to 1978 the former declined by 2½ per cent per annum and the latter by almost 5 per cent per annum following a period of modest growth up to 1973. Metal goods in contrast failed to expand very much between 1964 and 1973 and declined only by ½ per cent per annum thereafter. The employment response to recession is a little more varied, at least if we focus on the four largest sectors. The decline in mechanical engineering employment does not intensify after 1973 whereas for electrical (and instrument) engineering and motor vehicles the decline increases by 1½ per cent per annum. Only in metal goods is the change in employment growth commensurate with that in output growth.

The outcome for productivity in engineering as a whole and for two of its major components displaying very different trends is shown in Figure 7.2.

Occupational structure

Changes in the occupational structure of the engineering labour force are shown for 1967–77 in Table 7.2. Amongst those groups that have increased their relative importance over the period, three

Table 7.1 Growth in Engineering Output and Employment 1964–78

Per cent change per annum

		Mechanical engineering	Instrument engineering	Electrical engineering	Motor vehicles	Aerospace equipment	Vehicles n.e.s.	Metal goods	Engineering (excluding shipbuilding)
1964–73	Output	3.11	6.74	5.54	1.71	0.99	-3.18	0.06	2.60
	Employment	-0.67	0.31	0.04	0.88	-2.64	-6.81	-0.61	-0.44
1973–78	Output	-1.99	1.54	-0.94	-2.50	-4.83	-4.93	-0.47	-1.67
	Employment	-0.77	-1.51	-1.63	-0.55	-0.47	-0.25	-1.10	-1.02
1964–78	Output	1.92	4.88	3.23	0.21	-0.16	-3.80	-0.13	1.07
	Employment	-0.71	-0.34	-0.56	0.37	-1.86	-4.47	-0.50	-0.65
Gross output 1978 (£m, 1970 prices)		4,282	664	4,046	2,918	671	138	2,495	15,215
Employees in employment 1978 (thousands)		935	149	749	519	199	57	540	3,148

Source : MRG estimates

Figure 7.2 Productivity in Engineering 1964–85

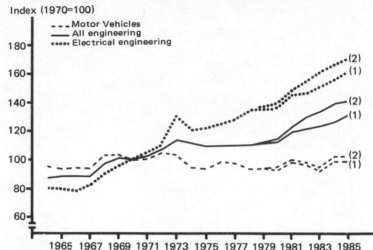

Note: Indices are derived from estimates of gross output per employee upto 1978 and from results of (1) the standard view and (2) the structural change simulation for 1979–85.

have also increased in absolute size: managers, administrative and professional staff, and supervisors and foremen. Scientists and technologists, technicians and draughtsmen, and operators have increased their proportions of the labour force but have declined in absolute terms. The major declines have taken place among craftsmen (176 thousand) and the unskilled manual workers (224 thousand).

Differences between the occupational structures of components of engineering and in changes observed during the recent recession are summarised in Table 7.3. The concentrations of certain occupations in particular industries, which underlie these aggregate figures, have been noted elsewhere (Wabe, 1977); for example,craftsmen in mechanical engineering, technicians, scientists and technologists in aerospace, semi-skilled workers in electrical engineering and motor vehicles. The changes in occupational proportions for the sector as a whole are not, perhaps, as great as one might expect during a period of major decline and are only slightly more noteworthy at the level of the individual industry. There is no marked evidence of dishoarding of one group rather than another but this is in the nature of occupational change in the industry, where the long-term shifts in occupational structure have taken place quite gradually with few dramatic cyclical variations (see Table 7.3).

Table 7.2 Occupational Structure of Engineering 1967–77

Per cent

Occupation	1967	1968	1969	1970	1971	1972	1973	1974	1975	1976	1977
Management	3.3	3.4	3.4	3.5	3.6	3.9	3.9	4.0	4.1	4.3	4.3
Scientists and technologists	1.7	1.9	1.9	1.9	1.9	1.8	1.8	1.8	1.8	1.9	1.9
Technicians and draughtsmen	7.0	7.3	7.2	7.4	7.5	7.6	7.5	7.3	7.3	7.5	7.4
Administrative and professional staff	3.5	3.7	3.9	4.1	4.2	4.3	4.4	4.4	4.5	4.8	4.9
Clerical and office staff	12.6	12.7	12.3	12.3	12.3	12.1	11.6	11.5	11.8	11.9	11.6
Supervisors and foremen	3.9	4.1	4.1	4.2	4.4	4.6	4.6	4.7	4.7	4.9	4.8
Craftsmen	21.1	20.8	20.2	19.6	19.5	19.9	19.4	18.8	18.3	18.3	18.5
Operators	31.3	32.1	33.7	34.4	34.0	33.2	34.1	35.2	35.9	35.4	35.1
All other (except canteen workers)	15.6	14.0	13.3	12.7	12.7	12.6	12.7	12.4	11.5	10.6	10.5
Total Employment (thousands)	3,415	3,371	3,408	3,422	3,322	3,106	3,127	3,173	3,072	2,892	2,934

Source: EITB annual reports and accounts.

Notes: Firms within EITB scope, excluding shipbuilding but includes marine engineering: EITB coverage of other industries does not correspond exactly with the Standard Industrial Classification used for official statistics.

Table 7.3 Broad Occupational Structure of Engineering Sectors 1973 and 1977.

Per cent

		Mechanical engineering	Instrument engineering	Electrical engineering	Motor vehicles	Aerospace equipment	Vehicles n.e.s.	Metal goods n.e.s.	Engineering
1	All administrative technical and clerical staff								
	1973	32.5	34.2	32.7	20.4	42.2	15.6	21.4	29.0
	1977	33.7	36.4	33.9	19.5	45.2	17.0	22.6	30.0
2	All craftsmen including all foremen								
	1973	35.1	24.3	17.4	26.0	37.0	39.7	25.8	27.4
	1977	34.4	22.3	19.1	28.0	34.9	43.9	27.8	28.2
3	All semi-skilled manual workers								
	1973	14.0	22.1	28.6	31.1	7.0	16.8	22.6	21.9
	1977	15.0	20.3	25.7	29.1	7.2	11.0	23.7	21.1
4	All other manual workers								
	1973	18.3	19.3	21.3	22.5	13.8	27.9	30.1	21.7
	1977	16.8	21.0	21.3	23.4	12.7	28.1	25.9	20.7

Source: DE survey: 'Occupations in engineering', DE *Gazette* (various).
Notes: Occupational data are not available for shipbuilding; engineering excludes shipbuilding. Category 1 is equivalent to part A, category 2 to parts B and C, category 3 to part D and category 4 to part E of the DE survey.

Recruitment of craft and technician trainees

The recruitment of craft trainees has been much more volatile as a proportion of the total labour force than has been the case for the employment of craftsmen. The elasticities of apprentice recruitment and apprentice employment with respect to craft employment for the decade up to 1973 were about $3^1/_2$ and 3 respectively.[6]

Two main explanations for this situation can be put forward bearing in mind that the dominant picture is one of declining craft employment, most likely due to a fall in demand for craftsmen. Had this been due to large numbers of craftsmen leaving for other jobs in engineering or outside, we would have expected to see firms attempting to increase the numbers of apprentices. Whether or not this would lead to an actual increase in apprentice numbers via net recruitment would depend on the supply of young people and this would to some extent be influenced by the same considerations that cause craftsmen to leave. However, should firms be successful in boosting apprentice numbers, one would expect a weak if not negative relationship between apprentice recruitment and craft employment, providing the situation is dynamically sustained over the decade studied. That is, dynamic excess demand for craftsmen arises mainly through a shifting supply schedule generating increased apprentice recruitment which does not catch up with demand because of the training lead-times involved. Instead, of course, we obtain a significant positive relationship between apprentice recruitment and craft employment and not only do both decline over this period but apprentice recruitment declines by much more than does craft employment. This would only occur if the supply of apprentice recruits was either falling through shifts in or moves along the supply schedule or, at the opposite extreme, if the profile of craft employment (and apprentice recruitment) was not in fact supply determined but demand determined. In the first case, the fact that apprentice recruitment was falling faster than craft employment would be due to a greater tightening in the labour market for apprentice recruits than in that for adult craftsmen (given appropriate assumptions about the shapes of supply and demand schedules). In the second case, this observation would follow if demand adjustments fall more upon the recruitment margin of a firm's craft labour force and especially upon the recruitment margin of a firm's *trainee* craft group.

From the vantage point of the late 1970s and evidence in Lindley (1974 and 1975), the second explanation above is more likely to be the correct one following the peak of craft employment in 1966. In general the employment of craftsmen and apprentices (and hence apprentice recruitment) would seem to have been demand determined, although in the short-run, craft employment could have been supply determined and apprentice recruitment demand determined. This would arise if firms, seeing the loss of craftsmen, decided to cut back on apprentice recruitment because they were unwilling to take the risk of loss of investment returns should newly trained men leave after only a short period with the firm as a fully qualified craftsman. This has been characterised by one of the authors as 'cleft stick myopia'.[7] The industry's reluctance to attract more craftsmen by altering the wage structure is combined with a reluctance to train its way out of the problem. One or other must be done in the short-run unless skill-saving capital equipment can be installed sufficiently quickly. Over the medium-run, the demand for craftsmen then continues to fall: short-run difficulties reflect the need to recruit from the external labour market in order to augment the supply of skilled labour to the firm. An extreme case of this occurred in the rapid up-turn of 1972/73. Such recruitment takes time and may encounter problems of marginal but significant skill mismatches where the craftsmen available have not got the required blend of skills and experience to be of immediate use to the firm.

The patterns of recruitment and completion of training as recorded in the statistics of the Engineering Industry Training Board (EITB) are shown in Table 7.4. The number registered fell sharply at the beginning of the 1970s and the EITB Award Scheme was introduced as a counter-cyclical training measure. The interpretation of changes in recruitment is complicated during this period by the raising of the school leaving age but in fact the large reduction in recruitment took place before the training year 1973/74 when the educational legislation would have had its main effect. On the other hand the recovery of craft employment in 1973–74, lagging somewhat behind output, would lead us to expect the normal belated response to the labour shortage situation of seeking to recruit young people for training programmes. And the circumstances suggest that employers did indeed have difficulties in meeting their requirements.[8]

Falling engineering output and rising unemployment among skilled workers would imply a continuing reduction in the recruitment of trainees. However, the fact that the cut back in 1972–74 had been very severe, and the presence of a lag in response to changes in

Table 7.4 Craft and Technician Trainees and TOPS Trainees

	First year craft and technician registration (1)	First year completers		Final year completers (2)		TOPS outflow (3)	
		Craft	Technician	Craft	Technician	Craft	Technician
1966/67	23,980	35,512	10,284	:	:	3,875	:
1967/68	27,539	30,632	8,846	:	:	4,486	:
1968/69	27,290	27,687	8,780	:	:	5,289	:
1969/70	26,552	26,392	8,460	:	:	5,853	:
1970/71	26,589	24,949	8,123	19,467(4)	6,073(4)	6,370	:
1971/72	21,942 (2,489)(5)	18,624	5,270	19,808(4)	6,200(4)	6,570	:
1972/73	16,788(5) (1,528)(5)	14,973	4,519	19,349	6,057	7,932	:
1973/74	16,920(5)	15,251	5,616	18,298	6,026	7,267	:
1974/75	23,496	22,145	6,346	16,352	5,201	7,030	:
1975/76	25,243 (3,436)	19,574	5,201	12,952	4,055	7,690	:
1976/77	24,478 (3,619)	17,811	5,570	12,240	3,832	7,690	:
1977/78	24,742 (3,400)	:	:	16,012	5,009	:	973
1978/79	:	:	:	18,021	5,636	:	:

Source: EITB Annual reports and accounts plus MRG estimates, MSC (Training Services Division).

Notes: (1) The numbers in brackets are those included in total registrations who are receiving an EITB award.
(2) Numbers finishing training are estimated from initial registration figures using observed losses during training, making allowances for those not registering with the EITB.
(3) Data refers to first year in question
(4) Figures for these years may be underestimates due to the discrepancy between registrations and completions in early years.
(5) The raising of the school leaving age (ROSLA) occurred in 1973.

the economy and labour market, probably accounts for the large increase in 1974/75. That the level reached was then sustained must
be attributed partly to the optimistic expectations and mounting
concern over possible manpower bottlenecks and by the direct
intervention of the EITB through its training awards.

Corresponding to the reduction in training in the early 1970s are
the low numbers of craft and technician trainees completing their
training in 1976 and 1977 when output and employment in engineering began to recover. This will have contributed significantly to
the increase in vacancies recorded in these years. Even so both vacancies and unemployment levels continue to indicate a far slacker
engineering labour market than has been experienced since the
Second World War. The geographical and specific occupational
patterns of vacancies and unemployment inevitably show very considerable variation with much tighter labour markets in the south-
east than in the north and for toolmakers and tool fitters than for
welders.

The result of the recruitment and qualifying patterns shown in
Table 7.4 is a more moderate fluctuation in employment of trainees
as a whole. This is shown in relation to the employment of trained
craftsmen and technicians in Figure 7.3. The employment of trained
craftsmen fell by 2 per cent per annum from 1967 to 1977 whereas
that of trained technicians reveals no significant trend. When trainees are included to form total craftsmen and technician groups the
rates of decline rise to 3 and 1½ per cent per annum respectively.
Within both occupational categories there are groups with divergent
behaviour, the most striking of which occurs between draughtsmen
and other technicians. According to the DE survey of occupations
in engineering, which distinguishes between the two, the employment of draughtsmen declined at a rate of 3 per cent per annum
throughout the last decade, turning up only in 1977 whereas other
technicians grew at almost 6 per cent per annum.

The linking of training programmes for craftsmen and technicians
through the common first year off-the-job training promoted by the
EITB has been an important step towards greater flexibility in this
labour market. It has certainly allowed for a greater degree of substitution between these two groups at least in the course of the training
process. At the same time the introduction of the module scheme by
which craftsmen may progressively qualify through systematic and
certified training in place of the traditional system has also enhanced the ability of the industry to adjust to changing skill require-

Figure 7.3 Craft and Technician Employment in Engineering 1967—85

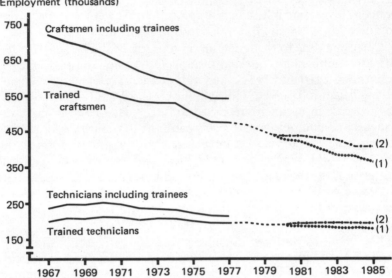

Employment (thousands)

Note: Figures for 1978—85 are taken from (1) the standard view and
         (2) the structural change simulation.

ments within the main craft groups (mechanical, electrical and
maintenance trades).

Earnings

Notwithstanding the comments made earlier about the role of relative earnings in this labour market, it is worth stressing the degree
to which fluctuations in industrial relativities have taken place in
recent years. Differences in earnings growth for construction and separate engineering industries relative to manufacturing are shown in
Figure 7.4 for 1971–78. Both construction and motor vehicles have
clearly been affected by the depth of recession experienced by them
since 1973. The situation in motor vehicles has particularly important implications for the supply of skilled manpower to other engineering industries given the historically large differential between the
earnings of its semi-skilled workers and those of skilled workers in
other industries and the very poor prospects for output over the me-

Figure 7.4 Differences in Earnings Growth: Engineering and Construction

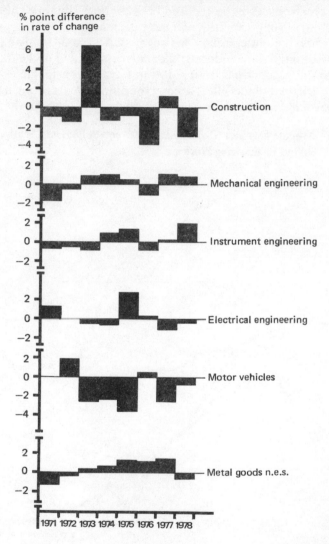

Source: Index of average earnings of all employees (older series), *Monthly Digest of Statistics.*

Note: The differences shown are percentage point differences between the annual rates of change of earnings in each industry and the corresponding rates of change for all manufacturing.

dium-term. One would expect the loss of skilled men to semi-skilled jobs in motor vehicles to be reduced because both the relevant differentials and job opportunities will have decreased.

As regards the differentials between skilled and semi-skilled workers within the same industry, the narrowing noted in the introduction to this chapter has been accompanied by considerable variation in the extent of this effect among the components of engineering, as shown in Figure 7.5 for selected industries. Moreover, the DE

Figure 7.5   Average Earnings Differentials between Skilled and Semi-Skilled Engineering Workers

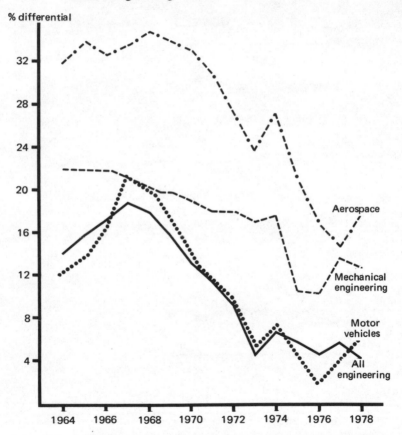

Source: "Average hourly earnings (excluding overtime) of time-workers in engineering at October of each year": DE *Gazette* (various).

(1979, p.434) has concluded that this narrowing has 'occured at times and on a scale that cannot be attributed to pay policy.'⁹ However, the DE does believe that 'the narrowing of differentials between 1967 and 1975 must rank with the length and depth of the industrial recession as one of the key changes in the economy that could contribute to skill shortages appearing at higher levels of unemployment than in the past'.

Thus pay and other working conditions attached to skilled jobs in engineering may well be in need of improvement before greater efficiency in the allocation of skilled manpower is achieved. An assessment of earnings prospects would, though, also take into account the probability of finding and retaining a skilled job. The study by MSC/ NEDO (1977) suggests that it is the fear of future redundancy that discourages redundant skilled workers from seeking further employment in engineering. This points to the need for changes in the relative conditions attached to white and blue collar jobs, particularly in relation to security, status and non-wage benefits in general.

7.2.2 Employment prospects for craftsmen and technicians

Output and aggregate employment

Sector Working Parties set up under the Industrial Strategy showed a very high propensity to perceive imminent manpower bottlenecks. But their optimism about prospects for recovery failed to mat⸰rialise and our projections for engineering suggest that we shall have to wait longer still.

Under the standard view, engineering (excluding shipbuilding) output falls at just below 1 per cent per annum and total employment at a rate of 3 per cent per annum between 1978 and 1985. By 1985 output is almost 6 per cent and total employment 20 per cent below the levels estimated for 1978 (See Figure 7.1 and Table 7.5). Slow growth in the world economy and at home and a continuing rise in import penetration are largely responsible for this decline. The fiscal stimulus does little to ameliorate the situation but the structural simulation, acting through increases in investment and productivity in selected manufacturing industries and increases in export demand elasticities, achieves a reversal of the downward trend. Engineering output rises by 12 per cent from 1978 to a level which is 2 per cent above the peak recorded in 1973. Employment, on the other hand, fails to increase from 1978, although its rate of decline is reduced by 40 per cent. The increase in productivity accompanying the structural measures leads to lower employment than would otherwise have been the case. Employment falls by 380 thousand instead of 630 thousand in the standard view.

In the standard view both output and employment changes are shared in roughly similar proportions between the two sub-periods 1978–81 and 1981–85. In the structural simulation the increase in productivity begins to act on employment before output receives its main stimulus. Productivity profiles for these simulations are shown in Figure 7.2.

Table 7.5 Predictions of Engineering Output and Employment 1978–85

	Output (£m 1970 prices)		Employees in Employment (thousands)	
	Standard view	Structural simulation	Standard view	Structural simulation
1978	15,213	15,213	3,148	3,148
1981	14,728	15,638	2,830	2,919
1985	14,375	16,960	2,519	2,773
% change				
1978–85	−5.5	11.5	−20.0	−11.9
1978–81	−3.2	2.8	−10.1	− 7.3
1981–85	−2.4	8.4	−11.0	− 5.0

Employment of trained craftsmen and technicians

Some indication of the prospects for employment of craftsmen and technicians has already been given in Chapter 4 using a very simple method of occupational analysis forced upon us by the lack of data for non-engineering industries. The projections given below exploit the additional information available for engineering. They imply similar patterns for future employment within engineering but, bearing in mind significant differences of occupational definition, the results presented in Figure 7.3 and Table 7.6 indicate a somewhat larger decline in craft employment and a smaller decline in technician employment than is expected from the projections using census of population data classified in terms of the Warwick Occupational Categories.

For both occupational groups, an employment function relating employment to output has been estimated. In the case of trained craftsmen the change in output per man for 1978–85 is slightly more than that implied for total engineering employment but more than three times greater than for trained technicians. Thus whereas engineering employment falls by 21 per cent between 1977 and 85 in the standard view, the number of trained craftsmen falls by 24 per cent and that of trained technicians by only 7 per cent.[10] Under the structural measures the marginal employment – output elasticities (calculated relative to the standard view) for these two groups lie close to 0.5 which is the elasticity for total employment. The value for craftsmen is slightly higher and that for technicians is lower. Thus the difference between the experiences of these occupations does not stem primarily from very different output elasticities but from the relative impact of technical progress upon the demand for their services over the longer run. This is captured via time trends in each equation.

Table 7.6 **Employment of Trained Craftsmen and Technicians 1977–85**

Thousands

	Trained craftsmen		Trained technicians	
	Standard view	Structural simulation	Standard view	Structural simulation
1977	475	475	195	195
1981	421	439	189	194
1985	361	404	181	194
% change				
1977–85	−24.0	−14.9	−7.2	−0.5
1977–81	−11.4	− 7.6	−3.1	−0.5
1981–85	−14.2	− 8.0	−4.2	−

Source: MRG forecasts based on EITB and DE data.

Whilst the general stance of our study of medium-term employment prospects is that the effects of micro-technology will not produce radical changes in overall productivity growth, we have already allowed for a substantial improvement up to 1985 relative to
the past 5 years (see Chapters 3 and 4). If anything the incorporation
of the new technology into both product and process innovations is
likely to affect mechanical engineering adversely and electrical engineering and electronics favourably. This will tend to reinforce the
projected decline in craft employment and the projected increase in
technician employment as shown in the structural simulation.

Components of skilled labour supply

Our statistical model of the training system in engineering accounts for the composition of trainees according to stage of training
reached and the different loss rates experienced during training. The
latter arise not only because of learning difficulties but also because
of voluntary quitting in favour of alternative employment and, increasingly, redundancy. The development of the EITB's module
scheme appears to be reducing wastage, however. No special provisions for greater redundancy in a period of higher unemployment or
lower wastage through changes in the training system have been allowed for in our projections of those qualifying as trained craftsmen.[11]

From 1975/76 the EITB has aimed to keep the number of first
year registrations of craft and technician trainees at about 24–25
thousand, supplementing the industry's own effort by means of
training awards where necessary. A continuation of this policy implies that from now until 1985 about 18,000 young people will complete craft training each year and about 5,500 will complete technician training. In addition about 10,000 people each year have been
receiving TOPS training in craft skills relevant to engineering with a
further 1,000 undergoing training as engineering technicians and
draughtsmen (see Table 7.4).

Starting from a position of high levels of unemployment amongst
engineering craftsmen, our uncertainty about the proportions of
these two newly qualified craft groups actually seeking jobs in the
engineering sector would not seem to be too important. This impression is strengthened when, even under the structural simulation,
craft employment is expected to fall by 70 thousand between 1978
and 1985.

There are other manpower flows which might upset this view but the available data suggest that their overall effect will not be sufficiently large. So deaths, retirements, occupational mobility within engineering (e.g. promotions to foreman) and net flows out of the industry will not combine to confound the indications of increasing surplus mentioned above. Even during a period of much lower unemployment amongst engineering workers and almost stable craft employment, these sources of loss amounted to less than 20 thousand at an annual rate.[12] Unfortunately we do not have a time series of such observations and so it is not possible to model the two potentially most significant flows – those due to occupational and industrial mobility – in relation to the state of the labour market.

7.3 Construction Trades

7.3.1 The construction industry 1967–78

The construction sector has, in recent years, accounted for an average of 7 per cent of all industrial output. The data in Table 7.7 indicate how this output has varied cyclically in the period since 1967. Output peaks in 1968 and 1973 contrast with troughs in 1970 and 1977; output measured in real terms fell by over 18 per cent between 1973 and 1977. Whilst the statistics for 1978 indicate that construction output has recovered from the nadir of the previous year, short-term output forecasts produced by construction specialists–for example, NEDO (1978)–suggest that output is not likely to return to 1973 peak levels in the near future.

The disaggregated data in Table 7.7 summarise output changes arising through the various private and public sector clients. The two private sector new work series – housing, and industrial and commercial buildings – exhibit the most volatile output profiles. The public sector new work series also demonstrate significant cyclical variability, although this is not quite as pronounced as for the private sector outputs. The most stable area of construction activity is that associated with repair and maintenance work (arising from both sectors) which, on average, has contributed about one third of all construction output. However, the statistics for 1978 indicate that it was an upsurge of output from this repair and maintenance sector which provided the major growth impetus to construction output in that year.

During the 1970s, public sector demand for construction work has sought to balance out some of the fluctuations arising from

Table 7.7 Construction Output 1967–78

£million at 1970 prices

Annual output	CSO UK total	DoE[1] GB total	DoE disaggregated outputs					
			Public new housing	Private new housing	Public other new work	Private industrial and commercial	All new work	All repair and maintenance
1967	6,502	5,531	793	832	1,196	1,111	3,932	1,599
1968	6,683	5,652	817	874	1,267	1,091	4,049	1,603
1969	6,592	5,621	784	802	1,300	1,170	4,057	1,565
1970	6,463	5,517	689	737	1,357	1,184	3,967	1,550
1971	6,650	5,611	635	853	1,313	1,222	4,023	1,588
1972	6,754	5,725	577	952	1,293	1,141	3,974	1,752
1973	6,935	5,987	593	1,018	1,345	1,163	4,119	1,868
1974	6,385	5,215	563	718	1,156	1,033	3,471	1,744
1975	5,861	4,760	591	632	1,038	931	3,192	1,568
1976	5,753	4,667	643	660	1,006	858	3,167	1,500
1977	5,664	4,599	562	604	978	944	3,087	1,511
1978(2)	6,002	4,960	469	735	978	1,009	3,191	1,769

Sources: MRG estimates; CSO *Monthly Digest of Statistics*; DoE *Housing and Construction Statistics* (*H & CS*).

Notes: (1) DoE output series have been deflated by the new series, given in *H & CS*, no. 25, Table I.
(2) Estimated values.

private sector demand, although the synchronisation has often been imperfect. When private sector demand was rising in the upturn phase of 1971–73, orders for public sector new housing, in particular, were constrained so that over this period the public sector's share of all new work averaged 47 per cent. After 1973 when private sector demand was declining, an increase in the public sector's new housing output occurred which served to cushion the recession in the industry. Equally, the level of output in public sector civil engineering (other new) work was stabilised over the period 1947–77. During these years, public clients accounted for slightly over 50 per cent of all new construction output. The recovery in 1978 has witnessed a resurgence in both types of private sector demand for new work, as well as growth in the demand for repair and maintenance in the private sector. However, there has been a corresponding decline in the demand for public sector output, especially local authority housing.

Amidst such cyclical variation it is difficult to identify clear longer run trends for different types of construction output. Simple extrapolation is not likely to prove very helpful and a fuller discussion of likely future trends in output is left until section 7.3.3.

The pattern of aggregate employment which has been determined by these observed trends in output is, not surprisingly, cyclical with a significant reduction in the number of construction workers in employment occurring in the period after 1973. The data in Table 7.8 show aggregate employment peaks in 1967 and 1973 and thereafter a decline in employment of about 14 per cent over the following 4 years. The preliminary employment returns for 1978 suggest that this downward trend has been halted, although there does not appear to have been any significant increase in construction employment to correspond with the average estimated 7 per cent increase in output which occurred in 1978.

Occupational structure

The disaggregated employment data presented in Table 7.8 clearly demonstrate how the recent reduction in construction employment has been concentrated on two main classes of worker – operatives employed by the private contractors and the self-employed worker. Whereas employed operatives in the private sector were reduced by 16 per cent over the period 1973–77, the equivalent reduction for public sector operatives was only 7 per cent. In comparison with operatives, the non-manual administrative, pro-

Table 7.8 Employment in Construction

Thousands

| Annual averages | All workers(1) | | Self-employed | Private contractors' employees | | DoE/GB based series | |
	DoE/GB(2) total	DE/UK total		Operatives	APTC staff	Public authorities' employees Operatives	APTC staff
1967	1,977	1,808	293	1,064	230	296	94
1968	1,948	1,796	306	1,033	233	278	98
1969	1,878	1,758	321	951	234	271	101
1970	1,789	1,649	337	869	223	255	105
1971	1,792	1,594	390	821	219	251	111
1972	1,870	1,673	440	839	224	253	114
1973	1,916	1,823	428	902	225	247	114
1974	1,883	1,766	427	874	240	233	110
1975	1,782	1,699	375	820	240	233	113
1976	1,715	1,660	341	788	237	236	114
1977	1,642	1,591	316	756	229	230	112
1978	1,641	1,594	327	749	230	224	111

Sources: DoE *H & CS*; DE *Gazette*.

Notes: (1) All workers include all employees in employment plus estimates of all self-employed.

(2) DoE estimates are for Great Britain but they include employees carrying out construction activities in establishments not classified to construction. Figures prior to 1973 are derived from DoE's annual October censuses, and are on a different basis from those for 1973 onwards, which rely on quarterly contractor returns and half-yearly returns from public sector authorities.

fessional, technical and clerical (APTC) staff in both sectors changed relatively little over this period. Examination of this employment data over the complete decade reveals a significant downward trend in the number of employed operatives in both private and public sectors. APTC staff on the other hand have, despite some fluctuations, remained reasonably constant in the private sector and have exhibited significant growth in the public sector.

The classification 'self-employed worker' in the construction industry is largely a residual category that includes working proprietors, self-employed sub-contractors who have a recognised status with the Inland Revenue and other self-employed workers who at any particular time may not be specifically known to the Inland Revenue or any other government agency responsible for preparing statistical (employment) returns. In particular, Phelps-Brown (1968) has sought to draw a distinction between the different types of construction worker who fall into the general category of self-employed. For present purposes, in assessing the trend in the self-employed, the series given in Table 7.8 must be treated with some caution as recent data necessarily contain estimates for some workers who are not known. In the wake of the Selective Employment Tax (SET) introduced in 1966 and prior to the tightening of the tax legislation governing payments to the self-employed construction worker, conditions favoured the growth of self-employment in the industry. Such a trend was reinforced with the boom in private housebuilding in the years up to 1973. The statistics on self-employment suggest that numbers grew by more than 50 per cent over the period 1967–72.

After 1973, the conditions which had favoured the rapid growth of the self-employed construction worker began to change significantly. SET was removed and a decline occurred in the output of private housing, the sector where 'lump' labour most readily finds employment.[13] In addition, changes in national employment legislation reduced the advantages of self-employment over employee status. In April 1977, the Inland Revenue revised the scheme for deducting sub-contractors' tax payments (714 Certificates) and this was considered likely to reduce the number of self-employed workers still further. Its effects have been monitored by the Construction Industry Manpower Board (1977) and from returns provided by the Inland Revenue it appears that between 1976 and 1977 some 18 per cent fewer tax certificates were issued to the self-employed.

The decline in the self-employed worker between 1973 and 1977 was estimated as some 26 per cent according to the statistics of Table 7.8. In looking to the future, it appears unlikely that this severe downward trend will continue; rather, a levelling-out in the number of self-employed construction workers can be expected in the medium-term. There is little likelihood of self-employment returning to pre–1973 levels but, now that the once-and-for-all effects of the legislative changes of 1977 have taken place, some stability in their numbers is the most probable outcome. The future for these self-employed workers is closely related to trends in the private new housing and repair and maintenance sectors.

From the various annual surveys conducted by the Department of the Environment (DoE) and, most recently, the Construction Industry Training Board (CITB), it is possible to present employment trends for selected occupations, which make up the general category of operatives. In Table 7.9 survey returns for both the private contractors and the local authorities have been combined to show employment profiles for specific occupational groups.

It is apparent that the general decline in operative employment over the last decade has not affected all trades equally. Most significantly, whilst employment of the semi-skilled and general labourers in the industry declined by over 40 per cent in the period 1967–77, the number of skilled craftsmen fell by just over 20 per cent. Of course, part of this result may be explained by changes in the classification of certain occupations, nevertheless this large difference between the experience of skilled and other operative grades does indicate a marked change in the balance between broad occupations. In 1967 the ratio of skilled to other operatives was 1.8 to 1; by 1977 it had risen to 2.5 to 1. The period after 1973 has witnessed a particularly severe decline in the numbers of unskilled workers employed in the industry. The decline in the number of general operatives has been less severe in the public sector than amongst private contractors.

Within the ranks of the skilled trades, all the main traditional crafts have suffered reductions in employment over the period since 1967. A comparison between 1967 and 1973, both years of peak construction activity, reveal how numbers in employment were falling in the numerically most important trades of carpentry, bricklaying and painting. Between 1967 and 1977 employment of carpenters and joiners fell by 32 per cent, bricklayers and masons by 26 per cent and painters and decorators by 32 per cent. Whilst some reco-

Table 7.9 Employment of Operatives[1] by Private Contractors and Local Authorities

Great Britain   *Thousands*

Census year	Craftsmen									Other (semi-skilled)	Unskilled labourers	All operatives
	Carpenters and joiners	Bricklayers and masons	Plasterers	Painters	Plumbers	Electricians	Scaffolders and steel workers	Other craftsmen	All craftsmen			
1967	184.3	108.6	27.8	130.8	62.1	68.2	26.2	200.1	808.1	75.9	374.4	1,258.4
1968	176.8	103.7	27.0	124.0	61.1	68.2	26.2	205.1	792.1	72.7	357.5	1,222.3
1969	165.3	91.6	23.8	111.8	57.3	67.8	25.6	199.2	742.4	79.1	312.1	1,133.6
1970	148.0	82.1	21.1	102.0	53.7	64.2	23.1	187.8	682.0	77.5	282.3	1,041.8
1971	141.3	81.1	20.5	96.6	53.1	62.0	20.4	182.1	657.1	337.6		994.7
1972	141.7	82.5	21.0	98.4	53.5	60.0	21.7	184.7	663.5	354.4		1,017.9
1973[2]	145.5	86.8	22.9	102.1	58.8	67.7	24.9	194.8	703.5	379.5		1,083.0
1974	144.5	88.2	23.5	95.0	52.7	59.1	28.2	188.6	679.8	342.3		1,022.1
1975	140.3	85.7	22.5	92.7	52.7	64.2	25.1	217.0	700.2	297.2		997.4
1976	133.7	83.6	22.1	91.9	48.3	61.2	25.5	204.2	670.5	276.9		947.4
1977[3]	125.9	80.2	19.6	89.1	46.1	61.0	27.7	200.1	649.7	265.2		914.9

Sources: DoE *H & CS*; DoE private contractors construction censuses; DoE *Monthly Bulletin of Construction Statistics* (prior to 1972); CITB levy returns.

Notes:
(1) Includes apprentices.
(2) Basis of register changed for 1973, causing a slight discontinuity in the series.
(3) From 1977 onwards, returns are collected by CITB rather than DoE. An adjustment has been made to correct for discrepancies in the two registers.

very from the 1977 low point is to be expected, the pronounced long-term downward trend appears well-established. The smaller trades of plasterer and plumber exhibit similar downward movements, but the reduction in the number of employed electricians has been less pronounced.

Of the individual crafts identified in Table 7.9 only the scaffolders, steel benders and steel erectors group shows an increase in employment for 1977 over 1967. Within the residual skill group of 'other craftsmen' – which incorporates such diverse skills as heating and ventilating specialists, mechanical plant operators and paviors – no significant downward trend is apparent. To some extent this might be explained by a limited amount of job reclassification from unskilled to skilled status. Most frequently, though, for 'other craftsmen' reductions in numbers in employment with private contractors have been offset by increases arising in the public sector.

In assessing the trends in employment in Tables 7.9 and 7.10 it should be remembered that the data refer only to employees of firms on the DoE registers at the time of the survey. The self-employed are not covered and for some crafts this component can be particularly important. Many skilled bricklayers have self-employed status and to some extent such workers are known to shift between self-employed and employee status from year to year. Equally in considering APTC staff (Table 7.10) it should be remembered that a significant proportion of professionals work for consulting firms not usually regarded as part of the construction industry and so are not included on the DoE registers,

In contrast to skilled operatives, APTC staff have been increasing over the period 1967–77 at the end of which they constituted almost 27 per cent of total employees. APTC employment has not been immune to fluctuations in construction output, but employment has varied far less than that for operatives. In particular, the local authorities continued to expand their employment of APTC staff even in the downturn after 1973.

Amongst professional occupations, the number of architects, surveyors and engineers has apparently changed very little over recent years. There has been some switching of employment opportunities out of the private sector and into local authorities but generally the number of such professionals in employment has remained relatively stable. The trend in the group classified as managers is confused by a reclassification of this category after 1970, but almost certainly there has been significant growth among managerial occupations during the 1970s.

Great Britain   *Thousands*

Table 7.10 Employment of Non-manual (APTC) Staff by Private Contractors and Local Authorities

Census year	Managers(1)	Architects	Surveyors	Engineers	Technical staff	Draughtsmen tracers	Foremen and supervisors	Clerical office and sales staff	All APTC staff	APTC% of total(2) employees
1967	51.8	6.6	16.9	25.9	26.7	14.5	47.2	118.3	307.9	19.7
1968	52.5	6.8	17.6	27.1	28.5	14.6	48.2	118.9	314.2	20.4
1969	57.8	6.9	16.4	27.7	31.7	13.9	48.0	116.3	318.7	21.9
1970	54.2	6.9	15.6	27.8	31.7	13.0	45.5	112.5	307.2	22.8
1971	44.1	6.9	16.1	28.2	31.8	13.0	47.4	111.3	298.8	23.1
1972	45.0	6.9	16.9	30.5	32.4	12.6	51.5	113.2	309.0	23.3
1973(3)	51.6	7.0	18.2	32.6	34.2	12.7	55.8	126.3	338.4	23.8
1974	54.1	6.6	18.9	31.4	37.5	11.6	55.5	124.0	339.6	24.9
1975	55.2		52.7 (4)		53.5	10.0	48.4	121.8	341.6	25.5
1976	55.1		52.2		52.5	9.5	46.5	118.3	334.1	26.1
1977	54.7		50.7		54.2	9.2	47.0	115.7	331.5	26.6

Sources: See Table 7.3.

Notes: (1) Managers are widely defined to include other professional staff n.e.s.; in 1971 a change in definitions resulted in about 10,000 private sector managers being re-classified as working proprietors (estimates of which are included with the self-employed, who are not recorded in this table).

(2) Total employees is the sum of all APTC staff and all operatives (as given in Table 7.3).

(3) Slight change in basis of the DoE register for 1973 onwards.

(4) As from 1975 there is a joint return for architects, surveyors and engineers. Figures for 1975–77 are shown under surveyors.

(5) Continuity adjustment made to render CITB returns compatible with DoE register.

The trend in employment in technical staff has been strongly positive throughout the last decade and, in particular, there was a large recorded upsurge in 1975 as more technical staff were apparently employed in both sectors. The fact that other non-manual occupational groups, especially foremen and supervisors, show a sharp decline at this time suggests that some of this observed increase may simply be due to a reclassification of occupations. The foremen and supervisors category exhibits rapid growth in the number of such employees in the early 1970s. Throughout the period under consideration, draughtsmen and tracers have been in slow decline, so that by 1977 their employment had been reduced by 37 per cent. The numerically largest APTC group is the residual category covering clerical, office and sales staff. Employment in these occupations follows industry output cycles quite closely and the 1973 peak witnessed a very strong increase. By 1977, employment had fallen back, but only by some 8 per cent from the peak level.

7.3.2 The current situation

An initial appraisal of the published statistics on unemployment and vacancy levels in the construction industry would suggest that over the last decade general labour shortages have rarely, if ever, been a serious problem. The data presented in Table 7.11 indicates that the lowest aggregate unemployment to vacancy ratio was experienced in the 1973 boom. In all other years the ratio was significantly higher and for 1978 was almost treble the 1973 value. The statistics for particular crafts do suggest that in the period 1972–74, carpenters, bricklayers, plasterers and electricians experienced relatively low unemployment rates, indicating that there may have been significant skill shortages in a number of regions. The data for craft unemployment in the subsequent years, including 1978, suggests that this problem of skill shortages has disappeared and that an excess supply of most types of craftsmen has been the main feature of the labour market.

In the light of these statistics, it is perhaps surprising to discover contractors, throughout 1978 and continuing into 1979, complaining of marked skill shortages and the impossibility in some regions of being able to recruit any craftsmen of a particular type. The National Federation of Building Trades Employers in their quarterly state of trade enquiry for the last quarter in 1978 (NFBTE, 1979) commented on how 76 per cent of the 600 contractors in the sample survey found it difficult, very difficult or virtually impossible to re-

Table 7.11 Unemployment and Vacancies in the Construction Industry

Great Britain — *Annual average (thousands)*

	Unemployed craftsmen(1)								Others	All un-employed	Unfilled vacancies
	Carpenters and joiners	Bricklayers(2)	Plasterers	Painters and decorators	Plumbers and glaziers	Electricians	Other craftsmen	All craftsmen			
1967	3.3	2.6	0.9	6.4	1.8	1.9	11.8	28.7	67.3	96	14
1968	3.3	2.6	1.0	6.7	2.2	2.1	13.0	30.9	71.1	102	14
1969	4.7	3.8	1.3	6.4	2.3	1.9	13.7	34.1	66.9	101	13
1970	5.4	3.9	1.4	6.6	2.8	2.0	15.0	37.2	68.8	106	13
1971	5.3	3.1	1.2	7.1	3.8	3.1	18.6	42.2	85.8	128	12
1972	3.6	2.0	0.9	6.5	3.7	3.3	17.6	37.6	95.3	133	18
1973	1.1	0.7	0.3	3.4	2.1	1.0	5.5	14.1	75.0	89	26
1974	2.1	2.6	0.8	4.1	3.0	1.2	6.9	20.7	83.4	104	17
1975	7.1	5.7	2.4	9.2	4.8	2.9	11.0	43.1	119.2	162	9
1976	10.0	7.1	3.1	12.2	6.5	3.4	15.4	57.7	152.5	210	9
1977	11.9	8.6	3.6	12.4	6.4	3.1	15.9	61.9	145.5	208	12
1978	9.4	6.7	3.0	10.7	5.3	2.8	13.7	52.0	134.7	186	18

Source: DE *Gazette* for relevant years.

Notes: (1) Craftsmen refer to men aged 18 and over for 1967–71; from 1972, craftsmen refer to men, women and young people.

(2) From 1976 total for bricklayers includes masons.

cruit bricklayers. Similarly, it was reported that plumbers, plasterers, and carpenters and joiners remained in quite short supply. A further indication of the severity of the skill shortage problem is the decision by the Building and Civil Engineering Economic Development Committee to set up a Skilled Manpower Steering Group in March 1979. The terms of reference for this group are primarily to investigate the nature and extent of shortages of skilled labour in the construction industry and to ascertain the underlying causes of any shortages or other related problems of labour supply.

Such apparent conflicts in evidence, as noted in the introduction, are not in fact unusual and a variety of explanations may be offered. It is well known that a minority of vacancies are reported by employers to the Department of Employment. As regards the degree to which unemployment of construction workers indicates the surplus manpower available, hearsay evidence of extensive 'moonlighting' and other forms of unrecorded working in the repair and maintenance sector are commonplace. Phelps Brown (1968) commented on this aspect of construction employment for an earlier decade. Moreover, the changes in the institutional structure of the labour market which have occurred in recent years following the reductions in the numbers of workers of self-employed status will also serve to distort recent unemployment statistics when set in an historical context.

The reported shortages of craftsmen, which are currently so prevalent in the industry, are essentially a short-term supply phenomenon and constitute a problem that will not necessarily be solved simply by increasing the longer-term supply of craftsmen. Given the falling demand for labour, some of the current shortages are attributable to the short-term immobility exhibited by craftsmen. In particular, it is felt that skilled construction workers are very reluctant to move outside their immediate locality in search of work.[14] Both Phelps Brown (1968) and DE (1965) provide evidence on this point and more up-to-date surveys into the mobility of operatives between both regions and employers are currently being carried out at University College, London. Not only are construction workers relatively immobile geographically, but many of the traditional building craftsmen are also rather occupationally immobile. It has been noted in NEDO (1976) how the number of years spent in a given craft in the industry are at a maximum for those trades exclusive to construction work (bricklayers and plasterers) and at a minimum for those used significantly in other industries (electricians and plumbers). A recent NEDO survey (1978a) found that 78 per cent of bricklayers in the sample whose first job was as a bricklayer in construction have always worked as such. The equivalent figure for carpenters and joiners was 42 per cent and there was a significant loss of men from this trade to other occupations.

A further insight into the nature of short-run shortages of skilled craftsmen arises from the observation that construction is an industry which traditionally experiences high labour turnover. Labour turnover rates tend to be directly related to the level of economic activity and when activity is increasing after a long period of slump, as in 1978, then significant movement between firms can be expected. Firms respond to such a situations by increasing both basic rates and bonus payments to try to maintain established craftsmen and attact new skilled workers. More craftsmen change employers in pursuit of higher earnings. The result is that the short-term perceived shortages of labour may well turn out to be higher than the actual shortage because of frictional mobility.

The problem of shortages amongst non-manual workers does not appear to be anywhere near as significant as that for craftsmen. In some regions, shortages of suitable foremen and supervisors have arisen recently, but the suggestion that this difficulty originates from such staff leaving the UK to work on contracts abroad is not supported by NEDO (1987a) evidence. This same NEDO study found that the professions (architects, surveyors and engineers) do not normally adjust to changing work loads through variations in the numbers employed, but rather they are able to modify their rate of working. In general, there also appears to be some downward flexibility between these professionals and their supporting technical staff so that, in the event of decreasing activity, it is the technician grades which are reduced, the professional groups taking on their work. When activity increases the professions return to their preferred functions and the technician grades are recruited in greater numbers.

The supply of construction craftsmen

The supply of craftsmen to the industry in the longer term is governed, in the first instance, by the intake of apprentices shown in Table 7.12. The principle formal scheme of apprenticeship for construction craft trainees is that monitored by the National Joint Council for the Building Industry (NJCBI). In addition to those ap-

Table 7.12   Apprentices and Trainees in the Construction Industry 1967–78

Thousands

	Trainees employed (GB)			Apprentices recruited NJCBI scheme	TOPS trainee completions(2) on construction-orientated schemes
	Private(1) sector	Local authorities	Total		
1967	103,492	9,180	112,672	13,839	..
1968	95,097	8,970	104,067	12,795	..
1969	86,310	8,261	94,571	12,358	..
1970	75,234	7,618	82,852	11,093	..
1971	68,300	7,405	75,705	8,793	..
1972	72,675	8,208	80,883	10,381	4,244
1973	79,325	8,345	87,670	14,251	5,802
1974	80,680	8,981	89,661	12,111	6,392
1975	77,225	10,420	87,645	13,093	6,925
1976	70,840	10,025	80,865	11,336	8,281
1977	61,880	10,025	70,612	10,249	8,280
1978	..	..	..	10,806	8,533

Source: DoE private contractors censuses;   DoE *H & CS*;   NJCBI statistics;   CITB annual reports.

Notes: (1) A discontinuity occurred after 1972, as a new basis for collecting these data was introduced. Since 1977 data are collected from CITB registered firms, the returns adjusted to ensure continuity with earlier DoE statistics.

(2) These are the totals for TOPS courses on masonry and paving, welding and pipecutting, woodworking and machining, bricklaying, carpentry and joinery, house-painting, plastering, plumbing, heating and ventilating, slating and roof-tiling and miscellaneous construction trades.

prenticeships which are formally registered with the NJCBI, there are many other unregistered apprentices taken into training.

Apprentice intake varies cyclically in accordance with both output and craft employment levels. The importance of these factors in determining variations has been evaluated in Briscoe (1976). The peak year for recruitment was 1973 but by 1977, the NJCBI intake had fallen by 28 per cent and was significantly lower than it had been 10 years earlier. It is noteworthy how the local authorities continued to increase their numbers of trainees up to 1975.

Aside from apprenticeships, the supply of craftsmen is enhanced by training programmes organised by both the Construction Industry Training Board (CITB) and the Training Opportunities Scheme (TOPS). The number seeking to gain craft status through shorter training schemes has increased significantly in the period since 1972 and industry recognition of such trainees has gained much wider acceptance. These trainees are likely to have found it easier to gain craft employment in the expansionary climate of 1978 than they did in the contraction of the preceding year.

A further supplement to the skilled workforce of the industry arises from informal training acquired on the job. Many workers who begin with semi-skilled status, for example as a bricklayer's mate, progress quite naturally to skilled status and this 'learning by doing' qualification is widely recognised in the industry. NEDO (1978a) comments on how significant numbers of both carpenters and bricklayers were late entrants to the skilled craft status and many of these received no formal training whatsoever.

The final main source of entrants to the ranks of the craftsmen is from other industries. Construction exchanges manpower particularly with such industries as engineering, timber and furniture, transport and communications, distributive trades, miscellaneous services and public administration (DE, 1970). It has been observed by Woodward-Smith (1979) and others, how a high proportion of those skilled men leaving construction are in the older age brackets and leave for the greater job security available in manufacturing.

A central determinant of the construction industry's ability to recruit skilled workers in the future is likely to reside in the rate of growth of relative earnings. In this respect an appreciation of how construction has compared in recent years with the all manufacturing average can be gained from Figure 7.4. Since 1970, weekly earnings have, overall, increased slightly more rapidly in construction than for the industrial average and they have grown at a comparable rate with earnings in manufacturing. In the period 1972–73 construction earnings were growing significantly faster than the industrial average, but with the downturn in construction activity following 1973 the differential advantage has almost been eroded.

In contrast to the position on relative earnings, construction workers typically have had to work longer average hours than the average worker in other industries but the differential appears to have been narrowing over time and this will clearly favour future recruitment to construction.

The supply to individual crafts within the construction sector is also likely to be influenced by relative earnings. It is apparent from Table 7.13 that differentials have shifted considerably over time. The difference between electricians and other trades has widened significantly during the last decade and bricklayers and carpenters exchanged positions in the earnings hierarchy. Identification of consistent trends is extremely difficult.

The quantitative effects of such changes in earnings and hours upon labour supply will not be established without much further research. Moreover these differentials cover very wide dispersions between the workers who constitute a single craft. Whilst Table 7.13 shows median values for each group, Table 7.14 shows

Table 7.13 Median Gross Weekly Earnings for Selected Construction Trades
Men over 21: £ per week and (index) all industry manual workers = 100

	1968	1973	1978
Carpenter	22.4 (100)	39.0 (107)	71.6 (93)
Bricklayer	21.9 (98)	38.0 (104)	73.2 (95)
Painter	21.7 (97)	34.9 (95)	70.0 (91)
Plumber	22.5 (100)	36.5 (100)	76.3 (99)
Electrician	24.8 (111)	38.3 (105)	90.5 (118)
Unskilled labourer	19.1 (85)	32.0 (87)	65.6 (85)
Craftsman's mate	—	32.9 (90)	63.5 (83)
All industries' manual workers[1]	22.4 (100)	36.6 (100)	76.8 (100)

Sources: *New Earnings Survey* for relevant years.

Note: (1) Manual workers over 21 years of age.

Table 7.14 Distribution of Gross Weekly Earnings in Selected Construction Trades 1978

								Per cent with earnings in range
	£49 or Less	£50–59	£60–69	£70–79	£80–89	£90–99	£100–119	£120 or more
Carpenter	1.7	18.6	25.7	21.0	12.0	8.9	8.2	3.9
Bricklayer	1.6	16.0	22.9	21.1	12.3	10.3	10.8	5.0
Painter	2.2	22.1	25.6	20.0	13.9	7.4	6.3	2.5
Plumber	1.4	11.5	21.0	22.9	13.9	10.0	9.5	9.8
Electrician	1.3	3.6	11.7	17.3	15.4	14.7	18.6	17.4
Unskilled labourer	16.6	21.2	20.3	17.1	11.7	6.3	5.2	1.6
Craftsman's mate	10.7	29.2	21.7	14.9	9.8	6.4	5.1	2.2
All industries' manual workers[1]	6.4	13.0	17.6	18.4	15.8	10.8	11.2	6.8

Source: *New Earnings Survey.*

Note: (1) Manual workers over 21 years of age.

the dispersion about the group medians for the most recent year, 1978. Thus, whilst the earnings data indicate that a bricklayer on average earns £73.2 per week compared with a craftman's mate who earns only £63.5, almost 20 per cent of bricklayers earn £60 or less and more than 20 per cent of craftsmen's mates earn more than £80.

7.3.3 Future employment prospects in construction

Aggregate employment prospects hinge critically, in the first instance, on the demand for the industry's output and, in particular,

Figure 7.6   Construction Output by Types of Work

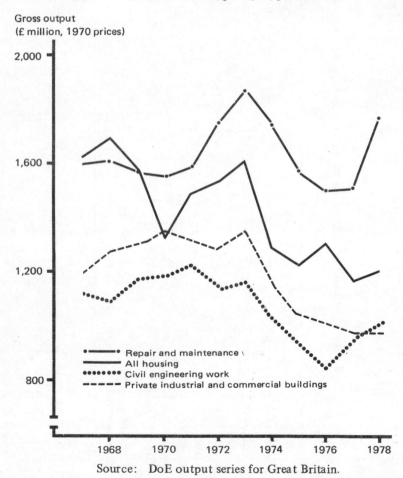

Source: DoE output series for Great Britain.

on the pattern of that output. Figure 7.6 shows the main trends in types of construction output discussed at the beginning of this section. Whilst all types of construction activity have behaved cyclically, both new housing and civil engineering work have, in recent years, followed downward trends. In assessing future output patterns it is useful to examine the determining factors which underlie the demand for each of the main types of construction output.

The output mix

Housing is the most important type of new construction activity and is especially significant for employment prospects because it is the most labour-intensive form of new building. In the longer-run, the number of houses built is set by the number of households relative to the available housing stock, after making due allowance for the type, condition and physical location of this stock. Already, according to the DoE (1977), by 1976 there were some 500 thousand more houses in existence in England and Wales than there were households. However, 15 per cent (2.7 million) of the total stock of housing units were deemed to be either physically unfit, substandard or were subject to overcrowding. In addition, there exist an unspecified number of other houses which are either in a state of serious disrepair or are essentially inadequate for the needs of the families currently living in them. Taking into account this backlog of unsuitable houses, the rate of depreciation of the present stock and the projected average rate of net new houshold formation, the DoE indicates that a minimum number of approximately 230 thousand housing units[15] will need to be built each year simply to maintain present standards in Great Britain.

Whilst considerations of minimal needs serve to set a floor on objectives for new housing output in the future, the actual levels achieved in each year will be determined by more short-term income and price factors. In the private sector, demand increases (inducing a lagged supply response) when real incomes are rising, mortgage finance is more plentiful and mortgage rates are lower. In the public sector, output is principally determined by revenue availability and local housing shortages which cannot be met by provision through private owner-occupation. In the 1970s there is some evidence that new housing output in the public sector varied to compensate for changes in private sector house building while the housing policy of the new Conservative government seems likely to restrict firmly the public sector to a residual role in housing provision. The main engine of any future growth in new house building in the medium-term is likely to be the private sector, where variations in real incomes and relative prices will play a decisive role.

New non-housing public sector work (civil engineering) covers a wide variety of output – educational buildings, structures for the health service, roads, buildings and works for nationalised undertakings and public utilities. All have in common the fact that they are commissioned and paid for by government (both central and local) and are thereby subject to the vicissitudes of fiscal policy. NEDO (1976) has examined in considerable detail the longer-run determinants of these various types of civil engineering work. The best guide to future output in this sector is provided by the White Papers detailing planned government construction expenditures. The 1979 White Paper provides for a small increase in new civil engineering work relative to 1978, mainly in the road building programme and in construction work for the nationalised industries – coal, gas and electricity in particular. Offsetting these increases are planned reductions in the provision of educational buildings. There is no likelihood of a return to the relatively high output levels of civil engineering experienced in the early 1970s. The prospects for the period after 1980 are for stable real output levels.

Buildings produced for private industry have been subject to some of the most pronounced cyclical variations in recent years and therefore they constitute one of the most difficult categories of output to predict. Currently, there is much optimism for a significant growth of output in the private industrial and commercial sector, following the revival of demand which has occurred over the past two years. Obviously, the demand for such buildings derives from the level of demand enjoyed by industry in general, notwithstanding the very complex lagged relationship between the two. However, it is by no means clear that higher final demands must necessarily translate themselves into demands for new or even extended buildings. Refurbishment of older buildings or adaption of existing but previously unused factories is an increasingly viable option, whilst the number of presently unoccupied office blocks is likely to inhibit new commercial developments. New technology will dictate a demand for some buildings, but innovations based on the microprocessor are unlikely to require large new structures to accommodate them, as did the large-frame computers, for example.

Currently, output based on repair and maintenance activity is experiencing a significant upsurge. Most of this increase in demand is attributable to housing repairs and more specifically to a change in policy heralded in DoE (1977). Policy has now moved away from demolition and new building – often with high rise flats replacing older terraced houses – in favour of renovation and improvement. In 1977 grant availability was extended and the level of such grants was significantly increased. The resulting increase in repair and maintenance work – much of it concentrated in the public sector – has been sustained. The prospects of these higher levels of repair and maintenance continuing in the future are considered to be good and since this is a very labour-intensive activity, it is very favourable portent for employment. However, taking repair and maintenance as a whole, more than 50 per cent of output arises from the public sector and since, unlike new building, it constitutes current expenditure, it is a prime target for spending cuts. General restraints on local authority current expenditure noted in Chapter 3 will serve to limit future growth of repair and maintenance output.

Productivity and employment

The implications of shifting patterns of work have been emphasised by NEDO (1976), where the demand for operatives was estimated to vary by 4 to 5 per cent, depending on whether output was housing intensive (high labour content) or civil engineering intensive (low labour content). More detailed studies carried out by the Building Research Establishment (Lemessany and Clapp, 1978) show how the labour requirements for a given real value of construction output vary significantly between different types of activity. These studies, for example, suggest that whilst the average operative man-day input for £1000 contract value at 1970 prices was 56.4 days for housing, it was only 49.6 days for private industrial buildings and a mere 27.2 days for road bulding projects.

The employment of individual trades is determined not only by the balance between the main types of construction activity undertaken but also by the method of construction chosen for each activity. Lemessany and Clapp demonstrate how with new housebuilding a very significant difference exists in the operative man-day inputs between houses constructed by traditional methods and those built using industrialised production. Bricklayers working on the construction of low-rise public sector dwellings on average put in 33.3 man-days per £1000 contract value when traditional construction methods are used, but where a non-traditional approach is

Table 7.15   Industrialised Dwellings: Local Authorities and New Towns:
England and Wales

	Number of starts (thousands)	Starts as a percentage of all local authority dwellings
1967	65.9	39.4
1968	61.4	41.3
1969	53.7	40.0
1970	28.8	25.1
1971	24.3	24.0
1972	18.0	19.8
1973	20.0	23.8
1974	22.9	20.5
1975	25.3	18.8
1976	17.7	14.0
1977	8 5	9.1
1978	3.5	4.5

Source: DoE *H & CS*.

adopted, this figure falls to only 16.2 man-days. Similar significant reductions also apply to plumbers, plasterers, electricians and general labourers. Overall the use of non-traditional instead of traditional building methods in public sector dwelling construction reduces the demand for operative employment by almost 30 per cent. Comparable analyses of alternative methods used in the construction of both educational and hospital buildings has produced broadly similar results.

Industrialised building methods are much more suited to large structures and civil engineering work than to low-level housebuilding. The statistics presented in Table 7.15 indicate how, in local authority housebuilding, industrialised production was already in decline in the early 1970s and more recently there has been a further steep reduction in the use of this method. Such a trend reflects the move away from high-rise dwellings and also the easier availability of traditional craft labour throughout most of the period under examination. A partial consequence of the downward trend has been an apparent lowering of productivity in the housebuilding sector. Whilst it seems most unlikely that industrialised building techniques in this country will ever regain their original popularity for housing construction, their further penetration both in very large structures and in housing components remains quite probable.

Trends in labour productivity constitute the second main determinant, after output, of the level of aggregate employment. Some general measures of recent productivity trends in the construction sector are shown in Figure 7.7. Whichever measure is adopted, it is clear that productivity behaves cyclically, falling when output is declining and rising when output is growing.[16] Whilst an underlying trend in productivity is revealed when a long span of data is considered, this trend is not immediately obvious from the data for the last decade. The use of industrialised building techniques, which raise labour productivity, tend to fluctuate with the output cycle, with contractors often only using this approach when confronted with real skill shortages.

Productivity gains in the industry are not solely related to industrialised building: there exist many other potential sources of such

Figure 7.7   Productivity in Construction.

Index (1970=100)

●●●●●●● Gross output per all man-hours
——— Gross output per operative hour
- - - - - Gross output per worker

gains. Clearly higher levels of investment in plant would be expected to produce increases in productivity. Inspection of published investment series, however, is not especially helpful since the construction industry acquires much of its plant not by purchasing but by hiring – frequently from another sector, such as the finance houses. Census of production analyses indicate that larger construction firms maintain relatively high capital-output ratios, although smaller firms inevitably are not capitalised to the same degree. The evidence suggests that the industry does not suffer from any shortage of plant; instead output is too low much of the time, to enable firms to fully utilise their existing plant.

Unlike many other manufacturing and service industries, it is not thought that construction will lose a large number of jobs as a result of new technologies deriving from the micro-processer. Jenkins and Sherman (1979) have suggested how future technological change will affect design and construction planning with some resulting job loss in the non-manual APTC occupations. Other specific crafts may be at risk as micro-electronic technology renders it more economic to produce building components which require appreciably less fixing and finishing than at present. In this context, the service trades, the electricians, plumbers and heating and ventilating engineers may experience some loss of jobs in the medium-term. However, leaving aside our doubts about the methodology of Jenkins and Sherman, they conclude that for construction 'we expect manpower demand to hold up well and even improve in the medium term as both industrial and house building are undertaken'.

Thus employment prospects in the medium-term hinge mainly on the future level and mix of output. On the basis of the discussion so far, it seems unlikely that productivity will grow strongly in the future unless large increases in output occur. Smaller gains in productivity may arise in response to local and short-term craft scarcities. There is unlikely to be any longer-term labour supply problem for the industry but almost inevitably activity fluctuations can be expected to create limited skill shortages. The solution to such shortages perhaps lies more with improving the mobility of existing craftsmen than with increasing their overall number.

The standard view of construction prospects

Aggregate predictions for the construction sector from the standard view simulation are given in Table 7.16. Construction output

Table 7.16 The Construction Sector 1978–85

	1978	1979	1980	1981	1982	1983	1984	1985
Gross output (£m 1970 prices)	6,086	6,003	5,810	5,974	5,954	6,195	6,389	6,452
Total employment (thousands)	1,612	1,615	1,617	1,635	1,642	1,663	1,685	1,697
Productivity (£ 1970 pr. per man)	3,775	3,717	3,593	3,654	3,626	3,725	3,792	3,801
Average weekly hours	42.5	42.3	42.1	41.8	41.6	41.4	41.2	41.0
Self-employment (thousands)	323	321	319	317	315	315	315	315
Output for all new work (£m 1970 prices)	4,093	4,100	3,968	4,052	4,036	4,258	4,429	4,488
Output of new private housing (£m 1970 prices)	1,041	1,058	1,052	1,127	1,180	1,332	1,373	1,404

Source: Standard view.

Figure 7.8 Construction Employment 1967–85

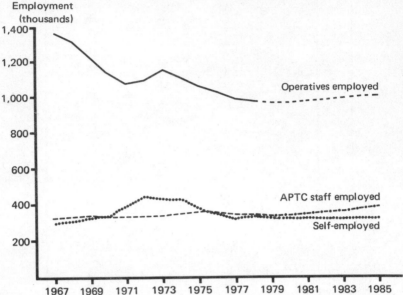

Note: From 1979 employment levels are based on the standard view.

is expected to fall slightly in the short-run to 1980 and thereafter to grow slowly with the most significant rise occurring in the period 1982–85. One of the main components of this growth is new house-building in the private sector, largely determined by the assumed lower rates of interest in the medium-term. Virtually all of the growth in the output of new work is expected to stem from the private sector. Expectations for public sector output are taken from the 1979 White Paper, modified as indicated in Chapter 3.

The resulting employment predictions indicate very little change over the period to 1985 (see Figure 7.8). Total employment is expected to increased by only 1 per cent per annum over the whole 7 year period and most of this increase is concentrated in the period 1982–85. In absolute terms, however, this rise of almost 100 thousand is to be welcomed in view of the poor prospects for employment in other production industries.

The modest fluctuations in output which are expected in the short-run are not likely to cause any significant variations in industry employment levels. No overall growth in productivity is expected in the construction industry up to 1985 and, indeed, some decline in productivity levels is likely in the short-run.

Employment levels in the construction sector are sensitive to medium-term changes in government policy. Certain variations from the standard view have been discussed in earlier chapters. The structural change simulation, for example, leads to higher investment in the economy and particularly benefits construction employment which rises by 1.6 per cent in 1985 relative to the standard view. However, if significant reductions in government capital expenditure programmes were to be introduced then lower levels of construction employment would result. The standard view assumption is for a fall in interest rates from the present high levels. Should this fail to materialise then construction employment levels would need to be revised downwards.

It is obviously desirable to proceed from the highly aggregate predictions of Table 7.16 to produce forecasts firstly for main types of construction worker and secondly for individual craft occupations. In order to accomplish this exercise it is necessary to explore the relationships that exist between the different categories of worker and the various types of output which these workers generate. Thereafter the outputs predicted by the macro-economic model can be used to forecast employment levels for individual occupational groups.

Relationships between disaggregated output and employment in the construction industry are complicated by the fact that the public sector maintains its own labour force which is capable of satisfying a small but significant part of its demand for output. Table 7.17 shows for 1977 how much of the output arising from public sector new housing, civil engineering work and, most important, repair and maintenance is produced by its own agents. Usually, all output originating from private sector clients is carried out by firms in the private sector. Whilst construction workers employed by public authorities produce output for the public sector, a large proportion of the workers employed by private contractors also produce for the public sector. Table 7.17 shows the number of operatives employed by private contractors who were producing output for public sector clients. It is not possible to allocate either APTC staff or self-employed workers to these types of work in the same way.

Matrices similar to those for 1977, have been prepared for each year for 1965–76 and the resulting data are being used to model relationships between various types of construction worker and the different categories of output shown in Table 7.17 The full results of this exercise will be published in due course. However, for present

Table 7.17 Construction Output and Employment Activity Matrix 1977

	Housing		Other new work	Repair and(1) maintenance		Industrial and commercial	All work	APTC staff	Self-employed workers
	Public	Private	Public	Public	Private	Private	Total		
Public authorities									
output(2) £m	36 (6.8)	—	41 (4.4)	472 (54.4)	—	—	549 (11.9)	..	..
employment 000s	15 (11.5)	—	15 (8.9)	200 (77.5)	—	—	230 (23.3)	112 (25.4)	..
Private contractors									
output(2) £m	526 (93.2)	604 (100)	937 (95.6)	395 (45.6)	644 (100)	944 (100)	4,050 (88.1)	..	316
employment 000s	116 (88.5)	85 (100)	153 (91.1)	58 (22.5)	166 (100)	178 (100)	756 (76.7)	229 (74.6)	316
Total industry									
output(2) £m	562	604	978	867	644	944	4,599	..	..
employment 000s	131	85	168	258	166	178	986	441	316

Sources: Output: MRG estimates based on DoE returns for third quarter 1977. Employment: MRG estimates based on DoE totals.

Notes: 'Public' and 'Private' refer to the client commissioning the work; figures in parentheses are the percentages carried out by each employing agency. Disaggregated employment figures relate to operatives only – see text for explanation.
(1) Assumes total repair and maintenance work on housing is allocated in same proportion to public and private sector housing stocks.
(2) 1970 prices.

purposes use can be made of preliminary results to provide a breakdown of the total employment projection into the numbers of self-employed workers, operatives and APTC staff employees. The estimated numbers are presented in Table 7.18. The historical upward trend in APTC staff is reflected in these projections although the downward trends in both the self-employed and operative series are significantly modified by the predicted increases in industry output in the early 1980s. Any marked deviation of future productivity levels from those achieved in the recent past would require these estimated breakdowns to be revised.

Table 7.18   Disaggregated Construction Employment: Standard View

				Thousands
	Self-employed	Operatives	APTC staff	Total employment
1978	323	963	326	1,612
1979	321	964	330	1,615
1980	319	962	336	1,617
1981	317	974	344	1,635
1982	315	976	351	1,642
1983	315	988	360	1,663
1984	315	999	371	1,685
1985	315	1,000	382	1,697

Suitable models for predicting individual skill employment have yet to be evolved. Simple extrapolation of historical trends is not particularly helpful since most operative skills have been in decline over the last decade, but the standard view prediction is for slowly increasing employment up to 1985. If the skill distribution of operative employment remains constant in the medium-term, then each craft will experience an overall rise of almost 4 per cent over the period 1978 to 1985. This would imply, for instance, an increase in employment of about 5 thousand carpenters and joiners and 3 thousand bricklayers. Chapter 4 demonstrates that although the group other transferable craftsmen is likely to fall by 88 thousand, to 1985, the industry effect, mainly coming from construction is positive, see Table 4.19. (Other transferable craftsmen is the group to which the majority of skilled craftsmen in construction are classified.) If, however, the future distribution favours more craftsmen and fewer semi-skilled and unskilled labourers, then these numbers could be significantly higher. The predicted 17 per cent increase in APTC staff between 1978 and 1985 is likely to be concentrated mainly on managerial and technical staff. The expected higher demand for private housing will also lead to a revival in clerical, office and sales staff employment levels after 1982.

Given the relatively slow rate at which aggregate construction employment is predicted to increase, it is not envisaged that any serious long-term supply deficiencies will arise. Nevertheless significant short-term problems may be expected. Models developed by Briscoe (1976) suggest that apprentice intakes are significantly related to current output levels and craft employment. In the period 1973–77 both output and craft employment were falling so that the number of apprentices taken on by private contractors experienced a corresponding decline as indicated in Table 7.12. Since it takes a full three years to complete apprentice training, the supply of newly qualified craftsmen to the construction labour market will be reduced, at least until 1980. As the number of trainees employed in the industry has fallen, so the number of completions on the TOPS construction – oriented courses has increased to partially compensate. Stagnating output and employment levels up until 1982 imply that the apprentice intake will be relatively low, so that if the predicted small but significant increase in output materialises after 1982, recruitment from the external labout market will be required. The delays involved may lead to temporary shortages of craftsmen in certain trades. Further TOPS training might play a roll in this situation but this raises more general issues which are discussed in the following section and in Chapter 9.

7.4 Conclusions

Quite fundamenal questions of training policy must be faced in view of the high levels of unemployment expected over the medium-term. Our discussion of past changes affecting skilled labour in engineering and construction suggests that the apparently common problem of recurrent shortages has been tackled rather differently in these two industries. The impact of the industrial training board system has been much greater in engineering whereas the importance of TOPS relative to the activities of the training board is greater in construction. The ITB system acts primarily through influencing the internal labour market operations of firms and TOPS affects more directly the external labour market. Both aim to stimulate the supply of newly trained workers but the EITB and CITB are mainly concerned with manipulating the intake of apprentice recruits whereas TOPS trainees are predominately adults engaged on short courses. Differences in the structures of these industries obviously explain this difference of emphasis – the encouragement of industrial training by small firms with high labour turnover presents organisational difficulties and it is perhaps to be expected that the-government Skillcentres would play a greater role in the provision of training places for construction trades.

As regards the employment situation over the medium-term for engineering the results discussed in Chapter 4 and the present chapter indicate that the decline in employment opportunities will continue but the fluctuations in output growth, which determine the profile of that decline, are likely to be much smaller in amplitude than has been the case since the early 1950s. Output could, itself, also decline slightly between 1978 and 1985. Unless major structural change can be brought about by government intervention, the form of which it is extremely difficult to specify in practical terms (but see Chapter 4), prospects for returning to pre-1973 growth rates are very bleak. Even if this were possible, the employment of craftsmen would certainly fall.

For construction trades, on the other hand, the situation is likely to be somewhat different. Even in the standard view the employment of operatives rises slightly and would benefit further under the structural simulation. This arises not only through a higher rate of growth of output but also because of very modest growth in productivity compared with engineering. Changes in technology and in the composition of construction output over the medium-term are expected to slow down the growth in productivity, notwithstanding the fact that the industry is already working well below capacity. In engineering the reverse is the case. If anything, pressure is building up for higher rates of productivity growth than those assumed in our simulations. This reflects the opportunities for gains through the introduction of microprocessors, although it will take some time for such applications to affect productivity trends at the aggregate industry level. The impact of import penetration upon engineering (a fact of life which has little influence upon construction) will continue to affect the most labour-intensive of sectors. Mechanical

engineering is, therefore, likely to decline through both unfavourable technological developments and foreign competition (increasingly from newly industrialising countries) and craft employment
will be severely affected.

Fluctuations in total construction output under the standard view
are also modest by past standards, although this is due partly to the
assumption we have made about the eventual fall in interest rates
which takes place quite smoothly.

The labour market situations likely to develop for these
important skill groups will be affected not only by the nature of
changes in demand but also by supply factors. The first of these
relates to the internal supply of new craftsmen trained through
apprenticeship schemes. Recently both industries have experienced
a fall in the numbers of young craftsmen because of reductions in
apprentice intakes in the 1970s. This will continue for longer in the
case of construction and might lead its firms to have greater recourse
to the external labour market than should be necessary for engineering where employment will, in any event, fall. The depressed state
of engineering may well make it increasingly difficult for the EITB
to maintain present levels of training without an exceptional use of
special awards, as firms revise downwards their expectations of
future demand and fears of labour shortages diminish. Increasing
the proportion of first-year craft/technician trainees who move on
to technician training is desirable but will not solve the problem of
determining the level of craft training to be promoted by the Board
over the medium-term.

Plans for TOPS training envisage no great change in the levels
of provision of training places for engineering and construction
trades. In construction, however, pressures for further adult training
or supplementary action by the CITB on apprentice training may
well mount up if employment of skilled men recovers as indicated
in the standard view. Should fluctuations in output growth in both
industries be quite moderate, then maintaining the link between the
recruitment of young apprentices and future demand may turn out
to be less of a problem than in the past. However, the high levels of
unemployment amongst skilled men and the localised nature of
those shortages which are likely to arise point to the need for devot-
ing resources to the most flexible forms of training. Particular emphasis on the responsiveness of TOPS to the needs of the labour
market and on reducing training lead-times associated with ITB ap-
proved courses would pay dividends in these circumstances.

On the other hand, manpower agencies should not accept too much of the responsibility for dealing with labour shortages. Poorly designed wage-systems, unnecessarily discriminating conditions of employment and the under-utilisation of skilled labour already employed are for employers and trade unions to tackle.

The role of government in providing an environment in which the manpower agencies can operate to best effect is also crucial and Chapter 9 will deal with these broader policy issues.

Notes

1 See MacKay *et al* (1971), Hunter (1978) and Lindley (1979) for further details.

2 See Lindley (1975) and Briscoe (1976).

3 See, for example, Bosworth (1974 and 1976), Lindley (1974 and 1975) and Wabe (1974 and 1977).

4 Note that shipbuilding is excluded from engineering throughout this chapter unless otherwise specified.

5 See Cowling *et al* (1980).

6 These estimates use the DE statistics on the entry of young people to employment and on occupations in engineering.

7 A more detailed treatment of the argument summarised here is given in Lindley (1976).

8 This obviously raises more general questions about the functioning of the labour market in relation to the employment of young people and research in this area is in progress within the Manpower Research Group.

9 Hawkesworth (1978), however, provides some very tentative econometric evidence of such an affect and discusses the results of other studies.

10 Estimates of craft and technician employment for 1978 are not yet available.

11 Increasingly, a spectrum of qualified craftsmen is being produced depending on the number of modules etc. undertaken after basic training. Our estimates provide guidance on the numbers of newly trained craftsmen completing, on average, two modules each.

12   See EITB (1975).

13   The term 'lump' refers to the lump-sum method of payment traditionally used to pay labour-only sub-contractors. Strictly it applies to all such self-employed workers, both those recognised by the Inland Revenue and those who are not. In common usage, however, the 'lump' is most often reserved to describe those workers who make a practice of tax avoidance and whose precise numbers are virtually impossible to determine.

14   Local registers maintained by Employment Offices provide information on local shortages which may often be in marked contrast to the labour supply position in other regional localities.

15   Forecasts of this kind are necessarily very hazardous since to some extent housing standards can be improved by programmes of rehabilitation (repair and maintenance work) rather than new building. Moreover, housing units have been getting smaller over time so that the real value of the average sized unit is probably significantly less now than it was a decade earlier.

16   The relationship between productivity and output in the construction sector is rendered complex by the slow adjustment of employment to changing output levels. Hence using measures of productivity which incorporate estimates for all types of construction worker in the denominator, productivity is shown in Figure 7.7 to be falling after 1971, at a time when output was continuing to rise to its peak 1973 value, However, examination of the alternative estimate which uses only operatives employed in the denominator indicates that productivity also continused to rise until 1973, and then fell back as output went into decline.

References

Bosworth, D.L. (1974). 'Production Functions and Skill Requirements'. In J. Stuart Wabe (ed.), 153–96.

——(1976). *Production Functions: A Theoretical and Empirical Study.* Farnborough: Saxon House.

Briscoe, G. (1976). 'Towards and Explanation of the Demand for Apprentices in the Construction Industry', Centre for Industrial Economic and Business Research Paper no. 67. Coventry:. University of Warwick. (mimeographed)

Construction Industry Manpower Board *(1977). Second Report to the Minister of Housing and Construction.* London: Department of Environment.

Cowling, K., P. Stoneman, J. Cubbin J. Cable, G. Hall, S. Domberger and P. Dutton (1980). *Mergers and Economic Performance.* Cambridge : Cambridge University Press.

Department of Employment (1965). 'Characteristics of Unemployed Skilled Construction Workers'. *Gazette,* 73, (November), 483–496.

——(1970). 'Approximate Estimates of the Flows of Employees Between Industries'. *Gazette,* 78, (April), 303–307).

——(1979). 'Skill Shortages in British Industry'. Gazette, 87, (May) 433–436.

Department of Environment (1977). *Housing Policy: A Consultative Document,* London: HMSO.

——(1979). *Housing Policy: A Consultative Document.* London: HMSO. ment. London : HMSO.

Engineering Industry Training Board (1975). *The Craftsman in Engineering (An Interim Report).* Research, Planning and Statistical research Paper no. 1. Watford : EITB.

Hawkesworth, R.I. (1978). 'The Movement of Skill Differentials in the U.K. Engineering Industry'. *British Journal of Industrial Relations.* 16, 3, 277–486

Hunter, L.C. (1978). *Labour Shortages and Manpower Policy.* Manpower Studies No. 19782. Manpower Services Commission. London : HMSO.

Jenkins, C. and B. Sherman (1979). *The Collapse of Work.* London : Eyre Methuen.

Lemessany, J. and M.A. Clapp (1978). 'Resource Inputs to Construction: the Labour Requirements of Housebuilding'. *Building Research Establishment Current Paper* no. 76.

Lindley, R.M. (1974). 'Manpower Movements and the Supply of Labour' in J. Stuart Wabe (ed.). 239–281.

——(1975). 'The Demand for Apprentice Recruits by the Engineering Industry, 1951–71. *Scottish Journal of Political Economy* 22, 1, 1–24.

——(1976). 'Aspects of the Labour Market for Skilled Engineering Craftsmen'. Research Report for the Engineering Industry Training Board. (mimeographed)

——(1978). (ed.) *Britain's Medium-Term Employment Prospects.* Coventry : Manpower Research Group, University of Warwick.

——(1979). 'Economic Decision-Making and Active Manpower Policies'. Paper presented to the European Consortium for Political Research. Free University of Brussels, April.

MacKay, D.I. *et al.* (1971). *Labour Markets Under Different Employment Conditions.* London: George Allen and Unwin.

Manpower Services Commission/National Economic Development Office (1977). *Engineering Craftsmen : Shortages and Related Problems.* Committee on the Supply and Utilisation of Skilled Engineering Manpower. London: NEDO.

National Economic Development Office (1976). *Construction into the Early 1980's.* Building and Civil Engineering EDCs. London : HMSO.

——(1978) Construction Forecasts Building and Civil Engineering Joint Forecasting Committee. London: HMSO.

——(1978a). *How Flexible is Construction ?* Buiding and Civil Engineering EDCs. London : HMSO.

National Federation of Building Trades Employers (1979). *Quarterly State of Trade Enquiry.* London : NFBTE.

Phelps Brown, E.H. (1968). *Report of the Committee of Inquiry into Certain Matters Concerning Labour in Building and Civil Engineering.* Cmnd. 3714. London : HMSO.

Wabe, J. Stuart (1974) (ed.) *Problems in Manpower Forecasting.* Farnborough: Saxon House.

——(1977). *Manpower Changes in the Engineering Industry.* Engineering Industry Training Board Research Report no. 5. Watford : EITB.

Woodward-Smith, N (1979). *A National Register of Craft Skills in the Building Industry.* London: Civic Trust.

8 The Labour Market for Scientists and Technologists

D.L. BOSWORTH AND R.A. WILSON

8.1 Introduction

In this chapter we turn our attention to the labour market for scientists and technologists (including engineers). There are a number of reasons for choosing to focus on this particular group. There has been a heated debate about the possibility of shortages of such types of manpower in the UK and the detrimental effect this imbalance might have on the dynamic performance of the economy. This question is of great importance, given the long training period required to produce this type of manpower and the large sums of money involved, much of it from the public purse.

At the outset it is important to define which individuals are involved in this labour market. A crucial distinction is between those *qualified* in scientific or technological subjects and those working in the occupational categories, *scientist* or *technologist*. This distinction is illustrated in Table 8.1 which shows the proportion of the stock of individuals qualified at degree level (QSEs)[1] who were employed as scientists or technologists (STs). On average, only about 44 per cent of QSEs were employed as scientists or technologists over this period while QSEs made up only about 48 per cent of the total number of STs.[2]

These overall figures disguise a marked difference between those qualified in science subjects and those qualified in engineering or technology. Only about 25 per cent of holders of science degrees find employment as scientists although some two-thirds of those who work as scientists are qualified at degree level. On the other hand, over 50 per cent of those qualified in engineering or technology are employed as engineers or technologists but less than one-third of those working in these occupations are qualified.

From Table 8.1 it is clear that in aggregate the proportion of people qualified in science or technology who take up employment in this area has been declining over time.[3] Perhaps surprisingly the percentage of scientists or technologists who are also QSEs also fell between 1961 and 1971 (although it rose slightly from 1966). This is in contrast with evidence from other sources which indicates an increasing tendency towards a qualified workforce.[4]

Table 8.1   Qualifications and Employment of Scientists and Technologists

		Per cent	
	1961	1966	1971
QSEs employed as STs	45.6	44.3	41.9
STs who were QSEs	51.3	45.4	46.7

Sources: OPCS *Census of Population,* (1961, 1966 and 1971).

It is clear that we are therefore dealing with two distinguishable but interdependent labour markets. It is relatively easy to identify the supply of QSEs, but much less straightforward to measure the extent to which this may be supplemented by unqualified persons who are capable of carrying out the job of ST. On the other hand, the demand for individuals is best analysed in terms of the occupational and functional dimensions of the labour input required. It is perhaps easier therefore to identify the demand for STs than that for QSEs. However, we have found it fruitful to formulate our analysis primarily in terms of the market for QSEs although we attempt to bear in mind the broader question of the demand and supply of occupational skills as well as qualifications.

The remainder of the chapter is divided into four sections. In section 8.2 we examine historical trends in the labour market for scientists and technologists, and consider the extent to which it has slackened in recent years. Section 8.3 discusses the problems involved in modelling the demand for and supply of QSEs while in section 8.4 the models developed in the previous section are used to make forecasts of likely changes in the labour market for QSEs in the 1980s. Our conclusions are contained in the final section.

8.2 Recent Trends in the Market for Scientists and Technologists

8.2.1 The supply of QSEs

Since 1959 the total stock of QSEs has more than doubled. The most rapid increase has been in the number of qualified scientists. As shown in Table 8.2, the latter rose from 122 to 307 thousands over the period 1959–76. The corresponding figures for qualified engineers exhibit a rather slower rate of growth, particularly after 1971.

Not all QSEs will be available for work. We need therefore to consider that part of the total stock who are economically active. This is

Table 8.2　Stocks of Qualified Scientists and Engineers 1959-76 [1]

Thousands

	Scientists		Engineers/technologists		Total	
	Total	Active	Total	Active	Total	Active
1959	122	100	133	125	255	225
1960	129	106	140	131	269	237
1961	137	112	147	137	284	249
1962	144	117	155	144	299	261
1963	151	123	162	150	313	273
1964	158	129	169	155	327	284
1965	166	135	175	161	341	296
1966	175	142	183	167	358	309
1967	185	149	191	174	376	323
1968	194	156	198	180	392	336
1969	205	165	208	188	413	353
1970	218	174	219	196	437	370
1971	231	184	230	205	461	389
1972	245	194	242	215	487	409
1973	260	205	254	223	514	428
1974	276	217	264	231	540	448
1975	292	228	272	237	564	465
1976	307	(240)[2]	278	(242)[2]	585	(482)[2]

Source:　Department of Industry (1977), pp. 5–7, Tables 1, 2 and 3.

Notes:　(1)　Persons possessing a degree or equivalent professional qualification in science or in engineering or technology respectively.

　　　　(2)　MRG estimates in parentheses.

also presented in Table 8.2. It shows a similar pattern of growth to the total stock but at a somewhat slower rate. Movements into and out of the active stock due to retirement etc. are encapsulated in the economic activity rate, showing the proportion of the total stock available for work. Table 8.3 shows that activity rates for both groups have declined over the period. This, however, has served only to offset slightly the growth in the total stock.

Table 8.3   Activity Rates for QSEs 1959-76

Per cent

	Scientists	Engineers & technologists
1959	82.2	94.0
1960	82.0	93.6
1961	81.8	93.2
1962	81.7	92.9
1963	81.5	92.6
1964	81.4	92.2
1965	81.2	91.9
1966	81.0	91.5
1967	80.8	91.1
1968	80.6	90.6
1969	80.3	90.1
1970	80.0	89.6
1971	79.7	89.1
1972	79.3	88.6
1973	78.9	88.1
1974	78.5	87.6
1975	78.2	87.1
1976	78.2	87.1

Source: Department of Industry (1977), Tables 2 and 3.

The decline in activity rates must be seen in the context of the overall trends in participation rates noted in Chapter 6. Activity rates for males have declined for most groups of workers and this dominates the picture for this group, particularly for qualified engineers. Analysis of data from the Census of Population shows that in contrast to males, activity rates for female QSEs have risen, albeit very slowly, over this period.[5] However, the proportion of QSEs

Table 8.4 Rates of Flow into and out of the Total Stock of QSEs: Great Britain 1959–1975

| | Rate of outflow | | Rate of inflow | | Rate of loss due to net emigration | Rate of loss due to death and net migration | Net rate of increase |
| | Emigration | Deaths | Immigration | New supply | | | |
	1	2	3	4	5	6	7
1959	2.3	0.9	2.6	5.7	-0.3	0.6	5.3
1960	2.1	0.9	2.5	6.1	-0.4	0.5	5.5
1961	2.6	0.9	2.8	5.9	-0.2	0.7	5.1
1962	2.6	0.9	2.7	5.7	-0.1	0.8	4.7
1963	2.8	0.9	2.3	5.9	0.5	1.5	4.4
1964	3.2	0.9	2.1	6.2	1.1	1.9	4.3
1965	3.3	0.9	2.5	6.5	0.8	1.7	4.9
1966	3.3	0.9	2.7	6.5	0.6	1.5	5.0
1967	3.7	0.8	2.3	6.5	1.4	2.2	4.3
1968	3.1	0.9	2.5	7.0	0.6	1.5	5.5
1969	3.1	0.9	2.6	7.0	0.5	1.4	5.7
1970	3.0	0.9	2.6	7.0	0.4	1.3	5.6
1971	2.5	0.9	2.2	6.7	0.3	1.2	5.6
1972	2.2	0.9	2.2	6.2	0.0	0.9	5.3
1973	2.9	0.9	2.3	5.9	0.6	0.7	5.2
1974	2.2	0.9	2.0	5.4	0.2	1.1	4.3
1975	2.5	0.8	2.0	5.2	0.5	1.3	3.9

Source: Department of Industry (1977).

Notes: Individual elements may not sum to totals due to rounding. Rates are expressed as a percentage of the opening stock.

Table 8.5 Functional Areas: Nature of Work

Nature of work	Professional scientists		Professional engineers					
	1968	1971	1966	1968	1971	1973	1975	1977
General management and technical administration	9.3	8.4	26.7	26.4	29.3	29.0	30.8	31.3
Research design and development	36.4	41.0[(1)]	30.6	29.8	30.1	28.6	26.8	21.4
Education and training	24.9	24.7	7.1	7.5	7.8	7.8	7.1	5.6
Other engineering/other scientific	27.8	22.6	33.9	32.1	30.9	30.4	32.4	39.7
Non-engineering/non-scientific	1.6	3.3	1.7	4.1	1.9	4.0	2.9	2.0
Total: all work	100.0	100.0	100.0	100.0	100.0	100.0	100.0	100.0

Sources: CEI surveys of professional engineers, 1968, 1971 and 1977; DTI surveys of professional scientists, 1968 and 1971.

Note: (1) Excludes a very small proportion of design activities.

who are females is low, forming less than 1 per cent of qualified engineers and less than 25 per cent of qualified scientists in 1971. Although there has been a tendency for these proportions to rise over time, this has had the effect of depressing overall activity rates since the activity rate for females is generally only about two-thirds of that for males. However, since changes in the proportion of females and in their activity rates have only been slight, they have not had a large impact.

Changes in the total stock of QSEs can be attributed to changes in the various flows into and out of this stock. The stock in period t, N(t), is related to that in the previous period by the accounting identity.

$$N(t) = N(t-1) + E(t-1, t) - M(t-1, t) - D(t-1,t). \quad . \quad . \quad . \quad (1)$$

where E(t–1,t) is the inflow of new entrants to the stock between t–1 and t, M(t–1,t) is the net outflow due to migration and D (t–1,t) is the outflow due to deaths.

Table 8.4 illustrates that throughout this period the rate of inflow[6] due to new supply has been well in excess of the rate·of loss due to deaths and net migration. The rate of loss due to deaths has remained virtually constant at just under 1 per cent per annum throughout the period. Migration flows, while more volatile, have remained quite small in net loss terms, rising to a maximum of 1 per cent or so in the mid-1960s. For scientists the period began with a net migratory inflow changing to a net outflow in the 1960s and finishing with a net inflow again at the end of the period. For engineers the pattern was similar although there was a net outflow throughout this period. For both groups however, the supply side has been dominated by the steady influx of new entrants. This is reflected in section 8.3 by the attention given to this particular flow as opposed to the other aspects of supply.

8.2.2 The demand for scientists and technologists – trends in employment

The demand for QSEs depends upon the levels of activity in the various functions that utilise their particular abilities. In many instances these functions are only indirectly linked to the process of production. In Table 8.5 we present information on the proportions of professional engineers working in different functional areas.

In addition to showing the main areas of employment, this table illustrates some of the main trends such as the move towards management and administration away from most other functions. Comparable data are not available for professional scientists for the whole period, but the table provides some indication of the similarities and differences. Notable is the much greater concentration of scientists in the R & D and educational and training functions than is the case for engineers and the greater proportion of engineers to be found in management and administration. While the period 1968 to 1971 for scientists is too short to isolate trends, it does appear that the pattern of functional employment was changing for the two groups so as to reinforce the observed differences.

Table 8.6   Employment of QSEs by Industry 1961, 1966 and 1971

Persons qualified in engineering and technology.	1961	1966 (thousands)	1971	1961	1966 (per cent of total)	1971
All industries	135.6	164.2	200.7	100.0	100.0	100.0
All manufacturing	64.1	73.5	88.4	47.3	44.8	44.1
Engineering	45.3	51.4	59.6	33.5	31.2	29.6
Manufacturing n.e.s.	18.9	22.3	28.9	14.0	13.8	14.5
Public utilities etc.[1]	19.0	21.9	25.1	13.9	13.3	12.6
Construction	8.6	14.1	16.4	6.4	8.6	8.2
Professional services	22.3	28.6	35.6	16.5	17.4	17.6
Public administration	12.7	13.6	19.9	9.4	8.3	9.9
Industries n.e.s.	9.0	12.6	15.2	6.6	7.6	7.6
Persons qualified in science						
All industries	110.7	139.6	179.5	100.0	100.0	100.0
All manufacturing	30.0	36.3	50.3	27.1	26.0	28.0
Engineering	9.4	12.3	17.0	8.6	8.9	9.6
Manufacturing n.e.s.	20.7	23.9	33.4	18.6	17.1	18.7
Public utilities etc.[1]	1.9	3.4	5.5	1.8	2.5	3.0
Construction	0.3	0.8	0.9	0.3	0.6	0.5
Professional services	58.8	74.0	89.0	53.2	53.0	49.6
Public administration	5.6	7.2	11.2	5.1	5.2	6.2
Industries n.e.s.	14.1	17.9	22.7	12.7	12.7	12.7

Source: Department of Industry (1977).

Note: (1) Includes transport and communications.

The industrial deployment of QSEs in employment is shown in Table 8.6. With the exception of agriculture and mining and quarrying which are included in industries n.e.s., all industries have shared in the substantial rise in QSEs employed between 1961 and 1971. The table also illustrates the concentration of qualified engineers in the production industries in general and of qualified scientists in professional (mainly educational) services and to a lesser extent in manufacturing. This growth in employment and the distribution of QSEs among industries is closely reflected in the numbers employed in the occupational categories scientist or engineer (see Bosworth and Wilson, 1978, Table 4). However, it may be the case that this pattern of growth and deployment across industries merely parallels total employment. That this is not the case is illustrated in Table 8.7

Table 8.7 Scientists and Technologists as a Percentage of Total Employment: Great Britain, 1951–71

	1951	1961	1966	1971
All technologists				
Engineering	1.26	2.60	3.30	3.82
Manufacturing n.e.s.	0.33	0.65	0.81	1.01
Public utilities etc.[1]	0.56	0.90	1.48	1.77
Construction	0.60	0.98	1.62	1.97
Professional services	2.66	4.89	5.17	5.64
Public administration	0.49	0.47	0.53	0.58
Industries n.e.s.	0.06	0.10	0.18	0.20
Scientists				
Engineering	0.16	0.19	0.17	0.16
Manufacturing n.e.s.	0.39	0.46	0.51	0.60
Public utilities n.e.s.[1]	0.06	0.08	0.14	0.17
Construction	0.01	0.01	0.02	0.02
Professional services	1.10	2.61	2.64	2.95
Public administration	0.23	0.25	0.29	0.36
Industries n.e.s.	0.04	0.03	0.05	0.04

Source: OPCS *Census of Population* (1951, 1961, 1966, and 1971).
Note: (1) See Table 8.6.

which shows the density of the occupational categories, scientist and technologist within the total workforce of each industry. The increase in the proportion of both these occupational categories in almost all industries is apparent, particularly for technologists. In addition, the much greater density of technologists in the engineering industry and of both scientists and technologists in professional services is illustrated.

In discussing the demand for this type of manpower, section 8.3 below concentrates upon QSEs rather than STs. The section begins with some naive models based primarily on time trend extrapolation or on industry output as the major explanatory variable but goes on to discuss briefly a model of the functional demand for QSEs. Consideration is therefore given to the importance of changes in both industrial structure and the pattern of functional employment on the demand for QSEs.

8.2.3   Labour market indicators for scientists and technologists

A crude comparison between the numbers of QSEs available for work and the number of STs actually employed reveals a growing gap as shown in Table 8.8. On the one hand, the number of engineer

Table 8.8   Gap between Supply of QSEs and number of Jobs for Scientists and Technologists

Thousands

	QSEs available for work		Jobs		Gap	
	Scientists	Engineers	Scientists	Engineers	Scientists	Engineers
1961	112	137	51	207	−61	70
1966	142	167	59	284	−83	117
1971	184	205	68	324	−116	119
1976	240	242	77	357	−163	115

Source: See text.

jobs has risen faster than the supply of qualified engineers. On the other hand, the supply of qualified scientists has grown much faster than the number of scientist jobs. This type of comparison appears to reinforce the widely held view that there are significant shortages of engineers.

However, previous work in this area, particularly for the United States, has shown the problems involved in assessing the extent of shortages (Arrow and Capron, 1959), while various studies for the

UK have emphasised the large degree of substitution possible, enabling firms to replace engineers by technicians or scientists (Mace and Taylor, 1975).

According to traditional theories of the labour market, the most likely indicators of a tightening market are increasing relative wages as employers compete with one another for a scarce resource, and a reduction in unemployment and a corresponding rise in vacancies.

No information on vacancies for QSEs is available. However, there are statistics available on the unemployment of newly qualified persons. Table 8.9 compares the percentage of new graduates

Table 8.9   **Comparison of Unemployment amongst QSEs with other workers (Males)**

| | | Per cent unemployed | | |
| | New graduates | | | |
	All graduates	Science	Engineering & technology	All workers
1963	2.69	2.82	1.48	2.32
1964	1.94	1.74	1.15	1.73
1965	1.44	1.29	0.93	1.68
1966	2.26	1.86	1.30	2.55
1967	3.38	2.76	1.65	3.18
1968	3.89	3.51	1.74	3.18
1969	4.19	4.00	2.23	3.39
1970	5.39	5.87	2.63	3.64
1971	7.79	8.41	6.77	5.20
1972	6.70	7.42	5.26	4.40
1973	6.20	6.38	3.14	2.95
1974	6.55	6.96	2.88	4.05
1975	9.74	8.28	3.88	6.45
1976	12.00	11.53	5.30	6.88
1977	12.00	11.72	4.79	7.22

Sources: Unemployment of new graduates from UGC, *First Destination of University Graduates* for relevant years.
Unemployment of all workers from DE *Gazette* for relevant years.

still searching for work in the December after graduation with the total unemployment rate. A significant slackening in the labour market is apparent for all groups but it is clear that the deterioration of the situation for new graduates in general has been worse than the average. Those qualified in science have also experienced increasing difficulty in obtaining suitable work. The situation for engineering graduates has been more favourable than that for other graduates but, in relation to the aggregate unemployment rate, shows a slight worsening since the early 1960s.

A similar picture emerges if vacancies and unemployment are compared for the occupational categories scientists and technologists from 1973 to 1978.[7] Although there are important and well documented problems with the approach, we can use the ratio of

Table 8.10   Unemployment and Vacancies for Scientists and Technologists 1973—78

Thousands

	Scientists			Technologists		
	U	V	U/V	U	V	U/V
1973	1.4	0.5	2.6	2.9	3.3	0.9
1974	1.1	0.4	2.8	2.8	3.2	0.9
1975	1.1	0.4	3.1	3.5	2.4	1.4
1976	1.7	0.3	6.4	4.8	2.3	2.1
1977	2.4	0.4	8.7	5.1	1.7	3.1
1978	2.5	0.2	14.0	4.2	1.6	2.6

	All professional and related occupations in science, engineering and technology and similar fields			All occupations		
	U	V	U/V	U	V	U/V
1973	8.6	9.7	0.9	529	323	1.6
1974	7.8	9.0	0.9	503	336	1.5
1975	10.5	6.0	1.8	796	159	5.0
1976	14.9	4.8	3.1	1127	125	9.0
1977	17.7	4.5	3.9	1209	167	7.3
1978	16.1	5.0	3.2	1202	226	5.3

Source: DE *Gazette* for relevant years.

Notes: Estimates are for June in each year.
          The U/V ratios are based on unrounded estimates of U and V.

unemployment to vacancies as an indicator of tightness in the labour market. In Table 8.10 all categories show the lowest U/V ratio in 1973 or 1974 following the peak in economic activity in 1973. After this date a very definite slackening is apparent for all groups up to 1976. The labour market as a whole tightened in 1977 and 1978. This is reflected in a tightening for the technologists and all professional and related categories. The situation for scientists is rather different however, with a continuous rise in U/V. The ratio for engineers is much less than that for other groups throughout, but comparisons of this statistic between occupational categories are fraught with difficulties. We would emphasise the similar pattern for all groups rather than use the data in Table 8.10 as evidence of a shortage of one particular type of manpower rather than another.

Table 8.11 reports data on the earnings of QSEs and other groups of workers. The series for professional engineers grows faster than the corresponding series for scientists over the entire period up to 1974, but since then scientists have overtaken them. In comparison with the index of average earnings, however, growth has been relatively slow in both cases. Also shown are the series for non-manual and manual employees, taken from the Department of Employment's six-monthly earnings enquiry. The manual series grows at a similar rate to the index of average earnings and faster than the non-manual series. However, since 1963 the latter shows a much faster rate of increase than the index for engineers and, more marked still, than the index for scientists.

On this evidence, there seems to be little reason to suspect an increasing shortage of qualified scientists or engineers. However, it must be emphasised that a large part of this erosion of differentials may have been the direct result of incomes policies which have consistently favoured the lower paid. If we reject the traditional theory of the labour market, shortages may exist despite the observed fall in relative pay. On the other hand, it is difficult to see why employers have not been able to raise their offers of remuneration between incomes policies if shortages were as serious as some commentators have suggested.[8]

An alternative way of assessing the relative states of various labour markets is to consider the rate of return to an individual of undertaking a course of education or training in order to qualify for a job as a scientist or engineer. This type of calculation takes into account changes in tax rates, grants and allowances, relative unemployment, etc. as well as movements in relative earnings. The method uses age earnings profiles at a point in time as an indicator of expected future earnings. Complete details of the methodology and results are given in Wilson (1980).

Table 8.12 shows that the rate of return to becoming a QSE has changed substantially over time. In 1968, an individual investing in himself in this way could expect a post-tax return of 14 per cent. By 1974 this had fallen to 9 per cent with little change since then.

Table 8.11   Comparison of Earnings of QSEs and Other Workers

Index nos. 1968=100

	Professional scientists	Professional engineers	Non-manual earnings (males)	Manual earnings (males)	Index of average earnings (all workers)
1960	67.8	60.8	64.1	63.9	..
1961	72.2	65.0	67.3	66.7	..
1962	76.8	69.6	71.0	69.0	..
1963	81.6	74.9	74.7	72.8	72.8
1964	86.4	79.4	79.0	78.7	78.3
1965	90.5	84.4	85.7	85.2	84.6
1966	94.0	89.2	89.6	88.3	88.6
1967	96.9	94.5	93.7	93.0	93.0
1968	100.0	100.0	100.0	100.0	100.0
1969	106.9	107.6	107.7	108.0	108.4
1970	115.0	115.6	121.3	122.0	123.2
1971	121.6	123.6	129.1	134.5	135.9
1972	133.1	137.3	144.1	155.7	156.6
1973	144.0	151.0	161.5	177.9	176.2
1974	154.8	176.0	182.7	211.4	213.7
1975	188.3	201.4	229.7	259.0	266.8
1976	223.4	228.8	274.0	291.2	299.9
1977	258.7	255.8	298.5	316.9	328.5

Sources: Data for professional scientists and engineers are taken from the surveys of members' earnings carried out by the professional institutions.

                The next two series are from the Department of Employment's six-monthly earnings enquiries.

                The fifth series is based on the index of average earnings published in the DE *Gazette*.

Again the evidence suggests a slackening of the labour market for both groups, particularly those qualified in science, reflecting the overall movement against graduates in the labour market. However, it may be the case that the current lower rates of return might depress the numbers and quality of potential entrants and result in shortages in the future. The question of the lagged response of supply to the current market situation becomes critical.

Table 8.12   Rate of Return to becoming a QSE[1]

Per cent

Those qualified in	1968	1971	1974	1975
Science	14.0	12.5	8.5	9.5
Engineering & technology	14.5	13.0	10.0[2]	9.0

Notes: (1)   Return to individual of undertaking a degree or equivalent qualification. Estimates rounded to nearest 0.5 per cent.

(2)   Average of figures calculated for 1973 and 1975.

Source: MRG estimates based on data from professional institutes.

In order to assess the market situation correctly in this context, a comprehensive treatment of supply and demand, including an examination of lagged adjustment is required. Studies of this type have been carried out for the United States by Freeman (1971). Our attempts to move in this direction are discussed in the next section.

8.3 Modelling the Labour Market for QSEs

8.3.1 Modelling supply

From the discussion of trends in supply in section 8.2, it is clear that the most important factor affecting the total numbers of QSEs has been the inflow of new entrants. Migration flows have also been of some importance but our attempts to model the latter in terms of economic variables have so far proved unsuccessful. For these reasons this section concentrates upon the flow of new entrants. Our basic approach has been to develop a demographic accounting model of the flow through the education system of students who eventually emerge as QSEs. Ideally one would like to be able to trace flows through school, further and higher education, but gaps and inconsistencies in the data limit what is possible in practice.

Newly qualified QSEs are composed of first degree university graduates, persons awarded degrees by the CNAA and persons obtaining professional qualifications. Since the majority of these are young people moving directly from school to university or college after taking A levels, for present purposes we can simplify the accounting model. Rather than attempting to trace all of the flows through the system, we can aggregate over different stages and across different routes to becoming a QSE. Thus instead of relating each flow to its

Table 8.13 Actual and Potential Flows of Newly Qualified Scientists and Engineers

Thousands

	Population of 18 year olds[1]	Qualified leavers[2]	Qualified leavers as % of 18 year olds	Flow of new QSEs[3]		New QSEs as % of qualified leavers	
				Scientists	Engineers	Scientists	Engineers
1960/61	700	43.0	6.1	..	..	..	..
1961/62	735	48.6	6.6	..	..	..	..
1962/63	749	56.6	7.6	8.1	9.8	18.8	22.8
1963/64	745	60.0	8.1	9.3	10.6	19.1	21.8
1964/65	848	68.3	8.1	10.1	11.6	17.8	20.5
1965/66	906	82.9	9.2	10.9	11.9	18.2	19.8
1966/67	834	85.5	10.3	11.7	12.1	17.1	17.7
1967/68	790	89.9	11.4	13.7	13.1	16.5	15.8
1968/69	763	94.5	12.4	14.6	13.5	17.1	15.8
1969/70	741	97.6	13.2	15.0	14.8	16.7	16.5
1970/71	744	102.4	13.8	15.3	14.6	16.2	15.5
1971/72	760	108.1	14.2	16.0	13.6	16.4	13.9
1972/73	752	109.9	14.6	16.5	12.9	16.1	12.6
1973/74	752	111.9	14.9	16.6	11.5	15.4	10.6
1974/75	776	113.1	14.6	17.0	11.5	15.5	10.5
1975/76	800	115.3	14.4	16.6	10.9	14.8	9.7
1976/77	822	122.2	14.9	16.5	11.4	14.6	10.1

Source: MRG estimates based on data from DES and Department of Industry.

Notes: (1) 18 year olds in the January of the previous academic year.
   (2) Qualified leavers from school or further education with 2 or more GCE 'A' levels or 3 or more Scottish 'H' levels.
   (3) As defined in the text.

opening stock we relate flows out of universities and further education to the stock of potential QSEs, the latter being measured by the number of persons obtaining certain A level qualifications τ years before, where τ reflects the length of the course. Table 8.13 illustrates the total population of 18 year olds and the numbers qualifying with two or more A levels in science subjects. The population of 18 year olds who provide the major part of the potential supply of new entrants to higher education has fluctuated quite sharply over this period as a result of demographic factors. The number rose up to 1965/66 and then fell again to 1969/70 before starting its present upward trend which will peak in the early 1980s. Not all of these 18 year olds are qualified to go into higher education. The second column in the table illustrates that the number of persons obtaining two or more A levels shows the same demographic cycles noted for the total population of 18 year olds. However, there is also a very strong upward trend in the proportion obtaining A levels as shown in column 3.

If the transition proportions or rates of flow through the educational system remained constant over time, we could explain the outflow of newly qualified graduates by equations of the form,

$$F(t) = a + bA(t-\tau) \qquad \qquad (2)$$

where $F(t)$ is the flow of QSEs from a certain course in year t; $A(t-\tau)$ is the number of persons obtaining the prerequisite A levels τ years earlier and τ reflects the length of the course. An alternative way of specifying this relationship would be to deflate $F(t)$ and $A(t-\tau)$ by the population of 18 year olds τ years earlier, $P(t-\tau)$

$$\frac{F(t)}{P(t-\tau)} = c \left[\frac{A(t-\tau)}{P(t-\tau)} \right]^d \qquad \qquad (3)$$

In equation (2), b represents the proportion of A level students who will emerge as QSEs. The parameter a reflects flows of new QSEs other than persons included in A $(t-\tau)$. In equation (3), d represents the extent to which the proportion of the population of 18 year olds who become new graduates responds to the proportion obtaining A levels. If this response is equiproportionate this coefficient will be unity and c will measure the transition proportion.

Equations (2) and (3) provide a good explanation of the new supply of QSEs. However, in both cases, the number or proportion of new QSEs is overestimated in recent years. The equations fail to pick up a decreased willingness of A level students to proceed into higher education (see Table 8.13, columns 6 and 7). This is reflected in the results by estimates of d well below unity and a severe problem of serial correlation.

An obvious explanation for this change in behaviour is that the declining rate of return to becoming a QSE has led to a falling proportion of qualified school-leavers carrying on their studies at a higher level. We do not have a complete time series of expected rates of return; however, a good indicator of this might be the relative earnings of scientists and engineers. Using the earnings data reported in Table 8.11, we computed estimates of the earnings of scientists and engineers relative to non-manual earnings. Adding this variable to equation (3) and taking logs we obtain:

$$\mathrm{Ln}\left[\frac{F(t)}{P(t-\tau)}\right] = e + f\mathrm{Ln}\left[\frac{A(t-\tau)}{P(t-\tau)}\right] + g\mathrm{Ln}\left[RE(t-\tau)\right] \quad \ldots \ldots (4)$$

where $RE(t-\tau)$ is a measure of relative earnings at the time an average individual would be making the decision whether or not to carry on into higher education. Equations of this type were found to fit the data very well by all the usual statistical criteria. Parameter values are in accord with *a priori* expectations and the problem of overestimation in the recent period disappears, as does the serial correlation. The coefficient f is insignificantly different from unity implying that a constant share of qualified school leavers will become new entrants to the stock of QSEs *ceteris paribus*. However, in recent years all other things have not been equal; in particular, the decline in relative earnings of QSEs has reduced the proportion of A level students following this type of career. The estimate of the elasticity of new supply with respect to earnings (g) is about 0.6 for scientists and 1.3 for engineers.

Ideally one would like to be able to establish whether other aspects of supply are also responsive to economic variables. We have already referred to problems in modelling migration flows; modelling the proportion of the total stock who are economically active is even more problematic. The basic difficulty is that we are limited to only three firm census observations, the remainder of the observations in Table 8.3 being very crude estimates. Until better data become available, it will not be possible to develop the treatment of total supply in line with our work on new supply.

8.3.2 Modelling demand

Traditional, profit maximising theory suggests that firms will demand an additional unit of labour if its contribution to the performance of the firm (i.e. the value of its marginal physical product) exceeds the going wage. The theory is essentially static: it deals with labour whose contribution is direct and immediate. The principle must be extended if it is to be applied to the decision to hire highly qualified technological manpower, because these workers are involved in both current (eg. direct production) and dynamic (eg. R & D) activities of the firm. The decision to hire such a worker is more of an investment decision: the firm incurs wage costs in the immediate period, but may not experience any tangible benefits for some time, perhaps not for many years. Given the presence of both current and dynamic contributions, the benefits of employing an additional scientist or engineer must be viewed as a stream of outputs or revenues stretching into the future. In a dynamic setting, the firm demands additional QSEs if the sum of discounted future revenues attributable to these workers exceeds the cost of hiring them (again, appropriately discounted back to the base period). At this stage, the information necessary to develop a complete model based on this type of approach is not available and we must be content with less ambitious goals.

As a first step toward a more complete understanding of the factors that influence demand, the employment of QSEs was related to time and then to the level of economic activity in each industry group. The employment data were drawn from Department of Trade and Industry (1971) and Department of Industry (1977) and provide information about eleven manufacturing and seven non-manufacturing industries in seven non-consecutive years. Using the time series observations for each industry, both linear and log-linear time trends were fitted through the observed levels of employment. The time trends appeared to fit reasonably well. The exponential functions provide direct estimates of the average rates of growth in QSE employment over the period 1958–71 and these are reported in Table 8.16. Within the manufacturing sector, food, drink and tobacco, other manufacturing and electrical engineering record the fastest average annual rates of growth. In the non-manufacturing sector, the fastest rates are in local government and public utilities. A number of groups exhibit a downward trend in employment; this is particularly strong in agriculture. Linear and log-linear specifications were also estimated in order to establish the relationship between the employment of QSEs and the level of activity in each sector. The results suggested that the relationships in which output appeared were generally inferior to the simple time trends. Attempts to include both output and time as explanatory variables were hampered by an inadequate number of observations. These regressions suffered from serious problems of autocorrelation and their overall explanatory power was not significantly better than for the simple time trends.

It is clear from data provided by the professional institutes (and reported in part, in Table 8. 5 above) that QSEs are employed in a wide variety of functions, many of which are only tenuously linked to the level of current production. This fact may to some extent explain why the simple regressions of employment on output were not wholly successful. In the light of this, a more rigorous model has been developed that allows the overall demand for QSEs to reflect the separate demands in each functional area. This model is explained in detail in Bosworth (1979) but its main characteristics are summarised below.

The model asserts that the demand in each area is related to the level of activity in that area and to the 'price' of QSEs in relation to other inputs. It was not possible to estimate separate demand relationships for each functional area as there were no official data on employment by function. Total employment of QSEs (ie. in all functions) was therefore related to the following variables: (a) the level of direct production activity, (b) expenditure on research and development, (c) investment activity, (d) marketing activity and (e) a time-trend to pick up any long-term trend effects. As this increases the number of explanatory variables in the model substantially, the time series observations by themselves were inadequate to test the model. In order to obtain sufficient observations, the time series and cross-sectional dimensions were combined to form a pool of 70 observations covering the manufacturing sector. There were further problems in obtaining measures of 'in-house' marketing activity and this variable consistently failed to make a significant contribution to the explanation of QSE employment (see Bosworth, 1979). The other variables were all statistically significant however, and they combined to give an acceptable explanation of QSE demand. Based on a fixed coefficient function, a 1 per cent increase in R & D activity results in a 0.9 per cent rise in QSE employment; a 1 per cent rise in production causes a 0.6 per cent rise in QSEs; and a 1 per cent rise in investment activity causes a 0.1 per cent rise in QSEs. Further research, however, has indicated that constraining the elasticity of substitution between inputs as in the fixed coefficient or Cobb-Douglas functions is not appropriate. Estimation of a generalised CES function indicates a degree of substitution for QSEs of around 0.2 to 0.3 (see Bosworth, 1979). This can be interpreted as tentative evidence that QSEs are difficult to replace in the functions that they undertake. In the exercises involving the more sophisticated model reported below, however, fixed coefficient relationships are assumed.

8.4 Forecasts for the 1980s

8.4.1 Forecasts of supply
Using the demographic accounting model developed earlier it is possible to make projections of the supply of QSEs, given the opening stock and assumptions about the various rates of flow and economic activity rates. Complete details of the methodology are given in Bosworth and Wilson (1978).

From Table 8.4 it is clear that the rate of outflow due to deaths has remained virtually constant. Obviously this flow will be dependent upon, among other things, the age structure of the stock of QSEs. This factor might be expected to cause a reduction in this flow as the influx of newly qualified persons in the 1960s and 1970s reduces the average age of the QSE population. For this reason we have adopted the assumption that this rate of flow is equal to its minimum historical value of 0.81 per cent for science and 0.83 per cent for engineering.

For migration we are on less firm ground. In the absence of anything better, we have assumed that individual emigration of immigration rates take on their historical average values. These imply a rate of net loss of 0.2 per cent and 0.6 per cent per annum for science and engineering respectively. In order to test the results for sensitivity to these assumptions, variations of ± 0.05 per cent on these rates were also used.

Finally, new supply was projected using equations of the same type as equation 4 in section 8.3. The number of newly qualified QSEs depends upon the population of 18 year olds, a projection of the proportion of 18 year olds who are qualified at A level and an assumption about the movement in the earnings of scientists and engineers relative to all non-manual workers.

The projection of the population of 18 year olds is taken from official projections by the Government Actuary's Department while the proportion of these people obtaining 2 or more A levels is based upon DES forecasts. Three different assumptions were made with respect to relative earnings. The basic assumption was of no change in relative earnings from the 1977 values. The alternatives were: first, a continued decline at the same rate as experienced in the 1960s and 1970s of about 1.5 per cent per annum, and second, a reversal of this decline with a restoration of relativities to the values observed in the mid–1960s by 1985. The impact of these alternative assumptions was a variation of ± 7.5 thousand in the total stock by 1985 in response to a variation in relative earnings of ± 10 per cent.

The alternative projections of the total numbers of QSEs are presented in Tables 8.14 and 8.15. The high and low variants combine the extreme assumptions with respect to relative earnings with those on death rates and net migration rates.

Table 8.14   The Future Supply of QSEs under Alternative Assumptions

	Total supply of QSEs			QSEs available for work		
	Central	High	Low	Central	High	Low
1976	584.8	. .	. .	482.1	. .	. .
1982	710.8	715.3	706.2	584.3	595.1	573.4
1985	784.3	797.0	772.1	643.7	662.0	625.9

Source: MRG estimates; see text for further details.

Table 8.15   Active Supply of QSEs: Science and Engineering

	Science			Engineering		
	Central	High	Low	Central	High	Low
1976	239.8	. .	. .	242.3	. .	. .
1981	294.5	299.8	289.3	271.4	275.8	267.0
1985	347.9	358.0	337.7	295.8	304.0	288.2

Not all of this stock of QSEs will in fact be available for work. In order to assess the total number of persons willing to supply themselves to the labour market, these projections need to be combined with projections of economic activity rates. Projections of activity rates will depend upon changes in the age structure of the population of QSEs, changes in the proportion of females, and changes in the activity rates of these subgroups within the population. Using past trends as a guide, these factors seem likely to offset one another over the next few years, leaving the total activity rates virtually unchanged; this therefore provides our basic assumption. A variation of ± 1 per cent is assumed to allow for a different proportion of females or a marked change in activity in response to changes in earnings. Combining these alternative assumptions with respect to economic activity rates with our high and low variants in respect of total numbers, gives our three final projections of the supply of QSEs available for work as shown in Table 8.14. In the central projection the total number of QSEs rises from 585 thousands in 1976 to 784 thousands by 1985. Of this growth, 125 thousand is accounted for by those qualified in science and 74 thousand by those qualified in engineering. Around this central projection, alternative assumptions with respect to earnings and migration make a difference of less than ± 2 per cent by 1985 for both those qualified in science and those qualified in engineering. In terms of those willing to work, the increase is 162 thousand in total, of which 108 thousand is accounted for by qualified scientists and 54 thousand by qualified engineers. The range around the central projections is now rather larger, about ± 3 per cent in total. Before commenting further on these results, we turn to our methods of projecting the demand for QSEs.

8.4.2 Forecasts of demand

The projections of QSE demand are much more tentative than those for supply for two main reasons. The first is that the modelling of demand is still in the very earliest stages of evolution. The second is that the most recent observation of QSE employment is 1971, which is far removed from our forecast period of 1978–85. Forecasting future demands under these conditions is clearly a hazardous business. Two sets of projections are presented. The first set consists of simple regressions based on time series data for each industry group of QSE employment on time and on output. The second set of results is based on pooled time series – cross-sectional data for manufacturing industry as a whole. We concentrate on the first set because, while estimating the more realistic model described in section 8.3.2 on the basis of pooled data is extremely revealing in describing past demands for QSEs, it has a number of important problems in a forecasting context. In particular, it becomes necessary to obtain forecasts of the independent variables before predictions for the dependent variable can be obtained. In the case of output and investment, their values are generated by the macroeconomic model, but in the case of R & D and advertising, exogenous forecasts must be obtained.

The first set of demand forecasts is based on time trends or on time series output data for each industry. The details of using both these models are reported in Bosworth and Wilson (1978, pp. 32–6). Our earlier comparison of the time trend and output regressions for each industry indicated that on balance the time trends performed substantially better than the output-based equations. A further basis of comparison between the two functions concerns the accuracy with which they predict the overall level of QSE employment in 1976. While this overall level of employment is not known precisely, we estimate that the active stock of QSEs was approximately 482 thousands in this year (see Table 8.14) and unemployment of this group was around the 3 per cent mark. Total employment of QSEs was therefore approximately 468 thousand. Comparison of the alternative predictions of total employment for 1976, shown as the all industry figures in Table 8.16 and 8.17, with the actual figure of 468 thousand, indicates the superiority of the time trend models, at least in aggregate. For all models, the forecasts for 1981 and 1985 relative to 1976 have been adjusted for each industry in proportion to the error exhibited in 1976 for total employment.

The revised estimates of the demand for QSEs based on the exponential time trends are reported in columns 3 to 5 and those based on the linear time trends appear in columns 7 to 9 of Table 8.16; the revised estimates based on trends in output are reported in columns 2 to 4 and 6 to 8 respectively in Table 8.17. Even now, after anchoring the various projections on the same total for 1976, the adjusted linear and log-linear projections based on simple time trends differ by over 10 per cent in the forecast year 1981 and by over 20 per cent by 1985. The revised projections based on output differ much less between the linear and log-linear versions. In addition, the results based on output are now much closer to the forecast employment of QSEs based on the linear trend. Even so, the implied rate of 'unemployment' (an accounting balance between our forecast levels of demand for and supply of QSEs in 1985) is going to differ substantially

Table 8.10 Annual Growth Rates and Time Trend Projections of QSE Employment

Thousands

Industry group	1976-85 % p.a.	Exponential time trends				Linear time trends			
		1976	Revised forecasts			1976	Revised forecasts		
			1976	1981	1985		1976	1981	1985
1. Food, drink and tobacco	5.8	8.1	7.8	10.4	13.1	7.1	7.5	8.9	9.9
2. Chemicals and allied	4.3	36.0	34.6	43.0	51.2	33.8	35.8	41.1	45.4
3. Metal manufacture	3.8	10.9	10.5	12.7	14.8	10.2	10.8	12.2	13.3
4. Scientific instruments	3.5	4.2	4.0	4.8	5.6	4.1	4.4	5.0	5.5
5. Mechanical engineering	3.3	31.3	30.2	35.6	40.7	29.7	31.4	35.1	38.2
6. Electrical engineering	5.2	41.9	40.3	52.3	64.4	37.2	39.3	45.5	50.6
7. Aerospace	-0.3	8.2	7.9	7.8	7.7	8.2	8.7	8.6	8.4
8. Motor vehicles	4.1	5.5	5.2	6.4	7.6	5.1	5.4	6.1	6.7
9. Other vehicles	3.3	3.9	3.7	4.4	5.0	3.7	3.9	4.4	4.8
10. Textiles etc.	2.1	5.9	5.7	6.3	6.9	5.7	6.1	6.6	7.0
11. Other manufacturing	5.7	15.3	14.7	19.6	24.6	13.3	14.1	16.5	18.5
Total manufacturing		171.1	164.7	203.4	241.6	158.3	167.3	190.0	208.2
12. Mining	-0.7	3.7	3.6	3.4	3.3	3.7	3.9	3.7	3.6
13. Agriculture	-3.9	2.6	2.5	2.1	1.8	2.3	2.4	1.6	0.9
14. Public utilities	5.0	35.8	34.5	44.4	54.3	32.3	34.2	39.6	44.0
15. Education	5.0	105.9	101.9	130.8	159.8	96.0	101.4	117.6	130.5
16. Health	3.7	13.8	13.3	15.9	18.5	13.0	13.7	15.5	16.9
17. Local government, construction	6.2	40.2	38.7	52.7	67.6	34.8	36.7	43.4	48.7
18. Other services, etc.	5.2	112.7	108.5	141.0	173.9	102.2	108.0	125.9	140.3
Total non-manufacturing		314.8	303.0	390.4	479.1	284.2	300.3	347.3	384.9
All industries		485.9	467.6	593.8	720.7	442.5	467.6	537.3	593.1

Source: MRG estimates; see text for details.

Table 8.17 Output-based Projections of QSE Employment

Thousands

| Industry group | Log-linear output | | | | Linear output | | | |
| | 1976 | Revised forecasts | | | 1976 | Revised forecasts | | |
		1976	1981	1985		1976	1981	1985
1. Food, drink and tobacco	7.4	8.2	9.0	11.5	7.0	7.8	8.4	10.0
2. Chemicals and allied	32.0	35.4	36.2	39.7	33.2	37.0	38.0	42.4
3. Metal manufacture	6.5	7.2	6.6	6.2	6.6	7.3	6.8	6.4
4. Scientific instruments	3.5	3.8	3.7	3.7	3.7	4.1	3.9	3.9
5. Mechanical engineering	24.0	26.5	24.8	23.8	24.0	26.7	25.1	24.0
6. Electrical engineering	35.7	39.4	45.5	48.2	34.5	38.5	43.6	45.9
7. Aerospace	8.9	9.8	10.8	11.9	8.9	9.9	10.6	11.1
8. Motor vehicles	3.8	4.2	4.2	4.0	3.8	4.2	4.2	4.1
9. Other vehicles	3.3	3.7	4.3	5.1	3.2	3.6	4.0	4.3
10. Textiles etc.	5.1	5.7	5.3	5.2	5.1	5.7	5.3	5.3
11. Other manufacturing	11.2	12.4	13.3	14.6	11.1	12.3	13.1	14.3
Total manufacturing	141.3	156.2	163.7	173.9	141.1	157.1	163.0	171.6
12. Mining	4.1	4.5	5.0	5.0	4.1	4.6	5.3	5.3
13. Agriculture	3.4	3.8	3.7	3.2	3.4	3.8	3.6	2.9
14. Public utilities	33.6	37.2	40.2	42.3	32.8	36.5	39.2	40.9
15. Education	106.3	117.5	116.6	120.5	103.9	115.7	114.9	118.5
16. Health	15.6	17.2	19.4	21.9	15.3	17.0	19.1	21.3
17. Local government, construction	23.7	26.1	27.6	31.5	23.9	26.6	28.0	31.5
18. Other services etc.	95.3	105.2	113.4	132.7	95.5	106.3	113.6	130.0
Total non-manufacturing	281.9	311.5	326.0	357.2	278.9	310.5	323.7	350.5
All industries	423.3	467.6	489.8	531.1	420.0	467.6	486.8	522.1

Source: MRC estimates; see text for details

depending on which functional form is chosen. These three, however, yield considerably smaller projections than the exponential time trend.

While output itself is to some extent trended with time, the output equations were generally statistically inferior to the time trends. Remembering our earlier discussion, current output is, after all, only one of a number of important explanatory variables, whose omission may lead to biased estimates and projections. While exactly the same sort of criticisms can be levelled at the time trend equations, they do seem slightly more reliable than the output equations at least in so far as fitting the past data is concerned. Of the two time trends, the linear model is likely to lead us less far astray than the exponential model.

A second set of forecasts was based on the more complicated functional model for manufacturing only, described in section 8.3.2. The projected values of output and investment generated by the macroeconomic model can be inserted into these QSE demand equations. These are derived from the results in our standard view (see chapter 4). In addition, however, predictions of real research and development (R & D) expenditure in 1981 and 1985 are also required. Ideally variations in R & D expenditure should be separately modelled and, indeed, work along these lines is in progress. At the present time, however, R & D expenditure was simulated around the most likely values of R & D based on observation of past trends over the period 1958–75 (see Bosworth 1979a). Almost all manufacturing industries exhibited a quadratic trend in R & D (and in R & D per unit of value added), generally reaching a peak during the late 1960s, being lower in the late-1950s and mid-1970s. Three basic assumptions were made with regard to R & D: (a) that it would rise steadily from its 1976 level to regain its highest post-war level; (b) it would follow a roughly average post-war level (i.e. at about its 1972 level); and (c) it would fall steadily back to its lowest known post-war level. With the most pessimistic of assumptions about R & D it was possible to generate levels of demand for QSEs in manufacturing below even the output-based forecasts reported in Table 8.17. With the more reasonable assumptions that R & D would rise to its average post-war level, the predicted demand for QSEs was very much on a par with the output-based forecasts for all manufacturing. On the optimistic assumptions that R & D activity will regain its previous highest postwar level, the forecast demand lies between the output and linear time trend predictions. We have therefore not reported these projections, confined as they are to manufacturing industries only.

Our supply equations are obviously simplistic and this criticism applies still more to even the most sophisticated of the demand models. The projections made at the current time have not allowed for the influence on demand of changes in relative wages, nor the ability of firms to substitute less qualified manpower for QSEs. However, the simulations undertaken for the more advanced demand model lead to quite different predictions in the demand for QSEs simply through the variation in R & D expenditure.

8.4.3. Comparison of future supply and demand

Our projections given in Table 8.14 indicate an economically active stock of 584 thousand out of a total stock of 711 persons holding a degree or equivalent qualification in science and technology in 1981 and 644 out of 784 thousand in 1985. Taken together with forecasts of demand, reported in Tables 8.16 and 8.17, this implies a substantial deviation between supply and demand. The exponential time trends suggest a position of excess demand for QSEs of less than 2 per cent in 1981 but of well over 10 per cent by 1985. Our feeling is that the tendency for this model to overestimate employment in 1976 increases as the forecast horizon is expanded (despite anchoring the projections to the fairly firm figure for 1976). The remaining three equations (i.e. the linear time trend and the output-based regressions) all indicate the more likely outcome of a position of excess supply of QSEs by 1981, a situation that does not appear to improve by the year 1985. Of the alternative naive models of demand tested we have a slight preference (in terms of fitting the observed data and the prediction for 1976) for the results of the linear time trends. This model suggests that demand grows according to the average annual increment in employment experienced during the period up to 1971. Using the figures in Table 8.16 this yields a projected level of QSE demand of 537 thousand in 1981 and 593 thousand in 1985. Comparison with the estimated active stock indicates an accounting imbalance between supply and demand of approximately 8 per cent in both 1981 and 1985. This prediction of excess supply, rather than excess demand, is reinforced further by the results of estimating the more complex model based on the composite of demands in each functional area. This model indicates a probable level of excess supply at some intermediate level, lying between the linear time trend and the output-based predictions.

Two further points should be made. First, the large range of possibilities only serves to emphasise the crude nature of the estimates produced. This can be attributed partly to inadequate data, particularly on the demand side, about the number of QSEs employed in various functions and of their contributions to output. Second, demand and supply forecasts have been undertaken quite separately, with no explicit mechanism by which either might adjust so as to remove imbalances in the QSE labour market. It was argued in section 8.3.1, for example, that relative earnings (partly a reflection of market forces) may have a significant (if lagged) influence on the supply of QSEs. It has been shown elsewhere (Bosworth, 1979) that wages also influence the demand for QSEs. Further research is therefore required to determine the extent to which imbalances might be eliminated by market forces and meanwhile we would underline the well-known caveats to be attached to comparisons of demand and supply forecasts of the kind made above.

8.4.4 Summary of future prospects

We have seen that in the past the demand for QSEs has followed a fairly steady time-trend. Demand seems to have risen to meet the steadily rising and substantial influx of new supply, although unemployment has also increased recently. Initial attempts to find a relationship between QSE employment and output have not been very successful. The more complex model for manufacturing that attempted to account directly for the different functions undertaken by QSEs was more acceptable from a theoretical standpoint and was more successful in explaining past trends, but data shortages in the sample period and the difficulties of forecasting the independent variables limit the usefulness of the model for forecasting at this stage. It is interesting to note that despite the depressed state of production and investment, and despite the downturn in real R & D activity (see Bosworth, 1979a), QSE employment has continued to rise unabated. This suggests that employers may have changed their patterns of demand for QSEs and qualified manpower in general, finding new areas to make use of such people.

Our projection based upon the linear time trend seems to give the most likely scenario for 1985. The projections of demand based on output appear to be too pessimistic, not reflecting changes in the relationship between QSE demand and output which have taken place since 1971. The projections that incorporate an exponential time-trend on the other hand appear to be overestimating the likely number of QSE jobs in 1985. By 1976, the latter imply 4 thousand more jobs than QSEs; yet as we have noted in earlier sections there appears to be little evidence of any general shortage, in fact, if anything, quite the reverse. While this equation fits the period of very rapid expansion of QSE employment between 1958 and 1971 well, it does not seem to give us a likely indication of job prospects in the period up to 1985. Thus, it is our view that the market for QSEs will probably move more in the direction of excess supply by 1981–85, particularly if the traditional functional activities of QSEs (eg. research and development) remain depressed or decline further. It is possible, however, that employers will continue to find new avenues of employment for QSEs by up-grading jobs and raising hiring standards. The main impact may not therefore be upon the more highly qualified, but may filter down the job hierarchy and worsen the plight of the less well-qualified workers.

8.5 Conclusions

The evidence examined in this study, although tentative, has painted a fairly consistent picture of the labour market for QSEs at least as far as the past is concerned. From figures on unemployment, vacancies and relative wages, the current indications are of an excess supply rather than shortages of QSEs. The rate of return to training as a QSE has fallen persistently over the period and would appear to undermine the incentive for potential entrants to follow this career route, although it must be added that this is possibly the case for all qualified professional workers. Our crude comparisons of supply and demand projections for 1985 also point, if anything, to a slowly growing excess supply of this type of labour. On this evidence we find it difficult to support the demand for increasing the new supply of QSEs above the present levels as advocated in, for example, the report by the British Association for the Advancement of Science (BAAS, 1977). Only a major investment strategy embodying a substantial increase in research and development activity would seem to warrant such a policy.

Two caveats must be added to this conclusion. Only the overall number of QSEs has been considered here; we have largely ignored *quality* and *composition*. The report by the BAAS (1977) shows a marked difference in the quality of candidates for university places in science and technology compared with other subjects as measured by A level scores (BAAS, 1977, Tables 10, 11, pp. 17–18). It may be that there is a shortage of well-qualified people. If this is the case, one does not have to look far for an explanation. It has already been seen in section 8.2 how relative pay and, consequently, the rate of return to becoming a QSE have declined. The BAAS report also quotes evidence of a survey of sixth formers' opinions which showed that scientific occupations are low down the ranking of status and salary (BAAS, 1977, Table 6, p.13). On our evidence these opinions are probably justified. Until employers and society are willing to pay QSEs relatively more, it is difficult to see how this situation can improve. There is no point in trying to persuade sixrh formers of the value and status of QSEs if employers obviously do not place such a high value on their services in practice. The problem of incomes policy constraining employers' behaviour has already been noted and it is clear that all salaried workers have suffered to some extent as a result, but if employers wish to recruit higher quality QSEs we cannot see how this can be achieved without a large increase in relative pay.

Although there is no evidence at present of a widespread shortage of QSEs, it seems clear that if individuals facing these low rates of return do choose *not* to follow this career path, then eventually we may observe the situation worsening in terms of absolute numbers as well as quality. Such a shortage could then build up in the absence of some action on the question of pay or alternative feedback response. The consequences of such dynamics are missing from our model at the current time. Our approach has to date largely failed to incorporate wage rates and other labour market variables in the supply and demand equations in a satisfactory manner. Nevertheless we have unearthed tentative evidence that supports the view that such a mechanism does operate to some extent and our future research will endeavour to make this explicit.

On the question of composition we would argue that while there may be no problem of shortages in aggregate the composition of the stock of QSEs may be out of balance with demand. Lack of data prevents us applying the type of analysis presented here to persons qualified in individual disciplines for which the market situation may be very different from that observed here for scientists and engineers. Finally it is worth emphasising that our evidence does suggest that we appear to be dealing with at least two distinct labour markets. Engineers seem to face a much tighter labour market than scientists. At the same time, while it would be unwise to talk of a shortage of QSEs, both scientists and engineers obviously face a much more favourable labour market situation than the average worker.

Notes

1. Including those possessing an equivalent professional qualification in science or technology.
2. More complete details of occupational classifications used are given in Appendix C. 'QSEs' is in common usage as an abbreviation for people qualified in science, engineering and technology. For the purpose of analysis this group is split into those qualified in science and those qualified in engineering and technology (engineering for short). In dealing with the occupational classification of people actually in employment we use the terms scientists and technologists, the latter embracing all engineers.
3. This decline occurs primarily for mechanical, electrical and electronic engineers. The dilution of qualified manpower in these occupational categories may reflect relatively bouyant demand causing firms to recruit people with lesser qualifications.
4. For example the results of the 1977 survey of professional engineers carried out by the Council of Engineering Institutions.
5. Department of Industry (1977), Table 19, p. 34.
6. Expressed as a percentage of the opening stock.
7. The period is limited by the need to maintain a consistent occupational classification.
8. The evidence presented in Table 8.11 indicates that the earnings of scientists have increased more rapidly than those for engineers in the 1970s, so it would appear that employers have been in a position to change relative pay to a considerable extent.

References

Arrow, K.J. and W.M. Capron (1959). 'Dynamic shortages and price rises: the engineer scientist case'. *Quarterly Journal of Economics,* 73, no. 2, 292–308.

Bosworth, D.L. (1979). 'The demand for Qualified Scientists and Engineers'. MRG Discussion Paper no. 7. Coventry Manpower Research Group University of Warwick. (mimeographed)

——(1979a). 'Recent Trends in Research and Development in the United Kingdom'. *Research Policy,* 8, no. 2, 164–85.

Bosworth, D.L. and R.A. Wilson (1978). 'The labour market for technicians, scientists and technologists'. Report prepared for the Manpower Services Commission. MRG Research Paper no. 32. Coventry Manpower Research Group University of Warwick. (mimeographed)

British Association for the Advancement of Science (1977). *Education, Engineers and Manufacturing Industry.* A Report to the British Association Co-ordinating Group. Birmingham: University of Aston.

Council of Engineering Institutions (1970). 'The Survey of Professional Engineers 1968'. (A joint survey by the Ministry of Technology and Council of Engineering institutions. See also surveys for 1966, 1971, 1973, 1975 and 1977.) London: HMSO.

Department of Industry (1976). *Persons with qualifications in engineering technology and science: Census of Population 1971, Great Britain* London: HMSO.

——(1977). *Changes in the population of persons with qualifications in engineering, technology and science, 1959 to 1976.* Studies in Technological Manpower no. 6. London: HMSO.

Department of Trade and Industry (1971). *Persons with qualifications in engineering, technology and science, 1959–1968.* Studies in Technological Manpower no. 3. London: HMSO.

Department of Trade and Industry and the Council of Science and Technology Institutes (1973). 'The Survey of Professional Scientists 1971'. (See in addition, the results of other surveys carried out over the years by the Council of Science and Technology Institutes and its individual member institutes.), London: HMSO.

Freeman, R.B. (1976). 'The Decline in the Economic Rewards to College Education'. *Review of Economics and Statistics,* 59, no. 1, 18–29.

Mace, J.D. and S.M. Taylor (1975). 'The Demand for Engineers in British Industry: Some Implications for Manpower Forecasting'. *British Journal of Industrial Relations,* 13, no. 2, 175–92.

Office of Population Censuses and Surveys (1970). *Classification of Occupations 1970.* London: HMSO.

Wilson, R.A. (1980). 'The Rate of Return to Becoming a Qualified Scientist or Engineer in Great Britain, 1966–1976'. *Scottish Journal of Political Economy,* 26, no. 4.

9 Employment Policy in Transition

R.M. LINDLEY

9.1 An Economy in the Doldrums

On present policies it is most unlikely that registered unemployment will be below 2 million in the early 1980s and the projections described in previous chapters suggest that substantially higher levels could be reached in the middle of the decade if the Government sticks to its manifesto. Accustomed as some may have become to the situation in recent years, for most people unemployment does constitute a major problem requiring government action and the prospect of an additional half to one million becoming unemployed should be taken very seriously.

What must be acknowledged, however, is that even under the stance of the previous government, unemployment would also have risen substantially. Riding high on electoral success, any government should be emboldened to implement its policies and in political terms it will become increasingly difficult for the new government to take radical steps as its term of office proceeds. Unfortunately there may be a tendency to blame the Conservative administration for the whole increase in unemployment. This would ignore fundamental weaknesses in the Labour government's economic and industrial strategy. These were identified in Lindley (1978) and the further analysis presented in Chapters 3 and 4 of the present study strengthens our previous argument.

The search for alternative economic strategies over the last few years has failed to produce a credible collection of policies able to reduce unemployment significantly below its current level. The imperatives of creating an atmosphere conducive to financial rectitude, moderation in pay negotiations and the control of inflation as a first priority have dominated political debate in the U K and other industrial countries. Both those who prefer the rough and tumble of prices and incomes policies and those who would have us wear the hair shirt of monetarism argue that employment will benefit in the long run. The former stress that their approach would avoid the short-run increases in unemployment associated with

330

monetarist prescriptions and the danger that the unemployment problem would reach a severity and duration which would be socially and politically unacceptable. The latter insist that the day of reckoning can be put off no longer: society has to decide what kind of economy it seeks to promote and then allow the logic of its operation to prevail.

This chapter is an essay on employment policy in transition. No attempt is made to review the voluminous and controversial literature on macroeconomic policy or to chronicle in detail the introduction of numerous employment and training measures in the last five years.[1] However, the shift in the intellectual climate during the 1970s and the evidence accumulating on the results of experiments in labour market intervention will naturally influence any discussion of the future path to be followed by policy-makers and these developments are dealt with, respectively, in the two sections to follow.

From this treatment, there emerge certain contradictions in present attitudes to employment policy which must be resolved if the response to fears of high unemployment is to be a constructive one. These 'themes of change' are identified in the fourth and final section, in which the prospects for adopting a coherent labour market policy are then considered. As a whole the chapter is concerned with the political economy of employment policy and is intended to be a fairly general treatment of ideas provoked by a review of past experience and future prospects.

The analysis of Chapter 3 suggests that the economy will be in the doldrums for some time to come. GDP could well grow on average at 1–1½ per cent per annum during the period 1978–85. Even allowing for exceptional endogenous wage and labour supply responses to the state of demand and for some relaxation of the fiscal stance, the level of registered unemployment should exceed 2 million in the 1980s. It is possible to be much more pessimistic but the reaction of participants in the labour market to circumstances which differ so much from the past is highly uncertain and there would seem no use in pressing our point any further.

With this scenario in mind it is extremely easy to reach for radical solutions which rest less upon the management of the economy in different ways and more upon winning the 'hearts and minds' of the electorate for social and political change. Stripped of their enthusiasm, these prescriptions display a lack of attention to detail which undermines their relevance to the problems facing the economy. With only a hazy view of their long-term implications it is all too easy to seek short-term employment gains which will be counter-productive. In our previous study, for example, we came to the following conclusion about one such option :

> 'It might appear that the most promising outlook for *employment* in the short and medium term corresponds to a situation in which import controls accompany a further fiscal stimulus but the higher level of productivity, associated with the structural measures evaluated here, does not materialise. Such a situation implies that the UK economy will trundle on into the 1980s, its caricature as a low real wage, low productivity economy becoming increasingly appropriate. No foundation would be laid for the eventual removal of import controls and for the depletion of our oil reserves. The inevitable adjustment, required sooner or later, would come as a much greater cultural shock than if the regeneration of manufacturing industry and the rest of the economy were to start proper in a period when the benefits of oil are able to cushion the employment effects. If, therefore, a successful industrial strategy is likely to exacerbate the problem of unemployment, this does not mean that there is a long-run alternative to improving UK competitiveness all round. The choice of, probably, higher employment and lower real income in the short and medium run is not one which would sustain the UK economy into the 1990s.' [2]

If import controls were to be introduced then we argued that 'they would need to be accompanied by specific industrial agreements to achieve a restructuring of the sectors concerned, higher productivity growth and wage restraint and by explicit government statements about the time-scale over which the controls would operate. Without such safeguards, import controls would fail to pave the way for their eventual removal.' [3]

That kind of industrial involvement would be anathema to the present government which has adopted a distinctly low key approach even to the modest notion of industrial strategy promoted by its predecessor. The new philosophy is not without its dangers, however. The main fear expressed in Chapter 3 is that the short-run effects of the monetary policy designed to pave the way for a resurgence of enterprise and efficiency, combined with a large switch from direct to indirect taxation, are likely to undermine the long-run strategy. This is partly because a much less confident view is taken of the impact of tax changes upon incentives and of incentives upon performance. It reflects also the feeling that the reduction in specific aid to industry, of which the measures included in the Budget were only a foretaste, might well be too severe a test of the ability of market forces to generate their own remedies. And on top of this to send industry into battle at the beginning of a world recession, the effects of which will be exacerbated by the Government's restraint on domestic demand, seems to increase the risk that many will not take up the fight.

The scene is now set for a major retrenchment in which firms will lower their demand expectations, gradually reduce employment to its desired level and invest only to make further labour-savings. If this process gathers momentum, the Government will find it difficult to reverse its direction. The psychology of managing the economy is as much a part of industrial policy as it is of monetary control and the cost, in terms of lost output and lower employment, of attempting to reduce inflation by too rapid a contraction of the PSBR could be very high.

Responses to this situation, if it were to materialise, would undoubtedly involve some relaxation of the fiscal stance by increasing disposable income and a return to some kind of industrial strategy in which government helps to finance investment directly or indirectly. The simulation results reported in Chapter 3 suggest that the medium-term effects of this would be significant but still quite modest in relation to the rise in unemployment. If fiscal policy is to favour reductions in planned expenditure combined with reductions in direct taxes and its relaxation primarily involves the latter, then the employment effect is likely to be relatively small. A more expansionary package may be rationalised by reference to a full employment budget position, slippery as that concept now is, or to the possibility of perverse effects upon the PSBR (largely resulting from exceptionally low activity in the economy) if too severe a posture is adopted. To see the problem in terms of fiscal or monetary policy alone would, however, be a mistake: the tax reductions included in the standard view or fiscal simulation rely on the support provided for the public sector financial account and the balance of payments by the production of North Sea oil and gas. Already under the fiscal stimulus not only do we fail to use this opportunity for investment which will bring future returns when oil production is beginning to decline but a large proportion of the consumption benefits go on imports.

We must instead address ourselves to the inadequacy of the structural measures. Why do these fail to resuscitate the manufacturing sector sufficiently to generate much higher output and employment? First, we are sufficiently sceptical of the autonomous investment response in the economy to have assumed that the government will need to finance the capital outlay and this affects the public sector deficit. Second, the effects of North Sea oil upon the international account are such that the impact of the potentially large increase in exports resulting from the strategy is, in a sense, nipped in the bud by an exchange rate appreciation which the authorities are unlikely to be able to prevent. Third, from the point of view of employment, large gains in productivity accompany the higher investment and this offsets some of the potential increase in jobs.

· At least in these circumstances, though, some ground is being prepared for faster growth in the future and in this cause a more reflationary posture would be worth the risk. Unfortunately the strategy which the Government is apparently beginning to follow is likely to increase the need for it to initiate the investment cycle at the same time as leaving less room for it to do so within its chosen limit for the PSBR. In placing so much emphasis on reducing direct taxation as a means of increasing incentives, its whole economic policy depends for its success not only upon the long-run effectiveness of these measures but also upon their timing in relation to what is left of the economic cycle. With a recession already upon us this would seem to be an inauspicious beginning. In addition, the blow dealt to investment in the short term is likely to be accompanied by a cut in industrial support when it is through these channels that government might exert its influence rather than through general tax cuts.[4]

The analysis of Britain's trade performance given in Chapter 4 underlines the complexity of past structural changes and the diversity of industrial response to domestic and international developments. Although fluctuations in price competitiveness in the past have led to favourable and unfavourable output effects in different industries and over different periods, they are expected to have a large negative effect upon output over the medium term. However, what most points to the long-term problem facing the manufacturing sector and the economy is the fact that the import demand elasticities are generally higher than the corresponding export demand elasticities. Quite apart from the general implication that this has for the equilibrium growth rate of the UK relative to the rest of the world, its consequence over the medium term when the world economy will be slow to recover is self-evident. In a sense this places a 'structural ceiling' upon the aspirations we might have for working through increased price competitiveness to achieve higher output. The fact that relative productivity growth and the effects of North Sea oil upon the exchange rate will lead to a loss of competitiveness in foreign markets over the medium term should not be allowed to obscure the underlying structural malaise indicated by the comparison of demand elasticities in the trade functions.

Although we have argued that skill shortages have not played a major role in the decline of the manufacturing sector, in the short run they are likely to have caused some loss of output and employment. Our view of the medium term is that general shortages of major groups of skills will not arise but that the presence of localised shortages will continue to niggle at the minds of policy-makers. A structural policy would not in itself reverse this conclusion but the stress upon developing manpower programmes which allow the agencies concerned to respond flexibly to labour shortages would be even greater than it is at present (see section 9.3). Thus we would not wish to play down the significance of certain types of skill for the introduction of new technology but this should not distract attention from the unemployment problem remaining even if the demands for these skills were quickly satisfied at little cost to the firms involved.

Chapter 5 showed that quite modest shifts in relative unemployment rates have occurred during the past decade despite large changes in the regional distribution of employment and the labour force. Only if account is taken of unregistered unemployment does this same conclusion apply to the period up to 1985. This distinction led us to provide some tentative estimates of regionally differentiated migration and labour force participation responses. At this stage the evidence points to the relatively minor importance of the former but to the potential significance of female labour supply adjustments. It may well be that supply responses to high regional unemployment rates will be such that the relative changes in registered unemployment rates are moderated. It may also be the case that the discouraged worker effect will bring the average levels of unemployment on either measure down below those given in our projections. But what of the demand responses? Our general conclusion, taking into account previous analysis of the workings of regional economies and the impact of policy, is that the relative changes in regional employment derived from our national projections are sufficiently large to dominate the offsetting effects of market forces. This means that with a UK registered unemployment rate exceeding 10 per cent, the regional rates would not converge *in extremis* and some British regions in addition to Northern Ireland could experience rates of 15 per cent or more. In these circumstances there would be immense social and political pressures upon central government to mitigate the problems of certain regions much more quickly than the normal operation of market forces would allow.

The relationship between unemployment rates among men and women is almost certainly linked to the labour supply responses which might be provoked by the evolving pattern of regional unemployment. Leaving this particular question to one side, however, the obvious conclusion from Chapter 6 is that the sex ratios observed in different occupations must surely change to favour the employment of more men. The corollary of which would be to expect that this might not only depress the male – female wage relativity from the new plateau established by the Equal Pay Act but also provide some downward pressure on the average wage level in the economy because of the product and labour market characteristics associated with traditionally female jobs. In addition, by shifting the burden of unemployment towards women, it might lower the average rate through the greater discouraged worker effect exhibited by those with more discretion to opt out of the labour force. These effects *may* temper the outcome envisaged in the projection in Chapter 6 where the female unemployment rate rises only slightly while the male rate doubles by 1985. But the importance of part-time working in many jobs done by women makes them unsuitable substitutes for the full-time jobs lost by men in manufacturing. In certain occupations there may be increases in the proportion of males among those seeking training and employment but in others the trend will continue to be in the opposite direction (small as the number of female engineering technicians, for example, will continue to be).

The movement towards greater equality of opportunity may be

checked somewhat in these circumstances by various forms of special pleading on behalf of unemployed males. Ironically, in the longer term the application of microprocessors is likely to affect many occupations in which women are highly concentrated. In the meantime chauvinistic reactions to the rising female labour force and relatively low female unemployment rates take no account of the occupational segregation which speaks plainly of lack of opportunity in employment. It also diverts attention away from the need for further changes in legislation on taxation, social security, pensions etc., the result of which would give members of households greater freedom to make sensible joint decisions about their participation in the labour market. Some of these changes could well increase the flexibility of the labour force.

Should higher levels of unemployment prevail in the future they will be accompanied by the inevitable paradox of skill shortages. Chapters 7 and 8 explored the general background to changes in employment of skilled manual workers in engineering and construction and of scientists and technologists in the economy as a whole. Throughout the last two decades industry has been criticised for failing to recruit scientists and technologists and use them in a wide variety of functions including marketing and sales. Firms themselves have complained of shortages but the scientific man-power committees, for example, discerned a much greater 'need' for such personnel than was recognised in practice by the average company. Some suggestions of ineffective use of scientists and technologists already in employment were also made but this was not of prime importance. Gannicott and Blaug (1969) took the scientific manpower committees to task for paying little attention to the way in which the labour market might be working. They argued that these committees were being paternalistic, that industry was not short of highly qualified manpower to anything like the extent claimed, otherwise it would have raised relative wages. Presumably, though, there are circumstances in which industry gets itself into a corner and, whilst these authors made their point most effectively, the marginalist case could fall when confronted with a considerable problem of industrial decline. Freeman (1978), in effect, bypasses the neoclassical position by concentrating upon the structural issue. Something has to be done about the competitive position of British industry. The market signals have failed to elicit an adequate response in the past. Even if this was due to distortions caused, encouraged or just allowed to persist by government, there is not

enough time for us to depend upon a strategy of making product and
labour markets competitive (if that were possible given the distribution of economic power) and sitting back to wait for the
economy to achieve its neoclassical bloom. After our poor
performance over the last two decades, the introduction of
microprocessors seems to be yet one more race which Britain is
liable to lose and the faster the pace the more strung-out the field
will become. This provides a rationale for government to boost the
supply of technicians, scientists and technologists – one which is
absent in the case of skilled manual trades. In that case, there has
been a growing realisation amongst policy-makers that underlying
the shortages of skilled manual labour is a major problem of poor
utilisation, the effects of which rival those of loss of craftsmen
through occupational mobility and inadequate recruitment of
trainees. The example of structural change included in our
simulations improves the situation for craftsmen relative to the
standard view, but does not prevent a substantial decline in employment.

Our simulation results indicate a worsening employment
situation even without searching for shadows cast by the potential
impact of new technology. If Britain were a closed economy this
need not be of fundamental concern although no doubt
we would expect there to be problems of adjustment. Instead, during
the late 1980s it is likely that the benefits of North Sea oil will begin
to decline and the application of microprocessors will be gathering
pace in an economy which is particularly dependent upon its trade
performance for sustaining growth. These two developments, both
somewhat beyond the main period under study, would seem to
clinch the case for a structural policy whatever the political
persuasion of the British government. Whilst this would
undoubtedly mean some compromise for the present government
which favours disengagement from industry, the encouragement of
incentives is only likely to bear fruit if linked to an industrial policy
which acknowledges the full complexity of the medium-term
structural problem. Moreover, given the productivity and exchange
rate effects likely to accompany a successful industrial policy it
would need to be supported by other measures to boost employment
at the same time as maintaining control of inflation.

9.2 Shifts in the Intellectual Climate

Cynics might say that the low unemployment objective has been abandoned by the political establishment only when it has become increasingly difficult to achieve. Theories purporting to show that its pursuit was, in any case, misguided have been wheeled out of storage in order to reduce the degree of embarrassment. It is true that some refurbishing of old concepts has been necessary in order to match the needs of a sophisticated market for economic ideas, but at root the rationalisation of political failure has taken its usual disreputable course.

For those in power, their officials and advisers, such reactions ignore the point that if the people want full employment then they must themselves act consistently with that aim. No obligation can be accepted unconditionally by government and its first responsibility is to establish a realistic appreciation of what is possible.

It is difficult not to sympathise with both attitudes. But underlying the debate about employment policy in recent years there have been presumptions about the functioning of the British economy which should themselves be raised as questions of policy rather than be treated as part of the framework within which economic issues are settled. If wage inflation and unemployment persist for longer than the Government thinks necessary, the perversity of the people will be blamed rather than the reliance of the Government upon a part of the economy whose function has been impaired for some time. Harsh lessons may be learnt to some purpose in these circumstances by the government standing firm if that is all it takes to get the labour market operating efficiently again. But to avoid wasteful social experiments on a grand scale it is worth looking at the empirical evidence both for the macroeconomy and for the labour market in order to get some idea of what is feasible in practice.

It is developments in macroeconomic theory, however, that have most conditioned the intellectual atmosphere governing debate about unemployment policy, rather than studies by labour economists. This applies particularly to the vogue for rational expectations equilibrium models of the macroeconomy. In Chapter 2 some doubts were expressed about the dangers of too obsessive an application of the neoclassical equilibrium concept in modelling the labour market. There appears to be a tendency to maintain the neoclassical hypothesis for longer than the evidence would justify, simply on the grounds that there is no other suitable scheme to apply to the analysis of a market which plays such a crucial part in the allocation of resources and the generation of price changes. The work of Malinvaud (1977), Dixit (1978) and others on the analysis of markets with rationing demonstrates clearly that this is not the case. Furthermore, Hahn (1978) shows that there is no need to abandon the notion of rational expectations in dealing with quantity-constrained equilibria. On the other hand Shiller (1978) expresses a number of doubts about the application of rational expectations models, particularly in relation to their assumptions about the sophisticated information possessed and processed by individuals as well as the likelihood of convergence to equilibrium in a reasonable period of time.[6] As with the simple neoclassical postulate of market clearing, the urge to adopt a rational expectations mechanism is partly conditioned by the lack of an adequate analytical alternative but it is quite possible that models which represent economic agents as having rather simple *ad hoc* ways of forming their expectations will perform better.

It would seem therefore that the case in favour of a straight-forward application of neoclassical theory buttressed by a rational expectations treatment of its dynamics is by no means cut and dried. To non-economists bemused by these technicalities the temptation to see the debate in terms of simple Keynesianism versus simple monetarism must be considerable. A better gambit for those concerned with the formation of economic policy would, however, place most emphasis upon the answers to empirical questions about the behaviour of the labour market.

The special relevance of these remarks for the development of employment policy is firstly that the rational expectations equilibrium bandwagon has begun to roll only quite recently in the UK. One of its initial contributions has been to help to legitimise further a simple form of monetarism, largely because the caveats expressed even by Friedman (1968) to say nothing of Lucas (1972) have not been enunciated clearly enough. For example, the need for gradualism in the introduction of a monetary rule has not been observed in recent policy changes. Combined with too direct a view of the relationship between money supply and the PSBR, this has led the Government to adopt an unnecessarily tight position on public expenditure in the short run.

The second point relates to where the debate about recent developments in macroeconomic theory has had one of its more constructive effects.

'Should this intellectual arbitrage prove successful, it will suggest important changes in the way we think about policy. Most fundamentally, it directs attention to the necessity of thinking of policy as the choice of stable "rules of the game", well understood by economic agents.'

Lucas and Sargent (1978, p.70)

It is true that in some hands this aspect has given place to neo-classical 'revisionism'. If considered more seriously, it implies that the increasing emphasis upon monetarist policies by both Labour and Conservative administrations must be accompanied by explicit statements on how government believes the labour market works at present, how it wants it to work and what policies are required to bring that situation about. In other words the 'rules of the game' do not merely relate to the choice of monetary targets to be followed through thick and thin. They should define government attitudes not only to aspects of the economy under its direct control but also to the functions it expects other parts of the economy to perform. Supplementary policy statements may then be required covering action intended to 'repair' the economic mechanism.

Unfortunately the new macroeconomics *assumes* that labour and product markets work on neoclassical lines. If they do not the conclusions about economic policy must be modified. Whilst one would like to think that people become 'simple monetarists' only after having satisfied themselves that these markets do work effectively, it seems more the case that they do so on the grounds that markets should be *made* to work. This imperative is then either forgotten or translated into some very straightforward caveat attached to pronouncements on policy – namely, that success is assured providing people in the labour market behave responsibly or sensibly. More sophisticated monetarists clearly appreciate that there is more to market failure than that but there is still a tendency to be rather easily persuaded of the innate competitiveness of the labour market.[7]

The third issue raised by the use of equilibrium models concerns the presumptions their results create about the relative importance of different components of the fiscal package. Various forms of expenditure and taxation are seen to distort decision-making in the labour market: for example, subsidies to training, employment and investment; payments of unemployment and social security benefits to certain groups; other transfer payments such as allowances to students, trainees etc.; housing subsidies; payroll taxes to finance the subsidised training; high levels of national insurance contributions from employers and employees; and, of course, taxes on income. If they are assessed assuming that the labour market is, in the first place, fairly competitive but now creaks under the weight of these measures then the new government's policy should include especially a reduction in this part of the fiscal package. The main growth area within the programme 'industry, energy, trade and employment' has been that covering the activities of the labour market agencies and the Department of Employment. However, manpower policy need not be written off as weak-minded fiscal policy. Even within the monetarist framework there is plenty of room for macroeconomic intervention to lower the 'natural rate' of unemployment but this follows only from recognising that a natural rate exceeding, say, 5 per cent or so is *prima facie* evidence of malfunctioning labour markets on a significant scale. There is however a suspicion that policies brought forward to reduce the natural rate or, more specifically, the non-accelerating inflation rate of unemployment (NAIRU) will fail to do so, but will instead, impede the adjustment of the labour market to the present value of that rate. In addition, it is argued that if past increases in NAIRU have followed from improvements in social welfare (e.g. unemployment benefit-induced increases), this is a consequence which should have been recognised and accepted at the outset. On the other hand, slow adjustment to a high NAIRU implies considerable loss of output and the prospect of speeding up the adjustment process alone could well be worth some loss of microeconomic efficiency. Thus before dispensing with the tools of employment policy, it is desirable to look more closely at the job they have been doing and might continue to do even under a monetarist regime.

9.3 Employment and Training Policies in the 1970s

Most economic policies impinge upon employment indirectly but some are specifically associated with employment and training objectives. Broadly speaking, this group includes industrial subsidies, job creation programmes, investment in human capital, incentives for geographical mobility and schemes for reducing labour supply. This section concentrates entirely upon the first three of these areas.[8] Details of the programmes and empirical studies of their effects are not generally given in what follows: the emphasis is more upon their implications for the overall style of employment policy.[9] However, a summary of the various special measures introduced during the 1970s is given in Table 9.1. The two main long-term programmes excluded from Table 9.1 but discussed below under 'investment in human capital' are the Training Opportunities Scheme (TOPS) and, introduced more recently, Training for Skills.

9.3.1. Employment subsidies

The Temporary Employment Subsidy (TES) was a job preservation subsidy designed to encourage firms to defer redundancies so as to hold down the level of unemployment and to preserve capacity for the economic upturn. It acted particularly as a net export subsidy to the textiles group of industries. At its peak it covered over 200 thousand employees about half of whom the DE estimates would have been registered as unemployed in the absence of the subsidy. Although eventually applied to the whole country, TES, like the Small Firms' Employment Subsidy (SFES) and the Adult Employment Subsidy (AES), was originally restricted to certain georgraphical locations identified in the course of administering regional policy. In that sense these subsidies began as developments of regional policy concentrating the employment effects on areas with the most severe unemployment problems. At the same time, an effect of limiting them to certain areas was to allow them to be introduced as experimental schemes perhaps capable of general application once they had been evaluated.[10] In contrast both the subsidies aimed at helping young people, the Recruitment Subsidy for School-Leavers (RSSL) and the Youth Employment Subsidy (YES), were applied throughout the country from the start.

From May 1978 TES support to the textiles group was limited to 70 per cent of an establishment's labour force for the first six months and 50 per cent for the second six months. A Short-time Working Compensation Scheme (STW) was introduced to 'offset any loss of TES support in the affected sectors'. Both schemes were closed for applications in March 1979 and replaced by the Temporary Short Time Working Compensation Scheme (TSTW), the first stage in the development of a more permanent scheme planned by the Labour government.

The present government may be inclined to draw a complete veil over the British experience of employment subsidies. Already it has closed SFES to manufacturing firms outside special Development

Table 9.1 Summary of Special Employment and Training Schemes

Scheme	Month introduced	Last month for applications	Peak of scheme Quarter	Average no. (thousands)	Average no. 1979 III (thousands)	Planned expenditure 1978/79 (£m 1978 pr.)	1979/80	Net cost per reduction in register (£ per week)	Register effect (%)
TES	Aug. 1975	March 1979	1977 III	204.7	44.3	155	69	–	50
STW	May 1978	March 1979	1979 II	9.8	3.8	12	42	n.a.	70
SFES	July 1977	March 1980	1979 III	59.2	59.2	14	10	25	25
RSSL	Oct. 1975	Sept. 1976	1976 I	20.4	–	–	–	20	15
YES	Oct. 1976	March 1978	1977 II	14.0	–	4	–	40	5
AES	Aug. 1978	June 1979	1979 II	0.9	0.6	1	3	n.a.	5
JCP	Oct. 1975	March 1978	1978 II	43.9	–	73	3	20	90
STEP	April 1978	n.a.	1979 III	18.4	18.4	10	76	17	100
WEP	Sept. 1976	March 1978	1977 IV	26.7	–	–	–	7	80
CI	April 1972	n.a.	1979 III	5.7	5.7	13	13	23	100
TSAYP	Jan. 1976	March 1978	1977 IV	7.3	–	–	–	5–15	95
YOP	April 1978	n.a.	1979 I	72.5	66.2	63	156	10	80–100
TI	Aug. 1975	n.a.	1977 II	30.5	25.3	41	27	15	70
JIS	July 1977	Feb. 1980	1979 I	0.2	0.2	n.a.	n.a.	n.a.	100
JRS	Jan. 1977	March 1980	1979 III	46.3	46.3	24	13	8–13	90

Sources: *The Government's Expenditure Plans 1979–80 to 1982–83.* Cmnd. 7439; *People and Work* (1978), Appendices 10 and 32; unpublished MSC data.

Notes: TES – Temporary Employment Subsidy, STW – Short-time Working Compensation Scheme, SFES – Small Firms' Employment Subsidy, RSSL – Recruitment Subsidy for School Leavers, YES – Youth Employment Subsidy, AES – Adult Employment Subsidy, JCP – Job Creation Programme, STEP – Special Temporary Employment Programme, WEP – Work Experience Programme, CI – Community Industry, TSAYP – TSA courses for young people, YOP – Youth Opportunities Programme, TI – Training places in industry, JIS – Job Introduction Scheme for disabled, JRS – Job Release Scheme.

(1) Additional provision for certain measures is included under the allocation of £200m to the permanent short-time working compensation scheme (not shown) in its initial year (1979/80), notably the cost of extending SFES from March 1979 to March 1980. TSTW itself covered about 49 thousand people on average during 1979 III. (see text).

(2) Figures for net cost per reduction in register are only intended to be roughly indicative of relative magnitudes and include estimates made in the early stages of some programmes.

(3) The register effect is the percentage of people covered by a scheme who are counted as a net reduction in the total number expected to register as unemployed in the absence of the scheme. Again these are very rough orders of magnitude used by the manpower agencies concerned for the purposes of estimating net costs. They do not take account of the full opportunity costs in terms of the benefits forgone by not undertaking other forms of public or private expenditure. See Lindley (1980) for a discussion of these estimates.

Areas and Development Areas and to non-manufacturing firms as a whole. The Restructuring Subsidy proposed by its predecessor has been dropped[11] and compensation under TSTW will be paid for 6 instead of 12 months. In the forthcoming White Paper on government expenditure it is most unlikely that Labour's new legislative scheme will be implemented. Sums exceeding £400 million (1978 survey prices) per year from 1980/81 had been allocated for this major initiative. A provision of £200 million for 1979/80 was also made under this heading to cater for alternative employment measures pending the full introduction of the new scheme. Even the continuation of SFES must be in question in the present climate, although if the Government were to go significantly beyond its general tax cuts to take special account of the needs of small businesses (a move which is not in fact proposed either in the Conservative election manifesto or the Queen's Speech), then the operation of subsidies and other forms of support to this sector may be dealt with on a more comprehensive basis – the case for which must now be a very strong one.

Policy on subsidies is likely to be affected by a number of considerations but, particularly, (a) the general stance on macroeconomic management, (b) expectations about where that stance will lead the economy in the short and medium term, (c) how much the distribution of employment opportunities and income matters to the Government, (d) evidence on the effects of past or existing subsidies and (e) the degree of separation of industrial and employment policy. The last of these relates to the tendency to take questions on employment subsidies separately from those on, for example, investment incentives, national insurance contributions and corporate taxation. No attempt to discuss these links will be made here but it seems important to stress that cutting the overt employment subsidies from public expenditure without dealing with these other elements of industrial and employment policy would reflect a distaste for direct *employment* subsidies *per se* which is at root irrational. This would apply within a monetarist framework as much as a Keynesian one. Thus, in considering (a), subsidising employment can be justified, under certain circumstances, as a means of lowering the natural rate of unemployment. Not only could this mean counteracting the possibly undesirable employment side-effects of subsidies to capital or taxes on labour but also seeking out certain groups for whom raising the probability of finding employment will not add significantly to the general inflationary pressure in the economy.

As regards (b), the prospects for employment envisaged in earlier chapters clearly bear upon the choice of subsidy. Focussing at the fairly aggregate level, the use of a job preservation subsidy, such as TES, for an industry experiencing long-term decline can only really be justified as a means of temporarily slowing down the impact of this upon the labour force, ironing out sharp changes in the situation facing domestic firms. For an industry in deep recession but where employment is likely to fall only slowly or rise in the medium term the maintenance of capacity and its enhancement could benefit from TES by allowing employment adjustments to be staged more effectively. Within an industry, however, the positions of individual firms can differ very considerably. In the case of motor vehicles this has led to drastic attempts to deal selectively with certain companies; in others, noted above, TES may have subsidised the weak at the expense of more robust exterprises. Matters of judgement on aid to specific firms cannot be avoided except by outright disengagement but there is a very strong case for differentiating an employment subsidy like TES according to industry, rather than leaving it to a complex of factors to produce a highly skewed distribution of expenditure which might nonetheless be inappropriate.

Subsidising job expansion sounds a much more promising activity, as portrayed by Mr. Albert Booth, the then Employment Secretary, in commenting on SFES:

'.... small firms, cashing-in on the brighter economic climate, will take advantage of this scheme to increase their work forces earlier than they might otherwise have done to meet increased demand for their products.'[12]

As an antidote to the nervousness of small businesses in recruiting labour given problematic demand recovery and the practicalities of employment protection, this may help. It depends for its success either upon advancing the point of expansion in the course of general economic recovery or upon manipulating the laws of natural selection by bribing employers to be a bit more ambitious without suffering the possibly unpleasant consequences of lowering their degree of risk aversion. As a *temporary* measure, SFES seems to have made a useful contribution but on a very small scale. Given the short-term economic outlook a much expanded SFES programme would probably have disappointing effects without implementing the kind of general policy towards small firms alluded to above. The notion that there are large *dynamic* effects to be exploited over the longer term rests, firstly, on a much greater scale of operation being envisaged and, secondly, on certain beliefs about the inherently innovative nature of the small business sector, struggling to escape from behind the barriers created by policy and institutions geared to the needs of large corporations. This is clearly not simply a matter of subsidising employment as such. There remain some doubts about the size of the employment effects in manufacturing and the difficulties of coping with the question of sub-contracting in parts of that sector. The work of Birch (1979) in the United States has created some excitement in the UK recently but his study identifies mainly the potential for growth within service industries and he is not at all clear on how it could be harnessed more effectively for the purposes of job generation.

Turning to (c), the distribution of employment opportunities and income, a notable aspect of the British experiments has been their favourable effects upon the employment of certain groups. Moreover, the impact of TES and SFES upon the situation facing females and the low paid generally is as relevant here as the impact of the specifically targetted schemes, RSSL, YES and AES. Ironically the effect of the latter to some extent undermined prospects for those who would have gained from the other subsidies. However, the targetted subsidies were on a much smaller scale and some official disillusionment with subsidies of this nature is evident. This is largely because all three were subsidies to recruitment flows with deadweight proportions of the order of 0.8 (the proportion of those covered who would have been recruited by the employer anyway). However, the DE/MSC estimate that SFES, subsidising an expansion in the stock of employment, also has a high deadweight proportion, of about 0.6.

Just as the two youth subsidies have been replaced by a major new programme for young people (see below), SFES may eventually be replaced by a comprehensive policy designed to increase incentives for small firms without necessarily subsidising employment directly. In both cases one would then have had a policy reaction which began by adjusting at the margin the financial circumstances governing employment decisions by the firms concerned and ended with a recognition that further marginal adaptation would not cope with the particularly acute situations likely to develop for the target groups, i.e. high youth unemployment and the risks of great financial difficulties for small firms, respectively. AES has operated in such a restricted manner that this experiment cannot be regarded as an adequate test of its potential as a redistributive instrument.

Whilst the special circumstances facing small firms might lead to the replacement of SFES with other incentives, it would be unwise to close the door on the use of employment subsidies in future. The evidence from British experiments with a mix of counter-cyclical and modestly targetted subsidies points in a rather different direction.

Counter-cyclical subsidies

It is no doubt far-fetched to imagine a judicious use of job preservation and expansion subsidies to temper the downturn and speed up the recovery in employment, for the *same* industry – that is, to increase cyclical labour hoarding without reducing the peak-to-peak rate of growth of productivity. A preference for one or other subsidy is likely to reflect not only some notion that an employment cycle does exist, the effects of which could be mitigated, but that this is imposed on a longer term trend. If the trend is downwards then the cyclical measure followed will tend to be a form of job preservation even though some firms in the industry concerned will be expanding. If the trend is upwards then attention will probably focus on job expansion. In the former case the subsidy is acting against the trend and in the latter it is attempting to intensify its effects. Seen in terms of controlling the pace of change so that labour can be absorbed into the expanding sectors without high levels of unemployment and unnecessary loss of output, this combination of different subsidies applied to different industries could have a constructive role to play when the major fear is one of rising unemployment rather than manpower bottlenecks. In that way, assessments of both the present state of the economy in relation to the business cycle and the longer term situation for different industries should determine the subsidy mix. Moreover they will determine the period for which payment is intended and the timing of announcements of the subsidies. In the UK, the use of temporary schemes reviewed each year or more frequently has lead to a degree of uncertainty about the potential gain from applying for a subsidy over and above that which is naturally associated with a counter-cyclical measure. This applies particularly to SFES which seeks to encourage employers to expand more quickly than they might otherwise have done.

The counter-cyclical job expansion subsidy proposed by Layard and Nickell (1979) differs significantly from SFES. They envisage a much longer time-scale with a take-up period of two years in the first instance followed by a four year period during which the subsidy would be gradually reduced. They argue that the measure would act initially through its effects on net exports; any direct stimulus to domestic demand or price effects upon investment activity would be relatively small. The importance attributed to the trade response does not, however, lead Layard and Nickell to suggest restricting the subsidy to those sectors producing tradeable goods and services or more specifically to those sectors most likely to be price-takers in international markets where the output and employment effects should be at their greatest.

Although proposed as a counter-cyclical measure these authors note (p.4) that 'If, of course, the gloomier forecasts of unemployment are right, then the subsidy could be extended later'. Here is a case, however, where the underlying long term trends are particularly relevant. Indeed they may begin to dominate the profile of employment over the medium term such that cyclical changes are unlikely to be accompanied by any significant increases in employment. Thus for a subsidy relying on the trade effects for its justification, there is the possibility that those industries most in a position to exploit the potential for gains in net exports will be those least able to generate employment increases because the growth of output cannot be stimulated sufficiently to overhaul the growth in productivity. One way of coping with this would be to reduce the base employment level from which 'additions' to employment are calculated at the start or in the course of the subsidy period but the proposal then becomes hedged around with administrative complications. In this respect a job preservation subsidy such as TES is of greater relevance to large areas of manufacturing, not as a counter-cyclical measure but as one designed to ameliorate a severe employment decline.

Long-run subsidies

This brings us to the question of long-run subsidies *per se*. In labour markets with rigid wage relativities, or flexible wages accompanied by distortions due to benefit payments, the economic case for long-run employment subsidies is not difficult to make nor would problems of implementation be insuperable. Jackman and Layard (1979) propose a tax-subsidy scheme for the UK in which

National Insurance contributions are turned into a progressive tax on non-overtime earnings. In a very general sense this implies a 'targetting' of the subsidy towards the lower paid. Clearly it cannot be used at all to encourage the employment of particular groups, such as young people and/or those with long durations of unemployment. The aim is simply to raise the demand for less skilled labour. However, the operation of the general tax-subsidy would not take into account the degree of distortion and wage rigidity, and relative variations in supply elasticities in different labour markets. As in the case of the counter-cyclical subsidies, the information on which to base an industrially differentiated scheme is also very limited.

An alternative approach would be to attach a long-run subsidy to the employment of a clearly defined section of the labour force: it is much easier to identify young people or those with durations of unemployment above a stated threshold than it is to target the tax-subsidy proposed by Jackman and Layard. The analysis of Baily and Tobin (1977) explores such a case 'in which the power of selective employment policies comes from exploiting differences among markets in wage responses'. Their model then rests upon the existence of certain groups for whom the Phillips curves are relatively flat so that reducing their unemployment would not lead to much additional inflationary pressure. The impact of this sort of subsidy upon the level of unemployment consistent with non-accelerating inflation is not likely to be large, however.

'Our general conclusion from the regressions is that the hypotheses necessary for success of direct job creation, wage subsidies and kindred policies are empirically supported, at least qualitatively. But our previous analysis makes us sceptical of the more extravagant hopes and claims for these policies, especially in the long run. Gains in GNP are harder to come by than reduction in unemployment counts. In the long run, displacements of workers from private employment, both in and outside the target population, will offset some of the direct employment gains. A large share of the case for direct job creation or selective subsidies depends on important effects not captured in aggregate measures of employment and production: *improved distribution of income and opportunity.*'[13]

This conclusion is a warning against exercising too much ingenuity in devising general schemes for the British economy which aim to lower unemployment over the long run as opposed to redistribute job opportunities. On the other hand, because subsidies for particular groups can promote greater equity and *may* help to reduce aggregate unemployment with little risk of increasing inflation, then the case for them would seem to be stronger than has been appreciated by governments in the UK. If they are phased out completely this will place a much greater burden upon forms of job creation with its larger component of public employment.

Compensation for short-time working

Finally, let us return to the short-time working compensation scheme proposed by Labour but likely to be dropped by the Conservatives. This subsidy bears the marks of TES, and the short-time working scheme which supplemented it (STW), but incorporates important new features. First, the scheme was intended to be permanent, covering public and private sectors without industrial or geographical restriction. Second, it was to provide compensation to employees rather than firms at a percentage of normal pay rather than a flat rate. Third, it was to be related specifically to short-time working arrangements. Fourth, the scheme incorporated two tiers, depending on the level of unemployment, whereby employers would receive a rebate of half of the compensation under the initial tier and a full rebate under the second tier at times of high unemployment. Fifth, compensation paid under the first tier would be financed equally by employers collectively and by the government.

The rationale for the proposed scheme was primarily to reduce redundancies and payments of unemployment benefits by encouraging short-time working. It would act as an economy-wide counter-cyclical job preservation scheme but with somewhat different effects upon different industries as noted in the general discussion above. The scheme in fact represented the culmination of the move away from targeted subsidies, apparently side-stepped objections to TES on Common Market treaty grounds, and introduced collective funding more akin to the arrangements made for redundancy payments. The Labour government anticipated the use of the second tier procedure from the start of its full introduction in 1980/81.

In some respects the proposal reflected the official taste for *ad hoc* employment policy, despite the notion of permanence attached to it. In the course of a recession of exceptional duration and surrounded by uncertainties about the prospects of recovery, the scheme was mooted with all the self-confidence of a government attuned to the cyclical regularities of the 1950s and 1960s. It is true that a second tier had been provided and was likely to be implemented quickly. But here was a scheme which dispensed entirely with the limited redistributive element embodied in earlier flat rate subsidies through which they scored their most obvious benefits. Instead it extended the job preservation element, in principle, for a much longer period during which the problem of policing the scheme would increase considerably. Moreover, the implications of the scheme for collective bargaining either over pay or shorter working hours had clearly not been thought out (although consultations with the CBI and TUC were to be sought).

As already noted, it is possible to conceive of many labour market situations in which efficiency and equity could be served by the introduction of a subsidy. Unfortunately there is a lack of evidence (especially for the UK) on the characteristics of labour market behaviour which would determine the relevance of these theories of labour market intervention. A very broad conclusion can be drawn, however, which also links the above discussion to that which follows on the development of job creation programmes. The trend in British employment policy away from the use of employment subsidies to improve the situation for specific groups of the labour force and, more recently, the reduction in the subsidy programme as a whole limit the marginal job generation process to forms of direct employment creation largely outside the market economy or under very artificial arrangements within it. Government must then rely on the non-market component of the public sector to bear the burden of providing the initiative for creating jobs, often of a very 'secondary' nature, rather than harness the energies of employing organisations in the market sector, especially in private firms. Only by setting its face against all forms of employment measure can a government avoid the choice between interfering in the market economy and promoting a secondary area of non-market employment in the public sector. If it is particularly concerned to avoid the latter, further discussion of employment subsidies is called for, given the prospects for employment over the medium term.

9.3.2 Job creation – constructive responses or 'wasteful mitigations'?

' "to dig holes in the ground", paid for out of earnings, will increase, not only employment but the real national dividend of useful goods and services. It is not reasonable, however, that a sensible community should be content to remain dependent on such fortuitous and often wasteful mitigations when once we understand the influence upon which effective demand depends.'

Keynes (1936, p.220)

Such are the shadows that follow officials organising job creation programmes. Even Keynes preferred alternative methods. Yet British experiments in this field during the 1970s bear little relation to the make-work activities in previous great recessions and none at all to the caricatures portrayed by the media in the early stages of development of the programme. The relevant schemes are listed in Table 9.1: the Job Creation Programme (JCP) and its successor, the Special Temporary Employment Programme (STEP). The Work Experience Programme (WEP) took over from JCP part of the responsibility for young people and this in turn was absorbed into the Youth Opportunities Programme (YOP). Both WEP and YOP are discussed below under 'investment in human capital', mainly because of the strong element of training and preparation for work embodied in these schemes, in addition to providing young people with some experience of regular if not permanent employment.

JCP was not merely an attempt to increase the demand for labour through financing particularly labour intensive projects. It provided temporary jobs for certain groups of the labour force. The mode of operation, in effect, suspended some of the legislation relating to employment protection, creating a new sector of the labour market in which jobs could be distributed amongst the groups so as to reduce the dispersion of unemployment experience between individuals. As in the case of STEP, WEP and YOP,

'when jobs are being provided for a limited duration, when some training is involved and when the jobs are being promoted in a sector of the economy where commercial comparisons are difficult to make, the result is obviously likely to reflect an amalgam of training, productive employment and social welfare objectives.'[14]

On the other hand sponsors of projects under JCP (public authorities, private employers, voluntary organisations or individuals) took on the responsibilities of employers in other respects than normally providing permanent employment – employees were paid wages according to local rates but were employed only for the length of the project or 52 weeks whichever was the shorter (projects averaged 32 weeks in duration). JCP grants covered wage costs plus up to 10 per cent of wage costs towards running costs in the absence of funds from other sources.

There are major problems in evaluating JCP. Various criticisms have been levelled at the programme and are reported in the Expenditure Committee's report[15] although many were associated with problems of developing the scheme from scratch and the Committee was on balance favourably impressed. The availability of information about the costs and effects of the scheme and its successor is still very unsatisfactory, however, when compared with that available on the different employment subsidies (incomplete as the latter is). The evaluation published in the *Gazette* (March 1977, pp.211-17) concentrates mainly on describing the types of projects, sponsors and the people employed on them. No mention is made of possible displacement effects upon the employment of other people.[16] No reference to alternative, more traditional, forms of public expenditure is made with a view to assessing the relative merits of JCP. This perhaps can be explained in part by the aspect of the programme already mentioned and which is reflected in the MSC's general conclusion to its evaluation (*ibid.*, p.217):

'... the primary objective of the programme is to create temporary jobs for selective groups of unemployed people who need them most, and it has achieved this goal. It has also enabled work of value to the community to be carried out which would otherwise have not been done.'

The official view of the net cost to public funds of JCP is that it amounted to about £1,040 per job per year. Bearing in mind the close comparison between JCP and certain forms of local authority expenditure and the fact that local authorities sponsored about 60 per cent of projects, one is drawn to compare this cost with that of conventional public expenditure on goods and services. No detailed estimates have been published by the Government but MRG simulations indicate that increases in non-defence expenditure would imply a PSBR cost per job of closer to £2,000 compared with a cost of about £7,000 for a policy of reflation through cutting the standard rate of tax.[17] JCP would seem much cheaper than even additions to general government consumption and bearing in mind the main objective of JCP, namely to help certain groups in the labour force on a temporary basis, it is understandable that this policy was favoured given the constraints on public expenditure growth. Indeed Mr. Albert Booth, when Employment Secretary, stated that

'An equivalent expenditure on general reflationary measures would have much less impact on unemployment. It is estimated that the cost of an extra job through general reflation is about ten times – approximately £13,000 – the cost of a job or training opportunity provided through special programmes.'[18]

Initial emphasis under JCP was placed on unemployed people aged 16–24 and 50 plus. Subsequently greater attention was given to those aged 25–49 who had been unemployed for at least 6 months. This partly reflected the introduction of WEP for young people.

STEP was introduced in April 1978 to replace JCP for those aged 19 and over who are unemployed. Priority is being given to areas of high unemployment (particularly inner cities) and to people aged 19 – 24 who have been unemployed for 6 months or more and to people aged 25 and over who have been unemployed for at least 12 months. The programme objective was to have been 30–35 thousand filled places by March 1980 in the country as a whole. Under the June 1979 public expenditure cuts this was reduced to 12–14 thousand places and the preferences for certain groups of the labour force and specific areas were turned into firm restrictions. Thus the Government has decided to hold the programme at the level reached in March 1979 at the end of its first year of operation, concentrating upon raising the proportion of long-term unemployed participating in the scheme from about 44 per cent to the two-thirds originally intended.

Set against the size of the (national) priority group of almost 400 thousand the initial target was clearly small. [19] The new one, taken together with the dropping of the tiny Adult Employment Subsidy, marks the near-eclipse of measures geared to the needs of long-term unemployed adults. The small scale of STEP established even in the original plan reflected fears that the more the programme was expanded the more likely would be the threat of substitution for permanent jobs.[20] This presumably relates to the fiscal substitution effect by which permanent public sector jobs are replaced by temporary ones concerned with less important work. There is also the problem that if the local rate for the job is paid, more unemployed workers may opt for STEP in preference to conventional employment. However, eligibility criteria and the limitations placed upon the duration of participation in the programme make this unlikely.

Thus in the strategy adopted by the new government, the switch away from public expenditure growth (covering, especially, public employment associated with government consumption) toward reductions in direct taxes has been given a further small twist by reducing that area of public or quasi-public employment which has the lowest net cost per job created and does not embody the commitment to permanence implied by the expansion of public employment in conventional areas. An alternative approach would have been to favour the expansion of STEP quite simply because it creates employment of a kind least likely to cause inflationary pressure, is more easily contracted and is much less expensive in terms of its PSBR implications. The prospects of rising unemployment among men made redundant from manufacturing industries imply further increases in the numbers of long-term unemployed. This situation would seem to warrant more than the dwindling policy response of the last two years.

Clearly, however, any proposal to reverse this trend must first tackle some basic questions. What will be the effects of continuing local authority involvement upon the conventional public sector labout market and how will these authorities use the independent powers for job creation which several have sought to obtain through introducing private bills to Parliament? What impact could the latter have on regional and industrial policy? How sustainable are the forms of 'non-profit-making enterpreneurship' which emerged under the job creation schemes? To what extent could our conception of the labour market be broadened by a systematic promotion of relatively small-scale enterprises organised through trusts or co-operatives? What effect would such a move be likely to have upon the small business sector? Would the employing organisations be any more forward looking in their planning of employment and training than is the case for the conventional sector once they have created an established pattern of project management? How would they respond to a progressive hardening of the financial criteria by which government were to treat them – could they only flourish within an artificially created public sector market for the goods and services they produce? Should policy deliberately encourage the introduction of conditions of employment (wages, hours of work, employment protection, etc.) which differ significantly from the rest of the labour market and what would be the industrial relations implications of this?

Alternatively should we regard job creation schemes as having no potential economic function by introducing innovative labour demand measures in a depressed labour market? Instead are they to be confined simply to providing a modest pool of job opportunities which can be used to take the edge off the unemployment experience of the diadvantaged or vulnerable groups of the labour force? In which case is not the scale currently planned still derisory? If efficiency is not particularly served, there would seem to be a strong argument, on grounds of low cost and equity, for the expansion of a carefully targetted version of STEP.

9.3.3 Investment in human capital

Labour supply will be reduced in the short run if those who would otherwise have sought jobs decide to extend their education or undertake vocational training outside the labour force. One consequence of recessions is that industrial training within companies is usually curtailed. This means that the individual faces both a deterioration in employment prospects and a reduction in opportunities for training which might help to place him or her in a stronger position to take advantage of the jobs that are still available and those which materialise when the economy starts to recover. The notion of counter-cyclical provision of training has been a major rationale for government manpower policy. Increasingly, however, it has become clear that

> 'counter-cyclical arguments for boosting vocational education and training are insufficient to warrant the scale of manpower programmes being developed. Notions of equity and social welfare are the main justification for intervening on an even larger scale to provide higher levels of industrial training and work

experience than the labour market could itself produce.'[21]

This conclusion applies with special force to the schemes for unemployed young people organised under the Youth Opportunities Programme. On the other hand, lingering on from the 1964 and 1973 legislation is the belief that not enough training is done in general and stimulating greater activity during recessions is not sufficient. If the present 'recession' represents rather more a fundamental adjustment to new circumstances than a somewhat severe cyclical phenomenon, further measures to promote training can be justified on long-term rather than counter-cyclical grounds. It can be argued that changes in occupational and industrial structure accompanying reductions in the demand for labour will generate a need for training and re-training which will more than make up for the effects of lower employment levels upon 'equilibrium' training requirements. This kind of shifting rationalisation has been a particular feature of training policy as it has emerged over the 1970s, especially in relation to skilled manual trades.

The emergence of Training for Skills

The Manpower Services Commission came to maturity in an environment which differed greatly from the one in which it was conceived. Chapter 7 concluded that the nature of manpower decision-making combined with certain characteristics of skilled labour markets should lead us to expect labour shortages even when unemployment is high. We should not be surprised that the Industrial Training Act (1964) and the Employment and Training Act (1973) focussed upon the need to tackle shortages of skilled workers rather than shortages of jobs for skilled workers. They were most concerned with influencing the behaviour of firms as opposed to the behaviour of workers. Policy was based implicitly on the sovereignty of demand to which supply was to respond more effectively than had been the case in the past. The main instrument of policy was a financial one but the administration of the system of industrial training boards was to provide a large degree of discretion over how this instrument was to be exercised. The targets of policy were (i) the quantity of training, (ii) the quality of training and (iii) the distribution of training costs across firms in the industries concerned.[22] Thus instruments and targets were related to the decision-making of the firm. In the case of the engineering industry the EITB concentrated its influence upon apprentice recruitment rather than on retraining or upgrading adults.

The orientation of policy in this way created a situation in which, when the problem manifestly became that of a prolonged labour surplus rather than current shortages, a thorough reassessment of the role of active manpower policy was required. The reaction to this apparent change in the nature of the manpower problem may be characterised as follows:

(i) A reluctance to recognise that a major change was taking place. In engineering this showed up as a tendency to disregard the evidence of short-run indicators and an unwillingness to reflect upon the obvious secular decline in the demand for skilled manual workers by the industry.

(ii) An unreasonable optimism about the prospects for rapid economic recovery and pessimism about the dangers of manpower bottlenecks to growth. In addition there was an intensification of the doctrine of the sovereignty of labour demand in which, as part of the Labour government's industrial strategy, manpower agencies were urged to take no risks of under-providing for the vital skills required by industry. This was the case even though one of the main objectives of the industrial strategy was to raise productivity.

(iii) A shift in the argument used previously to favour the maintenance of high levels of training, such as those reached in the late 1960s. The stress placed upon the general need to sustain the quantity of training began to give way to a stress upon the desirability of replenishing the stock of skills in the economy through *high quality* training programmes – usually involving the established apprentice schemes rather than supplementing the skills of those already qualified. This has the effect of continuing training at high levels. Combined with (i) this view plays down the significance of large numbers of unemployed skilled workers on the grounds that they are not as skilled as those being prepared under present training programmes. It also provides an excuse for the agencies concerned to take less notice of the increasing pool of 'skilled' people who have received their training in Skillcentres as adults (because their training is less comprehensive and is recognised to require a period of industrial experience before adequate skill is acquired). This general attitude tends to ignore the evidence that the skill content of many skilled manual jobs is falling.

(iv) An emphasis upon the loss of potential which would result in the event of a cutback in training of young people who dominate the intakes of most skilled manual training schemes. In times when there is a shortage of job opportunities for young people, industries which have in the past complained of a lack of 'suitably qualified' young entrants should make the most of the excess supply while they can. (This view may be linked to the one in (iii) on improving the quality of the skilled labour force.)

(v) An extension of the wasted potential argument in (iv) to encompass the social consequences of creating a large group of able, disillusioned, young unemployed and to justify providing them with a chance of finding a worthwhile job albeit perhaps at the expense of someone else already trained.

Clearly the last argument could be used to support exceptional increases in industrial training programmes, subject to the willingness of individuals to participate in them. In practice, training boards have tempered their enthusiasm for training according to some notion of the level of intake thought appropriate to satisfy the likely demand from their industries. In the case of apprenticeship schemes for young people, the Manpower Services Commission has accepted responsibility for financial support above a certain level agreed with the training board concerned (at least during the first year of off-the-job training). This has meant that the devotion of additional resources to apprentice training has been seen as part of the overall pattern of expenditure on this age group, as well as a part of general counter-cyclical training policy.

Thus, because the industrial training boards have placed great emphasis upon their identification with the interests of their industries (i.e. the firms covered) any policy leading to 'flooding' the labour market with skilled workers has been discouraged as being wasteful of resources and generally counter-productive from the industrial relations point of view.

There is, however, a further issue which must be raised before we can understand the actions of the various manpower agencies concerned with training. This is the long-term development of the training system itself. The Vital Skills Task Group emphasised the importance of reforms which would increase the efficiency of the labour market and remove some inequities in the provision of training.[23] Adopting the recommendations of the Group, the MSC has established certain criteria by which it will operate the new long-term Training for Skills programme, set up to 'maintain a consistent and permanent means to deal with training in important skills'. Amongst these criteria are guidelines intended to foster fundamental changes in attitudes towards entry to training in industry and its basic organisation. For some ITBs such developments were already under way. For example, the EITB has been building up the Craft Module system since the late 1960s and is now engaged in providing a forum in which progressive reform of the training of skilled engineering workers can be discussed by employers and unions.[24] Ultimately any new system must be settled through collective bargaining but the Board's role as midwife should be seen as perhaps the most significant case yet of the responsibilities of a manpower agency leading to it being involved in promoting profound institutional change in the labour market as perceived in industrial relations terms. The issue is not just the long-standing one of replacing the time-serving element in the training process by a form of certification but is primarily about the creation of a flexible training system from which a flexible and efficient labour force will emerge. This has implications for the relationships between different trade unions as well as those between unions and management.

From 1979–80 Training for Skills replaces assistance from the annual special measures programmes and grants for certain key training schemes. It remains to be seen how this new scheme will evolve, given the difficulties of marginal funding under the exceptional uncertainty of present economic conditions. The scale envisaged in the 1979 White Paper on government expenditure for 1979–80 was about that of the related special measures for the 1978 training year (£41 million). Whilst the counter-cyclical leanings of the new arrangements are clear enough there is also implied an intention to remedy the problems of under-training in the general sense noted above. For example, the Vital Skills Task Group made the following comment:

'If .... there is a case for replacing [the special measures] with a permanent means of redressing skill imbalances – at least those imbalances likely to have serious consequences for the economy as a whole – it would be necessary to distinguish clearly between the objectives of offsetting temporary cutbacks (which has been the aim of special training measures) and of making good a more deep-rooted shortfall in training levels. This distinction is crucial to the success of any new measures.'[25]

The practical problems of devising exemption criteria have been followed by those of deciding on the numbers of special training awards to offer. It is now likely that the whole levy-grant-exemption scheme will be affected by the Training for Skills programme and it is obviously desirable that the MSC's current review of progress made under the 1973 Employment and Training Act should include an assessment of the scheme's likely operation under Training for Skills and alternative possibilities for employer-government funding.[26]

Training Opportunities Scheme

The development of the training system as conventionally viewed by employers and unions is not the only perspective we might adopt. Its narrowness of focus stems not merely from the importance attached to the derived demand for labour but from certain presumptions about the best ways to provide training. The counter-cyclical justification for sometimes boosting the level of training has always been wedded to some notion of expected demand likely to emerge in the medium term. The presence of agencies trying to avoid drastic reductions in the recruitment of trainees during recessions should satisfy to some extent those who objected to the pre–1964 situation, on the grounds that not only was the growth of the economy being jeopardised in the upturn but able groups of young people were being denied for good the chance of skilled training in the main trades. At least there are now agencies provoking industries to consider their training decisions more seriously so that, if firms insist that the place for vocational training is in industry, the supply of such training will not be subject to such large fluctuations. Nonetheless, up to the early 1970s the supply was controlled largely by the firms and training boards. Individuals wishing to 'invest in themselves' by learning a skilled trade were unable to do so if it did not fit in with the plans of industrial organisations.[28] The expansion of government training envisaged in the Employment and Training Act (1973) was designed to deal with this problem but whilst it was recognised that this would also serve an economic purpose by increasing the 'capacity for real labour mobility in the economy', it was regarded quite separately from the issue capturing the greatest attention – the tendency for industry to under-train during recessions. Thus, from the point of view of dealing with periodic labour shortages, the emphasis at that stage was upon better anticipation of the future demand for labour by counter-cyclical action through the reformed but basically long-term training system. Much less stress was placed upon increasing the flexibility of the system itself through providing courses of shorter length for adults in industry or in special training centres run by the government.

While the development of TOPS does reflect an attempt to redress the balance between the interests of the individual and of the employers when devising national training policy,[29] there are some difficulties with the basic idea. Viewing the adult as a potential consumer of training and educational services the effect of TOPS has been to widen significantly the access to training for certain groups. The very imperfect market for these services in the UK has been characterised by periodic rationing during recessions. However, raising this constraint at the margin, even for skilled trades apparently in short supply, has not led to very high proportions of TOPS completers finding work in their new skill.[30] This and other features of the scheme together with the presence of shortages amidst high unemployment have led to a questioning of the role to be played by TOPS in the future. The *TOPS Review* (1978, p.49) recommended that:

> 'TOPS occupational training should be more closely related to employers' actual or prospective needs, and trainees' success in securing subsequent employment should be taken as a major indicator of the effectiveness of TOPS training although it should be applied less rigorously in evaluating work preparation courses than for occupational training.'

Thus although TOPS was initially regarded as a long-term development (a reform almost on a par with earlier reforms of parts of the post-school education system), it has been forged in a period of major recession. This has given it both the appearance and, to some extent, the reality of a counter-cyclical programme. In fact the original target of 100 thousand course completions 'as soon as possible' was put forward in 1972.[31] The MSC eventually set 1980 as the year for its achievement and then revised the objective to 90 thousand adult completions: about 70 thousand adults and 20 thousand young people completed courses in 1978/79.

The review of TOPS in effect concluded that its role in dealing with labour shortages in the short term should be given much greater emphasis, involving concerted action in local labour markets co-ordinated with the activities of employers, ITBs and educational establishments. It is not possible to do justice here to the variety of developments envisaged in the *TOPS Review*. The main point of relevance to the present discussion is that to a large extent these proposals have been provoked by the limitations placed upon the effectiveness of TOPS, as a scheme orientated towards the needs of individuals, by the institutional arrangements for entry to different occupations settled between employers and trade unions. At the same time, however, the future part to be played by TOPS seems to require the relaxation of some of the very restrictions – particularly relating to the recognition of TOPS training standards – which have given rise to the reassessment of its aims. Thus the *TOPS Review* (p.21) states that

> 'full implementation of proposals put forward in *Training for Skills* should eventually place adult training arrangements on a similar footing to those for young people and so give adult TOPS trainees a more certain place in the training system.'

It seems then that before entertaining targets for further expansion over the medium term, the pattern of TOPS involvement with the labour market is to change. In a sense the greatest price which employers might pay for more assistance from the public sector training services would be to pursue radical reform in their approach to skill training. The shift in TOPS strategy can be justified in any case where local labour markets are subject to major structural change.[32] But in less fraught circumstances it is particularly important that this price should be paid in full. Otherwise existing inadequacies in labour market operation will merely be underwritten by the tailoring of TOPS and the expansion of the 'direct training services' to the needs of ineffective employers.[33] The

MSC's operation of the Training for Skills programme as noted above provides a complementary lever in this respect.

Youth Opportunities Programme

The introduction of the Youth Opportunities Programme in April 1978 must be set against the reductions in explicit employment subsidies and job creation schemes described earlier and the tempering of TOPS expansion. YOP contains within it elements of all three main types of measure: subsidy, work experience and training. It is aimed at a particular group – those aged 18 and under who have been unemployed for six weeks or more – and has acquired a semi-permanent status. The scale of the operation required to mount the programme could only have been justified by assuming that unemployment would at least remain high and probably increase during the early 1980s. YOP is now the largest of the special measures.

The existence of YOP is a particularly obvious example of the kind of drive and flair which a public agency can bring to bear upon a problem which had for some years (in less extreme circumstances) apparently fallen outside the direct responsibilities of the two departments of state most obviously concerned: Education and Science, and Employment. The entry of young people into employment is particularly affected by severe recession. Perhaps the hallmark of the new programme was its eventual commitment that every unemployed school-leaver would be found a suitable opportunity under YOP not later than Easter 1979. This objective was 99 per cent fulfilled.[34]

Of the previous schemes, the Work Experience Programme and TSA courses for young people covered 60 and 20 thousand participants respectively during 1977/78. YOP effectively doubled the scale of this activity at the same time as increasing its variety. WEP originally developed separately to cater for unemployed young people but this affected the numbers participating in JCP. Its purpose was to give this group 'a chance to gain first hand experience of working life especially the various skills and disciplines'.[35] Employers received no payment for running a WEP scheme but the 'trainees' received an allowance: schemes lasted up to 52 weeks – most were 26 weeks in length. The significance of WEP and the relevant component of YOP is its use of employers to provide planned work experience in return for some benefit to the organisations concerned. The emphasis on training, the payment of an allowance rather than a wage, and the temporary nature of the employer's commitment sets it apart from the subsidies used to encourage the employment of young people. No evidence of the productive gains from such employment or possible displacement effects etc. has yet been published but on balance it would seem best to regard it as a training scheme with strong social welfare objectives. However, because of its closer association with employers who may be able to provide permanent employment, when compared with JCP or STEP, a much greater proportion of participants obtain jobs with their sponsors or elsewhere at the end of their spell in the programme.

One would expect the development of such a large-scale programme to have an impact on the labour market for young people itself. It is too early to evaluate its effects although several studies are in progress. The MSC's review points to possible difficulties in maintaining the momentum of YOP, the desire for a better working relationship with the further education system and the need to intensify efforts on behalf of the less able unemployed young people. But so little research has been done on the way in which this part of the UK labour market has operated that there is no reliable guide to how it might respond to the intervention represented by YOP. As noted earlier in this section, this problem bedevils the evaluation of most policies relating to employment and training.

9.4 Themes of Change – Transition to Labour Market Policy ?

There are few grounds for optimism about unemployment in the future. The respite provided by reductions in productivity growth in the latter part of the 1970s will not last for ever. Over the medium term there could well be additions to hidden unemployment, the counterpart of increases in registered unemployment which fail to match both the reductions in employment and additions to long-term labour supply. The welfare consequences of this state of affairs would differ from those of higher registered unemployment but not enough to absolve government of its responsibility for the underlying situation.

The areas of employment policy reviewed in the previous section have all undergone significant changes in strategy: an experimental period often confining the measures to certain geographical areas, sectors of the economy or groups of the labour force followed by programme expansion and/or development on new lines, leading to a period of reassessment the outcome of which has been to reduce the scale of operation. The exceptions amongst those discussed above are Training for Skills and the Youth Opportunities Programme. The difficulties faced by other industrialised countries in achieving sufficient growth to reduce unemployment have led to similar changes in the range and complexity of employment policy. They do not seem to have run out of steam to quite the extent experienced in the UK recently. Nonetheless, in the British case, this process has gone well beyond the conceptions of training policy embodied in the legislation of 1964 and 1973. The Department of Employment and Manpower Services Commission have been involved in a constructive response to a difficult situation but one which has, inevitably, left them somewhat vulnerable to criticism.

Economic arguments have been used loosely to support certain types of active manpower policy but the decisions of government and other bodies concerned with this field over the last 15 years reveal a rather incoherent view of the labour market, its place in the economy and the significance of alternative policies for its future development. This situation is partly a consequence of certain over-riding imperatives often generated in national negotiation: these concern the practice of industrial relations, prices and incomes control, industrial and regional policy, and the evolution of the public sector. Traditionally, manpower policy has been conceived within a framework of limitations placed upon it by the operation of these other policies. Collective agreements are difficult enough to reach, it is said, without interposing fundamental questions about the kind of labour market that should be promoted. The penchant for *ad hoc* prices and incomes controls places a premium upon simple rules which inevitably ride roughshod over the market mechanism such as it is. The relative emphasis upon and the specific content of industrial and regional policy has changed so much over the last two decades that it is virtually impossible, despite systematic research, to disentangle the separate effects of different policy instruments: manpower policy has been regarded as a subsidiary affair, as in the case of the support expected from it for the far-fetched growth targets 'adopted' in Labour's industrial strategy. But above all, the expansion of the public sector has been conducted with an utter disregard for its implications for both product markets and labour markets.

Training policy

The UK has now reached a major cross-roads in the progress of training policy. Eventually the introduction of certification and free entry regardless of age or employment status may come about through collective bargaining. Should this be the case it will pave the way for changes in the financial arrangements for training which could affect both firms and individuals, particularly in the provision of general training for 'transferable' skills. Until such progress is made, training policy will be difficult to rationalise in periods of prolonged recession. This problem will tend to be related to the distinction between 'economic' and 'social' objectives but in fact corresponds to the separation of the roles of 'meeting the needs of firms' and 'meeting the needs of individuals'. It is possible to adopt a partial equilibrium approach to the training strategy in which every thing that is done on the manpower front is subordinated to a stance on general economic policy even if the latter has manifestly failed to avoid high levels of unemployment. If taken to an extreme, and leaving aside the problem of localised skill shortages, such a policy would lead to increasing unemployment amongst less skilled workers as the aggregate supply of training in the economy were cut back in line with the expected medium-term trend in labour demand. As we stated in *Britain's Medium-Term Employment Prospects* (p.112):

> '.... even to the most hardened cost-benefit enthusiast, there is presumably little sense in allowing unemployment rates to rise more and more at the bottom of the occupational hierarchy, when .... there are significant differences in occupational demands resulting from different macroeconomic and industrial policies.'

This leads inevitably to the idea of training in order to reduce the dispersion between occupational unemployment rates and hence reduce the probability of skill bottlenecks and increase the probability of individuals finding jobs. Such a policy of spreading the labour surpluses up the occupational ladder will require government, manpower agencies, employers, trade unions and professional bodies to re-examine present agreements which limit access to vocational education and training. For the manpower agencies, in particular, future training policy should grasp this nettle very firmly. Indeed, a government with a taste for legislation on industrial relations would do better to look to this area of labour market policy rather than to concentrate upon the closed shop issue as indicated in the Queen's Speech (May, 1979). The latter for all its symbolic importance is unlikely to have any significant effect upon inflation or labour market equity. Staff in the manpower agencies might well shudder, however, at the prospect of such a shift in training policy.

To sum up then, there has yet to evolve a clear view of the status of the individual in relation to training policy despite the preoccupation with disadvantaged groups of the labour force at different stages during the recent period of high unemployment. The interests of the ordinary member of the labour force have not been at the focus of policy formation to the extent that this has been the case in education. In many respects it is at this level that the need for explicit discussion of the social, political and economic implications of alternative policies is greatest.

Employment subsidies and job creation

The experiments with subsidies and job creation implied new targets for policy administered through the Department of Employment and the Manpower Services Commission: notably, the manipulation of labour demand and the distribution of employment opportunities. This contrasts with the sovereignty of demand in relation to training policy, which concentrated upon manipulating supply. The continuation of the implicit subsidy and job creation elements alongside training as found in YOP would seem assured for some time to come. But their overt use depends on the future state of the economy. In a sense, just as the basic style of policy towards labour shortages survived, rather perversely, the transition from low to high unemployment, so the temporary demand measures survived for a while the transition from a period in which there were expectations of reflation occurring sooner rather than later to one in which such expectations began to fade. Only the Small Firms' Employment Subsidy has continued to prosper though. And even there the restrictions imposed by the new government threaten to limit its effectiveness, having confined it to manufacturing firms once again whereas the main potential employment growth appears to be associated with enterprises in the service sector.[36] However, this change may give way to more general assistance for small businesses. In fact perhaps the acid test of the

Government's policy on incentives and enterpeneurship is whether or not it makes significant provision for this group, though, of course, not even a counter-cyclical employment policy can be based on support for this sector alone.

With the prospect of rising unemployment over the medium term ministers are likely to come under considerable pressure to ameliorate the situation. Concerned as the Government is to promote the private sector, the use of employment subsidies would least compromise its general economic philosophy. A first stage might involve the targetting of subsidies towards certain groups of the labour force, largely as a means of redistributing employment opportunities but with the possibility of raising the aggregate demand for labour. The administration of the subsidies should provide firms with a medium-term planning horizon. A second stage would be to consider the introduction of more general job expansion subsidies at the beginning of the upturn expected at some point in the early 1980s. A third stage would be to consider an industrially differentiated job preservation subsidy *linked directly to industrial and regional policy.* Ideally, the whole question of industrial subsidies should be reviewed not simply with a view to a general cutback but weighing up the effects of different forms of assistance to industry and the extent to which they might be used to promote employment by altering the behaviour of firms at the margin. Wage rigidity or labour market distortions may prevent the wage adjustment process from working effectively but this does not mean that firms' output and employment decisions cannot be influenced by altering the cost of factor inputs. However, a major conclusion of our simulations is that great structural change is required and will only be achieved by the intervention of government. In the absence of this, the use of subsidies to lower significantly the level of unemployment consistent with non-accelerating inflation cannot be put forward with much confidence.

The manipulation of labour demand within an overall stance on budgetary policy hardly brings to mind the very small Special Temporary Employment Programme. Even at present levels of unemployment there would seem to be a case for increasing the scale of STEP. At higher levels, the employment benefits of additions to public expenditure would be increased by promoting labour intensive projects. This is not to underestimate the organisational difficulties of actually expanding a scheme to help the long-term unemployed in this way. But a mixed strategy is likely to be optimal and neither industrial training nor employment subsidies will suffice to deal with this particular aspect of the unemployment problem.

Incomes policy again ?

The introduction of employment subsidies is more in keeping with the idea of working through the market mechanism than is job creation. However, the more general the subsidy becomes the more likely it is to affect the wage bargaining process. This suggests that subsidies should be paid only on condition that wage increases do not exceed some norm over the period concerned. In the case of job preservation subsidies this would be quite feasible but for employment stock expansion subsidies (or, less favoured, recruitment flow subsidies) certain problems could be created because the income prospects of existing employees might suffer from the employment gains of new employees. It is probably true that only an independently administered incomes policy could remedy the situation.

The Conservative government's antipathy towards incomes policies, at least those tried in the past, has been firmly stated by ministers. Such intervention is believed to suspend both the workings of the labour market and the practice of responsible behaviour by unions and employers. Section 9.2 has already referred to the dangers of assuming that the market works rather better than it actually does. The microeconomic circumstances which govern wage bargains unconstrained by incomes policy provide no guarantee at all that those who make sacrifices will eventually recoup the benefits.

Thus it is likely that fiscal and monetary restraint will manage to cut the growth of current price GDP but will fail to control the division of this adjustment between output and price level effects in the way hoped for. Only some form of tax-based incomes policy would then preserve the commitment to working through the market (admittedly with some loss of microeconomic efficiency) at the same time as rewarding or penalising those who comply with or breach the rate of wage increases consistent with the Government's overall economic stance. As with employment subsidies there are a variety of possible tax-based incomes policies (TIP) and any scheme selected would amount to an important social experiment. But these are the choices which should now be debated. Seidman

(1978) in his review of the main alternatives shows that a TIP would lower the rate of wage increase granted by the average firm and hence help to reduce the rate of inflation associated with a given NAIRU. This transitional remedy would be enough to justify the use of TIP but Seidman goes on to argue that a *permanent* TIP would lower the NAIRU itself. Similar claims for certain types of employment subsidy have been made as noted in the previous section. What matters, however, is that even without such beneficial effects TIP would provide the Government with an instrument of policy broadly compatible with its monetarist view of the inflation process but recognising the need to cope with labour market imperfections. [37]

Government as the main labour market agent

The case for a medium-run policy on earnings and employment in the public sector has been argued in Lindley (1978, p.113). The failure of government to co-ordinate its actions particularly in relation to the different labour markets in which it operates has led to inconsistencies with stated aims of macroeconomic policy. A more coherent approach would involve reviewing the conditions attached to public sector purchasing contracts and all forms of assistance to industry. Where it is likely that the conscience of Parliament might otherwise impede an informal application of the government's bargaining strength (as occurred under the last Labour government) it may be necessary to seek appropriate powers through legislation. No conflict exists here with the Conservative policy on reducing the size of the public sector but the publication of a White Paper on government expenditure would be more illuminating if accompanied by a public sector manpower report to Parliament showing where reductions in employment are planned and their implications for the labour market. At present there is a danger that the squeeze on public spending combined with too severe a monetary policy will lead to arbitrary cuts across the board. In contrast the essence of Conservative objections to the size of the public sector is its inefficiency in certain areas which should, nonetheless, remain largely public and its unnecessary displacement of private sector activity in others. Moreover, the effects upon services to the public while cutting employment cannot be assessed without reference to employment levels. These will of course 'emerge' after pay agreements with trade unions have been reached followed by some juggling of cash limits and White Paper expenditure figures. But a proper analysis of the position on employment, earnings and public borrowing over the medium term requires a more systematic approach. In this respect the Government's direct influence on the real and financial sectors of the economy points to the need for published plans dealing with public employment and finance over the medium term. Both would help to avoid the unsettling effects of too much rhetoric about cutting the public sector and too much attention to short-term monetary targets.

Chapter 3 observed that the combination of restraint on public expenditure with a sharp switch from direct to indirect taxation had not only created undue tension in the short run but could well fail to achieve the long-term impact on initiative and efficiency which is being sought. The Government is also likely to face short-run difficulties in another area of policy related to managing public expenditure in pursuit of a long-term objective which its approach may well fail to deliver. This refers to Conservative attempts to dispense with the notion of incomes policy, even for the public sector, during a period when the Standing Commission on Pay Comparability set up by Labour continues to operate and cash limits are intended to limit the growth of expenditure quite significantly.

This situation is likely to generate confusion with the Government appearing to set expenditure levels in money terms and trade unions achieving much higher wage increases than the Government evidently thinks good for the economy. In effect the trade unions then seem to be deciding upon the level of service the public should receive. However committed to the free market, no government can avoid having an implicit policy on incomes in the public sector whatever its treatment of the private sector. Indeed, with the public sector covering at least 50 per cent of TUC membership, there is a strong case for the development of an explicit and quite sophisticated policy on incomes for this part of the economy. The present government is perhaps too inclined to assume that pay bargaining within the market-orientated public sector can proceed as in the private sector, and is reluctant to describe its approach to pay in the non-market public sector as an incomes policy. But the following quotation from *The Conservative Manifesto 1979* (p.10) points to a public sector labour market policy in embryo.

'Bargaining must also be put on a sounder economic footing, so that public sector wage settlements take full account of supply and demand and differences between regions, manning levels, job security and pension arrangements.'

Such a policy would take time to establish, certainly too long for those who would reform the labour market in a single Parliament. It would also need to break with the British tradition of setting up and disbanding bodies concerned with prices and incomes control with little regard for the loss of organisational efficiency and expertise which that entails.

The prospect of reductions in employment in central and local government has implications for job creation programmes. If this represents a longer term objective rather than a temporary restraint on spending then the use of STEP need not be seen as a diversion of badly needed funds away from worthier public sector projects. If there really is a great deal of wasted government expenditure, the expansion of STEP at a time of contraction in other areas of expenditure becomes primarily a redistribution of employment opportunities away from underemployed public servants towards unemployed workers generally. The arguments in favour of one rather than the other are then more finely balanced than the public sector unions might care to admit. The flexibility of STEP, its focus on disadvantaged workers and relatively low cost are strongly in its favour. The problem, of course, is to establish which of the activities regularly carried out by government should be curtailed as a matter of long-term policy. It is these which should be specifically identified in the report proposed above, together with plans for their reduction and the trends to be pursued in other areas of public service.

In many respects the institutional developments of the 1970s do indicate a greater degree of professionalism in government approaches to the labour market. On the other hand this has most clearly affected the provision of supporting services for such activities as vocational training and job search and placement. The extension of the range of government involvement with the labour market during the latter part of the 1970s has meant a period of experimentation during which there has been no explicit statement by government about what we should expect from the labour market itself. The new Conservative administration supports the view that labour market forces must be allowed to prevail within a framework of responsible free collective bargaining. Such a broad policy, strengthened by moves to reform certain aspects of the industrial relations system, is unlikely to be enough, bearing in mind the structural problems encountered already by the British economy and those to come, as indicated in previous chapters. The essence of a labour market policy attuned to the needs of the economy over the 1980s will be the attention it devotes to the structure of labour supply and demand. This type of approach is required whether a particular government adopts Keynesian or monetarist perspectives. Training schemes, employment subsidies and job creation programmes of the kind mentioned above draw their rationale from recognising, first, that there are deep-rooted imperfections in the labour market and, second, that these need to be tackled selectively rather than by switches of economic philosophy intended to purge the market of its inadequacies. In addition, a major factor in progress towards a national labour market policy will be the actions of government itself as the main participant in the labour market. In this respect the ascendancy of monetarism will have had a useful impact if it leads first to a sharpening of the debate about the public sector of the labour market and then to a serious reappraisal of the functioning of the labour market as a whole and the role its institutions might play in extracting Britain's economy from the doldrums. But we have a long way to go yet.

Notes

1 Both aspects will be covered in a forthcoming book by the author to be published in this series.

2 Lindley (1978), p.109.

3 *ibid.*

4 On the other hand there is a lack of firm empirical evidence on the effects of existing UK tax instruments and subsidies (and their inter-action) upon investment and employment. The difficulties of doing such work are well illustrated by the collection of papers edited by Whiting (1976).

5 In discussing the relevance of this for employment policy, Hahn (1979, pp.7–9) concludes:

   'In principle one can describe long run rational expectations conjectural equilibria in which agents are quantity constrained. It seems particularly the case that in labour markets the institutional setting is such that it becomes a rational conjecture to suppose that a quantity constrained worker cannot benefit from small wage reductions.'

6   Reviewing several studies Shiller asks (p.36):

'Can these authors seriously believe that unemployed workers really know this data or use professional forecasts which make use of this data? If anyone believes this, he should take a trip to the nearest unemployment compensation office and ask people standing in the line for the latest data on the growth of the money supply, the government surplus, or the latest inflation forecast by an econometric model.'

7   See Beenstock (1979) and Chapter 2.

8   The Employment Transfer Scheme operates on a very small scale to promote geographical mobility. Although, in principle, this would be a distinct alternative to training policy, especially for dealing with localised shortages in periods of high skilled unemployment, some reservations have been expressed about the effects of a major expansion of the scheme. See Beaumont (1979) for a discussion of the issues and some evidence. Reductions in labour supply have been achieved through earlier retirement under the Job Release Scheme (see Table 9.1).

In addition to the policy areas mentioned, there have been proposals for redistributing employment opportunities by the introduction of a shorter working week but no official support for the idea has been given. See *People and Work* (1978) and Lindley (1980) for a review of these and other policies aiming to manipulate (i) aggregate supply without altering directly the skill composition of the labour force or (ii) the link between hours worked and employment levels without altering aggregate demand as such. See also Layard (1979) on the selective measures introduced before August 1978 and OECD (1978).

9   See *People and Work* (1978), Manpower Services Commission (1978, 1978a, 1979 and 1979a) and *Gazette* articles cited elsewhere in this chapter for further information. Lindley (1980) provides a detailed assessment of the evidence on the effects of the selective measures given in Table 9.1.

10 Note that the Regional Employment Premium remained available until January 1977. For a review of its rationale and effects in the light of the new subsidies, see Lindley (1980).

11 This was to be an additional labour subsidy, the precise arrangements for which had not been announced but would be 'related to wage levels for the private sector and could be made available in some restructuring situations with the objective to preserve jobs which would otherwise disappear.' DE *Gazette,* March 1979, p.228.

12   DE *Gazette,* November 1978, p.1251.

13   Baily and Tobin (1977), p.539 – emphasis added.

14   Lindley (1978), p.19.

15   *The Jobs Creation Programme.* Seventh Report from the Expenditure Committee, May 1977.

16   Except to note the possible overlap between local authority projects sponsored under JCP and work which would have been done anyway, or the contrast with more important local authority work which had to be deferred under the public expenditure constraints.

17   These estimates were obtained with the exchange rate and average wages treated exogenously.

18   DE *Gazette,* October 1978, p.1131. Note that 'general reflation' is not defined and its effects are being compared, presumably, with some average effects of the special programmes rather than JCP.

19   *Review of the First Year of Special Programmes,* Manpower Services Commission (1979).

20   *People and Work,* Volume 1, p.39.

21   Lindley (1978), p.6.

22   This represents the usual view taken of the 1964 legislation. The 1973 Act altered the financial arrangements for training and provided for levy, grant and *exemption* (of small firms and, in addition, firms whose training is thought to be sufficient to meet their own needs as viewed by the ITB concerned) but the basic principles remain the same.

23   See *Training for Skills – a programme for action,* Manpower Services Commission (1978a).

24   See Engineering Industry Training Board (1979).

25   *Training for Skills,* p.20.

26   The collective funding proposal included in the original DE/MSC consultative document was dropped. See *Training for Vital Skills,* DE/MSC (1976).

27   *Training for Skills,* p.15.

28   The ITB system failed to prevent the large cut back in apprentice recruitment and other training during the first half of the decade (Lindley, 1978, p.22).

29 See *Towards a Comprehensive Manpower Policy,* Manpower Services Commission (1976).

30 The same is true, however, of more favoured areas of higher education. See Lindley (1978, pp.111-2) and also Chapter 8.

31 *Training for the Future.* Department of Employment (1972).

32 Hunter (1978) provides a valuable study of such a case where the role of public agencies as 'remedial agents and catalysts of change' should dominate its role in serving the needs of individuals.

33 See *TOPS Review* and MSC *Annual Report 1978–79.*

34 *Review of the First Year of Special Programmes,* Manpower Services Commission (1979), p.10.

35 Various aspects of WEP are discussed in DE *Gazette,* March 1978, pp.294–7 and DE *Gazette,* August 1978, pp.901–8.

36 See Chapters 3 and 4 and Fothergill and Gudgin (1979).

37 See Dildine and Sunley (1978) for a discussion of the administrative problems associated with TIPs.

References

Baily, M.N. and J. Tobin (1977). 'Macroeconomic Effects of Selective Public Employment and Wage Subsidies'. *Brooking's Papers on Economic Activity,* 2, 511–41.

Beaumont, P.B. (1979). 'An Examination of Assisted Labour Market Policy' in *Regional Policy: Past Experience and New Directions.* Eds. D. Maclennan and J.B. Parr. Oxford: Martin Robertson, 65–80.

Beenstock, M. (1979). 'Do UK Labour Markets Work?'. *Economic Outlook.* June/July, 21–31.

Birch, D.L. (1979). 'The Job Generation Process'. Cambridge, Mass.: M.I.T. Program on Neighborhood and Regional Change. (mimeographed)

Department of Employment (1972). *Training for the Future.* London : DE.

Department of Employment and Manpower Services Commission (1976). *Training for Vital Skills – A consultative document.* London: DE/MSC.

Dildine, L.L. and E.M. Sunley (1978). 'Administrative Problems of Tax-Based Incomes Policies'. *Brooking's Papers on Economic Activity*, 2, 363-89.

Dixit, Avinash (1978). 'The Balance of Trade in a Model of Temporary Equilibrium with Rationing'. *Review of Economic Studies*, 45, 393–404.

Engineering Industry Training Board (1979). *Annual Report and Accounts 1978/79*. Watford: EITB.

Fothergill, S. and G. Gudgin (1979). 'The Job Generation Process in Britain'. CES Research Series no. 32. London: Centre for Environmental Studies. (mimeographed)

Freeman, C. (1978). *Government Policies for Industrial Innovation*. Ninth J.D. Bernal Lecture. London: Birkbeck College.

Friedman, M. (1968). 'The Role of Monetary Policy'. *American Economic Review*, 58 (March), 1–17.

Gannicott, K.G. and M. Blaug (1969). 'Manpower Forecasting Since Robbins: A Science Lobby in Action'. *Higher Education Review*, 2,1,56–74.

The Government's Expenditure Plans 1979–80 to 1982–83 (1979). Cmnd 7439. London : HMSO.

Hahn, Frank (1978). 'On Non-Walrasian Equilibria'. *Review of Economic Studies*, 45, 1–17.

——(1979). 'Unemployment from a Theoretical Point of View'. Paper presented to US Department of Labor/Manpower Services Commission Conference on Unemployment and Unemployment Policy. London, May.

Hunter, L.C. with P.B. Beaumont (1978). *Labour Shortages and Manpower Policy*. Manpower Services Commission: Manpower Studies No. 19782. London: HMSO.

Jackman, R. and P.R.G. Layard (1979). 'The Efficiency Case for Targetted Labour Market Policies'. Paper presented to US Department of Labor/Manpower Services Commission Conference on Unemployment and Unemployment Policy. London, May.

The Jobs Creation Programme (1977). Seventh Report from the Expenditure Committee. London: HMSO.

Johnson, George E. (1979). 'The Theory of Labour Market Intervention'. Paper presented to US Department of Labor/Manpower Services Commission Conference on Unemployment and Unemployment Policy. London, May.

Keynes, J.M. (1936). *The General Theory of Employment, Interest and Money.* London: Macmillan.

Layard, P.R.G. (1979). 'The Costs and Benefits of Selective Employment Policies: The British Case'. *British Journal of Industrial Relations, 17* (July), 187–204.

Layard, P.R.G. and S.J. Nickell (1979). 'The Case for Subsidising Extra Jobs'. Paper presented to US Department of Labor/Manpower Services Commission Conference on Unemployment and Unemployment Policy. London, May.

Lindley, R.M. (1978) (ed.). *Britain's Medium-Term Employment Prospects.* Coventry: Manpower Research Group, University of Warwick.

—— (1980). 'Labour Market Policy in the UK: Special Measures'. MRG Discussion Paper. Coventry: Manpower Research Group, University of Warwick.

Lucas, R.E. (1972). 'Expectations and the Neutrality of Money'. *Journal of Economic Theory,* 4, 2, 103–24.

Lucas, R.E. and T.J. Sargent (1978). 'After Keynesian Macroeconomics' in *After the Phillips Curve: Persistence of High Inflation and High Unemployment.* Proceedings of a Federal Reserve Bank of Boston conference. Edgartown, Mass., June, 49–72.

Malinvaud, E. (1977). *The Theory of Unemployment Reconsidered.* Oxford: Basil Blackwell.

Manpower Services Commission (1976). *Towards a Comprehensive Manpower Policy.* London: MSC.

—— (1978). *TOPS Review.* London: MSC.

—— (1978a). *Training for Skills – a programme for action.* London: MSC.

—— (1979). *The Review of the First Year of Special Programmes.* London: MSC.

—— (1979a). *Annual Report 1978–79.* London: MSC.

Organisation for Economic Co-operation and Development (1978). *A Medium Term Strategy for Employment and Manpower Policies.* Paris: OECD.

People and Work: Prospects for Jobs and Training (1978). Thirteenth Report from the Expenditure Committee. London : HMSO.

Seidman, L.S. (1978). 'Tax-Based Incomes Policies'. *Brooking's Papers on Economic Activity,* 2, 301–48.

Shiller, R.J. (1978). 'Rational Expectations and the Dynamic Structure of Macroeconomic Models: A critical review'. *Journal of Monetary Economics,* 4, 1–44.

Whiting, A. (1976) (ed.). *The Economics of Industrial Subsidies.* Department of Industry. London: HMSO.

Appendices

Appendix A.   The Macroeconomic Model

This appendix gives a summary of the main features of our macroeconomic model. Some parts of our assessment work are highly formalised using fully specified models of sectors of the economy which are integrated for computer simulation: this obviously applies to the macroeconomic model. Other parts are the subject of model development but are currently in the form of a collection of separate sub-models or isolated equations: this is the case with the 'model' of manpower flows based on our demographic accounting system. It is important to recognise that econometric models are vehicles for analysis which involves a considerable amount of judgement. Thus it seems more appropriate to refer to the MRG's 'system of assessment' rather than to its 'model'.

In our previous study (Lindley, 1978) the macroeconomic model used was a development of the static model constructed by the Cambridge Growth Project and described in Barker (1976). The present study employs a similarly modified version of the dynamic model described by Barker, Peterson and Winters (1979). The changes we have made to these models concern particularly but not exclusively the treatment of the labour sector and this is summarised very briefly in Appendix B. Both models have a Keynesian structure incorporating an input-output system and concentrating on the determination of changes in the real sector of the economy. The level of disaggregation of commodities and industries is considerable by the standards of other models of the UK economy.

Primarily because of the degree of disaggregation, the model is a large one and comprises over 1,400 behavioural and technical relationships (excluding accounting identities). The main elements of the model are equations explaining consumption, investment, employment, exports, imports, prices and an input-output sector which deals with the flows of goods and services between industries and determines total industrial outputs. These equations are all solved together so that the final results are consistent with the various identities required by the national accounts. There are 49 employing activities distinguished by the model and these are listed in Appendix C together with the 16 aggregate groups normally used for the presentation of results.

Obviously the model does not explain every aspect of behaviour which affects the progress of the economy. Changes in the economy are viewed through changes in a large selection of economic variables. The model brings together the results of attempting to establish the relationships between these variables. However some are determined by what happens not just in the British economy but in many other economies (e.g. world commodity prices). Some variables are determined by complex social and political processes within the UK whose evolution economists cannot pretend to be able to forecast (e.g. government expenditure on health services; the structure of taxation). Some variables are determined by processes which economists believe are influenced by economic factors in a sufficiently direct fashion to enable them to aspire to modelling them, but satisfactory results have yet to emerge (e.g. general wage inflation and wage differentials). In the last case the balance between judgement, guesswork and formal modelling is in favour of the first two when producing forecasts. This applies particularly to the forecasting of wages when the medium term is likely to be affected by incomes policies not yet settled.

The three types of variable mentioned above are treated exogenously. In some cases the projected values are derived from independent forecasting equations such as those determining the levels of employment in public sector social services and public administration.

Exogenous variables can be classified into four main groups concerned with (i) the world economic environment, (ii) public expenditure, (iii) taxation and transfers of income and (iv) the labour market. The values of these variables projected to 1985 form the medium-term framework (described in Chapter 3) within which the model solves for the endogenous variables. The main exogenous and endogenous variables are listed in Tables A.1 and A.2.

The aspects of the model discussed so far have certain advantages and disadvantages associated with them and we comment briefly below upon those which particularly affect the presentation and analysis of our results.

The focus of the model upon the real sector reflects not so much a belief that financial and monetary flows are unimportant but more the stage reached in a research strategy orientated towards assessing medium-term employment prospects and identifying their structural characteristics. Thus the exchange rate and interest rate are not treated exogenously because it is assumed that they can be set at any

Table A.1 Major Exogenous Variables

1. Government current expenditure – 5 categories
2. Government capital expenditure – 5 categories
3. Investment by nationalised industries
4. Government employment – 5 categories
5. Employment by non-profit-making bodies and domestic service
6. Total labour supply
7. Total number self-employed
8. Number employed in HM forces
9. Average wage – whole economy
10. Wage differentials by industry (40 categories)
11. Average hours worked by industry (40 categories)
12. Exogenous productivity changes (40 categories)
13. Total population, U.K.
14. Export prices of competitors
15. Import prices in foreign currencies (57 categories)
16. Import tariffs (57 categories)
17. World production by area (10 categories)
18. Direct imports by consumers, industry and government
19. Exogenous imports, e.g. coal, gas, electricity etc.
20. Exogenous exports, e.g. natural oil, gems etc.
21. North Sea oil and gas production
22. North Sea oil tax allowance

23. Petroleum revenue tax
24. Royalty tax on North Sea oil and gas production
25. Foreign tourists' expenditure
26. Direct income tax rates (standard and other rates)
27. Corporation tax
28. Direct tax allowances – personal
29. Investment incentives – buildings and works
30. Investment incentives – plant, machinery and vehicles
31. National Insurance contributions
32. Rate contributions
33. Specific tax duties – consumers and industries
34. Ad valorem tax duties – consumers and industries
35. VAT – standard and differential rates
36. Subsidies – consumers and industries
37. Current transfers by government to persons
38. Current transfers by government abroad
39. Private transfers
40. Interest rate
41. Rent and property income of local authorities and public corporations
42. Capital transfers
43. Net lending
44. Exchange rate

Table A.2   Major Endogenous Variables

1. Consumers' expenditure (42 commodities)
2. Exports of goods (by 10 areas and 16 commodities)
3. Industry outputs (40 industries) — gross and net
4. Gross investment (3 assets and 40 industries)
5. Stockbuilding
6. Employment (40 industries)
7. Employment — whole economy
8. Unemployment — whole economy
9. Industry taxes — (40 industries and 6 categories of tax)
10. Imports (57 commodities)
11. Industrial demands for commodities (40 industries)
12. Total incomes by institutional sector (28 incomes, 7 institutional sectors)
13. Total expenditure by institutional sectors (23 expenditures, 7 institutional sectors)
14. Value of industrial inputs (40 industries, 9 inputs)
15. Industry prices and average wage bills (40 industries)
16. Export and import prices
17. Commodity demands and supplies (57 commodities)
18. Gross domestic product and its main components
19. The balance of trade
20. Personal disposable income

Note: This list of endogenous variables is not exhaustive. It is possible to deduce many more detailed results from the model, for example, one can make a fairly extensive analysis of tax incidence.

particular level simply by government decision, but because to make these variables endogenous in a medium term context requires further work on their determinants in order to produce credible explanatory relationships. Changes in institutional arrangements and the degree of government control are extremely difficult to cope with in this respect and the levels of the exchange rate and interest rate are at present established exogenously.

On the other hand our results are discussed in the light of any possible inconsistency between the values of exogenous and endogenous variables and the extent to which certain feedbacks from the latter to the former could be neutralised or at least delayed by government action.

The advantages of disaggregation accrue not only from the greater accuracy achieved in the simulation of aggregate economic quantities, such as GDP and its main components, but also through the value of the additional detail itself. Thus if the industrial groups are chosen so that nationalised industries and other industries particularly affected by government policy (for example, agriculture and construction) are identified separately, this makes it possible to distinguish the effects of different policies upon these specific industries. Moreover the peculiar circumstances of industries can be recognised, incorporating exogenous information which otherwise would be of little use.

The disadvantages of disaggregation relate not only to the increase in the amount of data preparation and estimation required, but also to the fact that this involves pushing diaggregated analysis to the limits of the reliability of the data. There are very practical problems in using such a model for projection purposes. First, the inevitable delay with which relatively detailed statistics are available means that the preparation of a base year view of the economy at a level distinguishing even our 16 aggregate groups of employing activities can only be done very provisionally for the immediate past year towards the end of the year following. For example, at the time of making our projections, final employment data for 1978 were not yet available. This problem applies to output, investment and employment by industry and all are of central importance to various judgements being made at the initial stage of simulation, for example, about the degree of below trend productivity and capacity usage in the base year and projected 'optimal' productivity.

The second main practical disadvantage of disaggregation is that it normally increases the number of exogenous inputs required to run the model. For example, if exports and imports have been disaggregated in some detail then so must, to some extent, the exogenous projections of world prices in order to provide the disaggregated equations with values of the relative price variables which help to determine these trade flows. Not only are there difficulties in obtaining recent past estimates of these variables but also a greater degree of judgement must be exercised in projecting values for the future.

Thus an important consequence of using a highly disaggregated model is a tendency to fall back on an earlier base year for analysis than would be the case when using an aggregate model.

When developing a disaggregated model for medium-term analysis it is almost inevitable with presently available data that the model-builder should decide to shift from quarterly to annual data. This means that the estimation of lag structures, which are usually difficult to identify properly, does not assume the importance applicable to short-run macroeconomic modelling. Nonetheless many important lag effects remain, for example in the determination of consumption, and do need to be modelled explicitly. A consequence of working with annual data is that the timing of policies and their effects will be less precise and residual adjustments to the early part of the projection period cannot be made as conveniently as in the case of short-run models. The results of a medium-term dynamic model are only generally indicative therefore of the profiles of economic change under alternative policies.

Appendix B.   Treatment of Labour Demand and Supply

Labour demand

A consequence of attempting to model the development of the economy in the medium-term is that certain types of estimated equation which appear to track short-term changes quite successfully begin to break down. The ubiquitous time trend is often at the root of the trouble and when included in equations embodying simple autoregressive lags (for example the Koyck adjustment mechanism), forecasting can be more than usually hazardous. Moreover, whilst over the short-term it may be reasonable to capture the growth of technical progress or even capital stock by such devices, this becomes increasingly unsatisfactory with the extension of the forecasting horizon.

The above comments apply with particular force to the projection of labour demand. Attempts to move closer to reality through the use of vintage production functions have yielded employment functions of the kind estimated by Wigley (1970) and Peterson (1976) in which employment is related to both output and the ratio of gross investment to output. These introduce the time trend implicitly but at one remove from its direct inclusion in the neo-classical short-term employment function. In vintage models it proxies the pace of productivity growth associated with successive vintages of capital. At the same time these vintage employment functions are somewhat awkward to evaluate because their rationale is directed basically at the explanation of productivity changes abstracting from cyclical fluctuations. The typical short-term employment function on the contrary is clearly mainly designed to explain these cyclical fluctuations about some trend.

The above comments are especially relevant to the problem of projecting the economy from 1978 to 1985. First the present recession has been characterised by its long duration so far and the slow recovery expected. This means that in spite of projecting over a span of seven years, the difference between the cyclical position in the base period and the trend value is highly significant relative to the trend increase over the projection period. Second, the bleak outlook for employment is likely to militate against the achievement of rapid productivity growth required to reach the long-run trend by 1985.

Present circumstances therefore seem to imply that the simulation of productivity growth in the medium term falls between the two situations for which the vintage and short-term employment functions are most suited. An alternative approach has been suggested by Hazledine (1978). In this model the adjustment of actual employment to short-run desired employment is distinguished explicitly from the adjustment of short-run desired employment to the 'technical optimal' level of employment. With the capital stock available it is argued that there is some optimal level of output which it was designed to produce and associated with this output level is an optimal level of man-hours of labour input which maximises productivity and minimises labour costs (per man-hour). Should demand be such that firms wish to produce more or less than their capital was designed to produce then desired employment in the short-run will differ from the technical optimal. Moreover the firm has then to adjust to this desired level.

Wilson (1979) gives a detailed comparison of the Hazledine approach with alternative models, including those discussed above, and this reveals that the Hazledine model provides a better explanation of past changes in employment and, more importantly, would seem to provide the best *ex ante* forecasts of employment change. As a result of these tests this model was used in our previous assessment (Lindley, 1978).

With such a model, forecasting involves, first, projecting the optimal levels of output, employment and hours. Second, defining the degree of technical optimality achieved in the horizon year and, third, estimating the adjustment of actual employment to the changes implied in 'optimal' and 'desired' employment in that year (and analogously for average hours worked). Because of difficulties in projecting the optimal levels of output and employment in the context of the dynamic version of the model we have developed a slightly different model for the current assessment. This new model is a synthesis of the Hazledine and conventional short-term employment functions which replaces the time trend in the latter by an exogenously determined growth of optimal productivity. The latter is obtained by observation of the growth in productivity between peaks in the economic cycle in each industry. It therefore grows discontinuously and at different rates in each sector. As in the previous assessment this is combined with a conventional partial adjustment mechanism to take into account the cost to firms of adjusting employment towards the desired levels implied by the underlying changes in optimal productivity.

Our forecasts for the current assessment therefore require an exogenous projection of the underlying growth in optimal productivity between 1978 and 1985, together with output levels in order to generate a projection of realised productivity growth.

Our projection of optimal productivity might be termed a 'behavioural optimum'. This is the level of productivity which might be achieved having regard to both the technical specifications of the capital stock and the social and economic environment in which productivity changes are evolving. Thus persistent high levels of unemployment will tend to adjust downwards the optimal level to which desired and actual employment are adjusting because this situation will sour the atmosphere in which productivity bargaining takes place. Our references to optimal productivity incorporate these additional considerations. We argue that the optimal level in 1985 will be lower than expected from an extrapolation through past productivity peaks not only because of the depth and duration of the present recession in investment, hence reducing the technical optimal, but also because the emerging situation of high unemployment is basically unfavourable to productivity grówth.

Optimal productivity growth is treated exogenously at present. In principle we should like to endogenise this, relating it to the technical optimal, perhaps as a function of past investment and other factors influencing the underlying rate of technological change and to the state of the labour market (via a bargaining model). Details of our assumptions together with the projections of optimal and realised average hours worked are given in Chapter 3.

The above outline of the method used to project employment is intended to serve only as a guide when discussing our exogenous assumptions and the simulation results. The model is applied to all the SAM employing activities except for non-profit-making bodies and the public sector services. The treatment of these groups involves the estimation of a set of relatively straightforward expenditure-employment functions.

Labour supply

Labour force estimates for the future are derived from projections of the total population by age group, sex and (for females) marital status for each mid-year from 1978 to 1985, prepared by GAD. Projections of labour force participation rates are applied to these to yield estimates of the size and demographic structure of the labour force up to 1985. Following DE practice, we initially define economic activity to include full-time students in making the above projections and then exclude this group from the labour force estimate using our estimates of the numbers of full-time students at each mid-year. Further discussion of the treatment of labour supply is given in the main text.

Occupational and regional employment projections

These projections are made by applying occupational and regional proportions to the industrial employment estimates derived from the macroeconomic model. The methods of estimating occupational and regional structure in 1985 involve the synthesis of various data sources and the use of simple models tempered by residual adjustments in the light of *ad hoc* information about future developments (for further details see Chapters 4 and 5).

Appendix C. Classification of Employing Activities and Occupations

Employing activities

The economy is classified according to 49 SAM employing activities, the first 40 of which cover agriculture, the index of production industries (mining, manufacturing, construction and public utilities) and the, mainly, commercial services sector. Services provided by government and private non-profit-making bodies are covered by the remaining 9 employing activities. Throughout this study the term 'industry' is used in its broadest sense and includes agriculture and the profit-making service sector. 'All industries' therefore refers to SAMs 1 to 40. Table C.1 defines the 16 SAM groups into which detail at the 49 SAM level has been aggregated in order to make the discussion and tabulation of results more manageable, without obscuring the most important disaggregate features.

Occupations

Table C.2 lists the main occupational groups which comprise the newly defined Warwick Occupational Categories (WOCs). They are aggregates of the Intermediate Occupational Groups (IOGs) which are themselves aggregated from the *Classification of Occupations 1970* (OPCS, 1971).

The IOGs were designed as a means of linking together the major existing sources of occupational data and of providing a stepping stone between them and the WOCs. Some notes on aggregation criteria applied to the IOGs are given below.

For manual occupations the main criteria are supply lead-times involved in training and the level of skill and transferability of skills between industries. It should be noted that the last criterion relates to individual SAM industries rather than to the aggregate SAM groups generally referred to in the tables of results. The non-manual occupations are aggregated according to the nature of the work performed in those occupations and the degree of similarity in the operation of occupational labour markets (e.g. civil, mechanical and electrical engineers are aggregated into the classification 'Engineers and scientists, etc.').

Table C.1 Aggregation of SAMs

SAM group	SAMs
1. Agriculture	Agriculture (1)
2. Mining	Coal mining (2), Oil and natural gas (3), Mining n.e.s. (4)
3. Food, drink and tobacco	Cereal processing (5), Food processing n.e.s. (6), Drink (7), Tobacco manufacture (8)
4. Chemicals etc.	Coke ovens (9), Mineral oil refining (10), Chemicals (11)
5. Metals	Iron and steel (12), Non-ferrous metals (13)
6. Engineering	Mechanical engineering (14), Instrument engineering (15), Electrical engineering (16), Shipbuilding (17), Motor vehicles (18), Aerospace equipment (19), Vehicles n.e.s. (20), Metal goods (21)
7. Textiles and clothing	Textile fibres (22), Textiles n.e.s. (23), Leather, clothing etc. (24)
8. Manufacture n.e.s.	Bricks (25), Timber and furniture (26), Paper and board (27), Printing and publishing (28), Rubber (29), Manufactures n.e.s. (30)
9. Construction	Construction (31)
10. Public utilities	Gas (32), Electricity (33), Water (34)
11. Transport and communication	Transport (35), Communications (36)
12. Distribution	Distribution (37)
13. Professional services	Insurance (38), Professional services (39)
14. Miscellaneous services	Miscellaneous services (40)
15. Health and education etc.	National Health Service (42), Public education (44), Private non-profit-making bodies (46)–(48), Private domestic service (49)
16. Public administration	Defence (41) Other central government (43), Other local government (45)
Manufacturing	SAM groups 3–8
Services	SAM groups 11–14

Table C.2 Warwick Occupational Categories

WOC	Title	Selected occupations within WOC
1.	Managers and administrators	Production, sales, personnel managers, proprietors, hotel managers, civil service executive officers.
2.	Education professions	University teachers, primary and secondary teachers; teachers n.e.c.
3.	Health professions etc.	Doctors, dentists, nurses, pharmacists, physiotherapists, public health inspectors, medical workers n.e.c., social welfare and related workers; clergy.
4.	Other professions	Valuers, financial agents, accountants, judges, solicitors, trade union officials, professional workers n.e.c.
5.	Literary, artistic and sports occupations	Athletes, trainers, authors, journalists, actors, musicians, artists, proprietors, managers and workers in service; sport and recreation n.e.c.
6.	Engineers, scientists, etc.	Civil, mechanical, electrical and electronic engineers; work study, progress, planning and production engineers; metallurgists, engineers n.e.c., chemists, physicists, biologists, etc., surveyors, architects.
7.	Technicians, draughtsmen	Technicians, draughtsmen, laboratory assistants, ships officers, pilots.
8.	Clerical occupations, etc.	Clerks, cashiers, office machine operators, typists, secretaries, telephone and telegraph operators.
9.	Sales occupations	Shop salesmen, roundsmen, commercial travellers, salesmen n.e.c.
10.	Supervisors, foremen	All supervisors and foremen (except with Census of Population statistics, for which this group includes only engineering foremen and transport inspectors).
11.	Engineering craftsmen	All skilled workers in engineering, electrical and electronic trades (e.g. turners, fitters, welders, tool-makers, motor mechanics, precision instrument makers).
12.	Other transferable craftsmen	Woodworkers, painters and decorators; bricklayers and masons; plasterers.
13.	Non-transferable craftsmen	All craft workers n.e.c. (e.g. miners, potters, furnacemen, jewellers; skilled textile and clothing workers.).
14.	Skilled operatives	Riggers, electroplaters, inspectors (metal and electrical), bakers, butchers, printers, other skilled workers n.e.c.
15.	Other operatives	Farmers, foresters, fishermen, surface mine and quarry workers; gas, coke and chemical makers; semi-skilled pottery workers, semi-skilled textile, construction and transport workers; fettlers, machine tool operators, assemblers, press workers, boilermen.
16.	Security occupations	Firemen, police, security guards.
17.	Personal service occupations	Porters, housekeepers, restauranteurs, waiters, bar staff, cooks, canteen assistants, kitchen hands, caretakers, cleaners, hairdressers, launderers, hospital ward orderlies, ambulance drivers.
18.	Other occupations	Labourers, inadequately described occupations

References for Appendices

Barker, T.S. (1976) (ed.). *Economic Structure and Policy.* Cambridge Studies in Applied Econometrics 2. London: Chapman and Hall.

Barker, T.S., W. Peterson and A. Winters (1979). 'The Cambridge Multisectoral Dynamic Model: Description and Analysis'. Paper presented to the Seventh International Conference on Input-Output Techniques, Innsbruck.

Hazledine, T. (1978). 'New Specifications for Employment and Hours Functions'. *Economica,* 45 (May), 179–93.

Lindley, R.M. (1978). (ed.). *Britain's Medium-Term Employment Prospects.* Coventry: Manpower Research Group, University of Warwick.

Peterson, W. (1976). 'Employment'. *Economic Structure and Policy,* ed. T.S. Barker. London: Chapman and Hall, 177–93.

Wigley, K.J. (1970). 'Production Models and Time Trends of Input-Output Coefficients'. *Input-Output in the United Kingdom,* ed. E.F. Gossling. London: Frank Cass, 89–118.

Wilson, R.A. (1979). 'Comparative Forecasting Performance of Disaggregated Employment Models'. Discussion Paper no. 3. Coventry: Manpower Research Group, University of Warwick. (mimeographed)